DEBATE AND ARGUMENT

A Systems Approach to Advocacy

DEBATE AND ARGUMENT

A Systems Approach
to Advocacy

Michael Pfau
Augustana College

David A. Thomas
University of Richmond

Walter Ulrich
Vanderbilt University

Scott, Foresman and Company
Glenview, Illinois
London, England

Library of Congress Cataloging-in-Publication Data

Pfau, Michael.
  Debate and argument.

  Includes bibliographies and index.
  1. Debates and debating.   I. Thomas, David Allen,
  II. Ulrich, Walter.   III. Title.
PN4181.P44   1987   808.5′3   87–4859
ISBN 0–673–18163–4

123456 – MPC – 929190898887

PREFACE

It is now commonplace to note that we have entered an "Information Age," characterized by an explosion of new data and a rapidly accelerating rate of change, and fueled by electronic communication and computer technologies. New knowledge, as represented by published research in articles and books, doubles each decade, while the growth of electronic data storage, retrieval, and transmission makes its access and use easier than ever before.

Today's students are responding to this information revolution by seeking courses that will help them deal with an increasingly complex and rapidly changing world. They recognize the need to improve their critical thinking, evaluation, and decision-making skills. Curricular offerings in debate and argument, as well as collegiate and high school co-curricular programs in debate, are among the most effective vehicles to enhance these skills. We have written *Debate and Argument: A Systems Approach to Advocacy* for both uses. We believe that this book provides a sound, thorough, and challenging treatment of debate and argument, appropriate as a text for curricular use and valuable as a resource for co-curricular use.

Debate and Argument is a comprehensive textbook on the theory and practice of argumentation and debate. Our goal has been to accommodate the main currents of contemporary debate practices. Our approach is based on policy systems analysis. Recent surveys of coaches and debaters in the National Debate Tournaments found that two-thirds or more of the respondents claim to belong to the policy systems school of debate. To explain briefly the distinctiveness of this approach, the traditional approach to debate was dominated for decades by "stock issues analysis," in which the affirmative advocate had the "burden of proof" to prove certain arguments as part of an overall "*prima facie* case." These were the basic issues: Is there a need for a change? Is there a plan that will solve the need? Is the plan desirable? Traditionally, the arguments in a debate focused on the affirmative's success or failure in trying to prove those stock issues. The negative side, thus, needed only to overthrow the affirmative's case on one or more of those issues. This technique proved inadequate for in-depth examining of contemporary issues or for determining rational policy decisions as real decision makers do. Since the 1970s, policy systems analysis has become better understood and more widely accepted and practiced.

The policy systems approach to analysis suggests that in the real world of decision making, such as in Congress, decisions do not hinge on whether the advocate for the proposed new legislation can carry the stock issues. Rather, decisions in this context are based on whether or not the proposal can be demonstrated to be the best system for managing problems. Therefore, in a debate, the negative side has more responsibility than simply to test the logic and evidence of the affirmative case for fallacies. The negative side must also support an alternative system for dealing with the problem under discussion.

These two approaches are very different in the varying demands they place on opposing debaters in their analysis of the issues, their selection of cases and proof, and their strategies and tactics for refutation. Today's debaters and their coaches seem to prefer the policy systems approach over the stock issues approach, and yet none of the other argumentation and debate textbooks on the market is centered on policy systems analysis as its organizing approach. A textbook is needed to meet the requirements of today's instructors, students, coaches, and debaters for a useful, practical, and relevant resource. This textbook meets that need.

Debate and Argument is an integration of modern argumentation theory and competitive debate theory. The primary practical emphasis of the book is oriented more to competitive debate than to general argumentation. Yet the debate application is always related to sound argumentation within the policy systems framework, and that application is reflected in this book.

Debate and Argument is organized in three parts. Part One offers a general overview of debate, the policy systems approach, and the decision-making process. Part Two examines research, briefing, tools, evidence, and reasoning. Part Three provides practical instruction on affirmative and negative case construction, strategies and tactics, refutation, cross examination, and style.

Our goal has been not to write a textbook that incorporates all approaches to debate and argument, but one that meets the highest standards of practical, relevant content and method. Today's students demand and deserve nothing less for developing their intellectual capacity and leadership skills. Society is driven not by technology but by people with extraordinary skills of thought, analysis, problem solving, and communication. To that end, we have devoted our best efforts in writing *Debate and Argument*.

Acknowledgments

It would be impossible to acknowledge all of our colleagues who have exerted some degree of influence on our thinking about argumentation and debate. Nonetheless, we would be remiss if we failed to single out those few who have played a particularly instrumental role in our own growth as debaters, coaches, and teachers of argumentation and debate.

We first acknowledge the late Daniel M. Rohrer. He played a significant role in the formative stages of this project. Further, because he contributed so much to each of our thinking about argumentation and debate, his ideas are embodied in the text itself. We owe him much; we miss him even more.

We are particularly grateful to those who influenced us during the formative years. Our high school and collegiate debate coaches, Bernard L. Brock, Everett E. Chapman, William English, DeWitte T. Holland, J. C. Larkin, Donn W. Parson, and Wilburn L. Sims inspired our interest in and shaped our thinking about argumentation and debate.

Later, during our own tenures as teachers, scholars, and forensic coaches, a number of our colleagues have exerted special influence on our intellectual development, including (in addition to those acknowledged previously): Jerry M. Anderson, Wayne Brockriede, Judee K. Burgoon, Michael Burgoon, James W. Chesebro, Jerry Corsi, Randall Fisher, Thomas J. Hynes, Ted R. Jackson, Kassian Kovalcheck, Allan J. Lichtman, Malcolm Sillars, William Southworth, James J. Unger, Joseph W. Wenzel, Charles A. Willard, and David Zarefsky.

We acknowledge the assistance of our reviewers for their suggestions on fine-tuning the manuscript: John S. Gossett, North Texas State University; Bruce E. Gronbeck, The University of Iowa; Dale Herbeck, Boston College; Thomas J. Hynes, Jr., University of Louisville; Donn W. Parson, The University of Kansas; and Neil Phillips, University of Northern Iowa.

We also thank Scott, Foresman for its commitment to and leadership in speech communication, and for its support of this book on debate and argument. We are particularly grateful to two individuals: Barbara Muller, acquisitions editor, for her vision and support from the outset; and Carol Leon, project editor, for her overall supervision and attention to detail during the editing phase.

Finally, we acknowledge our students. They make teaching and coaching worth-while. We have been fortunate in having an opportunity to work with many warm, talented, and conscientious students. Some of them claim that we exerted an important impact on their lives. This may or may not be true. What is clear is that our students influenced us more than they will ever know. We thank them.

Michael Pfau
David A. Thomas
Walter Ulrich

CONTENTS

PART TWO
PREPARATION FOR ADVOCACY · 51

DEBATE AND ARGUMENT

A Systems Approach
to Advocacy

PART ONE

APPROACH
TO
ADVOCACY

CHAPTER ONE

A FIRST LOOK AT DEBATE

Debate is a decision-making process that emphasizes the use of reasoning when you disagree with others. As a school activity, debate is a part of a co-curricular program devoted to improving the intellectual and literary abilities of high school and college students. Traditionally, academic debate has been sponsored for student participation. Outside of school, debate has been conducted in legislative groups, courtrooms, and business conference rooms for many centuries as a civilized method for making decisions.

Ideally, the way students are taught to debate in contests or in classrooms should consist of the procedures that govern civilized, reasonable decision making in actual practice. This book is aimed at helping you learn to debate in keeping with that ideal. It leads the aspiring debater through a progressive sequence of information and skills in order to develop a mastery of debating ability. In the chapters that follow, you will be guided through argumentation and debate in various conflict settings, and you will see how to debate, step by step, in academic contests. The aim of this book is to make your exposure to debate as comprehensive, yet as practical and understandable, as possible.

THE NATURE OF DEBATE

To many people, debate is a loosely defined concept that covers almost all situations where people verbally disagree with one another. During a presidential election campaign, the candidates may appear in a televised debate. In a courtroom trial, the lawyers engage in a debate before the judge or jury over the case being tried. William F. Buckley, Jr., may be seen on his television program, "The Firing Line," debating against liberals on the issues of the day. After a controversial documentary or dramatic program, a panel of experts (carefully chosen by the networks to represent both sides) conduct a debate on the meaning of what was just shown.

A corporate board of directors may debate whether to begin negotiations with another company concerning a possible merger. The President sends U.S. troops into a "hot spot" somewhere in the world, and Congress then debates the wisdom or necessity of his action. The United Nations General Assembly also holds a debate over what to do as an international peace-keeping organization in that same "hot spot," and whether to endorse or condemn the U.S. for intervening there.

These situations share some elements that let us put them into the pigeonhole called debating. They also resemble other kinds of activities, such as discussing, arguing, or negotiating. These general uses of the term are understood in everyday conversations, but they are a little too broad for an understanding of debate as an activity you would like to learn to do better.

Situational Elements of Debate

Let us look a bit closer at the situations mentioned above and attempt to glean some of the factors they have in common.

1. *A decision must be made.* In every instance, there is a pressing problem or issue that will not go away by itself. Unless a decision is made, things are likely to get worse. The nature of the decision calls for looking at the facts and drawing rational conclusions. Flipping a coin or drawing straws is not a satisfactory method for making the decision. Should you buy a condominium or a house? Merge the companies? Invade another country? These decisions are not trivial ones.

2. *The need for decision stems from a conflict between people.* Someone disagrees with someone else, and a decision must be made. Debate is not so much a puzzle-solving activity done in solitude as it is a conflict between two competing alternatives, both of which seek to be accepted but only one of which can be. A company targeted for acquisition by a larger conglomerate may not want to be taken over. International diplomats must take into account conflicting views of world events.

3. *The decision is debatable.* Each side can make a case that justifies its position. The issues debated are not cut-and-dried, universal "truths." Rather, they are about matters that are fundamentally uncertain, tentative, or open to question. Although there may be some undisputed facts related to the issue, the facts themselves do not lead to a final, inevitable conclusion, as in a measurement problem in mathematics. If perfect agreement existed, there would be no debate. There is always a dimension of judgment or interpretation, which is why we use the phrase, "a debatable issue."

4. *The process is based on a desire to settle the issue, or at least to obtain a decision peacefully.* None of the process we call *debate* involves the use of physical force or coercion. An element of persuasion is always involved. When the President intervenes with troops in a combat zone, that is force; when Congress talks over whether or not it was right for him to do it, that is *debate.*

5. *The process is based on a desire to decide rationally.* Those in disagreement would rather come to a decision after considering all the facts. It is not enough to reach an emotional decision. One of the key distinctions of debate, as opposed to mere discussion, is that good reasoning and hard evidence count for more than bad reasoning

and personal opinions. It is this rational quality that sets debate apart from quarreling and quibbling. The young couple must look at the hard facts of their income and their other obligations when considering their desire to live in a new and more comfortable dwelling. Diplomats must use rationality to keep strong international tensions within bounds.

6. *Usually, those in disagreement do not want to give in to their opponents on points to which they are committed.* A debate occurs when both sides are committed to their own viewpoints, which happen to oppose each other. This quality distinguishes between debate and negotiation, because negotiators follow rules of compromise and trade-offs to reach an ultimate decision that both sides can live with until the next negotiating session.

7. *The decision is usually made by an outside party after hearing both sides present their cases.* The courtroom trial is a prime example of debate between opposing sides, each of which is committed to prevailing over the other side. However, both sides must abide by the final ruling of the judge and jury—an outside decision-maker. The final decision may not be one with which the parties agree, but it is one they must accept after the debate has worked its way to a conclusion. Though absolute truth may not be reached, debates must come to conclusions, and conflicts must be decided for the moment at least. At the end of a courtroom trial, the jury deliberates over the evidence and arguments in order to reach a single decision: guilty or not guilty. The only thing that can be done when a verdict is reached is to obey the ruling of the court, or appeal it to a higher court. An appeal, of course, begins a new debate, this time on the issue of whether the first decision was just according to the rules of due process.

A Definition of Debate

Putting these seven characteristics of debate together, we can tentatively compose a definition of *debate. Debate is a process in which people argue for opposing sides of a conflict, using rational rules and methods in preference to force or emotions, in order to obtain a decision for one side or the other by an objective third party.*

The final decision is always based on the notion that the winning side is *probably* the one that should be accepted, based on the arguments given; but there is never an absolutely certain conclusion in the kinds of issues that lead to debate. Usually, the choice is actually made by some third party. For this reason, often the debate process may not succeed in putting the issue to rest once and for all. Since the losing side may not be content with the decision, some issues are debated perennially, it seems. The topics of abortion, gun control, and capital punishment generate new debates (or repeat the same old debates) year after year.

So debate is a decision-making process in an ongoing argument that allows for decisions to be made when decisions are needed. The process involves people who are committed to their viewpoints and use rational rules and methods to construct their cases. Debates in the real world must usually be presented to third parties for the "final" decision. A third party is someone who is willing to listen to both sides and make a judgment based on the arguments given. To a large extent, the skill involved in presenting the arguments to the decision-maker goes a long way toward influencing the outcome of the decision itself. That, in a nutshell, is the reason why schools teach debate, and why students enroll in debate courses and participate in debate contests: so that students can learn to develop the ability to debate more effectively, and thus determine more of their own destinies.

DECISION-MAKING PARADIGMS

As we have seen, one of the leading characteristics of debate as a decision process is that arguments proceed according to rules or principles of reasoning. But what constitutes reasonable rules? The answer to this question is very important to the conduct of debate as a decision process in the many areas of human action and controversy.

At the outset, it should be made clear that the rules and principles of rational decision making can and do vary from one arena of conflict to another. For example, the rules that govern courtroom debate are very strict and detailed. The whole trial process is set up to provide an adversarial situation between parties. Each side has to follow certain procedures in making its case. Motions must be filed in the proper way and at the proper time before there can be a hearing or ruling on them, and evidence is carefully examined and monitored by the court to make sure it is relevant to the case and that it meets the standards for admissibility. Hearsay evidence may not be admitted as part of a case against a defendant. Everything must conform to the rules of due process, or the whole case can be thrown out of court.

The rules of courtroom argumentation do not apply in most other arenas of controversy. A different set of rules applies in the scientific laboratory. Unlike lawyers, scientists do not try the charges against a defendant. Rather, they experiment and test whether a given theory is an accurate explanation of the part of the world being studied. There are no formal adversaries pitted against each other; there is only the scientist, designing and conducting his or her experiment. Yet the rules for scientific experimentation are every bit as strict and rigidly enforced in the laboratory as the rules of due process are in court.

The example of the scientific laboratory experiment suggests an underlying principle of argumentation now coming into prominence in debate theory and practice. That is the notion of the paradigm for decision making. More will be made of this notion throughout this textbook, because it is a key to understanding how to build and maintain cases for your position in any debate. For now, we will focus closely on the meaning of the paradigm as a guide to rational rules for decision making through debate.

Kuhn's Theory of Scientific Paradigms

The leading source of information about the concept of paradigms is *The Structure of Scientific Revolutions,*[1] a book by Thomas S. Kuhn, a philosopher of science. Kuhn began with the premise that science as a field of knowledge is based on the primary objectives of building theory. Normally, scientists who agree on that objective within their own specialty (say, physics) make up a community of scholars who are familiar with the same essential facts.

Whenever a scientific discipline is united, as physics is, around a commonly understood goal, and the members of that discipline are also agreed on what should be studied and what methods should be used in doing those studies, that discipline can be considered a "normal" science. In that situation, scientific research proceeds in a uniform way toward solving a commonly understood set of problems in the field, using certain standardized experimental methods accepted by all the members of that discipline as valid and reliable.

The commonly accepted way to organize a field is called a "paradigm," and it serves as a metaphor or model for the field to use in visualizing its goals and specifying what methods serve to achieve those goals. A field's paradigm, or model, is helpful to everyone in clarifying what specific methods for pursuing knowledge are appropriate to the field, and what sorts of information or data are considered to be acceptable as answers to the questions asked in the research paradigm.

Thus, a community of scholars subscribes to a field orientation that consists of (1) a generally understood goal or goals, (2) a paradigm (or model) that depicts how that goal or goals should be pursued, (3) a strategic framework or operational design thought to be most appropriate for conducting the research or decision making within the field to achieve the goal, and, finally, (4) a set of specific techniques or methods that implement the design. The community of scientific study can be diagrammed as shown in Figure 1–1.

To add one further thought inspired by Kuhn's writings, a given field of scholarship does not make its greatest advances in learning simply by conducting more and more studies using the specific approved techniques and methods. This "puzzle solving" approach to finding new knowledge is effective but slow. The essence of a "normal science" is this slow but steady advance in the accumulation of knowledge. It is also very uncreative, in that it places a higher premium on producing work *using the approved method* than on the value of the product of that work.

Kuhn suggested that a field makes its greatest advances when a new paradigm is introduced. Especially when the research done by scientists in the "normal" paradigm produces unexpected or unexplainable results, a new, unorthodox "revolutionary paradigm" may be suggested. The prime example is when Galileo proposed the revolutionary notion that the earth revolves around the sun, because in his observations, the old geocentric paradigm that the earth is the stationary center of the universe failed to explain the evidence he saw. For a more recent example, look again at the field of physics. Before Einstein, the field of physics was a "normal science." Its conceptual hierarchy for research was well accepted, and research was indeed proceeding routinely. Einstein, however, challenged the normal conceptions of physical science by introducing his revolutionary Theory of Special Relativity and its famous formula, $E = MC^2$. As Einstein's theory became better known, it caused a major shift in the whole field of physics. Thus, science proceeds most rapidly by changing its basic paradigms or models for understanding, not by conducting standardized research projects designed to find out information needed to "flesh out" the gaps seen in the old paradigm.

Debate is generated by shifts in paradigms. During the period of transition between the era dominated by the "normal" paradigm, and the new era when the

FIGURE 1–1 HIERARCHY OF METHODOLOGIES FOR INVESTIGATION IN THE FIELD OF PHYSICS

1. Goal: To extend the theory of physics so that more is known about the physical laws of the world and the universe
2. Paradigm (or Model) for Study: The Scientific Method
3. Operational Design for Implementing Studies: Hypothesis Testing
4. Methods: Laboratory Experiments to Test Hypotheses

alternative paradigm replaces it, many controversies and debates are conducted over the whole nature of the field and the specific methods used to study and advance the field. There is a clash between the old and the new paradigms, so that a field of study in such a situation may be considered to have not one, but two (or even more) competing paradigms.

Paradigms in Social Sciences

In the social sciences, such as political science, sociology, and communication studies, it is not difficult to see competing paradigms today. This is also true in the field of law. For example, the goal of the Supreme Court is to hand down justice in America through an evaluation of the cases appealed to it. An overriding paradigm governed the decision-making process used by the Supreme Court from the days of Chief Justice Marshall (after the American Revolution legitimized the Constitution itself) right up to the middle of the twentieth century. That paradigm was the notion that laws should be measured against the Constitution. The Supreme Court, upon hearing an appeal, would determine whether the law being applied in the given case was within the meaning of the Constitution, either by direct comparison, or by indirect comparison by means of consulting previous decisions they had made in similar cases. Precedents were used to guide the Justices as they considered whether a law was constitutional or not. Over the decades of American legal history, Supreme Court precedents came to possess almost the same power as the Constitution itself.

Then, in 1954, the Supreme Court had to decide a case dealing with racial discrimination. The case concerned whether a School Board in Topeka, Kansas, could maintain separate (but equal) schools for black and white children. For the first time in a major decision, the Supreme Court decided to overthrow a clear precedent, the previous Supreme Court decision called *Plessy vs. Ferguson* that had stood for decades. To support this reversal of the *Plessy* decision, the Court turned to evidence from other sources, such as psychologists and social workers, about the effects of separate schooling on the children.

As a matter of fact, the "normal" paradigm for Supreme Court decision making was questioned long before the 1954 case. When Louis Brandeis was a lawyer in the early 1900s, he filed briefs with the Supreme Court urging that it should expand its methods of legal reasoning. For our purposes here, the important point is that in 1954 the Supreme Court launched a new paradigm for appellate decision making. Whereas formerly, the paradigm was to revere precedent as a clear guide to the present, in 1954 the Court introduced a new paradigm to allow modern social theories to be used to determine whether a law can be considered within the meaning or intent of the Constitution. Since that 1954 decision of *Brown vs. the Board of Education,* the Supreme Court has turned to non-legal sources to help it evaluate the validity of many other cases. For instance, the Supreme Court used medical evidence from the Mayo Clinic in its decision on state abortion laws in the case of *Roe vs. Wade.* The Supreme Court also used extra-legal, precedent-overturning evidence in the important legislative reapportionment case of *Baker vs. Carr.* A diagram of the competing paradigms now seen in Supreme Court decision making is given in Figure 1–2.

Other examples of competing paradigms for achieving the goals within various fields of social science can also be seen readily. In management theory, the overall goal is to increase a company's profit and productivity. The two leading paradigms for running large or small businesses are either authoritarian direction, or democratic and humanized approaches. Douglas McGregor called these alternatives "Theory X" and "Theory Y."[2] According to Theory X, the management of a company is based exclusively on economic interests, such as production and profit. With respect to people, this means controlling their behavior to fit the needs of the company. Theory Y takes a more positive view of people and their motives. Management can enhance productivity best by making the organizational environment most congenial to the human interests of those who work in it.

The competing paradigms are applied in everyday company operations by differing methods for handling personnel. Under the strong, centralized approach, it is likely that a single executive officer will make most or all of the company's decisions, without much regard for the effects of those decisions on the fate of the people who work for the company. In fact, automation and robots may even be brought in to replace personnel. Under the Theory Y paradigm for management, human resources are considered to be more important and more productive in the long run than profits. Specific managerial methods include profit sharing plans for increasing motivation to work for the company, and team building and quality circles to enliven the interest level and increase the decision-making authority of individual workers in a company. So far, in American businesses, the two approaches each seem to have had their successes and their failures, and both paradigms are currently in strong competition.

Another example, similar to the management example just discussed, may be seen in public administration.[3] In today's society, the federal government has passed many laws to regulate a wide range of businesses and other activities thought to have a bearing on the health, safety, or welfare of the citizens. Pollution laws, medical care, food and drug laws, and many other examples come to mind. In order to implement these regulations, a whole new branch of government has recently emerged: the regulatory agencies. Congress passes general laws to regulate businesses, and the executive branch appoints administrative agencies to carry them out according to the policies thought to be most efficient, or economical, or otherwise within the broad mandates of the law. Within the field of public administration, there are currently

---

FIGURE 1-2 HIERARCHY OF DECISION METHODS IN SUPREME COURT CASES

1. Goal: To achieve justice in decisions appealed to the Supreme Court
2. Old Paradigm: Strict construction of the literal meaning and intent of the Constitution
3. Operational Design: Hear cases in litigation appealed to the Supreme Court
4. Methods: Apply precedent as the basis for overturning laws as being unconstitutional

OR

1. Goal: To achieve justice in decisions appealed to the Supreme Court, as before
2. New Paradigm: Revisionist approach to meaning and intent of Constitution
3. Operational Strategy: Litigation appealed to the Supreme Court, as before
4. Methods: Overturn precedents thought to be outmoded by applying theories, facts, and information gleaned from relevant sources outside the law itself

---

competing paradigms for carrying out these regulations. Just as the field of management has a centralized viewpoint on one hand, and a democratic or human resources viewpoint on the other, so, too, the regulatory agencies may operate under a bureaucratic, "hard-line" approach, or a decentralized, flexible, open approach.

Different agencies may operate more in one paradigm than in others. Law enforcement agencies are more likely to be regimented and bureaucratic, almost military, in their approach to carrying out their duties. Likewise, the Internal Revenue Service is very single-minded in its approach to collecting taxes. On the other hand, the Department of Health and Human Services is much more "people oriented," less domineering and "cold," and correspondingly less efficient.

Two important points are that (1) different fields of concern have their own paradigms for gathering information and making decisions, and (2) within any given field, there may be competing paradigms for accomplishing those purposes. Thus debate is conducted within the fields over what methods its members should be using to achieve the goals, and what types of evidence and arguments "count" toward determining solutions to their conflicts. These points are extremely relevant to the subject of what rules or principles of rationality apply in debates over controversies that arise within any field of decision making. Rather than apply an ad hoc, arbitrary set of rhetorical principles to all controversies, we should seek to identify the principles of decision making actually employed by the responsible decision makers whose methods we take as our paradigms and models for debate.

It is important to identify the paradigms used by policy decision makers and apply their methods for investigating and arguing. In this book, we attempt to do these things as we examine various examples of arguments and debates. Our approach is coherent and rational, and we hope it proves to be a more relevant form of analysis and advocacy for students to learn than the methods heretofore followed in classrooms and tournaments. At the same time, our approach is not radical or unknown. Nor does it ignore the traditional approaches previously followed, or the innovative approaches currently being propounded by others in our discipline. Hopefully, our approach will serve to clarify and to unify the principles and rules of debating in the academic environment, and thus provide a better basis for students to become more effective debaters and advocates in whatever disciplines they may choose to enter.

EVOLUTION OF THE POLICY SYSTEMS APPROACH IN DEBATE

We shall provide a full discussion of the paradigms used in academic debate today in chapter 2. At this point, we shall provide a basic orientation to the question of what paradigms are best suited for academic debate.

Historical Overview of Academic Debate

As speech departments began to develop in colleges and universities in the first half of this century, academic debating was established as an organized and sponsored educational activity, as opposed to a club or student pastime. Debate was viewed as an excellent drill for teaching argumentation and rhetoric. Also, students were attracted to debate groups in schools because they found it to be a very enjoyable and stimulating activity. A circular process soon developed. As more students were attracted to enter tournaments, more tournaments were launched by more speech departments. Rules were devised to accommodate swelling student participation in the burgeoning new outlets of interscholastic contests.

Debates were organized in such a way that two-person teams could enter a tournament and engage in a schedule of several debates on a weekend. The format for the debate contest was streamlined to allow for more debate rounds to be scheduled. Speeches were strictly limited in time, which was one of the major changes from the old days of the literary societies when a single intersectional debate might occupy an entire day. Within the short time limits for speeches, debaters soon learned to be very selective about the arguments they felt they should make in order to win. Without time to be eloquent, debates became more stylized. Debaters had to adapt their techniques in deciding what to say and how to say it in a very short speech.

The basic model used by debaters at first was the courtroom style, in which opposing lawyers made their cases for and against an accused person. Some of the rules of courtroom debate, transferred to school debates early on, included the notions of "presumption" and "burden of proof," as well as the rules that contentions and indictments must be supported by adequate evidence. Along with this analogy between a school debate and a trial, the main rules for constructing cases and arguments about the resolution were drawn from formal Classical logic, the writings of the European positivists, and the pragmatic American philosophers like John Dewey and Walter Lippmann.

One convention of debate that developed into a routine, expected feature of academic debating was that the subject for debate was always phrased as a policy resolution. For several decades, until very recently, academic debate tournaments were contests in which the subject for debate was some version of "Resolved: That the Federal Government Should (adopt a particular policy)." Even though a policy proposal had little in common with an accused person in a trial, still the student debaters followed rules for building cases and refuting opponents, drawn from the judicial model and supplemented with other principles that seemed reasonable. As the practices persisted, textbooks were written to institutionalize and elaborate on this particular hybrid model between legal rules of argument (and evidence) and political/ legislative controversies.

The Development of the Policy Systems Approach

During the 1970s, a series of articles and papers by debate theorists appeared in journals and at the professional conferences of the forensics community. Bernard Brock and three of his graduate students at the University of Minnesota, James Klumpp, James Chesebro, and John Cragan, wrote a book in 1972 entitled *Public Policy Decision Making: Systems Analysis and Comparative Advantages Debate.*[4] Concurrently, two other theorists, Allan Lichtman and Daniel M. Rohrer, were producing a voluminous series of articles on the same subject.[5] These authors were innovators at the time, though in retrospect they seem to have been articulating what was actually a simple concept. They proposed a better method for debaters to use in analyzing policy resolutions. Following the practices then used in actual legislative hearings and developed in political science theories, they advocated a new approach called "policy systems analysis."

In policy systems analysis, the affirmative team makes a policy proposal based on the rationale that the benefits of adopting it would probably outweigh its costs. This new approach deviated in several ways from the traditional approach it sought to replace. One important difference was that in policy systems analysis, the negative team is expected to take a stand for some alternative policy position of their own, and not to rely purely on the legal concept of "presumption" of the *status quo* to win. That alternative position might be a counterplan, or it might be the present system. The crucial requirement is that whatever policy system the negative upholds as superior to the affirmative plan, it must be developed and supported in the same way, and for the same reasons, that affirmative teams defend their plans and proposals.

Several of the terms used in the preceding paragraph are rather technical, relating to the special arena of academic debate and its rules. It is not important to try to learn their specific meanings at this point, because they will be explained and exemplified fully in later chapters of this book. More importantly, the policy systems analysis approach sought to develop its basic proofs among the kinds of research and evidence in use in actual policy decision making. For instance, new emphasis was placed on scientific studies that permitted quantifiable predictions of the consequences of policy change, rather than on the conclusionary opinions and testimony of authorities, or on philosophical refutation of logical fallacies in the opponents' case.

Lichtman and Rohrer's contribution can be likened to a paradigm shift in academic debate. Whereas the "normal" school of thought held that academic debate was an exercise in logic and rhetoric, the "revolutionary" approach of the policy systems analysis views debate as an exercise in political and legislative decision-making techniques. This new "paradigm" for academic debate has developed a large constituency among the coaches and debaters actively participating in tournaments today. The older approach has not disappeared from use, but it is certainly less prominent than it was. Recent surveys of coaches and participants in debate programs disclose that a majority of those who respond consider themselves to be within the "policy systems" school of thought.

Policy systems analysis is not a unanimously accepted approach. One reason is that students in a debate tournament are neither legislators nor social scientists, and debate judges are not "real" lawmakers whose decisions will determine the fate of the proposed policy change being debated. There is room for other approaches to the debate contest in terms of what argument rules and principles may be used. New proposals along these lines appear from time to time, and are accepted to a greater or lesser extent by participants.

Another problem with policy systems analysis is that debate tournaments are not as exclusively dedicated to policy resolutions as they were when Lichtman and Rohrer first made their contribution. New debate leagues have emerged at both the high school and intercollegiate levels. Some tournaments are centered on non-policy issues, such as value resolutions. In a debate over a non-policy resolution, much of what Lichtman and Rohrer advocated for rational policy decision making has less relevance. Other analytical decision methods may be more appropriate in "value debates." The "hypothesis testing" paradigm, advocated by David Zarefsky,[6] seems to be attracting considerable attention as a viable approach for non-policy debates.

It should be clearly understood by the reader that the perspective of this textbook is oriented toward the policy systems paradigm for debating and deliberation. We believe it is consistent with and in some ways superior to other leading paradigms for debate. We recognize that competing paradigms for debate can and do exist today,[7] but our preference is for the policy systems analysis perspective articulated first by Lichtman and Rohrer. This does not mean that we believe it is the only paradigm, nor even the best in all controversies that people debate about, either in the real world or in academic tournaments. But it is certainly the perspective used in political and legislative controversies, and it is also the perspective used in academic debates in a majority of tournaments by most debaters and forensics educators. Because the policy systems analysis perspective is comprehensive, coherent, relevant, and understandable, our approach to the elements of debate theory and practice will emphasize it. We shall attempt to keep our treatment as balanced as possible, and to explain alternative approaches where they are appropriate.

THE BENEFITS OF DEBATING

Students who wish to participate in academic debate, either in a class or in a competitive tournament, should expect certain things to be true of their experience. Most of these observations are predictions of benefits to be gained, but some are cautions to heed. These predictions are both immediate and long range.

1. You will immediately *improve your ability to analyze problems* of the sort you are assigned to debate. The fundamental quality of debate is its analytical approach to policy systems, with their essential elements, interactive relationships, and consequences. Therefore, the first thing you will study is the way to analyze a problem area, devise solutions, and make rational discriminations among competing alternatives.

2. In the long run, you will find that this analytical outlook will lead you to *be a better citizen.* At the least, you will be a more informed member of your community and nation for understanding the dynamics of policy formation and policy change. Possibly, you will become an active leader and contributor to public life in some capacity. All of the co-authors of this textbook are active forensics educators and have been for years. Each of us can recall former students who are now lawyers and government leaders, or are involved in various other professional positions that draw heavily from their experiences as debaters. Many surveys have revealed the pervasiveness of debate training as a part of the backgrounds of leading citizens. A majority of the members of Congress were either high school or college debaters. A large proportion of those listed in *Who's Who in America* were formerly debaters.

3. You will immediately *improve your ability to communicate.* The skills of organizing your case, producing relevant evidence to your claims, listening and making sensible responses to your opponents' cases, and speaking in public are fundamental to academic debate.

4. In the long run, you will find that you will improve your communication skills, including the ability to organize your thoughts, compose logical and compelling messages, assert yourself in adverse situations, and speak with confidence and force. These *skills will be transferable to any goal you have in life.* You will find these skills will help your grades in most other courses, and they will help you succeed in almost any career.

5. You will immediately *become a better library researcher.* In academic debate, a heavy emphasis is placed on proving your points with evidence, which is accomplished by using direct quotations from publications found in the library. You will become familiar with the card catalog, the *Readers' Guide to Periodic Literature,* the leading newspapers and opinion magazines, and many professional and scholarly journals. You will also become familiar with government documents. Also, as more libraries install computerized catalog access terminals, along with access to major research database information retrieving systems, you will be more likely to utilize these facilities for doing research not only for debate, but for all other needs.

Here is a caution to heed: Academic debate is time-consuming because of the heavy demands to produce evidence through research. This is not as true of preparing an assignment for a classroom debate as it is of preparing to debate as a member of the school's team in competitive tournaments. You will find that, as a general rule, the time required to study for a typical course in argumentation and debate is not equal to other advanced courses in communications or English. For most students, it amounts to much more.

Participation in competitive debate requires even more commitment than does a course in argumentation and debate. A significant difference exists between preparing to present a single side of one classroom debate (usually in collaboration with the students who will be your opponents for the event), and preparing to enter a tournament where you will be expected to debate on both sides of the resolution for six or eight debates. You have no way of anticipating what your opponents' cases may be except for your analysis of all the possible arguments that could reasonably be made. (This is the same situation that exists in actual argument situations, such as courtroom trials.) Even with a coordinated, cooperative team effort to brainstorm ideas and compile evidence into a centralized, shared file, you can expect to devote many hours to preparation activities alone. In addition, a tournament will require an entire weekend, along with the time needed for travel to and from its location.

A majority of participants in academic debate never enter a tournament in high school or college. Of those who do, a majority only enter tournaments during one semester, or one year. But for most contestants, the activity of debating is enjoyable and alluring. A few become varsity debaters at the national championship level. For those who limit their experience, it is usually not because the activity is unenjoyable or unrewarding, but because they lack the time required to excel in it.

Like anything else, you get out of debate what you put into it. At the classroom assignment level, you will gain the important abilities to analyze, communicate, and do more effective library research. The amount of these skills you gain may be less than those of a committed varsity debater; but it will be more than those who do not take the course.

6. You will immediately be *better prepared to enter a professional school*—in particular, a law school—or other course of advanced or graduate training. Other things being equal, you will find that having had debate experience will give you a significant advantage over other applicants to law school or graduate school in some fields. Admission officials for law schools often place a premium on one extracurricular activity: debate.

7. In the long run, if you enter law school, you will have a *competitive edge over your classmates,* other factors being equal. This is true for several reasons. First, the analytical techniques and the subject matter for debate are akin to the types of research, analysis, and problem areas you will study in law school. Second, a record of success in academic debate marks you as a diligent, hard worker with high motivation to succeed. Third, it shows a natural aptitude and interest in the career field of law practice or other public service. Even though "pre-law" is not a formal major, *per se,* at most undergraduate institutions, you will find that most pre-law academic counselors recommend a course in argumentation and debate as a part of every undergraduate degree program, regardless of the choice of major field of study.

The preceding paragraphs should not be misinterpreted. We do not claim that academic debate will make you a better lawyer. Most practicing lawyers do not make courtroom speeches or engage in formal debates. Our point is that law schools conduct their courses very much along the lines that academic debaters follow in the course of their normal participation and study. Once in law school, former debaters have a real advantage over non-debaters. Other things being equal, former debaters are often preferred over other applicants to law school. This is a more limited claim for one of the benefits of debate, but it appears to be a very substantial benefit for anyone planning to go to law school.

8. You will *enjoy a competitive, challenging intellectual game.* By no means do we intend to promote academic debate on the basis of gamesmanship. However, we see no reason to ignore the fact that most students who participate are motivated by the pleasure of joining in—and possibly winning—a game of wits. Furthermore, the more involved you become in debate, the more fun it is. It is especially fun if you learn the secrets of winning more debates than you lose.

9. In the long run, you will find that your competitive experiences will *provide you with a more tolerant and flexible approach to life.* Daniel M. Rohrer wrote that an intrinsic value of debate is that it concentrates on the growth of the individual in self-understanding, and in understanding others.[8] Sometimes you win and sometimes you lose, even when you think you probably deserve the opposite result. To learn how to lose is a valuable lesson in humility, but to learn how to win is a treasure of exhilaration.

Beyond the qualities of flexibility and adaptation to the fortunes of life, you will also expand your limits of intellectual tolerance for ideas. If academic debate teaches nothing else, you learn about the complexities that underlie issues and make them debatable. You will be a less dogmatic thinker, even while your powers of analysis and critical judgment are sharpened by the training and discipline inherent in debate.

In summary, Colburt and Biggers recently surveyed the literature of the educational benefits of debate. They concluded: "The literature suggests that debaters benefit in at least three areas. First, forensic competition improves the students' communication skills. Second, forensics provides a unique educational experience because of the way it promotes depth of study, complex analysis and focused critical thinking. Third, forensics offers excellent pre-professional preparation."[9]

SUMMARY

Debate is a decision-making process which emphasizes reasoning as a tool for making decisions in argumentative situations. It is useful and appropriate in situations when a decision must be made, there is conflict between people, the decision is uncertain, peaceful and rational means are preferred, and the parties to the disagreement are committed to their own side. Under these conditions, the decision-making process calls for a third party to be an objective critic and judge of the debate. Therefore, debate is defined as a process in which people argue for opposing sides of a conflict, using rational rules and methods in preference to force or emotions, to obtain a decision for one side or the other by an objective third party.

Argumentation and debate may occur in numerous forums or arenas for decision-making. Some of these include the courtroom, the scientific laboratory, and the halls of Congress, among many others. Each argumentative or decision-making forum proceeds according to a paradigm, or pattern for guiding the choice of what counts as evidence, and what rules of inference are followed in arriving at conclusions.

We subscribe to the policy decision-making paradigm as the best one available for studying argumentation and debate. It is modeled on actual decision-making procedures in public forums of debate, such as the legislative hearing. In terms of academic debate for classroom use or tournament competition, the policy systems paradigm is also the most widely known and used one. Yet it is flexible enough to allow the incorporation of other paradigms as well.

Throughout this book, many of the points we have raised here will be fully elaborated. In three major parts, this book will explain our approach to advocacy, how to prepare for advocacy, the process of advocacy, and how to apply these principles of advocacy in argumentation and debate.

In Part One, we discuss the policy systems paradigm and some corollary principles of effective decision making. In Part Two, we discuss the methods of conducting research for information, the topics of evidence and reasoning, the techniques of composing argumentative briefs and blocks, and the essential tools for advocacy. In Part Three, the specific steps in the process of advocacy are examined, including both affirmative and negative cases, strategies, and tactics, along with refutation, cross-examination, and style.

Notes

[1]Thomas S. Kuhn, *The Structure of Scientific Revolution, 2d Ed.* (Chicago: Univ. of Chicago Press, 1970).

[2]Douglas McGregor, *The Human Side of Enterprise* (NY: McGraw-Hill, 1960).

[3]Vincent Ostrom, *The Intellectual Crisis in Public Administration* (University, AL: Univ. of Alabama Press, 1973) 17.

[4]Bernard L. Brock, James W. Chesebro, John F. Cragan, and James F. Klumpp, *Public Policy Decision-Making: Systems Analysis and Comparative Advantages Debate* (NY: Harper & Row, 1973).

[5]Allan J. Lichtman and Daniel M. Rohrer, "Role of the Criteria Case in the Conceptual Framework of Academic Debate, Parts 1–5" five successive installments in *Debate Issues,* Jan.–May 1970. A frequently quoted article by Lichtman and Rohrer is "The Logic of Policy Disputes," *Journal of the American Forensic Association* 16 (1980), 236–47. Several important articles by Lichtman and Rohrer (and others) are reprinted in David A. Thomas and Jack Hart (eds.), *Advanced Debate: Readings in Theory, Practice, and Teaching, 3rd Ed.* (Lincolnwood: National Textbook, 1987). A special forum on policy systems analysis, edited by David A. Thomas, appeared in the *Journal of the American Forensic Association,* 23 (Winter 1986).

[6]David Zarefsky, "Argument as Hypothesis Testing," in *Advanced Debate,* 205–15. A special forum on hypothesis testing appeared in the *Journal of the American Forensic Association,* 19 (Winter 1983), 158–90. See also J.W. Patterson and David Zarefsky, *Contemporary Debate* (Boston: Houghton Mifflin, 1983).

[7]See the special forum on debate paradigms featuring an article by Robert C. Rowland, "Standards of Paradigm Evaluation," together with three articles in response, in *Journal of the American Forensic Association* 18 (Winter 1982), 133–60.

[8]Daniel M. Rohrer, "Debate as a Liberal Art," in *Advanced Debate,* 3–11.

[9]Kent Colbert and Thompson Biggers, "Why Should We Support Debate?" *Journal of the American Forensic Association,* 21 (Spring 1985), 237.

CHAPTER TWO

POLICY SYSTEMS

Argument plays an important role in our society. Every day we engage in arguments with other individuals, and the outcome of these arguments affects the way we live. Some of these arguments are relatively trivial, such as those we may have about where to eat, or which team will win a football game. Other arguments, such as those in Congress about defense spending, economic policy, or energy programs, may influence the futures of millions of individuals. Between these two extremes are arguments made in corporations, courtrooms, churches, and classrooms that affect numerous people. Given its pervasive impact in our society, an understanding of argumentation is important for any individual attempting to interact with other people.

We think that it is important to understand the situations in which arguments arise, because the situations have much to do with the way we make and evaluate arguments. We argue with our spouses or other loved ones in interpersonal situations, and we argue formally in courtrooms. Obviously, we do not argue in those two situations in exactly the same way, nor do we react the same way to arguments that take place in different environments. We may see political candidates debate on television during an election campaign and we also see elected officials debate bills in Congressional hearings on cable television, or on the network news coverage of legislative action. The arguments in these two environments differ in their nature and in their interest to the public, even though the same individuals are involved, often speaking about exactly the same topics. It is the situation that is different: in the election campaign, the candidate is trying to arouse the voters' interest and persuade them to cast votes; but in the hearings, he or she is trying to conform to the technical requirements of actual legislative rules and to be effective within that body.

We are particularly interested in studying public argumentation in situations where policies are at stake. Here, the most promising approach to the study of argument is the policy systems analysis model. This perspective attempts to evaluate alternative courses of action by examining the policies being advocated as being detailed sets of changes that are made within a larger political or social system. Alternative policies are examined in a rigorous manner in order to determine the best course of action. The various effects of these alternative policies are examined and weighed in an attempt to accurately predict the implications of the alternatives available to the policy maker. To understand the nature of this approach to argument, it is necessary to understand two related concepts: that of a *system* and that of a *policy system*.

THE NATURE OF A SYSTEM

Systems analysis has become a very popular method for explaining the subject matter in many academic subjects during the last decade or so. Since the philosopher of science, Ludwig von Bertalanffy,[1] introduced his theory of "general systems analysis," practically every introductory or survey course in the college catalog has applied it to its subject matter. Von Bertalanffy observed that the different branches of science were being studied—and taught—in a very fragmented fashion. Yet, in his view (which he explained very simply), there were some general principles that apply to all sciences, with all of them using the same notion of nature as a systemic organization of components in operation together in some dynamic process to produce a predictable outcome. It takes little imagination to cross-apply his notion of systems analysis— identifying the components, observing their dynamics, deducing their rules and effects—to other subjects in non-technical areas such as the social sciences, and even, with a little creativity, to some of the arts and humanities.

Let us take a closer look at systems analysis in general, and see how it can help clarify our thinking about a subject. Later, in the next section of this chapter, we can work through the process of applying the principles of systems analysis to decision making in policy formation and policy change.

First, let us define a system. A system is a set of interrelated components (or items) that operate in an environment to achieve a goal. Any effort to solve a problem, or to make changes in a system, may require that we alter one or more of these components of a system. However, changing components will inevitably result in numerous other effects. Before we act, therefore, it is important to understand the nature of the system in which we operate.

There are five elements of any system: its components or parts; the relationships between the parts; the environment of the system; the goal of the system; and the management of the relationships between the parts of the system.[2]

Individual Components of a System

The first element of a system consists of the *individual components* of that system. Any system has individual parts that, taken together, help make up the whole system. To understand how a system works, it is important that we first identify the parts that combine to make up the system. For example, if we were to analyze a university as a system, we would probably start by identifying the individual components of the university. These components would consist of such things as the faculty, the students, the administrative staff, and so on. Similarly, if we were to view the legal system from a systems perspective, we would need to examine the lawyers, the judges, the defendants, the witnesses, the parole officers, etc.

The parts, or components, of a complex system may include subsystems of their own. For example, an analysis of the government of the United States would require an understanding of its components, including Congress, the executive branch, administrative agencies, the court system, and state and local governments. In turn, each of these components could also be viewed as a system. Congress, for example, is composed of numerous committees, and each member of Congress has an individual staff. Similarly, the international system consists of both individual nations and international organizations. Each of these components, in turn, is a complex system.

Interrelationships of the Components

The second element of a system is the *relationship between the components* of the system. The components of a system do not operate in isolation; instead they interact with each other. In a University system, the faculty interacts with the students, and the administrative staff interacts with the faculty. Similarly, in any system, as in any complex society, no individual component can act without affecting numerous other components of that system. For example, many environmentalists argue that any change in the population of one species of animals may affect the entire animal population. If one species of animal becomes extinct, those animals that feed on the extinct animal may become threatened with starvation. In addition, those animals that, in the past, had been threatened by the newly extinct animal may start multiplying more rapidly, affecting numerous other animals. This complex set of interrelationships would spread out until almost all animals would be affected in some manner.

To understand fully how a system works, it is important to understand how the components of a system relate to each other. How does a change in component X affect component Y? What components are vital to the functioning of component Z? How many components are interacting together? What counter-forces are there to hinder or moderate a given interaction? Is a relationship between two components direct, or indirect? Without this knowledge, it is difficult to predict the exact effects of alterations of the system. Systems analysis helps us probe the interrelationships between elements of a system and helps us organize our knowledge of the system in a meaningful manner.

Components in the system are often arranged in a hierarchy. Larger components are composed of smaller components. The Federal government, for example, is composed of three independent branches (legislative, executive, and judicial). The branches are composed of smaller components (individual departments, for example, or committees), which are composed of still smaller components.

Environment of a System

The third element in a system is its *environment*. A system does not operate in a vacuum; instead it is a part of a larger environment. The university operates within the larger community in which it is located, and it also operates as one institution in the state's university system. The United States operates within the context of the world political system. To look at a system from the narrow perspective of only its own components will cause us to lose track of the broader context within which our decisions must be made. While we may not be able to control these external factors, they can control the success or failure of the policies we seek to evaluate. The legal system, for example, is often influenced by a number of external elements. The state of the economy influences the number of individuals who will commit crimes. The political environment controls the amount of resources that the court systems can use to combat crime, as well as the restrictions that are placed upon people acting within the legal environment. While the legal system, or any system, may have distinct boundaries, it is influenced by factors beyond its control.

The environment consists of several elements, and the relevant parts of the environment often depend on the nature of the system we are examining. This environment can include natural forces such as rain, floods, climatic forces, and so on. It can also include the political climate that surrounds the system, or the economic, material, and personnel resources available to the system.

In examining the relationship between a system and its environment, it is important to understand that there are two types of systems, an open system and a closed system. The open system will draw in resources from its environment and return resources to the environment in which it operates; the system interacts with the world around it. Examples of this type of system would include almost any living animal, the American economic system, or any private corporation. In all these instances, the system does not operate in isolation; it draws from and interacts with the environment around it, whether it be the physical atmosphere or the economy of other countries. A closed system, on the other hand, is a self-sufficient system that does not interact directly with its environment. A submarine, for example, may be viewed as a relatively closed system since it provides all its own air, food and energy, and it disposes of most of its wastes within its own system. While the submarine functions within an environment, that environment has only a marginal effect on the way the submarine operates.

There are very few examples of a true closed system. Even a submarine needs to surface for air, replace crew members, or obtain supplies, and it is sensitive to outside water pressure and temperature changes. In social sciences and public-policy decision making, the types of systems that are altered are open systems, with each component being interrelated with numerous other components of the system. In order to understand how the open system operates and to predict the effects of an alteration of the system, it is necessary to examine these complex interrelationships.

Goal of a System

The fourth element of a system is its *goal*. Systems do not operate randomly; they are created for some purpose. To understand a system fully we need to understand why the system was created and what goals the system attempts to achieve. These goals may be stated goals, as is the case with many organizations or governments, or they may be unstated goals that we can only discover by examining how the system works and what objectives the organization seems to be seeking.

Management of a System

The final element of a system is the *management* of the system. There is usually some part of the system that controls the activity within it. Someone or something oversees the system and determines how it will work. In an organization, this may be a single individual or a group of individuals who make the decisions about how the system should work and attempt to place these decisions into force. In a social system, the management of the system would be comprised of those individuals who control the way the system operates. When we talk about a social system there may be no single individual who is responsible for overseeing the operation of the system, but there may be a set of guidelines that govern the operation of the system. In some cases, the management will consist of a set of natural rules that govern how the system interacts.

These last two elements of a system, the goals and the management, are especially important in human organizations. While natural systems such as the solar system and the ecological system may be said to have goals and management only in a broad sense of the terms, these components are important for human-created systems. Humans create social systems to achieve specific goals, and they develop specific methods for ensuring that these goals are carried out.

It is clear that, in order to describe any system fully, we need to examine the components of that system, the relationships between those components, the environment within which the system operates, the goals of the system, and the management of the system.

THE NATURE OF A POLICY SYSTEM

A system can be compared to a policy system, which is a subset of the larger system. A policy system is set of interrelated actions (for example, rules, regulations, court decisions, or laws) set up to govern behavior within a jurisdiction that has power to formulate and enforce the action. A policy system can refer to either an existing system of rules, or a proposed alteration in the way we do things. Schools have dress codes, businesses have credit policies, and governments have laws. All of these policies are binding within the limits of the established jurisdiction and are changeable according to rules of procedures that govern the jurisdiction. Policies may be totally opposite in adjacent jurisdictions.

Individual Components of a Policy System

The five elements of a policy system are the same as those of a general system. First, a policy system has components. The components include the specific rules, statutes, decisions, and so on that make up the policy. In examining our foreign policy system, we would examine the economic, diplomatic, and military policies. Our economic policy includes our tax, trade, employment, and monetary policies, etc.

When an advocate defends a new policy system, that policy system often includes a portion of the existing system, as well as specific alterations in the existing system. The advocate of a new military weapon does not usually suggest that the weapon replace our entire military policy; instead it is proposed as a substitute for a portion of the old defense policy, or an addition to the old policy. The new policy contains elements of the old policy.

The advocate of a policy should outline all of the components of the policy system that is being defended. This not only ensures that the advocate has thought out all the implications of the policy, but it also makes sure that the audience understands what exactly is being defended. It is often easy for policy makers to agree on a general goal, but they may disagree on the specific approach to the problem. We may all agree that something should be done about the economy, or that the federal budget should be reduced, but when specific policies are advocated we begin to disagree about what should be done. Some individuals will advocate decreases in defense expenditures, while others will advocate decreases in welfare programs. While there may be agreement on general principles, the support for specific policies will vary. If the debate remains at the general level, we may have some agreement about the subject being debated, but at the same time no concrete solution will be reached. The only way to deal productively with a problem is to focus the debate on the specific alternatives that are available to the policy maker.

Relationships Between the Components

The components of a policy system are also interrelated. These *interrelationships* affect the ways that policies operate. The various branches of government help check and balance the operations of other branches. The judiciary can declare laws passed by Congress unconstitutional, thus providing a check on Congress. Congress oversees the executive branch in order to check abuses of power. The President can veto legislation and can appoint, with the approval of Congress, members of the court system. Each branch of government acts as a check on the other branches. Checks and balances ensure that the policy system achieves its intended goals and does what it is supposed to do. They also prevent the policy from doing things that it was not designed to do.

Environment of a Policy System

Policy systems operate within a larger *environment,* and they are designed to alter that environment. For example, our legal policies are designed to alter the social environment by decreasing conflict. One of the goals of our energy policies is to minimize the impact of energy production on the ecological environment. Part of the analysis of any policy is the prediction of the probable effects of that policy on the environment. What problems will the policy eliminate? What new problems will it create?

The environment of a policy system is very complex. Public opinion may restrict the effectiveness of a policy. The mass media, lobbies, social movements, and other forces may affect the outcome of a policy. Economic swings, international tensions, and political pressures will all affect the way the policy system operates.

The effect of a policy system on its environment can be predicted in a number of ways. We may first attempt to look at the nature of the system in which the policy will operate, in order to understand how the larger system operates. By identifying the causes of various elements of that system, we can predict the results of a new policy. For example, if in examining the nature of the American educational system, we determine that the cause of low test scores is that teachers do not spend enough time on basic skills, the solution to the problem would be to develop a policy system that causes teachers to spend more time teaching those skills. The goal of the advocate would be to establish the cause of a problem and to indicate that the proposed policy would eliminate this cause. Another way to predict the effect of a policy would be to examine the effect of similar policies in other environments. Often a policy that is being advocated has been attempted in another jurisdiction or in a pilot study. Finally, we can predict the effect of a policy on its environment by examining the testimony of experts about the effects of those policies.

Goals of a Policy System

A policy system also will have *goals*. We do not create policy systems randomly; they are designed to promote a certain value or to achieve a certain objective. School systems are designed to educate students. The legal system is designed to promote justice. These goals often come into conflict, as is the case, for example, when the goal of law and order conflicts with the goal of preserving individual liberty, or when the goal of economic growth conflicts with the goal of preventing inflation. In these cases the decision maker must establish a hierarchy of values in order to set priorities for the competing goals. Many policy disputes revolve around the resolution of these conflicts: Is law and order more important than justice? Is the right to a fair trial more important than freedom of the press? Is the protection of the environment more important than economic growth? The policy system will reflect the policy maker's hierarchy of values. Any policy decision will inevitably require a choice between competing values; the value system of the advocate determines how this choice is made.

In addition, portions of a policy system may conflict with other parts of the system. The federal government assists tobacco farmers while attempting to decrease the number of smokers. We may increase tariffs (hurting other countries) while increasing economic aid to those countries. We may sell weapons to both sides of a conflict. These conflicts often require modifications of policy systems. This is often accomplished through small changes designed to fine tune the policies and minimize conflicts.

There are numerous types of value systems available to an advocate. The choice of the appropriate system is often made in a subconscious manner, but given its importance, it is desirable that the wise evaluator of policy devote time to determining the most appropriate value system. Three value systems are frequently used by policy makers.

1. Utilitarianism (or pragmatism). The impulse to be practical and efficient is strong in American culture, and it is reinforced by the success that pragmatic, hard-headed people have had in applying this set of values. Pragmatists make decisions based on usefulness or profit. Undistracted by abstract considerations over profound ethical questions, engineers follow very practical systems to build bridges and roads, or fly airplanes. Following sound, conservative fiscal principles, bankers know how to make money. American foreign economic policy, by and large, is based on the utilitar-ian principle of self-interest in world trade and international security. The problem with utilitarianism is that, in its singleminded pursuit of getting a job done, it sometimes places little weight on intangible values. Utilitarianism develops a frame-work for analyzing values, but it does not provide guidance as to how these values should be evaluated. In addition, some have argued that there are certain rights that should not be violated regardless of the consequences.[3]

2. Natural law (abstract ethical practices). The natural law perspective argues that there are certain universal values that should not be violated. For example, this view of values would suggest that certain values, such as the right to privacy, the right to a fair trial, the freedom of speech, and so on, are guaranteed to individuals regardless of their consequences. Some theorists suggest that these rights cannot be denied to an individual, except in a few narrowly defined conditions. For example, from this perspective, the right to a trial could not be denied to an individual simply because it would be convenient for society to deny the right. The right to a trial, and other rights, are guaranteed to the individual regardless of their cost to society. Similarly, according to this perspective, our foreign policy should be based on international law, not what is in the best interest of the United States.

The natural law approach to values has some problems. Some have argued that there are cases where some rights may need to be violated in order to promote the good of society. Others have indicated that, even if natural law, in theory, is desirable, it is impossible to determine which values or rights comprise the natural law. How do we know that the right to privacy is a natural law right? Is the right to an education a natural law? The right to know? Intelligent individuals may disagree on the answers to these questions, and there is no rational way to resolve these disputes.[4]

3. Contemporary American Values. Americans share a fairly large number of values. These values include democracy, liberty, individuality, the Puritan work ethic, family life, and so on. Most (although not all) Americans feel that these values are desirable and that they should be promoted. From this perspective, policies that promote these values are desirable; those that do not are viewed as being undesirable.

While the contemporary American values perspective has some advantages, there are limitations to this approach. First, it does not explain how to resolve value conflicts. Contemporary American values often come into conflict. We accept both individuality and conformity as values, for example, but they are in direct conflict. Other values such as liberty and security or economic growth and the environment may conflict in specific cases. There is no clear method of resolving such conflicts within this value system. In addition, many of these values are accepted uncritically by the public. Simply because Americans (or any group of individuals) think that a value *is* desirable does not mean that the value *should be viewed* as being desirable. Some of our values have been attacked in recent years. The desirability of economic growth, for example, has been criticized by numerous theorists who are concerned about the economic, ecological, and political implications of economic growth. From this perspective, while some American values may be desirable, it is quite possible that some of the values may need to be modified or discarded.[5]

Management of a Policy System

The final part of a policy system is the *management* of the policy. Laws and regulations do not operate by themselves; they need agents who will implement, interpret and enforce their provisions. It is important for any decision maker to examine the nature of the individuals who manage the policy system. Many policy arguments focus on the issue of *who* manages a policy. Should the federal government become involved in education, or should education be regulated by the states? Should social policy be managed by Congress or by the Supreme Court? The individual responsible for the management of a policy system plays a vital role in determining the effectiveness of that policy.

IMPLICATIONS FOR ARGUMENT

Emphasis on Alternative Policies

The systems approach to arguments about policy has at least four major implications for the student of argument.[6] First, systems analysis emphasizes the comparison of alternative policies. Advocates defend specific policy proposals or bills. The process of formulating policy is devoted to comparing these competing proposals. From this perspective, the decision maker must decide between alternative policies. It is not enough simply to reject one policy because the decision maker lacks enough information to be totally certain of its wisdom or because the policy, in the abstract, would create some problems. A policy should be rejected only if there are superior policies available to the critic of the argument. To reject a policy is to tacitly accept an alternative policy. One cannot decide not to decide; that choice, in itself, is a decision to accept a policy (the present system). For example, if a policy maker decides to reject a policy that would prevent the introduction of a new medical drug on the market, that decision would have the effect of permitting the drug to be introduced. The decision not to institute a new program is, in effect, supporting the decision to continue with existing programs, no matter what they are or how ineffective they may be.

The emphasis on alternative policies is important. It means that any advocate must determine what policy system he or she will defend. This policy system should be developed in sufficient detail to permit the target audience to make an intelligent choice between the alternatives being proposed by the advocates. In addition, it means that the participants in a dispute need to develop competing policies; they must defend policies that are mutually exclusive. The basis for policy dispute is that the critic of argument is forced to make a choice between the policy defended by an advocate compared to the policy defended by other advocates; it should be impossible for the critic to support both positions. If an individual advocates the use of air bags to decrease injuries resulting from car accidents, and an opponent advocate responds with a policy system that requires all drivers to wear seat belts, these two systems would not be competitive; the critic could support both systems. Instead, the advocates should force the decision maker to choose between two policy systems that either cannot or should not simultaneously coexist. The essence of policy analysis is the comparison of two or more alternative solutions to a problem.

The emphasis on alternatives also shifts the focus of the debate away from the problem being addressed to the choices available to decision makers. Rather than starting with the problem and asking what can be done, policy makers begin with the available choices and ask which one is the most desirable. In a sense, this outlook is an optimistic one. To focus on individual problems may lead to frustration if the problem cannot be solved completely. To look at a problem and orient our efforts to attempting to solve the inevitable could result in wasted effort. Instead, the systems approach emphasizes the search for the alternatives that are open to us as decision makers. The advocate seeks out alternatives and selects the most desirable policy. While examining problems may be useful in generating and weighing alternative courses of action, the focus is on potential policies and the outcomes of those policies.

Emphasis on Multiple Causes and Multiple Effects

The second implication of systems analysis is its emphasis on multiple causes and multiple effects. The traditional approach to argument often emphasized a single problem and attempted to discover a single cause of that problem. Policy analysis assumes that any individual problem will have multiple causes. Inflation may be caused by excessive government spending, shortages of materials, labor pressures, growth in the money supply, high interest rates, and numerous other factors. Instead of identifying one of these factors as the cause of inflation, policy analysis would examine a single policy and would determine the effect of that policy on inflation, recognizing that any single action may affect only one of the causes of that problem. The recognition of multiple causes of a problem will also suggest that multiple potential solutions should be evaluated.

Policy analysis also recognizes that any action will have multiple effects. A single governmental policy may affect a host of other components in the system being examined. These effects can be complex. Many policies will draw resources from other programs. A significant increase in spending in one program may require decreased expenditures in other programs (or increased taxes or a larger deficit). The political resources needed to mobilize votes to pass a bill may require concessions on other pieces of legislation. A law may have a symbolic effect that either increases or decreases the likelihood of mobilizing support for other legislation.

Emphasis on Risk Analysis

The third implication of systems analysis for argumentation is the increased emphasis on risk analysis.[7] Policy disputes are rarely black or white issues. The very fact that an issue is the subject of debate suggests that there is some evidence to support both sides of a position. Policy analysis recognizes this by emphasizing the probability of the effects of a policy, without requiring that these effects be determined as being certainties.

We live in a world in which there is much uncertainty. Conflicting studies exist on the effects of certain foods on our health, on the risks created by various energy sources, and on the effects of proposed policies. There is little that can be done to eliminate these uncertainties, even though we can attempt to minimize their degree. In war, we must decide how to fight a battle without always knowing the exact strength or location of opposing forces. We may need to implement some social programs without a full understanding of all the causes of a problem. In essence, we are often required to act under uncertainty; we rarely have the luxury of having all the facts necessary to predict the effects of our policies.

Policy analysis recognizes this limitation, and attempts to develop a logic for making decisions under uncertainty. The policy analyst attempts to discover possible effects of a policy system. The analyst then attempts to determine the probability of each effect by weighing the evidence supporting the effect with the evidence undermining the probability of the effect. For example, in a debate over the effects of cigarette smoking on cancer, the critic would not resolve the issue by saying that one advocate "proves" with a 100 percent certainty that cigarette smoking is or is not harmful simply because one side read more studies to support their view or because one study was slightly better than another; rather the judge would look at the evidence and then assign a probability of between 0 and 100 percent that cigarette smoking is harmful. This would permit the weighing of this effect even if the probability of the effect is less than 100 percent.

One problem facing many policy makers concerns what to do with extremely low-level risks. Suppose, for example, the risk of an effect resulting from a policy is not 10 percent or 5 percent but .001 percent. Should this effect be given any weight, or should it be ignored? This is an important issue, since if the disadvantage to a policy has a large effect, even a small risk of that disadvantage may be viewed as having a greater importance than a more certain, but smaller, advantage. The method for weighing effects is to employ a formula of impact equals risk times harm (or benefit). Thus a policy with a 50 percent chance of costing $10,000 is viewed as having the same impact as a policy that is certain to cost $5,000 (.5 × $10,000 = $5,000). Thus, if a policy has a potential effect of producing gigantic harms, even if the risk is small, the harm left by multiplying risk times harm may still dwarf other factors. For example, a nuclear war will probably kill over 100,000,000 people. If a policy has a one in 100,000 (.00001) chance of preventing a nuclear war, by this analysis it should be selected over a policy that will save 990 people with a 100 percent certainty (100,000,000 × .00001 = 1,000, while 990 × 1 = 990).

Those who argue that low-risk arguments should be weighed like any other arguments note that catastrophic events do happen, and that unless we consider the possibility that a policy may produce a catastrophic effect, we are doomed to repeat past errors. We have had depressions and wars, and it is likely that many of those effects were, at the time, viewed as low-risk effects of policies. Today we are faced with potential problems of enormous impact, ranging from overpopulation, climatic shifts, and nuclear war, to massive deprivation of liberty. According to many people, it would be foolish to ignore the risks of these events simply because the risks are low.

Other individuals suggest that, below a certain level, we should ignore low-level probability harms. This view would suggest that, unless there is at least a .05 likelihood of a harm, we should ignore that effect of a policy. This standard would make the decision-making process easier, since it would eliminate numerous marginally relevant effects of a policy. It is also arguable that determining the risk of an effect, always a difficult task, is even more inaccurate at low levels. After all, how can one tell that a .001 risk of nuclear war is not really a .000000000001 risk? In addition, small risks can work both ways; if there is a very slight risk of policy A causing a nuclear war, there may also be a slight risk of policy A making nuclear war less likely. To deal with such low-level probabilities simply diverts our attention from those effects that we are sure will result from the policies being examined. In the long run, it is also arguable that the positive and negative low-probability effects of a policy either cancel each other out, or they are so complicated that it is impossible for us to predict the ultimate result of a policy fully if we look at all low-probability results of a policy.

Method of Assigning Presumption

The final implication of systems analysis for debate is that it assigns presumption with the least risky policy.[8] Presumption is the assumption that, other factors being equal, one policy should be accepted instead of another. Presumption is an important concept in argumentation theory because it determines the decision maker's *predisposition to believe,* or what is presumed to be true before the argument is played out to its end. Without knowing what is presumed to be true, you do not know what you have to prove by your argumentation. Traditionally, there has been a presumption for the present policy system (also known as the *status quo*). It has been assumed that, without a strong reason to change, we should continue to do things the way we traditionally have done them. This presumption has placed a significant burden on those who have advocated a change in policy; not only must they demonstrate that the present system is inadequate, they must prove that there is a significant reason to adopt a new policy.

Since systemic decision making is a comparison of alternative policies, the policy systems approach does not arbitrarily assign presumption to either side of a dispute. Instead, presumption is placed with the side that advocates a policy that involves the least amount of risk. The reason for this method of assigning presumption is that, for a policy analyst, the purpose of presumption is to allow the advocates to account for the influence of unknown factors on the success of a policy. The less we know about a policy, the greater the risk that either the policy will produce unknown disadvantages, or the policy will fail to function as predicted. It is true that there is also the possibility that a risky policy will also produce unforeseen advantages or that the policy will be more successful than anticipated. However, experience with prior policies suggests that unknown desirable effects of a policy are less likely than unknown *un*desirable effects of a policy. In addition, the greater the change that is proposed, the greater the risk of these unknown and undesirable side effects.

To account for these unknown side effects, it is wise to assign presumption with the least risky policy. Generally, the amount of risk a policy entails can be calculated by examining the amount of the change proposed, the importance of the system being altered, the permanence of the change, and the amount of information we have about the effect of the change.

Many factors are used to determine the amount of risk entailed in adopting a policy. For example, we may want to look at the extent of the change involved. The greater the amount of change, the greater the risk of undesirable side effects. Thus a policy altering the method of making welfare payments would entail less risk than a new program providing for a guaranteed annual income for all citizens.

Another way to measure the amount of risk that a policy entails is to look at the importance of the affected system. If a policy alters an important part of a system, then that policy should be viewed as being more risky than one that alters a minor part of the system. For example, a policy that altered the design of the helmets worn by soldiers in Europe would be less risky than a policy that altered the targeting of our nuclear weapons in Europe simply because the nuclear weapons are a more important part of our defense efforts than are the helmets.

A third approach to measuring risk involves examining the state of the present system. If conditions are adequate under the existing programs, then it would make sense to stay with the current system unless the new system is clearly superior. On the other hand, if current conditions are poor, it may be worth the risk to try out a new policy since it is unlikely that the new policy could be much worse than the existing program.

The fourth way to measure risk is to examine the reversability of the advocated policy. Some policies commit us to follow a course of action over a period of several years, while other policies can be modified or reversed if we discover that the initial decision was incorrect. Declaring war, for example, would be a decision that would be very hard to reverse, while an economic sanction or a diplomatic overture could be withdrawn easily. The less the opportunity to reverse a policy exists, the greater the risk of the policy.

Finally, we may wish to examine the amount of information available on a given policy alternative. Some policies will be supported by much high-quality information and we may have the analytic tools needed to predict accurately what the effect of that policy will be with much certainty. Other policies are more speculative; we may have little basis for predicting the effects of the policy and we may have no way of predicting what the policy will do. In this case, it would seem obvious that the policy that we know more about is much less risky; the other policy has a high risk of unknown disadvantages.

In a few cases, presumption in our society is assigned to reflect the values held by society and/or the decision maker. For example, our judicial system is based on the premise that avoiding the conviction of innocent people is more important than convicting guilty individuals. For that reason, we assign a presumption of innocence to an individual accused with a crime. A similar presumption operates in science (presumption is placed against an experimental hypothesis). In the majority of cases, however, these values are reflected in the debates about the policy being evaluated, instead of being arbitrarily assigned prior to the dispute.

A SYSTEMS APPROACH TO A MODEL OF ARGUMENT

So far, we have discussed systems analysis from the perspective of an individual who seeks to develop an understanding of a decision-making situation to determine the best policy to advocate, and from the perspective of the evaluator of argument who seeks to analyze the arguments made by several advocates. These perspectives will be further developed in the later sections of this book. It is important to recognize, however, that arguments do not take place in a vacuum; rather, argument is a type of social interaction between two or more individuals, operating within certain constraints.

Systems analysis can also help us understand the nature of the forum in which argument takes place. A forum is an outlet for discussion of an issue. For example, in law the courtroom acts as a forum for discussing legal issues; in academia journals and conventions act as forums for the examination of new (and old) ideas, and the floor of Congress is one of many forums for the discussion of public policy. Arguments take place in a forum with rules, time limits, and other constraints on the advocate. These constraints preclude some arguments from being developed fully, and they create the opportunities for an advocate to develop strategies to promote other arguments. In addition, each forum develops its own standards for reaching decisions. In order to take full advantage of the opportunities provided by an argumentative forum, it is important to examine the forum as a system of argument.

Whenever we engage in an argument, we do so in an environment that both limits our ability to argue and governs the nature of our arguments. While we often argue without thinking about the system in which we are arguing, understanding that system can usually help us recognize the limitations and the potentials of the argumentation system.

Components of an Argumentative System

From the perspective of the advocate, there are at least four major components of an argumentative system. First, there is the *advocate*. The advocate brings certain skills, background, abilities, and other characteristics into the argumentative situation. Before engaging in an argument, it would be helpful for an advocate to analyze his or her strengths and weaknesses as an advocate. What types of arguments does the advocate present effectively? What weaknesses will the opponents attempt to exploit? What are the beliefs of the advocate? The answers to these and other questions may be useful in developing an argumentative strategy for the advocate.

The advocate faces an *opponent,* who may or may not have similar abilities. A wise advocate attempts to discover the strengths and weaknesses of the opponent so that an appropriate strategy can be developed. What arguments will the opponents be prepared to answer? How well researched will the opponents be? What types of arguments will the other side raise? Knowing the answers to these questions can provide much assistance in preparing for a dispute.

The advocate will also frequently have some individuals who will act as *allies;* they support the position that the advocate advances. These allies can help the advocate present a position, but they can sometimes hinder the advocate's position. The allies may, for example, support more extreme positions than the advocate would like, forcing the advocate to modify his or her position. A candidate for president may be forced to defend the statements of the candidate for vice-president. Proponents of rights for women may be forced to defend some extreme positions with which they may personally disagree because the public may perceive the feminist movement as supportive of these positions. In short, a speaker may be identified with positions, not necessarily because the speaker believes these positions, but because the groups supporting the speaker believe them. This forces the advocate either to support the positions or to make it clear that the beliefs of the allies are not the same as those of the advocate.

Finally, the system includes the *critic;* that individual or group of individuals that decides how an argument should be resolved. This may be a single person, or it could be a large audience. The arguments of the advocate are directed toward this component of the system. The complexity of the argument and the tone of the argument will be influenced by the nature of the critic. In addition, the reliability of the decision will depend on the competence and impartiality of the critic.

Relationships Between the Components

After we have identified the components of an argumentative system, we next need to examine the *relationships* between these elements. Frequently, for example, the judge and the opponent are the same individual, as is the case in many interpersonal arguments. When I argue with a friend, for example, my friend is both an opponent (responding to my arguments) and a critic (determining the strength of my arguments compared to his or her counterarguments). When our opponents are also our critics, our argumentative strategies would be different than if the critic were someone else; for example, we may need to treat weak arguments with more respect and to change the tone of our arguments.

There are other aspects of the relationships between the components of the argumentative system that could affect the nature of the dispute. The two opposing advocates could be able to communicate with each other directly, or they could be restricted to indirect forms of communication. For example, in many social movements, the members of the opposing movements communicate mainly through the mass media. Obviously, the more communication that exists between advocates, the easier it is for the advocates to coordinate strategies. These relationships may also help determine the tone of the dispute.

Environment of an Argumentative System

The third element of an argumentative system is its environment. Argument does not take place in isolation—it takes place in a real-world environment. Some aspects of this environment (the development of new political events, for example) may influence the effectiveness of an argument. Advocates will attempt to gather information from the environment to support the positions that they are defending and, once a policy is adopted, the effects of that policy may become the substance for future arguments.

Goals of an Argumentative System

As we have discussed before, any system operates to achieve certain goals. Frequently these goals will help provide guidelines for the arguments that take place within the system. People engage in argument for a number of reasons. These goals often reflect the values of the individuals engaged in argument. Many of the ethical guidelines accepted by advocates will depend on the goal of the activity. The reasons for engaging in argument affect the type of system that is appropriate for the advocates. There are at least four reasons why people argue. First, some people argue to *discover the truth*. An argument between scholars, for example, often has the goal of discovering what view of reality is most accurate. We argue in classrooms in order to understand the subject under discussion. Many public debates attempt to expose the audience to a variety of viewpoints to enable the audience to understand the issues involved.

Seeking the truth is not the only possible goal of argument, however. A second potential goal of argument is to *select the best possible policy* open to an individual. This goal would acknowledge that any choice must be made using a limited amount of information, and this limitation makes truth an unrealistic expectation. Debates in Congress are directed at discovering the best possible legislation. Debates in a legal setting are often directed not at discovering the truth, but at applying the principles of law to a set of litigants.

A third goal of argument is to *convince other individuals of the validity of a position* that the advocate has already accepted as being true. A political candidate, for example, is not seeking to discover the truth when arguing before a potential voter, nor is the candidate interested in determining the best policy. The candidate has already formulated opinions on these issues, and he or she is attempting to convince the population that his or her opinions are true. A sales clerk would also use argument, not to discover the truth, but to convince a customer to buy something. In both of these cases, the advocate has reached a decision before engaging in an argument; the argument is used to convince others that this decision is correct.

A fourth goal of argument is to *promote social interaction*. We sometimes argue with other individuals, not to change their views towards an object, but to act as the basis for an extended interaction. A person may engage in an argument with another person in an attempt to start (or continue) a conversation. Some psychologists suggest that arguments between marriage partners may be useful in clearing the air and in promoting a healthy long-term relationship. Some arguments serve as a social outlet; they have no serious purpose other than providing entertainment for the participants.

Each of these goals of argument will suggest a different approach to the study of argument. If the goal of argument is to discover the truth, then the advocate should emphasize rational arguments and a rigorous testing of all viewpoints. If the goal is to determine the best policy, then a detailed method of policy analysis should be used. If persuasion is the goal, then the advocate may select arguments that, though irrational, are effective in altering opinions. Finally, if the goal of argument is to promote social interaction, then rules of rationality would be of little importance (and they sometimes might be deliberately ignored), while rules promoting a harmonious interpersonal relationship would be very important. The purpose of argument thus affects the way that we examine argument.

Some forums of argument are ideally suited to the search for the truth. The existence of opposing advocates, each defending a view of reality, allows various opinions to be subjected to thorough testing. It is assumed that if all viewpoints are permitted to be voiced, eventually the truth will emerge from the discussion. If an opinion is false, it should be easy to demonstrate that the view is incorrect. And if a position is partially true and partially false, by subjecting that position to critical scrutiny we can modify the initial position so that it is closer to the truth.

Management of an Argumentative System

Not only are components of the argumentative situation interrelated, but they are managed by some external force. All argumentative situations have certain rules that govern their conduct. A trial, for example, is governed by many regulations governing who may speak, when they can speak, what they can talk about. The judge makes rulings on motions, objections, and other procedural matters and, by doing so, manages the nature of the arguments at the trial. Congress has many regulations governing its debates. Even informal arguments have certain unwritten rules about who may interrupt whom at what time; what may be argued, and so on. In general, these rules govern who may speak, when they may speak (or the order of the speeches), how long they may speak, what rules govern the admissibility of evidence, the amount of advance notice of the subject of the argument, as well as other procedures. Every argumentation system is different, and it would be wise for an advocate to understand what these restrictions are for the system in which the argument takes place. These restrictions are the basis for the strategies of an advocate, and they play an important role in planning of an argumentative campaign.

The purpose of this discussion is to illustrate that no two argumentative systems are identical. This means that a wise advocate will attempt to discover the nature of the argumentative system before starting an argument. This knowledge may help the advocate structure his or her argument to take advantage of the system. Such choices as the timing of an argument, the choice of positions, the tone of the argument, and so on may be based upon the nature of the argumentative forum. Additionally, an advocate may wish to alter the argumentative system to promote the goals of either the advocate or the argumentative system.

▬ SUMMARY ▬

The systems approach to argument is very useful for a student of argument. This chapter has introduced a few of the major components of the systems approach to argument; many of these concepts will be discussed in greater detail in later chapters. We began with a discussion of the nature of a system. A system includes components, their interrelationships, an environment, a system of management, and goals. This was contrasted with a policy system, which contains goals, means, checks and balances, and effects. Debate consists of a comparison of alternative policy systems and the examination of how these policy systems operate within a larger system. This approach has at least four implications for the advocate; it focuses the debate on the comparison of alternatives, it stresses the multiple causes of problems and the multiple effects of policies; it emphasizes the use of risk analysis in weighing alternative courses of action, and it emphasizes a type of presumption that is based upon the risk of the policies being compared.

The systems approach can also be used to analyze the forum in which argument takes place. People do not argue in a vacuum; the arguments take place in an argumentative system. This system controls who may speak, when they may speak, the topic of debate, who evaluates the debate, the goal of the argument, and so on. These factors shape the choices available to an advocate and form the basis for any strategic choices.

Notes

[1] Ludwig von Bertalanffy, *General Systems Theory*. Rev. ed. (New York: George Braziller, 1968).

[2] For a more detailed discussion of systems, see F.E. Emery, ed., *Systems Thinking* (Baltimore: Penguin books, 1969); Ervin Lazlo, ed., *The Relevance of General Systems Theory* (New York: George Braziller, 1972); Ervin Lazlo, *Introduction to Systems Philosophy* (New York: Harper & Row, 1972); and C. West Churchman, *The Systems Approach,* 2nd ed. (New York: Laurel, 1979).

[3] For a defense of utilitarianism, see John Stuart Mill, *Utilitarianism with Critical Essays,* Samuel Gorovitz, ed. (New York: Bobbs-Merrill Company, Inc., 1971). See also J.J.C. Smart and Bernard Williams, *Utilitarianism: For and Against* (Cambridge: Cambridge University Press, 1973).

[4] For a more detailed discussion of natural law, see Thomas Morawetz, *The Philosophy of Law: An Introduction* (New York: Macmillan Publishing Co., Inc., 1980), pp. 59–75.

[5] See Edward D. Steele and W. Charles Redding, "The American Value System: Premises for Persuasion," *Western Speech,* 26 (1962), 83–91. See also Richard D. Rieke and Malcolm D. Sillars, *Argumentation and the Decision Making Process,* 2nd ed. (Glenview, IL: Scott, Foresman and Company, 1984).

[6] Allan J. Lichtman and Daniel M. Rohrer, "The Logic of Policy Dispute," *Journal of the American Forensic Association,* 16 (Spring 1980), 235–47; and Allan J. Lichtman, Daniel M.

Rohrer, and Jerome Corsi, "Policy Systems Analysis in Debate," in *Advanced Debate, 3rd ed.,* David A. Thomas and Jack Hart (eds.) (Lincolnwood: National Textbook Company, 1987). pp. 216–30.

[7]Vincent Follert, "Risk Analysis: Its Application to Argumentation and Decision-Making," *Journal of the American Forensic Association,* 18 (Fall 1981), 99–108.

[8]Allan J. Lichtman and Daniel M. Rohrer, "Decision Rules in Debate: Presumption and Burden of Proof," in Thomas and Hart, pp. 347–72.

CHAPTER THREE

DECISION
MAKING

Before an advocate can begin to develop a case, it is necessary to understand the nature of the issues being debated. An effective advocate devotes much time and energy to preparing for an argument. It is not uncommon, for example, for lawyers to spend the vast majority of their time preparing for trial—researching, analyzing legal issues, preparing cases—and very little time actually arguing the case. Any advocate should devote a significant amount of effort to analyzing the issues in a dispute. In order to be an effective advocate, an individual must know which position is worth defending. Ideally, one does not argue for the sake of arguing; one argues because an analysis of the facts has revealed that a certain position is worthy of the advocate's support. The question becomes, how does one decide what positions warrant our active advocacy?

In answering this question, it is important to distinguish between several related analytical concepts. Some of our analysis is problem solving in nature: we are confronted with a problem, and we attempt to develop certain solutions to minimize or eliminate the problem. A school board faced with declining test scores, for example, may meet in order to develop effective strategies to solve the problem. Problem solving is distinguished from decision making, which is oriented toward making choices among potential actions. More than one possible action is made available to an individual (or a group), and one of these actions is selected. Decision making may or may not occur in response to a specific problem. For example, an industry considering expanding its markets will consider several alternatives and then make a decision as to which alternative should be taken. This decision may not be in response to a problem; it may simply be made to improve the strength of the industry.

Policy making is a broader concept than either problem solving or decision making. Policy making involves the translation of broad decisions into specific policies. We may have decided to do something about poverty; policy making translates that desire into specific action and then attempts to implement the action.

We are faced with important choices every day. As we make these decisions, it is important that we develop a systemic approach to the problems that we face. If we use an unsystematic decision-making process, the result can be disastrous. The question becomes: what are the characteristics of a rational decision-making process?[1]

There are six critical stages in the decision-making process. First, the policy maker must identify the problem. Next, the policy maker selects an appropriate strategy for approaching the problem. Third, the policy maker generates several possible alternative methods of solving the problem, and then the policy maker determines the effects of adopting each proposed alternative. Fifth, the best alternative is selected. Finally, the decision maker implements the chosen policy. These stages may not always be separate and recognizable, but they are essential for effective decision making. Each of these stages warrants a more detailed examination.

IDENTIFYING THE PROBLEM

Before any policy maker can address any issue, he or she must first notice that there is the need to make a choice about something. Every day we are faced with hundreds of potential choices, ranging from the trivial to those choices that affect our entire future. The first problem facing any policy maker is to decide which choices are worthy of the attention of the advocate and which choices should be neglected. Which issues should we devote time and effort to in order to be prepared to argue? The policy maker is faced with a problem of having an infinite number of potential choices and a finite amount of time to devote to those choices. The question is, how should the limited time of the policy maker be allocated?

This problem is faced by all decision makers. Congress is faced with the problem of agenda building. Congress has jurisdiction over many problems, yet in every session our representatives can devote energy to only a small number of these issues. Often issues such as health care, legal reform, and political reform are neglected, not because these issues are unworthy of attention, but because there are more pressing problems that face Congress. The Supreme Court has jurisdiction over thousands of cases which are appealed to it every term, yet the Court can only deliberate on about a hundred of these cases if it plans to devote adequate time to each case. A newspaper reporter can report on any of thousands of potential news items, yet he or she has time to cover only a fraction of these news events. In deciding what issues are worthy of attention, the policy maker assigns a set of priorities to the range of possible subjects demanding time, effort, and action.

This problem is a difficult one to resolve. Paradoxically, the task of determining what issues are worthy of one's attention diverts time from the actual decision-making process—indeed, some have argued that often the Supreme Court has spent more effort deciding what cases to hear than in actually deliberating on the cases it finally hears. This effort is well spent, however. Just as one can make an error by adopting the wrong policy, a person can make an error by failing to notice a problem that exists and thereby not even considering what steps to take. Some scientists have argued that the problem with our energy policy before 1973 was not that the arguments advanced by the advocates discussing the energy policy were poor, but that no one considered the energy policy worthy of their attention until the energy crisis was serious. The problem with the arguments on the crisis was that there *were* no arguments about the energy problem. It is often suggested that many policy makers have a crisis mentality, that is, the fault of ignoring a problem until it becomes serious and then attempting to develop stopgap methods to eliminate the problem. This is an issue with the problem-solving approach to issues. If we wait until a crisis is imminent, it may be too late to avert the problem. A wiser strategy would be to consider the choices that confront us and to determine which choices are worthy of being examined. Like an ideal legislative body, we need to examine the problems surrounding us—both current and future—and decide which of these problems we should seek to address.[2]

There is no clear-cut way to make this choice. The choice of which issues to address will often reflect the values of the decision maker. Sometimes the choice of topic is made for the advocate by someone else. For example, in academic debate, the topic for debate is decided prior to a tournament. There are some factors, however, that should be taken into consideration before an individual decides either to examine the options available to him or her, or to decide that a choice is inconsequential.

Significance of the Decision.　First, the decision maker may wish to examine the importance of the issue. While this may be hard to do until the policy maker conducts additional research into the problem, it would be worthwhile to examine whether the problem has the potential to be significant. For example, our nuclear weapons policy obviously has the potential to shape the future of the entire world. That would make it a very high-priority issue. On the other hand, the choice of America's national bird, while important to a few individuals, is unlikely to drastically affect the future of America.

Controversy.　A policy maker may also look at the controversial nature of the problem. A problem that generates much controversy should probably receive more of our attention than a problem that many individuals view as being unworthy of discussion. The fact that many individuals are concerned with issues like abortion, prayer in the school, and educational policies suggests that these issues are worthy of our attention. While some issues that are of little interest to the population may also be important (DNA research, for example), the other standards can be used to call our attention to these policies. In general, someone who overlooks issues with wide popular interest risks missing important areas of controversy.

Permanence.　The policy maker should devote more attention to a recurring problem than to a temporary problem. Some issues are temporary in nature; once they are decided the energy we spent deciding these issues will be of no further use. In other cases a decision we make may have implications for future decisions. For example, more time should be devoted to attempting to minimize traffic congestion caused by urbanization of an area (which is permanent) than to solve congestion caused by a temporary influx of visitors. The more likely a choice is to be repeated in the future, the more important the choice.

Immediacy.   A problem that is of current interest or that requires immediate action is more likely to warrant our attention than a problem that was either important only long ago or will be far in the future. While some long-term planning is often desirable, we should not be so concerned about the future that we forget about today's problems. Deciding what to do in the distant future may be futile in some cases; conditions may change so much in the interim that the choice we make today may be outdated by the time we plan to act. On the other hand, if we fail to decide on current problems, they may continue while we put off our decision making. Future problems can often (but not always) be put aside while we consider immediate issues.

Availability of Information.   The availability of information may influence the amount of energy we spend on a problem. For some choices, the information required for making a rational decision may not be available until sometime in the future. This may suggest that the advocate delay consideration of this issue until the information becomes available. It may be desirable to withhold judgment on a legal issue until the courts have gathered all the information and decided the issue; at that point we can determine if the court made the correct decision. The Supreme Court decided in the late 1970s, for example, to delay a decision on the use of television cameras in the courtroom until additional studies had been conducted on the effects of cameras on trials. Deciding an issue before we have adequate information may lead to undesirable decisions.

Complexity.   The complexity of an issue may also influence the desirability of investigating a problem. The time required to reach a decision on a complex issue may be better spent deliberating on several less-complicated issues. Congress has, on occasion, delayed debating patent law reform because the issue was so complex that some members were unsure that they could understand all the details of the debate. If a problem is extremely complex, an individual may research the topic only to discover that he or she knew no more about the topic after researching the topic than before. The complexity of the topic could result in wasted energy.

Control over Outcome.   The decision maker should limit deliberations to those issues that are under his or her control. While the issue of whether Japan should develop a nuclear weapon may be more important than the decision about where a student should attend graduate school, for the student the second decision has a higher priority since that student can have some control over that decision, while it is unlikely a single student could have much of an influence over Japanese nuclear policy. It makes sense to concentrate our energy on issues we can do something about, instead of issues that we cannot affect.

All of these factors need to be taken into account when determining what issues are worthy of a higher priority to solve. The control of the public forum's agenda can be just as important in guaranteeing that a wise policy is adopted as the arguments on these issues. Not only will a good advocate promote good arguments on an issue, the advocate should attempt to ensure that the important problem areas are discussed. In this manner, decision makers can be sure their attention and efforts are not diverted to low-priority subjects at the expense of neglecting higher priority situations that demand a decision.

SELECTING A DECISION-MAKING STRATEGY

Once an advocate has decided that an issue is worthy of attention, the next step is to develop an appropriate strategy for deciding what should be done. The advocate can determine that a problem is worthy of only minor attention, and thus the problem may be given only perfunctory analysis. For a high-priority issue, the advocate may decide that the problem requires extensive analysis. In order to make this determination, however, the advocate needs to be familiar with the potential decision-making options available. There are five major decision-making strategies open to a policy maker: optimizing, satisficing, incrementalism, mixed scanning, and intuition.

Optimizing Strategy

The optimizing strategy seeks to discover the best possible solution to a problem. The goal of this strategy is to seek out the solution that produces the best results. To that end, the decision maker attempts to consider all possible alternatives to a problem, collects all available information on the topic, and then processes all the information in order to discover the best possible solution. This type of decision-making strategy is not used very often, for reasons that will soon be discussed. A few complex court cases consider a relatively limited issue, but both sides attempt to introduce all available information into the court in order to ensure the "best" possible decision.

While this approach may produce the best solution to a problem, there are some problems with this decision-making strategy. First, optimizing requires considerable time, money, and effort. To explore all alternatives fully would require far too many resources to make this strategy practical for most decisions. For example, a high government official in Canada once asked a research institute to propose the optimized system for national taxation. The project was quickly abandoned when the researchers submitted an estimate that the total costs of doing a study guaranteed to produce an optimized taxation system would exceed the expected tax revenue for a year. Second, even if all the information on all the options available to us could be collected, it is unlikely that any individual could absorb or organize all of this information in any meaningful manner. We have a limit to the amount of information that we can process, and the optimizing strategy requires that we process an amount of information that greatly exceeds our mental capability in many cases. Finally, the optimizing strategy assumes that we can quantify the impact of all our decisions; an assumption that we soon will see may be unwarranted. While it is possible in theory to optimize a solution to any given problem, in practice only the simplest and smallest systems may be treated optimally. Therefore, *suboptimal* decisions are the usual result of decision-making processes. When analysts describe a decision as *suboptimal,* they do not mean to imply that it is inferior or slipshod. Rather, they mean the suboptimal decision-making methods are based on the use of *best estimates* of data instead of actual data. It is more feasible to make reasonable estimates than to pay the high costs of obtaining huge volumes of complex information. Clearly, suboptimal solutions are more limited than the optimized solution; but suboptimal decision making may still be regarded as better than unsystematic methods.

Satisficing Strategy

A second decision-making strategy is the satisficing strategy.[3] Satisficing is a good example of a suboptimal decision-making strategy that is very feasible and popular. Instead of attempting to discover the best policy, this strategy attempts to discover a policy that meets certain minimum requirements; it seeks a policy that is "good enough" to be adopted, even though it is not perfect. For example, in hiring a worker, some industries do not look for the "ideal" worker; as soon as a satisfactory applicant applies for a job, he or she is hired. The industry seeks a satisfactory solution to its problem, not necessarily the best solution. This goal is accomplished by generating a moderate number of alternatives (although, unlike the optimizing strategy, not all alternatives are examined), establishing certain minimum requirements for a solution, and then adopting the policy that best meets these minimal requirements. This approach requires less time than does the optimizing strategy, although it also produces a result that is less than perfect. Some have suggested that the satisficing strategy also emphasizes short-term values over long-term effects since the minimal requirements are stated as short-term effects.

Incremental Strategy

A third approach to decision making is the incremental approach.[4] This approach suggests that any problem should be addressed by emphasizing small changes in existing policies, instead of making drastic changes or adopting new policies that significantly alter the way we do things. We should seek to change the present slowly, according to this viewpoint, one step at a time, rather than attempting major policy alterations. This approach would cause the decision maker to start with the existing system and it would limit the options considered to the minor changes that can be made without altering fundamental values. For example, some have argued that our attack on the problems of poverty has been incremental in nature. Instead of developing a comprehensive poverty program, we have passed relatively small, piecemeal programs. If a specific failure of poverty programs is identified, we pass small laws designed to eliminate that specific problem. Eligibility requirements are raised or lowered in an attempt to adjust our policies to the conditions of society. Our policies have emphasized small, incremental changes.

This is not the case in other areas. There are some cases of large, non-incremental policies. When President Kennedy decided to increase federal support for the space program, he pushed for large increases in spending and radical shifts in the direction of the program. While, since that time, many changes in our space program have been incremental, the initial creation of the space program was an example of a non-incremental policy.

Incrementalism has several advantages. Since the changes made are small, it means that the resources that we have invested in current structures are maintained. To adopt a radically new program to replace existing ones would waste all that we have invested in current programs. In addition, the small changes suggested by incrementalism increase the certainty that we can predict the effects of a policy. If the small changes produce bad side effects, we can return to the earlier ways of doing things without much difficulty. This allows us to better manage both the policy and the effects of the policy.

At the same time, incrementalism does have some weaknesses. Since it promotes change through small increments, it is an extremely slow process. Because it uses existing policies as a starting place, it often perpetuates existing value systems and favors the values of the powerful more than the values of the powerless. Some have suggested that in some areas, radical changes are needed to solve our problems. Advocates of a nuclear arms freeze, for example, suggest that the solution to an arms race is not minor alteration in our nuclear weapons policy, but a complete revision of our way of looking at nuclear war.

The incremental decision-making strategy is a cautious, conservative, "fine-tuning" approach. Therefore it is also a continuous, ongoing process. Its actions and decisions always appear in the form of compromises between interested parties or factions. Incrementalism is best suited for large, complex organizations in which rapid or revolutionary changes are not feasible or desirable. For example, General Motors Corporation engages in incremental decision making all the time when it plans annual changes in its numerous automobile models. The great majority of changes in a given auto model are small. Only rarely does GMC announce the introduction of a totally new car or the total elimination of one of its models.

Mixed Scanning Strategy

The fourth approach to decision making is called mixed scanning. Developed by sociologist Amitai Etzioni,[5] it is an attempt to integrate many of the other decision-making strategies into a single strategy having strengths of the other approaches without their weaknesses. While the complete explanation of the strategy is complex, the essential characteristics of mixed scanning are as follows: First, the decision maker lists all the relevant alternatives to the problem. Then he or she eliminates all those alternatives that have an obvious crippling objection such as high cost, ethical problems, or major political problems. After this stage is completed, the decision maker goes through the list of alternatives that remain in greater detail, eliminating those that have less serious objections. This process is repeated, each time with higher and higher standards for the policies, until at last only one policy remains.

Once only one policy is left, it is divided into individual sections and is implemented incrementally, one step at a time. While the policy is being implemented, the policy maker seeks out information to discover whether the policy is having its intended results. If the results are negative, the policy maker reviews both the initial decision and the implementation of that decision.

This type of decision making is similar to the type implemented by a chess player. A chess player does not consider the effect of all possible moves; usually only a small number of moves are considered; the others are quickly ruled out due to clear problems. Once the player has narrowed the choices to a few moves, each alternative move is evaluated. Finally, a choice is made, and the player moves a piece. The player acts cautiously, moving only one piece at a time. If an initial move turns out to be unwise, the player can abandon that plan and begin another. While the player may decide on a strategy involving dozens of moves, the strategy is re-examined after each move and, if the overall strategy appears to be unwise after a few moves, it is quickly modified.

Since mixed scanning is a combination of some of the elements of the earlier strategies, it shares their strengths and weaknesses; it has the advantage of processing a large amount of information rapidly. At the same time, if the preliminary screening is done carelessly, potentially desirable solutions could be eliminated prematurely.

Intuitive Strategy

The final decision-making strategy involves simply relying on the intuition of the policy maker. This process involves having the decision maker act based on whatever he or she subconsciously thinks is correct. This decision-making mode has the advantage of saving time, and it frequently will produce an adequate decision. Thus, it is usually the best method for making minor decisions, such as where to eat lunch or what clothes to wear. On the other hand, this strategy hardly exposes the decision to any rigorous testing. The risk that critical information will be overlooked, or that the decision will be based on what the advocate *hopes* is the best policy instead of what *is* the best policy is magnified.

The decision as to which of these decision-making modes should be used depends on the nature of the decision being made. The more important the decision, the more rigorous the method of decision making that should be used. Time may also restrict the advocate to a less reliable but faster strategy. Finally, it should be noted that the time allocated to any single decision is time that cannot be devoted to other decisions that may be more important. At any rate, a wise decision maker selects a decision-making strategy that is appropriate to the problem being faced.

GENERATING ALTERNATIVES

Regardless of the decision-making strategy selected by an advocate, one important step in the process is to select the potential alternative solutions to the problem at hand. While the number of alternatives that need to be generated may vary from strategy to strategy, it is usually desirable to generate as many alternatives as possible. It should be noted that one potential alternative is the present system (i.e., that no action should be taken).

One way to generate numerous alternatives is a technique known as brainstorming. This process involves setting aside a time devoted entirely to generating alternative policies, with the goal of generating as many as possible. This is accomplished by listing as many ideas as can be imagined (either by all members of a group or by one individual acting alone). Because the emphasis at this stage of the decision-making process should be on coming up with numerous alternatives, no criticism of any of these possibilities should be presented at the brainstorming stage. It is easy to eliminate bad alternatives later in the process. Criticism of any of the alternatives at an early stage may intimidate individuals and inhibit them from presenting other, desirable alternatives. It is also possible that an absurd alternative may provide the inspiration for a workable solution to the problem. Presenting one idea may inspire a second idea that may lead to a third idea. While many of the ideas generated through this process may be of little worth, it is likely that the process will generate some valuable ideas that otherwise would have been overlooked.

Suppose, for example, we wanted to decide upon a nominee for the Supreme Court. If we used the brainstorming method, everybody involved would think of as many potential nominees as possible. No candidate would be evaluated until all candidates have been listed. This process should generate an extremely comprehensive list. Individuals proposed by one person might suggest other possible candidates to another person.

The types of ideas generated will be influenced by the policy maker who will make the final decision. Thus, if a federal policy maker is being addressed, that policy maker can only consider potential pieces of federal legislation that can be adopted. If the audience being addressed is a group of private citizens, then the only policies they can adopt are policies of individual action. Thus the types of alternatives that an individual seeks to generate should depend on the perspective of the potential decision maker.

DETERMINING THE EFFECTS OF ALTERNATIVE POLICIES

Once the available options have been identified by the policy maker, it is important to predict what the results of implementing a policy will be. This stage requires making two determinations: the possible effects of a policy, and the probability of these effects.

Discovering the Effects

Any policy will have multiple effects on its environment. The effects may be both direct and indirect. The decision to build a mass transportation system, for example, will have an impact on the level of pollution in a city, the cost of housing in both the city and in the suburbs, the tax base of the city, the amount of money available for other governmental programs (since the program will probably need to be funded through cuts in other programs), the amount of business in downtown areas, as well as a host of other social interactions. A good decision maker will attempt to discover as many of these effects as possible in order to determine which policy system has, on balance, the most desirable effects. In predicting these effects, it is important to discover all the effects of a system, not simply those effects that are easiest to quantify. Many of the effects of a policy may not be tangible; they may involve restrictions on freedom of movement, dignity, or privacy. While we can't attach a numerical value to these effects, they are important to us as human beings. Although we may not be able to explain exactly how much liberty is to be weighed, we would probably all consider any policy that results in the loss of liberty as having at least some negative effect.

The problem thus involves determining what negative and positive effects will result from the implementation of a policy. Some of these effects may be easily discovered or predicted. A new hospital will clearly require money for the building costs, which is a negative effect of such a decision. A new factory may mean pollution. In other cases, however, many of the effects of a policy will be less clear (and even a policy with some clear effects may also have indirect effects that are not obvious). Many of these effects may be predictable only if we conduct extensive research on a policy.

This research should seek out several types of information. Experts in the field may offer predictions about the effects of a policy. History may be consulted to see what effects similar policies have produced. Sometimes, the policy being examined (or similar policies) may have been adopted in similar jurisdictions, and the results in these jurisdictions may be useful in predicting the effect of the proposed policy. Sometimes pilot studies may be conducted to see what the effect of the policy, carried out on a small scale, will be. Computer simulations may be of some use, assuming the model used is an accurate one. Some effects of a policy can be predicted by using common sense, while others require an extensive analysis of the system that is being altered. How does the system work? Why do existing problems continue? Why do existing policies fail? Who benefits from the existing policies? The answers to these questions can begin to help us understand the nature of the system and this will help us predict the effects of future policies.

Calculating the Probability

It is not enough to predict simply what the result of a policy will be. A wise decision maker also asks what the probability is of any given result. Most of the decisions we make are reached in a climate of uncertainty—we may have an idea about what effects a policy could produce, but the degree of confidence we have in these predictions may vary.

The way to distinguish between the argument that indicates that an alternative will almost certainly produce an effect (for example, that closing down a factory will cause some unemployment) and an argument that indicates a lower level of probability (for example, that a nuclear power plant will have a meltdown), is to develop a method to make an accurate estimate of the probability of each effect being examined. There are numerous ways to attempt to estimate the probability of these effects. For example, one may look at the evidence supporting the effect of a policy. What is the quality of the evidence? How much evidence supports the effect? Is all the evidence from similar sources, or does it come from a variety of independent sources? If there is a large amount of evidence from a variety of reliable sources which indicate that the policy will produce a certain effect, the probability of that effect is greater than an effect supported by only one unreliable source of information. The strength of the evidence should also be examined. How confident are your sources of their predictions? What probability do they assign to the effect? For example, in arguing about the safety of nuclear reactors, almost everyone will agree that there is some risk that a nuclear reactor will eventually have a meltdown that will release radiation. Opponents of the reactors, however, argue that the risk of such a meltdown is very high, perhaps one meltdown every ten years.

Proponents of nuclear power argue that the risk is very low; perhaps about one in several million. Obviously, depending upon which figure is accurate, nuclear power plants are either very risky or very safe.

The probability of a policy having an effect may also depend on other factors. For example, in order for any policy to have an effect, it must be feasible. Thus an advocate should examine the policy to see if there are any problems with the implementation of the program that may reduce the ability of the policy to produce an expected result.

DETERMINING THE BEST ALTERNATIVE

After the effects of all the alternatives have been analyzed, it is necessary to select the appropriate policy. The decision maker does not have the option of refusing to select a policy; to do so is to agree tacitly to continue with the existing policies. Instead, the decision maker must select the best policy of those available. Initially, some of the policies may be eliminated because they fail to meet the minimum requirements of the policy maker. For example, if you were buying a car, there are certain absolute requirements that must be met before you would even consider making the purchase; the car must be affordable, it must meet state and local safety standards, and so on. Similar minimum requirements exist for other policies; they must be financially feasible; they must be politically possible, etc. Any policy that does not meet these absolute requirements can be eliminated from consideration.

Once those policies that do not meet our minimum requirements are eliminated, several other policies will remain. The decision maker should evaluate these policies by examining the potential effects of these policies and the probability of these effects. The policy maker needs to select the policy with the best cost-benefit ratio. In doing this, the policy maker should keep several things in mind.

Considering Non-Quantifiable Effects

First, the policy maker should be careful not to ignore non-quantifiable effects of a policy. There is a tendency for some policy makers to restrict their analysis of a policy to those effects which can be quantified. This may cause the policy maker to ignore important effects that are not easily translated into numbers — such things as the policy's effect on individual liberties, the aesthetic characteristics of a policy, and the effect of a policy on the quality of life. At the decision-making stage, it is important that these effects be given an appropriate weight. As noted in the last chapter, some values will be more important than others, and a wise decision maker will recognize this in balancing the effects of competing policies.

Relying on Numerical Certainty

Second, the decision maker should be cautious about relying on numerical certainty. While much of this discussion has assumed that a numerical value can be assigned to the probability of an effect being produced by adopting a policy or to the value of that effect, it should be noted that these numerical figures are often arbitrary and may be inaccurate. This does not mean that the numerical assignment of probabilities and values is of no importance; such a determination can help eliminate ill-advised decisions and can often help in providing a framework for making intelligent ones. It is important to recognize that, while basic systems analysis can help promote a rigorous test of policies, it does have some limitations. Policy makers should recognize these limitations, attempt to minimize them, and use the framework of analysis to the maximum extent possible, given these limitations. The value of risk analysis is that it provides an organized method of structuring the information necessary for rational decisions.

Weighing the Effects

Third, the decision maker should consider *who* should do the weighing of the effect of a policy. Sometimes it is desirable to have individuals besides a policy maker weigh the effects of various policies. For example, instead of having a policy maker in Washington, D.C., decide whether the benefits of additional jobs in a specific city outweigh the disadvantages, it might be wise to let the citizens in that community do the weighing. There is often a temptation for people with power to make decisions for those affected by the decision without consulting the individuals directly involved. For example, one of the arguments against government regulation of consumer products is that the individual consumer should make the decision about whether increased safety is worth an additional expense; that is not a decision to be made by government. While there are numerous responses to this issue (for example, it is suggested that the consumers do not have sufficient information to make a rational choice), the evaluator of a policy should at least consider *who* should perform the weighing of different values.

Identifying Presumption

Often, there may be two or more policies that have similar abilities to solve a problem, and the policy maker is forced to develop some method of choosing between the two policies. In these cases, the decision maker should attempt to identify the policy that has presumption, i.e., the policy that, other factors being equal, should be adopted. Presumption is simply a rule that allows us to choose between two or more similar policies. In law, for example, there is a presumption that an individual is innocent until proven guilty. This rule is accepted by the legal system to promote the value of the individual, to force the prosecutor to initiate argument, and to guide the court in case of conflicting evidence. Similar presumptions exist in policy argument to guide our choices when two policies seem to have equal merit. In those cases where two or more policies are judged to be equal, the decision maker should select the policy having presumption.

For a policy maker, presumption is assigned to the policy that contains the least amount of risk. The assumption behind this view is that risk is an undesirable quality of a policy. If we do not know something about the effects of a policy, there is a good chance that the policy will produce undesirable side effects. Unknown elements of a policy may interfere with the effects, or worse, they may have detrimental effects.

Thus, the least risky policy is the one that should be adopted, assuming the two policies are equal in other respects. As noted in the last chapter, the relative risk of a policy can be determined by looking at the extent of the change made, the importance of the affected system, the state of the current policy, the reversability of the change, and the availability of information about the policy.

Analyzing Risk of Unknown Effects

In analyzing the risk of unknown side effects, two factors should be considered. First, it is important to discover which policy has the greatest amount of risk associated with it. Second, it would be wise to estimate the amount of risk each policy entails. Sometimes, the difference in risk between the two policies will be small, in which case the risk element serves as little more than a tie-breaking function. In other cases, one policy will be much more risky than another. In these cases, not only must the more risky policy be superior to the less risky one, but this margin of superiority must be enough to outweigh the greater amount of risk associated with that policy.

IMPLEMENTING THE POLICY

Once the best policy has been identified, it is necessary to ensure that the policy is put into effect. A growing amount of literature in political science suggests that one major problem with many social programs is not that the programs had problems in their design, but that the implementation was inadequate. A wise policy maker thus should attempt to adopt implementation strategies to ensure that the goals of the policy are fulfilled. Often policies are adopted, only to never be carried out. For example, when the Supreme Court decided the case of *Brown v. Topeka Board of Education,* it ruled that segregation was unlawful. Unfortunately, the Court did not develop any strategies for ensuring that its orders were carried out; as a result, segregation continued for years after the case was decided.

Ensuring the implementation of a policy requires several measures. The details of the proposed policies should be specific enough to guarantee that the intended policies are implemented. The policy maker should determine who will implement the policy, as well as the specific actions that need to be carried out. The policy maker should also provide for checks on the agent responsible for the policy's implementation, to ensure that the provisions are carried out. This may include an agent who checks out the compliance of the administrators of the plan with its mandates, as well as a systematic method for evaluation.

Since most policies have both desirable and undesirable side effects, it would also be useful to develop a strategy that would minimize the harmful side effects of a policy. While these harmful side effects may be identified in an earlier stage of the decision-making process, the decision maker should take steps to minimize their effects. For example, he or she may wish to incorporate advocated provisions designed to mini-mize the harmful side effects of the policy. When Congress passed laws altering our trade policies for the textile industry, for example, it recognized that the new policies might cause economic hardships to some individuals. To minimize that problem, Congress included a provision that guaranteed economic assistance to those hurt by the act.

The policy maker may also wish to develop contingency plans either to prevent harmful side effects or to minimize the side effects if they do materialize. In this manner, the negative impacts of the policy are minimized. For example, suppose a policy maker decided it was necessary to invade another country. It would be helpful to consider all the possible undesirable side effects of that policy (escalation, failure of the intervention, domestic problems, etc.) and then decide what to do in case of each contingency. That way, if any of the undesirable effects of a policy materialize, the policy maker would be prepared to take action to minimize the effect.

SUMMARY

This chapter has discussed the general strategies used by an advocate before entering into a dispute. Before we engage in advocacy, we should be sure that the position we defend is worthy of defense. This requires a systemic examination of the world around us. The process requires an advocate to identify the nature of a problem, to select an appropriate decision-making strategy, to generate potential alternatives, to predict the effects of those alternatives, to select the best alternative, and then to implement the chosen alternative. The amount of our energy that should be devoted to this stage of advocacy depends on numerous factors, but it is important that this choice be made in a rational manner.

Notes

[1]There have been a number of attempts to address this problem. See, for example, John Dewey, *How We Think, Rev. ed.* (Boston: Heath, 1933); Irving L. Janis and Leon Mann, *Decision Making* (New York: Free Press, 1977): John D. Arnold, *The Art of Decision Making* (New York: AMACOM, 1978); Alexander H. Cornell, *The Decision-Maker's Handbook* (Englewood Cliffs, NJ: Prentice-Hall, Inc., 1980); and E. Frank Harrison, *The Managerial Decision-Making Process,* 2nd Ed. (Boston: Houghton Mifflin Co., 1981).

[2]Walter Ulrich, "Determining What Arguments are Critical," in *Dimensions of Argument: Proceedings of the Second Summer Conference on Argumentation,* edited by George Ziegelmueller and Jack Rhodes (Annandale, VA: Speech Communication Association, 1981), pp. 544–53.

[3]Herbert A. Simon, *Models of Man* (New York: Wiley, 1957).

[4]Charles E. Lindblom, "The Science of 'Muddling Through,'" *Public Administration Review,* 19 (1959), 79–99.

[5]Amitai Etzioni, *The Active Society* (New York: Free Press, 1968).

PART TWO

PREPARATION
FOR
ADVOCACY

CHAPTER FOUR

RESEARCH

The ability to research is one of the most important skills of an effective advocate. Without knowledge of the facts in a dispute, argument can degenerate into mere assertion and counterassertion. For argument to be worthwhile, it is important that the advocates understand the nature of the problem being examined, and that they be familiar with the background of the problem. This requires two types of research skills. The advocate must be able to locate material on a specific topic, and to evaluate and defend the evidence on that topic. This chapter will examine the first skill; chapter 7 will analyze the problems involved in evaluating evidence.

WHY RESEARCH?

There are many reasons why it is important for an advocate to develop effective research skills. Research can help generate ideas. When an advocate is first confronted with a topic, there are many issues that are relevant to the topic, but which may not be apparent to someone who is not familiar with the topic. Someone researching nuclear power, for example, could probably be expected to anticipate some of the more familiar issues involved in the discussion of nuclear power (such as the problems of radioactivity, waste disposal, and accidents). Other issues (such as the effect of our nuclear power program on nuclear proliferation, climatic effects of nuclear power, shortages of uranium, and so on) may not be as clear. Only after conducting an extensive research program can an advocate be expected to understand all these issues, as well as the arguments for and against each position.

Effective research skills can also help an advocate anticipate and prepare for potential arguments against his or her position. By reading material on a topic, it is possible to predict the types of arguments that the other side may make. This forewarning will allow the debater to prepare defenses against these positions instead of being surprised by new arguments (see chapter 5). Finally, research skills help advocates support their positions. Instead of relying on assertions to prove an argument, an advocate with effective research skills will be able to provide statistics and expert opinions to support his or her position. This increases the strength of the advocate's case.

After discovering the position that the advocate will be defending, he or she should start gathering background information on the topic. At this stage, the advocate is primarily interested in gaining a general overview of the topic, so research should emphasize background information. Initially, the critical issues involved in debating the topic may be unclear. Much of the material read during this phase of the research effort will seem to be irrelevant. Despite these problems, it is necessary to continue reading material on the topic; eventually the issues will become clearer. At the end of this stage of the research process, the advocate should start determining what arguments to research and what evidence is needed. It is usually desirable to keep a list of case ideas and negative arguments that should be researched as the season progresses; this will enable the advocate to determine which areas need more research. It will also help the advocate establish research priorities as the season progresses.

After the advocate begins to understand the nature of a topic, more specific research is required. At this stage, he or she begins to look for evidence to support specific arguments or to fill in gaps in research. Debaters may wish to look up sources that have been quoted by opponents or mentioned in the footnotes of books and articles on the topic that they have researched. It is sometimes necessary to go back to sources that have already been read by the researcher; often the relevance of some articles may not be clear until after other information has been examined and the researcher has a better understanding of the topic. It is then necessary to go back to articles to obtain quotations that were missed during the first reading.

Research should be a continuous process. Effective advocates continue to research a topic long after the initial research effort has been completed. An advocate who stops researching the topic will soon discover that hardworking opponents will have more recent and superior evidence. It is necessary to continually update evidence and to become aware of developments in the topic area. There may be many new developments over the course of a single season. New court cases may alter the nature of a problem area. Congress could pass new laws that minimize the harms claimed by an advocate. New studies on a problem may be published, or new information on old studies may become available. An advocate who is not aware of these developments may be unpleasantly surprised by an opponent who has done more extensive research.

Not all research conducted by a debater is topic-specific research. A good advocate is well read in numerous fields besides the one being debated. Knowledge of economics, philosophy, psychology, law, and other disciplines may prove useful in debating almost any topic. Many issues are interrelated, and a debater with a broad background may be able to see how the issues raised by the topic are affected by other factors. For example, to understand the effects of a new law altering the legal system, one should be familiar not only with law, but with psychology, sociology, political science, and a host of other fields of study. Debaters should not restrict their research to the narrow area covered by the topic; a broader knowledge of the way society works can often lead a debater to discover useful strategies in a debate round.

SOURCES OF EVIDENCE

Advocates should consult a wide range of materials when they begin to research any topic. To conduct an effective program of research, it is necessary to understand the nature of the materials available, as well as the indexes that can help the debater locate evidence on a topic. This section will examine the various sources of evidence commonly used by advocates. The exploration will include a discussion of the advantages and disadvantages of each type of evidence, as well as a list of the indexes available to the researcher using these types of evidence.

Books

Advocates frequently rely on books to locate information on a topic. While there are many types of books—ranging from the college textbook to the popular trade book to the scholarly book published by a university press—several characteristics are shared by most books. Many of these features of books make them attractive sources for evidence.

Advantages of Books   Books are often detailed. The author of a book is able to examine the subject of the book in great depth. Unlike the author of a newspaper or journal article, the author of a book has almost unlimited space available. If the author wishes to develop an argument in a great amount of detail, there is nothing preventing the use of several pages to explore the issue. In a short article, on the other hand, the author may decide to either ignore an argument or to treat it in a superficial manner because of space limitations. This in-depth treatment of a subject is extremely useful for a debater seeking to locate information on a topic.

Not only do books provide a detailed discussion of a topic, many books also contain footnotes (or endnotes). A footnote indicates where the author found information on a topic. Footnotes are helpful for researchers for several reasons. First, they allow the researcher to evaluate the conclusions of an author. If a book contains a statement that is critical to an argument, an advocate may wish to consult the source mentioned in the footnotes to determine if the original source was credible. In many books, the conclusions of the author are based in part on the research of other individuals. Whether any given statement in a book should be accepted may depend on the credibility of the evidence the author used to support his or her conclusion. The author of a book on the Middle East may rely on an almanac for information on the population of a country instead of conducting an independent census. If that almanac is inaccurate, errors will be repeated in the author's book. A footnote allows the researcher to discover where the author found the material used in the book, and the advocate can then check the original source of a conclusion to ensure that it is accurate. For example, if a book contains the statement that a certain product is harmful, the advocate may wish to consult the source the author of the book cites to discover the methodology used to reach the conclusion reported in the book.

Footnotes also help researchers locate other information on a topic. The author of a book has frequently conducted an in-depth search of the material available on a topic. The footnotes of a book list those sources that the author has found to be helpful in writing the book. Advocates should use the footnotes to provide leads to other sources of information on the topic. The advocate can start with a few books, and then use the footnotes to discover other sources of information. These sources may, in turn, lead to additional sources of information. The process of looking up sources listed in footnotes can thus provide an advocate with an extensive bibliography on a topic being debated.

Disadvantages of Books   There are some problems with using books. First, materials in books are frequently dated. It takes a long time to write a book and often, by the time a book is published, portions of the book are out of date. The process of publishing a book is a long one; the author must research the topic, find a publisher, write and revise the manuscript, and check the final copy. From the time the author has stopped researching a topic until the time a book is published, many new developments may have taken place. It is not unusual for the material in a book to be well over a year old by the time it is published simply because of the delays inherent in the publishing process. While there are occasional books on issues of current interest that are published with a shorter time lag (the Pentagon Papers were published a few weeks after they were released, for example), most books are not very useful for locating information about extremely recent events.

Another problem with using books is that it is easy to rely too heavily on a single book when researching a topic. Since some books do contain a wealth of material and since they are often detailed, some debaters cease researching after they discover a single book that contains all the information needed for a case. This temptation to rely on a single book for a case is dangerous. It may encourage the advocate to take a distorted view of reality. Any author can only reflect one view of the world; a wise researcher recognizes this and attempts to discover other perspectives on a problem to ensure that potential weaknesses in a position are not ignored. While books are a useful tool for a researcher, they should not be viewed as a stopping point in the research process.

Locating Relevant Books   Several useful tools are available for locating books on a topic. The most frequently used tool is the card catalog. The card catalog can be found in any library and, as its name suggests, it is an index of cards containing the author, title, and subject matter of all the books contained in the library. The cards are arranged alphabetically, usually by author, title, and/or subject matter. Each card will also contain a code indicating where the book can be found in the library. For books not available in a local library, a researcher may wish to consult *Books in Print,* which contains information about books currently available for purchase. Most libraries and major bookstores have this reference, which has individual volumes organized by author, title, and subject matter. Debaters interested in finding out what experts in the field think about a book should consult either the *Book Review Digest* or the *Book*

Review Index. These sources direct the advocate to magazines and journals where the books have been reviewed. Both the *New York Times Book Review* and the *New York Review of Books* also contain useful reviews of many of the more influential books published in English.

When using any index, it is important to recognize that information on a topic may be listed under several potential headings. Researchers are often tempted to look up a topic under one heading and to stop using an index if there are no entries listed under the first heading examined. An advocate researching prison reform, for example, may look in an index under the heading "penal reform" and, finding no entries, will assume that there are no books or articles on penal reform listed. The problem with this approach is that indexes may list articles or books about a topic under several headings. Material on penal reform may be listed under "justice" or "law enforcement" or "prisons" or even "United States—prisons." To further complicate matters, one index may list all articles on a topic under one heading and another index may use another heading. Researchers using indexes need to anticipate alternative key words that may be used to classify articles and books on the topic. Advocates researching pollution control, for example, should look under a wide variety of headings, including "environment," "ecology," "air pollution," "United States—pollution," and "United States—Environmental Protection Agency," as well as any other headings that could lead the debater to information on the topic. Two sources are useful in locating possible headings in indexes. The *Library of Congress Subject Headings* provides cross-references to many potential headings on a topic. *ERIC Thesaurus of Descriptors* lists possible headings for subjects in education.

It is also important for a researcher to learn how to skim material. It is usually not necessary to read all the material in a book (or in any other source) when researching. Much of the material in any source will be irrelevant to the advocate. A researcher should consult the table of contents or index of a book to locate the relevant material. Other parts of the book can be skimmed in order to see if there is any relevant material elsewhere.

Many libraries have developed a computerized catalog for the books in their library. These systems will permit the researcher to locate books held in the library by typing in the subject, author, or title of the books. The computer will list all the books in the library's holdings included in the category, along with the location of the book, and sometimes whether or not the book is checked out. In using these computerized card catalogs, it is important to enter as many headings as possible to ensure that material on the topic is not overlooked.

Newspapers

Newspapers are a popular source of information for millions of Americans. The quality of newspapers varies greatly from city to city. Certain newspapers, including the *Washington Post, The New York Times,* the *Los Angeles Times,* and the *Christian Science Monitor* are considered national in scope and have strong reputations among journalists.[1] The *New York Times,* for example, is thought by many to be the best newspaper in the country; its Sunday "News of the Week in Review" is a useful summary of current events. The *Wall Street Journal* is considered a high quality newspaper on financial issues. *USA Today* is a relatively new newspaper with a national circulation that tends to give most issues superficial treatment, although it will treat one issue in some depth every day. Several international newspapers are also considered extremely influential, including the London *Times,* the *Manchester Guardian,* the *Neue Zurcher Zeitung* (Switzerland), *Le Monde* (France) and *ABC* (Spain). At the other extreme are local papers which often act more as public relations outlets for local businesses than examples of high-quality journalism. Obviously not all local newspapers fall into this category, but it is important for advocates to recognize that many local newspapers do not have the staff or money needed to support the type of investigative reporting conducted by the major national newspapers.

Advantages of Newspapers   While the quality of newspapers varies greatly, there are some common characteristics of many newspapers. Newspapers are very current. Most are published daily or, at worst, once a week. This permits newspapers to provide information on current events before it is dated. If a researcher wishes to discover what happened in the world yesterday, a high-quality newspaper is a good source to consult. Papers like the *New York Times* frequently carry transcripts of important speeches or short documents the day after they are released, and any major paper will contain up-to-date information on current events. The national newspapers will also contain a wealth of material on topics of current concern. The national newspapers like the *New York Times* and the *Washington Post* have access to much information about the way the government operates, and a reader of these newspapers can learn much about what is happening in the country. One leading governmental official commented that 95% of all the information a citizen needs to make a rational decision about public policy can be found in the *New York Times*. President John Kennedy noted that, during the Bay of Pigs crisis, he got a better idea of what was going on in the world by reading *The New York Times* than by reading the reports from the CIA.[2] The influence of these newspapers is indicated by the large number of governmental leaders who regularly read them.

Weaknesses of Newspapers   Newspapers are not without their weaknesses. The fact that newspapers operate under the pressure of deadlines may adversely affect their quality. Some newspapers will be tempted to publish stories before they can be verified to prevent other news sources from "scooping" them. In 1980, for example, the *Atlanta Constitution,* one of the country's most distinguished newspapers, published a story the morning after an election proclaiming that an incumbent Senator had been reelected. The story turned out to be premature; by the time all the ballots had been counted, it turned out that the Senator had been defeated. The pressure to print the story before all the votes were tabulated turned out to be too strong to resist, and the newspaper ended up publishing an inaccurate story.

In other cases, time pressures may encourage journalists to publish stories without checking out all the facts. Often, journalists may be under pressure to produce facts rapidly; people are interested in knowing what is happening in the world today, not what happened a month ago. As a result, journalists may be tempted to rely on inaccurate sources. During the 1982 Israeli invasion of Lebanon, for example, many journalists relied on statistics provided by the Palestinian Red Crescent for estimates of the number of casualties in the war; it turned out that the organization was run by the brother of Yasser Arafat, the leader of the group the Israelis were attempting to evict from Lebanon. Subsequent studies by impartial groups have suggested that the number of casualties in the war were far less than those published in newspapers.[3] This distortion was not intentional on the part of the newspapers; they were simply unable to confirm all the statistics before the papers were scheduled to be published.

Sometimes, however, newspapers will intentionally present a slanted view of the news. The owners of newspapers will often have strong political views, and these views may be reflected in the editorials of a newspaper, as well as the content of news stories. During the Vietnam War, for example, conservative newspapers would tend to publish stories about the successes of the American military in Vietnam; liberal papers would publish stories presenting a more pessimistic view of the war. The choice of the stories to be included in the newspaper as well as the selection of language in the story may reflect the bias of the reporter and the editor.

Locating Material in Newspapers   Several reference tools are useful in finding material in newspapers. Most of the major newspapers have indexes. The most prominent indexes are the *New York Times Index,* the (London) *Times Index,* the *Wall Street Journal Index,* and the *Christian Science Monitor Index.* The *Newspaper Index* has volumes that index a variety of major national newspapers. For advocates interested in obtaining articles from local papers, there are several sources available in certain libraries. *Editorials on File* provides copies of editorials published in local newspapers on major current issues. *Newsbank* and *Update* index clippings of articles on a wide variety of subjects published in local newspapers. These clippings are stored on microforms. In addition, most newspapers keep copies of old issues of their own paper, often clipped and filed by topic (stored in places sometimes called "morgues"). Researchers interested in discovering how newspapers in other countries react to news events may wish to read the *World Press Review.* This magazine publishes English translations of news stories from newspapers in all parts of the world, and it is an extremely useful source for any foreign-policy topic. Finally, for advocates who wish to read critical reviews of the way newspapers cover the news, two journals, the *Columbia Journalism Review* and the *Washington Journalism Review,* should be helpful.

Magazines

Another popular source of information for many people is magazines. These periodicals provide a wide range of information on many issues. For researchers seeking information on public policy, the most popular magazines include *Time, Newsweek,* and *U.S. News & World Report,* with such magazines as the *Economist* (England), the *National Review,* and the *New Republic* following in popularity.

Advantages of Magazines   Magazines have many advantages as sources of information. They are fairly current; the magazine will usually be published within a week or a month of the events covered. This makes the magazine a good source of information on current events. The major newsmagazines are also read by many individuals, so they help advocates predict the types of arguments that they can anticipate hearing from their opponents. In addition, newsmagazines are perceived to be credible by many individuals; if something is reported in *Time,* people assume that it is true, even if this belief is not warranted.

Disadvantages of Magazines   There are several problems involved with using magazines for research. Since magazines are aimed at a large audience, they are often forced to simplify complex stories. As a result, many journalists consider magazines to emphasize style over content. Some journalists view magazines as low-quality news sources, often more interested in entertainment than in facts. Robert Newman, of the University of Pittsburgh, went so far as to label two of the more well-known national magazines as "the weekly fiction magazines."[4] In addition, the major magazines often reflect a strong bias on political issues. Stories are often slanted in such a way as to reinforce the magazines' editorial positions. Favorable causes are presented in a favorable light, while undesirable causes are placed in a less favorable light. Magazines like *The New Republic, Progressive,* and *National Review* are designed to promote particular views of the world; they reflect political beliefs in their selection and coverage of issues. Even magazines like *Time, Newsweek,* and *U.S. News & World Report* reflect a certain perspective in their presentation of national and world events. The magazines often present slanted stories on an issue.

Locating Material in Magazines   There are several good indexes for magazines. The most widely used index is the *Readers' Guide to Periodical Literature.* This work indexes most of the major magazines that are usually found in libraries. Included in the index are *Time, Newsweek,* and *U.S. News & World Report.* The *P.A.I.S.* (Public Affairs Information Service) *Bulletin* indexes selected magazines, books, documents, pamphlets, and other information related to economic, social, and political issues. Two other sources, the *Popular Periodical Index* and *Access,* index periodicals with a wide circulation that are not included in the *Readers' Guide.* This would include periodicals such as *The Rolling Stone* which are read by many people but are not available in many academic libraries. The *Utne Reader* publishes key articles from 1,000 more obscure magazines.

Journals

Advantages of Journals   A journal is a specialized publication, similar to a magazine, written by and for professionals in a field. Examples of journals include the *Journal of the American Forensic Association, Political Science Quarterly,* the *Journal of Conflict Resolution,* and the *Harvard Law Review.* Since these journals are intended for a very sophisticated audience, they often contain extremely detailed information on a topic. The authors of a journal article are generally well qualified in their fields, and articles in journals are usually screened by a panel of experts in the field before they are published. This process helps produce very high-quality documents. In addition, journal articles will usually have footnotes, with all the resulting advantages previously mentioned.

Disadvantages of Journals   At the same time, the complexity of journal articles presents unique problems for debaters. Since the articles are designed to be read by professionals in the field, many will be too complex for some individuals. It is usually best to consult journal articles only after gaining an understanding of the major issues of the debate topic. Journal articles may also vary in complexity; one article may require a sophisticated knowledge of statistical methodology, while another article might make sense to a high school student with little knowledge of the subject. The implication of this is that a researcher should not ignore journal articles simply because he or she does not understand the first one located on a topic; it is likely that many of the others will be easier to understand.

Journal articles present other problems to advocates. They are often difficult to locate. While most libraries will subscribe to many magazines and newspapers, journals are often located only in the libraries of major universities. In addition, like books, journal articles are often extremely dated. It may take several months from the time an author finishes an article until the time that article is reviewed and accepted for publication. Even after the article is accepted, there may be a time lag from a few months to a few years before the article is finally published. As a result, by the time an article is published in a journal, the material may be outdated and thus journals are of limited use on current events.

Locating Material in Journals   There are several useful journal indexes. The *Humanities Index* and the *Social Sciences Index* will be helpful on many topics. The *ABC* or *Advanced Bibliography of Contents—Political Science* indexes many articles on law and government. On economic topics, both the *Index to Economic Articles* and the *Journal of Economic Literature* are useful (as well as *The Business Periodicals Index,* which indexes publications with characteristics of both periodicals and journals). In addition, many other fields of study have indexes devoted to their journals. Some have a type of reference tool known as an abstract. An abstract provides all the information found in an index (author, title, and the location of the article), as well as a brief summary of the content of the article. This summary is very helpful in that it can help determine if an article contains any useful material on a topic. Some of the more popular abstracts include the *Psychological Abstracts* and the *Sociological Abstracts.* If a debater is uncertain where a journal is indexed, the best source to consult is *Ulrich's International Periodicals Directory,* which tells where all the major periodicals and journals are indexed.

A final research tool for journals is a citation index. A citation index locates articles that have referred to (or cited) an earlier article. Suppose, for example, that in researching a topic a researcher discovers that five years ago there was a critical article written on the topic. It would be useful to find out if other individuals who have read this article have responded to it. The citation index will locate any article that has mentioned the original article in a footnote. This is extremely useful for locating other articles on a topic or for discovering attacks on an article. There are several excellent citation indexes, including the *Social Sciences Citation Index,* and *Shepard's Citations* (for legal material).

Government Documents

Government documents are an extremely useful source for information on many topics. The United States Government Printing Office is the largest publisher in the United States, and much of the material it publishes is available at a moderate price. In addition, by law every congressional district has at least one library that contains most of the major federal government publications.

There are three major types of government documents of use to researchers. The first type transcribes Congressional debates. The *Congressional Record* is the official transcript of these debates. The second type of government document transcribes congressional hearings. The government printing office publishes a record of the hearings of congressional subcommittees on proposed legislation. Finally, there are executive documents. Executive agencies such as the Department of Justice or the State Department will also frequently publish reports and other material of use to researchers.

Advantages of Government Documents   There are many advantages to using government documents. Government documents contain a wealth of materials on many subjects. Congressional hearings often contain the testimony of a wide variety of individuals as well as copies of articles, court cases, and other material useful to advocates. The *Congressional Record* will contain transcripts of the Congressional debates on proposed laws, as well as reprints of major speeches and articles of public interest. Many government documents include material from a wide variety of viewpoints; congressional hearings have witnesses representing several viewpoints, and many varied opinions will be expressed in the debates in Congress. Government documents are also relatively current; the *Congressional Record* is available within a few days of the congressional debates, and the material from hearings is usually available a few months after they are held. Since there is no need to pay the authors of the documents for writing the document and since the government printing office does not need to make a profit, government documents are also relatively inexpensive (in fact, many documents may be obtained free from the issuing agency or from a member of Congress).

Disadvantages of Government Documents   While there is much good information in many government documents, there are many problems encountered in using them. Many government documents are poorly organized. The organization of congressional hearings, for example, is by witness, not by subject matter. It thus may be necessary to read through much irrelevant material to locate useful evidence. The credibility of the evidence in government documents will often vary greatly. Many government statistics, for example, may be distorted in a way to make the administra-

FIGURE 4-1   RESEARCH TOOLS

BOOKS
  Card Catalog
  Books in Print
  Book Review Index
  Current Book Review Citations
  Book Review Digest
NEWSPAPERS
  New York Times Index
  Christian Science Monitor Index
  Washington Post Index
  Wall Street Journal Index
  (London) *Times Index*
  Alternative Press Index
  Editorials on File
MAGAZINES
  Readers' Guide to Periodical Literature
  Popular Periodicals Index
  P.A.I.S.
  Ulrich's International Periodicals Directory
JOURNALS
  General
    Social Science Index
    Social Science Citation Index
  Political Science
    ABC-Political Science
    International Political Science Abstract
    U.S. Political Science Documents
  Economics
    Business Periodicals Index
    Index of Economic Articles
    Journal of Economic Literature

tion look good. The witnesses who testify before a congressional subcommittee may range from the top authorities in the field to unqualified individuals who have requested the opportunity to address the subcommittee. It is thus important to discover the qualifications of the individual being quoted in the government document in order to assess the reliability of the testimony.

Locating Material in Government Documents   There are several useful indexes of government documents. The *Congressional Record Index* indexes the deliberations of Congress. There are two editions of the *Congressional Record:* an edition that is published every day that Congress is in session, and an annual edition that contains a permanent record of Congressional debates. The *Monthly Catalog of*

Education
  Education Index
  Current Index to Journals in Education
  ERIC
Miscellaneous
  Philosopher's Index
  Sociological Abstracts
  Psychological Abstracts
  Index Medicus
GOVERNMENT DOCUMENTS
  Monthly Catalog of U.S. Government Documents
  C.I.S. Index
  American Statistics Index
  Congressional Record Index
LEGAL MATERIALS
  Index to Legal Periodicals
  Index to Periodicals Related to Law
  Corpus Juris Secundum; American Jurisprudence
  United States Code, Annotated
  Shepard's Citations
MISCELLANEOUS
  Television News Index and Abstracts
  Facts on File
  Dissertation Abstracts International
  Dialog

United States Government Publications indexes both the major publications of the executive branch of government and the congressional hearings. The *Congressional Information Service Index* provides both an index and an abstract (organized by individual testimony) of all major congressional hearings. There is also an index of publications of the General Accounting Office. The *Index to U.S. Government Periodicals*, as its title suggests, indexes the major periodicals published by the federal government. State governmental publications can be located in the *Checklist of State Publications*.

Legal Material

Many controversial topics have legal implications that are worth researching. Legal material is often of great use for any topic involving major social policy. The *Index to Legal Periodicals* indexes law review articles. This index is supplemented by the *Current Law Index*, the *Legal Resource Index*, Harvard Law School's annual *Legal Bibliography*, the *Index to Foreign Legal Periodicals*, and the *Index to Periodical Articles Related to Law. Corpus Juris Secundum* and *American Jurisprudence* are legal encyclopedias that provide a detailed introduction to the current status of the law. The *United States Code Annotated (U.S.C.A.)* contains the text of the federal laws currently in effect and it also includes summaries of the court cases that have interpreted the law. All law libraries will also contain copies of all the Supreme Court decisions (and sometimes the briefs for both sides in the court case), as well as many other court decisions. There are several books that provide more detailed information about using legal information, including Morris Cohen's *Legal Research in a Nutshell.*[5]

Other Sources of Information

There are many other sources of information on debate topics. Television can provide some background information on a topic, although television news is usually superficial (the transcript of a 30-minute newscast would fill less than one page of the *New York Times*), and television news often emphasizes the dramatic. The *Television News Index and Abstracts* can assist the researcher in locating material that has appeared on television newscasts. The *Educational Resources Information Clearinghouse (ERIC)* index locates material related to education; information in this index can be found on microforms. Many specialized reference works such as dictionaries, encyclopedias, biographical works, almanacs, and so on may be of use to debaters. For information on these types of materials, the debater may wish to consult such reference materials as Winchell's *Guide to Reference Books*[6] or may wish to ask the reference librarian at a local library for more specialized sources.

Advocates should also recognize that there are many sources of information besides the library. Special interest groups such as the National Rifle Association and the American Civil Liberties Union may provide the debater with much information (although this information is usually extremely biased). Researchers may also wish to interview individuals with some expertise in the field, ranging from Senators and Representatives to university professors (this type of research should normally be conducted after the researcher has conducted some preliminary research; it can provide useful leads). Since interviews are not written and thus cannot be verified, advocates should not quote from the interview in a debate round, although interviews can be useful in gathering background information on a topic and in gaining leads for additional information.

Researchers with access to computers can use several of the computerized databases. *The Source* and *Dialog* provide access to a large number of the indexes already discussed. The Dow Jones service may be useful on economic topics, and more computer-related information retrieval systems become available every day. *Lexis* can help locate court cases on a topic. Clearly there are many sources that an advocate can consult in researching a topic.

When conducting research, advocates should recognize that almost all of the indexes mentioned in this chapter will be dated. Usually, anywhere from a few weeks to a year will elapse between the time an article is published and when the article is indexed. For recent events, then, a debater may wish to skim recent issues of publications related to the topic. This not only helps the advocate stay informed about developments, but it may also help the advocate discover new ideas for arguments. Browsing through government documents, books, or journals may result in discovering ideas and/or articles that may prove useful. Many ideas can be generated by leaving the index table and simply browsing through the library; new relationships may be discovered by looking at seemingly unrelated issues and attempting to see relationships between these issues and the subject being debated.

ETHICS OF EVIDENCE

While researching a topic, advocates are often tempted to take shortcuts in order to win an argument. Some of these shortcuts involve practices that are generally considered to be unethical. It is important for researchers to understand that many of the choices made while researching a topic have ethical implications. The use of evidence that does not conform to ethical standards can undermine the entire decision-making process. Evidence that is distorted or taken out of context could result in an inferior decision if that evidence is accepted by the critic of an argument. It is in everyone's interest to promote the use of evidence that conforms to a common ethical standard.

Fabricated Evidence

There are three major ethical violations that a debater should avoid. The first violation is fabrication of evidence. A few advocates find it easier to manufacture evidence instead of taking the time to go to a library to gather accurate information on the topic. Not knowing a statistic, for example, they may decide to arbitrarily create a number that is then used to support an argument. While this practice is not common, it does happen in some arguments. One debate team lost a critical round at the national debate tournament because their opponents read a damaging piece of evidence that turned out to be manufactured; in other cases teams reaching the final round of the college national debate tournament have been caught reading manufactured and/or distorted evidence. Fabricating evidence takes place in all types of debate. One presidential candidate in the 1980 election was accused by several individuals of making up statistics that advanced his cause. When journalists attempted to verify these statistics, they discovered that they were not based on any objective measures; the candidate simply made up figures that he thought would be useful.[7]

Rational decisions should not be based on mythical evidence. We should attempt to make sure that all evidence introduced in a debate round is accurate. The importance of accurate evidence is shown by the efforts of the national debate organizations to regulate the use of evidence. Both the National Forensic League and the American Forensic Association have adopted codes of ethics that punish teams that use fabricated evidence with a loss and zero speaker points. Even outside debate rounds individuals who often manufacture evidence lose credibility with their audiences. It is also important to note that an advocate is responsible for any evidence he or she introduces into an argument, even if the advocate did not personally research the evidence. When advocates read evidence, they are indicating that the evidence is legitimate and that they are willing to defend its integrity. If this were not the case, any advocate who was caught using evidence that was manufactured could escape punishment by blaming the poor-quality evidence on another person (who usually is not around to defend himself or herself). This would make it almost impossible to punish anyone who manufactured evidence since the type of person who would manufacture evidence would usually have no difficulty lying about the name of the person who conducted the original research. More important than this consideration is the obligation of an advocate to be honest with an audience, and to be sure that statements made in an argument are accurate.

Distorted Evidence

A second type of ethical violation is more difficult to evaluate. Advocates should not use evidence that is distorted. When an advocate reads evidence, he or she is using the words of the source of the evidence to support a position. While it is not possible to read everything that an author has said about a subject in a speech, the advocate should make sure that the statements that are read in their speeches accurately represent the beliefs of the individual quoted. A good guideline would be to ask, would the authors agree with the statements that I attribute to them? If an advocate must leave out a part of a sentence (a practice that should be avoided, if possible), he or she should make sure that the omitted words do not change the meaning of the sentence. Leaving out words like "not" could change the meaning of a sentence (for example, in 1631, the Oxford University Press printed an edition of the Bible that accidently left out the word "not" from one of the Ten Commandments; this obviously changed the meaning of that commandment). The researcher should also be careful not to phrase evidence in a manner that suggests greater certainty than was intended by the author. Words like "could" should not be changed to "will." The rhetorical force of the quote should not be "power worded" in such a way as to make the evidence seem more forceful and persuasive than it was expressed by the author. The key principle is to make sure that caution is exercised in copying evidence and using it to support a position.

Plagiarized Material

A third ethical problem with the use of evidence is plagiarism. Plagiarism involves using another person's idea without attributing the idea to that individual. When someone writes a paper or presents a speech, it is assumed that unless otherwise noted, the ideas and language of that paper or speech are the product of the original thought of the person making the presentation. If an individual quotes another person, the fact that the material is quoted should be noted and the source of the quotation should be given. This is especially critical when an advocate quotes an individual word-for-word. A person who copied an essay from a magazine or encyclopedia, for example, would clearly be guilty of plagiarism; similarly an advocate who quotes another person without indicating the source is guilty of plagiarism.

The reason plagiarism is discouraged is that a person's ideas belong to him or her.

FIGURE 4-2   STRUCTURE OF A TYPICAL NOTECARD

```
(1) Heading                    (2) Index Number

(3) Source of evidence (qualifications)
    Title, date, page number(s)        (4) Initials

(5) Quotation




(6) Comments
```

To use someone else's ideas without attributing them to that individual is a form of stealing. We should show our respect for the source of our ideas by explaining where we found our material. We should give credit to those individuals who assisted us in discovering arguments for our debates. In addition, letting the audience know the source of our information allows the audience to critically evaluate the strength of our evidence. To claim that an idea is our own when, in reality, it came from another person is dishonest.

FORMAT OF EVIDENCE

After a researcher has located evidence, he or she must then develop a method of taking notes and organizing evidence in a usable form. The easiest method of organizing evidence is to record it on notecards. The advocate should read material on a topic, and then place all usable evidence on notecards for use in an argument. It is easiest to use a relatively small notecard; either a 3″ × 5″ or a 4″ × 6″ notecard is used by many debaters. A typical notecard will have the structure shown above.

All parts of the notecard have a purpose. The heading (1) briefly summarizes the contents of the card. This saves the advocate time when preparing an argument since the advocate need only read the label of the card to find out if the card is useful. The index number (2) corresponds to the file section in which the card will be organized (see chapter 6). After gathering a large amount of evidence, the advocate will want to develop a detailed filing system, and this number tells the advocate where to file the evidence after the round.

FIGURE 4-3   A TYPICAL NOTECARD

More study of energy sources needed   A-13

John P. Holdren (Professor of Energy, U. of Calif.-
Berkeley), *Technology Review,* April, 1982,
p. 38.   WAU

"Sensible choices about energy sources will
require both better information about
environmental characteristics and better use of
this information in the selection of energy
options."

(for the study counterplan)

The source of the evidence (3) is an extremely important part of the evidence card. Every card should contain enough information to permit the researcher to locate the original document from which the evidence was copied. For a book, this information would include the author, title, date of publication, and page number. For a journal article, this would include, at a minimum, the author, journal, exact date, and page number. In addition, it is often desirable to include the title of the article. In short, given the information on the evidence card, it should be possible to locate the original source of the evidence in order to verify its content. Thus, *New York Times,* 1983 would be an inadequate citation, since it does not include the exact date or the page number of the quotation.

This information is useful for two reasons. First, it assists in locating material. Often the first time a researcher reads a document he or she will miss material that initially does not seem to be relevant, but after further research has been conducted, the material may seem to serve a purpose. The citation on the notecard will permit the researcher to locate the original source so that the material may be re-read in order to locate quotations that may have been overlooked in the first stages of the research effort.

The citation on the notecard can also prevent false accusations of unethical practices. If an advocate is accused of manufacturing evidence or distorting material, the complete citation permits a researcher to locate the original source of a quotation, which should disprove any false ethical accusations.

A complete citation should include not only enough information to locate the original source, but also information about the qualifications of the individual being quoted. Evidence is no more reliable than the person who made the statement. It is important that we understand why the person being quoted should be believed. Often the qualifications of that individual can be found in the original source; most journals will provide the qualifications of the authors of their articles, and books and government documents will often provide background material of their sources. When this information cannot be found in the original material, it is sometimes possible to find this material in such sources as *Who's Who in America,* the *Directory of American Scholars,* the *National Faculty Directory,* the *Biography Index* and the *United States Government Manual.*

It is often desirable to include on notecards the initials of the person who researched the evidence (4). Many times, advocates will read evidence researched by others, in addition to their own research. The initials reveal who researched the evidence. While a speaker is responsible for all evidence he or she reads, regardless of who originally researched it, this information may be useful in checking out the context of evidence or in locating the original source (for example, when the original researcher owns a copy of a source).

The most important part of the evidence card is, of course, the evidence itself. Each evidence card should contain one (and only one) major idea. If a source has several good arguments, it is best to place each major idea on a separate notecard. This permits the advocate to organize the evidence in a manner consistent with the way arguments are being presented in the debate round; this pattern may not correspond with the way the author organizes his or her material. It is also useful to attempt to keep the evidence as short as possible. If the evidence is too long, it may be difficult to read in the round; it would take too much time to read an extremely long evidence card. The evidence should be as specific as possible, giving the reasons behind conclusions as well as the conclusions themselves.

All evidence should be copied on evidence cards with the advocate keeping in mind how the evidence can be used in an argument. What arguments can the evidence help support? What arguments can the evidence help refute? The evidence should be cut (i.e., copied on a notecard) in a manner that promotes these goals. Each evidence card should be understandable in isolation. This means that the meaning of an evidence card should be clear. For example, an evidence card that says "This program will cost $30 billion" is unclear. What program is it referring to? The evidence may be clear in context, but in the heat of an argument the individual who researched the evidence may have forgotten what it was referring to. Thus the card should read "This program [National Health Insurance] will cost $30 billion." By including the phrase "National Health Insurance" in brackets, it is clear which program the evidence is talking about (in this case, since there are many versions of this particular program, it would be even better if the specific bill mentioned in the evidence was included). Including a phrase in brackets indicates that the words in the brackets did not appear in the original source.

Sometimes it may be necessary to leave material out of a quotation. This should be done with caution because of the risk of misusing this technique. When words are left out of a quotation, the debater should indicate that words were left out by using ellipses (. . .). For example, suppose an advocate wanted to prove that Pakistan had the capability of exploding a nuclear weapon and his or her research found someone who wrote, "Several nations have the capability of exploding a nuclear weapon, including Argentina, Israel, South Africa, Pakistan, and West Germany." The evidence supports the position that Pakistan could explode a nuclear bomb, but it includes much irrelevant information. It would be reasonable to cut out some of the irrelevant material so the evidence would read: "Several nations have the capability of exploding a nuclear weapon, including . . . Pakistan . . ." This evidence is shorter, but it contains all the critical information needed by the advocate. While some material is left out, the material that is deleted does not change the meaning of what is left in the quotation. In addition, it is clear that the author of the quotation would agree with the statement attributed to him or her.

The final part of a notecard is the comment section (6). This section is optional, but it can be useful for some evidence. The comment section provides additional information about the evidence. An advocate may wish to include on the evidence card how the evidence should be used, or what arguments the evidence is to be used against. Information about the context of the evidence should also be included where appropriate.

SUMMARY

The ability to research is obviously an important skill for any advocate. Researching a topic requires much effort on the part of a debater—there is no substitute for hard work and long hours in a library. Fortunately, the more energy that is spent on researching, the easier researching becomes. Advocates quickly develop efficient methods for finding materials, and they develop a sixth sense about where to locate critical information. This skill not only helps the advocate prepare for argument, but it also can help the advocate locate useful material for work, school, and other activities. In short, developing effective research skills is a very important step in many activities.

Once the advocate has located material and placed that evidence on notecards, it is important to evaluate the credibility of that evidence. All the evidence in the world will do little good to an advocate if he or she does not know how to use the evidence effectively. Chapter 7 will examine how an advocate should determine the strength of evidence.

Notes

[1] See, for example, John C. Merrill and Harrold A. Fisher, *The World's Great Dailies* (New York: Hastings House, 1980); William L. Rivers, *The Opinionmakers* (Boston: Beacon Press, 1967); and Ray White, "Government VIP's Rate the Washington Press," *Washington Journalism Review*, January/February, 1982, pp. 37–40.

[2] Rivers, p. 78.

[3] Max Lerner, "Media Vulnerability Evident in Casualty Gaffe," *National Comment*, September, 1982, pp. 76–7.

[4] Robert P. Newman and Dale R. Newman, *Evidence* (Boston: Houghton Mifflin Company, 1969), 131–163.

[5]Morris L. Cohen, *Legal Research in a Nutshell,* 3rd ed. (St. Paul Minn.: West Publishing Co., 1978).

[6]Constance M. Winchell, *Guide to Reference Books,* 8th ed. (Chicago: American Library Association, 1967).

[7]"Where Did He Get Those Figures?" *Time,* April 14, 1980, p. 31.

CHAPTER FIVE

BRIEFING
ARGUMENTS

Once an advocate has conducted the initial research on a topic, the evidence must be organized in a usable manner. The best way to organize and structure a large amount of material on a topic is to place the evidence on briefs. A brief is an organized set of arguments and evidence designed to either defend or attack a position. A brief can act as an outline of major arguments that an advocate can present during a dispute. To develop a well-structured brief, the advocate goes through a period of preparation that requires much thought about the potential issues in a dispute, the potential responses to these positions, the best support for these responses, and the interrelationships between the potential responses open to an advocate. This process can be extremely time-consuming, but if the advocate takes the time to develop a good set of briefs on a topic, the preparation can prove to be worthwhile.

THE IMPORTANCE OF BRIEFING ARGUMENTS

There are several reasons why it is important to prepare briefs on a topic before the debate. First, the process of blocking out arguments allows the advocate to organize his or her positions. If a person were asked, with no advance warning, to develop responses to an argument, that person would probably start randomly listing responses to that position. Many of these arguments would be repetitive, poorly developed, and poorly phrased. On the other hand, if that same individual were told in advance that he or she would be asked to respond to a certain position, the person would be able to list potential arguments and then could review all the possible responses to that position, eliminating the weak ones, developing the strong ones, and then structuring the responses into a strong, well-organized position. A brief operates in the same manner. By anticipating the issues likely to emerge in a dispute and by planning how to respond to those positions, the advocate is able to structure his or her responses to the other side's case. Just as preplanning is desirable for an essay or a test, blocking out responses is helpful to the advocate. For example, during the 1960 presidential campaign, a series of debates between the two nominees, Richard Nixon and John F. Kennedy, were arranged. Kennedy devoted much time to "blocking out" potential questions. He attempted to anticipate the major issues that would be raised during the debates, and then wrote down responses to those issues on notecards, along with facts and statistics that supported his responses. He continually reviewed these cards before the debates and, as a result, he was prepared to answer the questions with confidence.[1] Similarly, in more recent political debates, candidates have developed briefing books on potential questions so that they can be prepared to respond to those issues likely to be raised during the debates.

Blocking out potential responses also helps save time. If an advocate has organized a position before engaging in a dispute, then he or she need not spend time finding evidence, thinking of what to say, and structuring a response once the debate has begun. By blocking out arguments, the well-organized advocate performs the tasks that many less-organized debaters will need to do during the heat of a dispute. As a result, the advocate who has blocked out arguments before the dispute will have more time to think about the issues in the controversy, take notes, and to select the best possible positions.

Blocking arguments also saves time during speeches. By preparing responses to an argument before it begins, the advocate has ample time to eliminate excess rhetoric from an argument, to select the best evidence to introduce into the dispute, to eliminate any unnecessary arguments, to eliminate wordy evidence, and so on. As a result, the arguments on a brief may be more concise than those developed extemporaneously during a dispute. A well-briefed advocate can present more high-quality arguments in a shorter amount of time than an advocate who is unprepared to argue.

Briefs can also prevent an advocate from forgetting a response. Many times a debater will become involved in a dispute and, an hour later, think of a good response to an issue that he or she forgot to present. After the argument is over, it is too late to present this response, but by blocking out responses in advance, the advocate is able to minimize the omission of an important argument.

The briefing process occurs over a long period of time. This enables the advocates to outline the arguments against a position when they have time to think about the position in a relaxed atmosphere, with no distracting pressures. After the brief is finished, it can be modified if the advocate thinks of another argument. Thus the advocate is unlikely to forget any major response to an issue on the brief.

Briefing also prevents the debater from making major argumentative errors. By selecting which arguments to present before a round, the advocate has time to think about the implications of arguments. Two positions that contradict may be discovered, and the advocate can decide which position should be dropped. The team members may wish to talk with each other in an attempt to develop a consistent position and to coordinate arguments. Briefing arguments also helps minimize the risk that important evidence will be lost or misfiled.

Finally, briefing arguments helps direct research efforts. When an advocate begins preparing briefs, it will soon become clear which arguments he or she is prepared to attack. It is better to discover these strengths and weaknesses *before* beginning to speak, instead of after the argument has begun. After discovering gaps in the research efforts, the advocate can either investigate the areas of weaknesses, or develop a strategy that diverts the focus of the dispute to the areas that the advocate is prepared to defend. Briefing can thus be directly tied to the research efforts of the advocate.

THE PROCESS OF BRIEFING

Given the importance of blocking out arguments, it is important that every advocate learn how to develop a brief. While some briefing may begin at an early stage in the research process, generally most blocking occurs after the advocate has conducted much of the initial research on a topic. There are three steps an advocate should follow in creating briefs on a topic. First, an advocate should determine what briefs are needed. Second, the advocate should gather ideas and evidence to use on the briefs. Finally, the briefs should be organized and placed in their final form.

Determining Necessary Briefs

The first stage in blocking out arguments is to determine which arguments need to be blocked. At this stage, it is usually wise to use a notebook or a sheet of paper to write down every possible argument that an advocate should be prepared to address. The advocate should try to anticipate what the other side will argue. This information can be gained in many ways. While researching a topic, for example, an advocate should not only read to gain support for his or her case, but should also be looking for arguments that the other side may raise. The advocate may wish to brainstorm for possible arguments the other side may present. Past debates should be examined. What did the other side argue against similar cases? What strategies have been used in prior debates?

In preparing for a political debate, for example, the advocate should look at past political debates for potential issues that might be raised by the press or an opponent. Current newspapers and magazines should be read in order to discover new issues. Press statements and campaign literature from both sides should be examined to locate potential issues. Information on those participating in the debates should be located. What interests do they have? What issues do they think are important? All this information can help generate a list of potential issues that need to be anticipated and briefed out.

The stock issues may also be useful to some advocates in anticipating responses to a case. An advocate may wish to decide what programs exist to solve a problem, what evidence on minimizing the harm exists, and what possible disadvantages and solvency attacks can be raised against the policy. The negative advocate should attempt to think of all the possible affirmative plans, advantages, and inherencies. Suppose that an advocate were debating the resolution, "Resolved, that the federal government should provide employment opportunities to all United States citizens." An affirmative

FIGURE 5-1

HARMS OF UNEMPLOYMENT
  Health
  Crime
  Poverty
  Stress
  Housing
SIGNIFICANCE
  Level of unemployment
  Length of unemployment
  Unemployment will continue
INHERENCY
  Federal job programs
  Monetary policy
  Private job programs
  State and local job programs
  Welfare
DISADVANTAGES
  Employment causes inflation
  Cost
  Low unemployment hurts military recruiting
  Low unemployment hurts colleges
  Socialism
  Federal jobs will replace civilian jobs

advocate might develop a list of potential briefs by listing all the possible harms of unemployment, potential programs that could help minimize unemployment, potential disadvantages to those programs, and so on. A partial list might look like the one in Figure 5–1.

A negative advocate should anticipate potential affirmative policies and advantages. While the affirmative advocate has the advantage of knowing what case will be the focus of the debate, the negative advocate must be prepared for all potential cases. The negative advocate's list of briefs might look like the one in Figure 5–1, but it might also include other categories not on that list. For example, it might include a list of specific areas of employment that an affirmative advocate might use in its plan (for example, some advocates might argue that we should employ individuals in the military, Peace Corps, agricultural industries, or in energy-related areas, and then claim advantages from the type of work these individuals performed.) The negative would need to be prepared to argue against these policies.

The briefing process does not require that *all* potential arguments be briefed out. Advocates should make choices in the briefing process about which arguments they will present and which they will ignore. The affirmative advocate, for example, might choose to discuss only one harm of unemployment, making briefs on the other harms of unemployment unnecessary. The negative advocate might decide to focus attention on one of the disadvantages instead of spreading research efforts out among all of the areas. There are limits to this concentration, of course. An advocate must be prepared to respond to those issues raised by the other side; the affirmative needs to be prepared to respond to *all* potential disadvantages, just as the negative needs (usually) to be prepared to respond to all potential advantages. In some cases, responses to one disadvantage apply to a whole series of other arguments, which can help minimize the number of briefs required by an advocate. For example, rather than developing a brief against individual welfare programs (Medicare, Medicaid, food stamps, etc.), it might be easier to prepare one brief explaining why welfare programs, in general, cannot solve the unemployment problem.

Gathering Material for the Brief

After determining the potential arguments that he or she may face, the advocate should gather material and arguments on these issues. One way to do this is to create a notecard or a notebook page for each issue. At the top of the card or page, the debater will write the issue to be refuted. The debater then spreads out the cards and goes through the evidence, placing the evidence behind the card noting the position that the evidence helps defeat. Against some positions, the debater may wish to make an argument that is not supported with evidence. In these cases the debater may wish to jot down this argument on the notecard containing the name of the argument being refuted. At the end of this stage, the debater should have sorted out the evidence into groups corresponding to the argument that the evidence is designed to attack.

Structuring the Brief

Once the advocate has gathered together all the information on an issue, the brief should then be organized into its final form. The brief in debate is slightly different from the type of brief found in other fields of study, for example, law. In law, the brief used is a complete brief that contains, in one document, the background for a case and all the major arguments being advanced.[2] In academic debate, on the other hand, each individual argument is the subject of its own separate brief. The reason for this difference is simple. In law, the lawyers know all the issues that they will be forced to address and often they know all of the other side's arguments as well as their structure of attack. In addition, the legal brief can be prepared at a leisurely pace, and is generally not limited by time or space constraints. On the other hand, a debate brief is designed to be used as a tool for the debater. It is not intended to be comprehensive in itself, but to be used by the debater to help in presenting a case. By the end of a season, most debaters have developed far more briefs than they could read in a single debate (or at a single tournament). Indeed, in many rounds most of the briefs will be irrelevant, since they are directed toward a specific argument. If the argument addressed by the brief is not raised in the debate, there is little reason to read the brief. In addition, the order of presenting a brief may vary. In some rounds, a debater may wish to read brief A first; in

FIGURE 5-2

AFFIRMATIVE (or NEGATIVE)
TITLE OF BRIEF (e.g., UNEMPLOYMENT IS INCREASING)
I. FIRST ARGUMENT (this should be a complete, concise sentence)
    A. SUBPOINT (if needed)
        Source of Evidence (you should include the complete citation for all evidence on the brief. This would include the source, qualifications, page numbers, and so on. If a source is cited twice on a brief, the complete citation should be given both times. Do not use *Ibid., op. cit.* or other similar terms.)

        "Present the evidence in quotes. If the evidence is paraphrased, note this on the brief. If words have been deleted or added, use ellipses (. . .) or brackets. Try to keep this to a minimum (see chapter 4). The evidence should also be cut so that irrelevant information is not on the brief."

        (Use more than one piece of evidence per subpoint if necessary. Place the best evidence first. Some arguments may have several quotations and statistics to support them.)
    B. SUBPOINT (If needed. If there is an A subpoint, there should be a B subpoint)
        Evidence, as before
II. SECOND ARGUMENT
    A. SUBPOINT
        Evidence
    B. SUBPOINT
        Evidence

other debates the brief may be read at the end of a speech, or never at all. To that end, it is best that each brief deal with a single issue, unlike the more comprehensive briefs in law.

The goal of a good brief is to include the best analysis and the best evidence on an issue in a clear, concise, and well-organized document. When organizing the final brief, the debater should think about how useful the brief will be in an actual round and attempt to make the brief as usable as possible. The brief should contain several parts. A finished brief should look somewhat like the example in Figure 5–2.

While the exact format will vary from brief to brief, (for example, some briefs will have no substructure; others will have more structure), they all have certain characteristics.

First, the briefs make extensive use of indentation. Most briefs are similar to an outline, with all the major positions beginning at the left-hand margin and sub-arguments and evidence indented. This makes it easier for the debater to find arguments and evidence on the brief (as may be the case if an advocate decided to read only one of the arguments during a speech), and to visualize the relationships between the major ideas.

FIGURE 5-3

AFFIRMATIVE

UNEMPLOYMENT IS HARMFUL

I.   Unemployment leads to death.

Therman Evans (MD) "Unemployment and Health," *Journal of the American Medical Association,* May 2, 1977, p. 1965.

"According to Dr. Brenner's study, a 1.4 percent increase (about 1½ million people) in the number of unemployed, sustained over the 6-year period between 1970 and 1975, resulted in 20,240 heart and kidney disease deaths, 495 liver cirrhosis deaths, 920 suicides, and 648 homicides. In all, there were 36,887 deaths (27% were of blacks) from various causes."

M. Harvey Brenner (Professor, Operations Research, Johns Hopkins University), "Health Costs and Benefits of Economic Policy," *International Journal of Health Services,* 1977, p. 615.

"Unemployment plays a significant (if not major) statistical role in increasing social trauma for all indices of social cost and for virtually all ages, both sexes, and for whites and nonwhites in the United States."

"Lies, Damn Lies and Statistics," *Time,* July 9, 1984, p. 67.

". . . M. Harvey Brenner of the Johns Hopkins School of Public Health, linked the sharp rise in unemployment during the 1973–74 recession to a subsequent 2.8% rise in deaths from heart attacks."

II. Unemployment increases crime.

Representative John Conyers, Jr. (Michigan) "Journal's Guide for Women Crimefighters," *Congressional Record,* March 24, 1977, p. 9066.

"Today, even the most conservative crime theorists acknowledge the close relation between crime and unemployment. Data from Congressional Research Service, Congressional Budget Office, and Joint Economic Committee studies show a clear relationship between unemployment and imprisonment rates for both State and Federal prison systems. A recent CBO study, for example, documented a 94-percent positive correlation between unemployment and Federal prison admissions."

III. Unemployment harms self-esteem.

Leonard Greene, (Institute for Socioeconomic Studies), *Free Enterprise Without Poverty,* 1981, p. 68.

"Yes, the despair and frustration of a person unable to find work is emotionally crippling."

The brief also contains both arguments and evidence. With all the material in one place, the brief is easy to use. Sometimes, an argument may need no supporting evidence (for example, if an advocate makes a logical response that needs no support), and in other cases the brief may refer to evidence that has been read earlier by the advocate (the affirmative, for example, may wish to refer to evidence in the initial affirmative speech in the briefs instead of reading it a second time.) It may also be wise to include back-up evidence in the brief. Many advocates will include several evidence cards for each subpoint, in case one card cannot be used for some reason, or to provide additional support for the argument. In other cases, an advocate may anticipate

---

FIGURE 5-4

AFFIRMATIVE

BRENNER'S STUDY IS GOOD.

I.   Brenner's study is the best available.

Peter Draper, Jenney Griffiths, John Dennis, James Partridge, and Jean Popay (Unit for the Study of Health Policy, Guy's Hospital Medical School, London), "Microprocessors, Macro-Economic Policy, and Public Health," *The Lancet,* February 17, 1979, p. 373.

"Probably the largest and most statistically elaborate inquiries into the effects of unemployment and health on other social indicators in different countries (including the U.K.) has been carried out by an American Medical sociologist, Dr. Harvey Brenner, and his colleagues of Johns Hopkins University."

II. Brenner *underestimates* the harms of unemployment.

M. Harvey Brenner (Johns Hopkins University), "Estimating the Social Costs of National Economic Policy: Implications for Mental and Physical Health, and Criminal Aggression," in Joint Economic Committee, United States Congress, *Achieving the Goals of the Employment Act of 1946 — Thirtieth Anniversary Review,* October 26, 1976, p. 97.

". . . these measurement problems would tend to significantly bias downward the size size of the impact of unemployment on a given social problem as measured by the coefficient associated with it. This necessitates regarding the quantitative estimates of impact of the unemployment with caution and with the awareness of possible substantial under-estimates."

III. Other studies confirm Brenner.

A. The Bunn Study

William Check, (editor, *Journal of the American Medical Association*), "Do Economic Slumps Increase Illness?" *JAMA,* September 21, 1979, p. 1241.

"Alfred Bunn, DSR, BCom, MEc, of the School of Economic and Financial Studies in New South Wales, carried out the analysis of Australian coronary mortality data. He found that changes in age- and sex-specific IHD (Ischemic heart disease) mortality were highly correlated with unemployment in three time periods— the years preceding, during, and following the Great Depression, which began about 1930."

B. The Fox and Goldblatt Study

Ian Mills (Senior Fellow, Science Policy Research Unit, University of Sussex), "Joblessness and Health," *World Press Review,* July, 1983, p. 58.

"A study by John Fox and Peter Goldblatt of City University, London, shows that men unemployed at the time of the 1971 census were much more likely to have died over the subsequent four years. Most startling was the conclusion that death rates from accidents and violence (with suicide a major component) were more than twice those of employed men."

---

responses to the arguments on the brief, and the brief will contain responses to these anticipated responses. If these responses are extensive, it might be useful to develop a series of back-up briefs. An example of a brief is given in Figure 5–3. A potential back-up brief is given in Figure 5–4.

FIGURE 5-5

I. Nuclear power is undesirable because of accidents, radiation, and terrorism.

The major arguments on the brief should be clearly phrased. The labels on the brief should be concise and specific. The advocate should also make sure that the evidence under a label supports the argument implied by the label. In addition, each label should contain one, and only one, idea. If an advocate wishes to make three arguments, each of those arguments should have its own separate subpoint, although they can be combined under one brief or major heading. For example, instead of having one subpoint like the one in Figure 5-5, it would be better to divide the argument into three parts and to develop it as in Figure 5-6.

This second pattern clearly divides the harm area into three, independent arguments that will be easy to defend as independent positions. If one of these three arguments is lost, it would be easy to continue to defend the other two arguments. Similarly, if an advocate decides to make only one of the three arguments, this would be simple to do with the brief in Figure 5-6, but it would be extremely difficult with the brief in Figure 5-5, since locating the best evidence would be a slow process.

The evidence on the briefs should meet all the requirements discussed in chapter 3. Since the advocate may choose to read only part of the brief in a round, each individual quotation should have the complete citation. The advocate should only read that portion of the evidence that supports the subpoint being defended; irrelevant portions of the evidence should be edited out (or "cut"). This obviously does not mean that the advocate should distort the evidence; only that the advocate need not read parts of evidence that are irrelevant to the position being defended. This process was discussed in more detail in chapter 3.

The brief should also be designed to be used in an argument. This means that it should not be too long. A 15-page brief may be fine in law, but in a normal argument it would require an entire speech to read that brief. The advocate should either subdivide

FIGURE 5-6

I. Nuclear power is undesirable.
   A. Nuclear power plants may be involved in accidents.
   B. Nuclear power plants emit harmful radioactivity.
   C. Nuclear power plants are vulnerable to terrorist attacks.

FIGURE 5-7

NEGATIVE

The volunteer army is working
1. Enlistments are increasing. # #
2. The quality of the soldiers is up. #
3. Turnover is declining. #
4. Studies support the viability of the army.
    A. Defense Manpower Commission #
    B. Brookings Institute Study #

or edit the brief, leaving out weaker responses and evidence. This process is best done before an argument, not during the debate. In addition, the advocate should consider the order of the arguments on the brief. Many times, an advocate will not read an entire brief during an argument; often only the first few responses can be read. To prepare for this contingency, one should make sure that the best arguments are made. In the heat of an argument, the advocate frequently reads only the first few responses on a brief. For this reason, it would be wise to make sure that the strongest arguments are listed first on a brief, or at least to clearly mark these responses on the brief.

Debaters may also wish to experiment with the format of the briefs they use. While we have presented a suggested format for briefs, some debaters will use less formal ones, especially if they are in a hurry to develop briefs. For example, some debaters use file folders for briefs, stapling or taping evidence to the folder instead of retyping the evidence on a brief. In other cases, debaters may wish to use index cards for their briefs. As mentioned earlier, when John F. Kennedy was preparing for his debate with Richard Nixon, he would carry around several notecards, each containing a topic, as well as facts about that topic.

Debaters may wish to use notecards if they are in a hurry and do not have the time to type several briefs. Each notecard would contain the argument being made, along with the arguments designed to refute that position. The cover card might look something like Figure 5-7.

The top card would indicate the arguments to be made supporting the position that the debater wished to defend. A symbol (#) would be used to indicate that there is

---

FIGURE 5-8

NEGATIVE

COURTS CAN PREVENT THE MEDIA FROM INFLUENCING JURORS.

I.   The jury-selection process can remove biased jurors.

II.   The trial can be removed to another city.

III. Juries can be instructed to ignore publicity.

IV.   Juries can be kept isolated from the media.

V.   The court can issue a "gag order."

---

evidence to support the argument. The evidence would be numbered to correspond with the argument it is to support, and all evidence related to the brief would be clipped to the cover card.

TYPES OF BRIEFS

While there are certain common characteristics of all briefs, in the final analysis, each advocate needs to decide for himself or herself the best way to organize the material into blocks. There are two general approaches an advocate can take to developing a brief. The first approach is to use a horizontal brief. A horizontal brief is one that includes several unrelated arguments against a position. A vertical brief takes one issue and develops it in depth. For example, suppose that an advocate wished to prove that cigarette smoking is harmful. With a horizontal brief, the advocate would present several studies supporting the position that smoking is harmful, with each study supported by a single quotation. A vertical brief, on the other hand, might take one study proving that cigarette smoking is harmful, and then provide a wealth of material explaining why that study was a good one. The horizontal brief emphasizes numerous positions, while the vertical brief develops a few arguments in depth.

If a negative advocate were facing a case that argued that the coverage of trials by the media influenced prospective jurors, an outline of a horizontal brief might look like Figure 5-8.

A vertical brief, on the other hand, might take one of these positions and develop it in depth. An outline of such a brief might look like the one in Figure 5-9.

The second brief is much more developed than the first brief. This development is desirable in many ways. The development increases the credibility of the argument. It also ensures that the argument is not easily dismissed or ignored. At the same time, there is the risk that the opposition may be able to dismiss the argument with a response that had not been anticipated. For this reason, it is usually best to be sure about the strength of an argument before constructing a vertical brief on the subject.

FIGURE 5-9

NEGATIVE

JURIES CAN BE INSTRUCTED TO IGNORE PUBLICITY.

I. Courts have the legal ability to instruct jurors to ignore newspaper coverage of the case.
    A. Federal courts
    B. State courts
II. Courts are willing to instruct jurors.
    A. Federal Courts
    B. State Courts
III. Jury instructions are effective.
    A. Jurors listen to jury instructions.
    B. Jurors will ignore media coverage if they are told to do so.
       1. Study #1
       2. Study #2
       3. Study #3
IV. Jury instructions are desirable.
    A. They do not infringe on the freedom of the press.
    B. They allow input from the attorneys.

USING BRIEFS

It is not enough to develop an extensive collection of briefs; the advocate needs to know how to effectively use those briefs. One of the most frequent criticisms of many advocates—in academic, political, and legal debates—is that they do not know how to use their briefs and, as a result, they mishandle arguments.

Updating Briefs

Initially, it is important for advocates to continually update briefs. A brief that was adequate in September may be hopelessly outdated by January. Much may happen between the day a brief is constructed and the time it is used in an argument; the advocate needs to keep up with these developments and to alter the brief if these developments require such a revision. Hopefully, the advocate will discover newer and better evidence on an issue as the advocate continues researching the topic; this evidence should replace the old evidence on a brief. In addition, as briefs are used, advocates may discover weaknesses in the way they were organized or developed. Some arguments may be more difficult to defend than the advocate initially anticipated. Other arguments may be harder to explain than originally predicted. These arguments need either to be replaced with newer positions, or they need to be restructured to eliminate their weaknesses.

Avoiding the Predictable

In addition, when an advocate advances the same positions in every dispute, they become predictable. Other advocates begin to anticipate positions and they know when to expect their opponents' arguments. This allows them to research the advocate's position in depth and to prepare strategies that exploit weaknesses in those positions. It would be better if the advocate kept modifying his or her positions and arguments, to cause the opposition to be unsure about the arguments they will face.

Adapting the Brief

Even if advocates continually modify their briefs, there are other problems that an overreliance on briefs can cause. For example, many advocates allow briefs to substitute for original thought. Once they enter the advocacy situation, all thinking stops, and they mindlessly read briefs, whether or not they apply. Sometimes the advocate will simply react to key words. If an advocate is confronted with a case dealing with Pakistan, the advocate will pull out the "Pakistan" briefs and read them, ignoring whether the case is concerned with the Pakistani-Indian arms race, human rights violations, or Pakistani economic development. This happens outside academic debate rounds. In the 1976 presidential debates, for example, both Gerald Ford and Jimmy Carter prepared for potential questions, but both failed, at least to some degree, to adapt those responses to the questions that were asked.[3] A candidate might have a short response to questions about nuclear power, for example, but the response would be the same to a question that asked "How do you feel about nuclear power?" as to the question, "What can be done about the waste from nuclear power plants?" Instead of adapting a brief to a specific argument, advocates read the brief and hope that it applies.

To prevent this misuse of briefs, it is important for the advocate to understand the briefs, as well as the evidence on the brief. The adaptation of a brief to a specific case requires knowing the details and fine distinctions in the evidence. To effectively argue about the importance of the First Amendment, for example, it is not enough to know a few quotations about the importance of free speech; it is necessary to know something about the philosophy behind both the Amendment and the quotations. The brief can provide an outline of the advocate's arguments as well as some evidence that supports this position, but the explanation of the argument as well as the defense of the argument requires that the advocate know the assumptions behind the argument.

This is not how briefs should be used. Instead of substituting for original thought, briefs should help supplement it. They should allow the advocates time to think about other potential arguments, confident that they will have something to say. The advocates should listen to what is being said and they should determine which brief, if any, should be used. The advocate, after all, need not read all the evidence contained on the brief in any given round; often only a portion of the brief will need to be read. In making this determination, the advocate needs to think about the opposition's position. How does this case differ from the case that the brief was designed for? What sections of the brief will be most effective? Should the brief be restructured for this case? Instead of simply reading the brief, the advocate should use the time in the round to determine its best use.

SUMMARY

The briefing and blocking process is important for any advocate. This process takes a series of seemingly unrelated ideas and evidence, and structures them into a usable tool. There are several types of briefs; determining which type is best depends upon the nature of the argument, the amount of time available, and the nature of the opposition. To be an effective advocate, however, it is necessary to be able to apply the briefs to a specific set of arguments. The advocate thus needs to develop the skills of listening and taking careful notes. This will enable the debater to make intelligent choices about what arguments to present, and when to present them. These skills will be discussed in the next chapter.

Notes

[1]Theodore H. White, *The Making of the President: 1960* (New York: Atheneum, 1961), pp. 322–23.

[2]Mario Pittoni, *Brief Writing and Argumentation,* 3rd edition (Brooklyn: Foundation Press, 1967).

[3]Lloyd Bitzer and Theodore Rueter, *Carter vs. Ford: The Counterfeit Debates of 1976* (Madison: University of Wisconsin Press, 1980), pp. 198–204.

CHAPTER SIX

ESSENTIAL
TOOLS

Understanding how to construct, present, and defend an argumentative position embodies the heart and soul of the process of advocacy. Yet, the process of advocacy involves more than this, because understanding alone will not produce an effective advocate. The missing ingredient consists of the tools of the advocate's trade. These essential tools must be more than merely understood; they must be internalized, so that they become almost second nature to the advocate.

This chapter will focus on three essential tools of the trade: effective listening; complete, accurate, and efficient notetaking; and proficient organization of materials. We will examine each of these tools, with particular emphasis on listening and notetaking. We will indicate the role that each plays in advocacy, and we will suggest specific techniques which should be understood and internalized to start the student on the road toward mastery.

EFFECTIVE LISTENING

Importance of Listening

Listening is a very important skill. We spend approximately 80 percent of our waking hours in communication; of this time, nearly half is spent listening.[1] Among nearly all groups that have been studied, listening is the most prevalent communication function, surpassing speaking, writing, and reading.

At first glance it doesn't seem possible that we spend so much time listening. We only need to visualize those situations in which we typically find ourselves in order to comprehend the proportion of time that we spend listening. Students listen to lectures from their teachers during most class periods. Church or synagogue members listen to sermons during religious services. Businesspeople frequently participate in meetings where they must listen to others present reports. In each of these situations, listening takes place in a group setting. Although communication is the joint responsibility of the speaker *and* the receiver, in a group setting the speaker must assume a disproportionate share of the burden for insuring that the receiver understands the message. Thus, the speaker must take pains to hold the receiver's attention and interest, simplify items, and repeat main points.

Another component of our daily communication activity involves the electronic media. The average American spends about seven hours per day in front of the television set.[2] The electronic media pose additional challenges for the receiver. We are accustomed to processing commercial messages which run from 15 to 30 seconds, and digesting news stories that typically run less than one minute in length. Through the techniques of brevity, simplification, and repetition, the electronic media ordinarily aims programming at the lowest common denominator.

Furthermore, listening skills are integral to our success or failure among our peers, within the family, and on the job. It would be fair to conclude that listening is the most important element of communication in most people's lives.

Reasons for Poor Listening

Given the importance of listening, it is ironic that most Americans are poor listeners. Studies indicate that the average person listens at only a 25 percent effectiveness level.[3] Furthermore, the average person's listening effectiveness will decline with age. As we mature, growing from children to adults (a process that results in ever-increasing capacities in most areas of endeavor), we become increasingly less effective listeners. Studies confirm that, when confronted with a simple message from a teacher, listening retention tends to fall off in a linear pattern as age increases.[4]

Why are Americans such poor listeners? There are many possible answers to this question. Three important causal factors are:

Lack of Formal Training. Most Americans have never experienced formal instruction in listening, regardless of the level of education attained. As a Sperry advertisement claims, ". . . listening is the one communication skill that we're never really taught. We're taught how to read, to write, to speak—but not to listen."[5]

Listening Is Not Valued. Our society does not value listening skills. This is evident in a variety of ways. For example, Americans tend to reinforce ineffective listening. We don't require that people accept the consequences of poor listening. We repeat instructions, we follow-up to see if the instructions were carried out, and, if someone misunderstands us, we tend to give him or her a second chance. This is especially evident in our educational practices. It also shows up in the consumer realm. A number of lawsuits have been won by consumers who disregarded a product's instructions for proper use, were injured, and who then sued the company for damages, claiming that the product was unsafe.

Our culture also conditions us to speak, not to listen. When we are not actually talking, we are preparing for what we will say next. Listening requires a substantial effort; that isn't possible if the individual is actively preparing to talk during the time that he or she isn't actually speaking. Finally, our society offers very limited opportunities for formal instruction in listening. We stress reading and writing in the elementary years, and reading, writing, and speaking in the high school and collegiate years. Some colleges and universities now offer elective courses in listening, but there is no systematic effort to impart listening skills to all students.

Difficulty of Effective Listening.   The third reason why Americans are poor listeners is the fact that listening is a complex and difficult process. We communicate orally via the exchange of symbols. Yet, a symbol is not a direct representation of an object. Symbols require interpretation, initially on the part of the sender of the message, and finally on the part of the receiver. Interpretations, of course, are anything but definitive. They are unique to each of us, a product of our individual experiences. For example, the words, "detente," "inflation," "pornography," "freedom," "abortion," or "poverty," produce very distinct images for different people. Thus, the listener may receive the specified symbol from the speaker, but may decode it (assign meaning to it) in such a way that it bears little resemblance to the meaning that the speaker was attempting to convey.

The listening process itself offers ample opportunities for the misinterpretation of a message. Between the speaker and the receiver, environmental interference (e.g., a competing message, noise, poor acoustics, etc.) may impair accurate reception of the message. Once the message reaches the receiver, internal interference (e.g., a headcold, lack of concentration, an inability to decode one or more of the symbols received, etc.) may block accurate reception of the message. If the message is able to overcome these barriers, it must still hurdle various stumbling blocks within the receiver. For example, the message must be processed both verbally and visually, possibly with incongruous results. Hearing and seeing are both involved in listening. Once a message is received, it is visually processed, and meaning is assigned; similarly, meaning is assigned when a message is verbally processed. Meaning is then evaluated, retained for future utilization and a response is made.

We have simplified the listening process considerably with the preceding explanation. The point is this: listening is a very complex process. It stands to reason, then, that listening is a difficult task. One of the reasons that this society does not stress listening more is the misconception that listening is like breathing—an automatic, physiological function. Nothing could be further from the truth. This misconception confuses the mere physical act of hearing with the mental process of listening. Listening is very difficult; it requires preparation and substantial effort.

Speaking Rate and Listening Effectiveness

The average American speaks at a rate of 125 to 150 words per minute.[6] This pace has been steadily increasing during the past two decades. Accomplished intercollegiate debaters speak at an even faster rate.

What effect does speaking rate have on listening effectiveness? Contrary to conventional wisdom, increased speaking rate does not significantly impair—and can enhance—comprehension. A broad consensus among researchers supports the claim that speaking rates can be doubled (over the norm) with less than a 10 percent decline in listening comprehension.[7] This places the maximum threshold at approximately 280 words per minute. Beyond this point, comprehension declines sharply. A speaking rate of 280 words per minute could be viewed as an optimal threshold in those circumstances in which time is an especially scarce commodity. For example, in tournament debate competition, where the pressure exists to present a substantial amount of material within a fixed period, or in the procurement and use of expensive radio and/or television advertising time, it makes sense to increase the speaking rate, as long as target audience comprehension and acceptance are maintained.

In most circumstances, receivers prefer a slightly quickened speaking rate (above the national norm of 125 to 150 words per minute). This is because the normal speaking rate hardly begins to tax the capacity of the mind to process verbal messages. We think at about 500 words per minute;[8] few, if any, humans can speak faster than 300 words per minute, while most talk at less than half of this rate. As a result, many listeners "tune out" a speaker's message. They grow bored and distracted, and listening effectiveness declines. We have all experienced situations in which the speaker proceeded at a painfully slow pace. When this happens, it is difficult to concentrate on the message; the receiver's mind wanders, and most of what is said gets lost. In such circumstances, a quickened speaking rate can actually facilitate listening comprehension.

Academic debate is an exercise in oral argumentation. It differs from everyday speaking situations such as classroom lectures, church sermons, or mass media presentations. The speakers in a debate are required to carry a high content load. Each speaker must complete coverage of those arguments that make up his or her share of the elements in the case. In addition, academic debate is not addressed to a general audience of laypersons, but to specialists who are trained in the art of encoding, processing, and evaluating argument. Finally, the time limits are strictly enforced in debate.

Under these circumstances, even novice debaters quickly cast off their acquired habits of conventional speech. Advocates in a debate speak at a faster rate than they would in any other situation. Accomplished intercollegiate debaters speak at an average rate of nearly 270 words per minute.[9] This pace has been steadily increasing in recent years (indeed, some intercollegiate debaters have been clocked at approximately 300 words per minute).

It follows, then, that listening is a crucial skill for the debater. Former participants frequently cite improved listening as one of the most important benefits of debate.

Importance of Listening in Advocacy

Listening skills are an absolute prerequisite to a mastery of the process of advocacy. Initially, you must know precisely what the opposing speaker said in order to refute his or her arguments. For example, you may wish to argue that a peacetime draft registration is both unnecessary and undesirable. Your opponent claims that a peacetime draft registration is essential, because (1) regional "hot spots" can escalate without warning, requiring the rapid deployment, and possibly the sustained use, of

U.S. conventional forces; the all-volunteer force, without the backing of a draft registration system for rapid mobilization in an emergency, cannot respond in a crisis. And, (2) all youth have an obligation of service to their country; that draft registration is the price we should be willing to pay for the benefits of U.S. citizenship. In order to defend your position, it is necessary to refute both of the arguments offered by your opponent. If you didn't hear, or if you misconstrued, either of the opponent's arguments, it could prove to be very difficult to sustain your position. The failure to hear an opponent's argument will cause a substantial disfunction in advocacy.

But, hearing each argument is only the first step. The advocate must also listen for slight nuances in the opponent's position. For example, it makes a big difference whether the speaker advocates the *legalization or* the *decriminalization* of the possession of small quantities of marijuana. The rationale used to support either position would be similar. However, the implications for argument are quite distinct.

In addition to listening to your opponent's claims, you must also listen carefully for the warrants (explanations) in support of the opponent's position. To respond effectively you need to know the reasons offered in support of the opponent's claim. Each warrant provides a unique set of argumentative options. For example, if an opponent claims that a "tough" United States resolve will curb Soviet adventurism, it is important to listen for the supporting rationale. If no reason is given, the claim represents nothing more than a simple assertion and can be dismissed quite easily. If an explanation is provided, its nature determines response possibilities. The speaker might bolster the claim, explaining that the Soviets respect strength; if the U.S. toughens its military capacities, and takes a "hardline" position in response to the U.S.S.R., then the Soviets will act more cautiously in the international arena. This particular explanation sets up a strong response. You can argue that Soviet leadership is at a crossroads, looking closely to U.S. cues before deciding on future policy directions. If the U.S. takes a "hardline" position, the Soviets will respond in kind; conversely, if the U.S. adopts a conciliatory posture, important breakthroughs are possible which would reduce superpower tension and facilitate nuclear force reductions. In this instance, the opponent's explanation serves as the catalyst for a strong argumentative response. If you fail to catch the explanation, this prospect will be lost.

Finally, the advocate must pay meticulous attention to the backing (evidenciary support) for an opponent's position. Some of the best arguments are products of an opponent's miscue. In deciding on an appropriate response, the advocate must initially determine if this claim was supported with evidence. If not, the claim can be dismissed as a mere assertion.

For example, an opponent might argue that the government of El Salvador has made substantial progress in reducing human rights violations against its own people. If that argument was backed up with evidence, the advocate must first discover the nature of the proof. Did the evidence consist of mere opinion or empirical verification? The answer determines argumentative options. Then, the appropriateness of the source must be examined. Was the evidence an official statement by the U.S. Department of State? If so, a charge of bias could be made, since the Department is interested in supporting existing policy toward El Salvador, and has a track record of "playing down" that government's human rights excesses. Or, did the evidence consist of an official pronouncement of Amnesty International, an organization committed to ascertaining the human rights record of the world's governments? The former can be dismissed as biased; the latter will require a much stronger answer. In each instance, it is important to listen to the evidence; it opens up, and closes off, argumentative possibilities.

Suggestions to Improve Listening

Effective listening does not come easily—it is not an automatic function, analogous to breathing. Instead, individuals must cultivate their listening skills. The following suggestions, while not exhaustive, can improve listening effectiveness.

Concentrate.   First, work on concentration. Listening is hard work. It requires a concerted effort. As indicated previously, environmental and internal interferences can impede listening. Some distractions emanate from the communication environment, such as the sound of other people talking, noise from automobiles passing on the street outside, or poor acoustics. Learn to block out, or compensate for, these distractions. Other distractions originate within the listener, such as musing or allowing the mind to dwell on visual irrelevancies (i.e., the speaker's attire, characteristics of the room, etc.). The listener can, quite literally, force a total immersion in the speaker's message. Such is the power of self-discipline, and it holds the key to concentration.

Use Available Time.   Second, make full use of spare time. We have already noted that the mind processes information at a rate of 500 words per minute; no speaker can begin to approach this rate. The difference between what Ralph G. Nichols terms "thought speed" and "speech speed" offers difficulty and/or opportunity, depending on how the listener uses this increment of time.[10] It is a source of difficulty if it breaks the listener's concentration, thus impeding comprehension. Conversely, spare time offers a valuable opportunity if used wisely. It allows the listener to tie up loose ends (this is especially important to effective notetaking, as we will observe shortly), reflect on the message, and anticipate upcoming development. It is up to the listener to optimize spare time.

Prepare for Listening.   Finally, prepare thoroughly for listening. This consists of a personal effort designed to improve memory, enhance vocabulary, and become familiar with the topic, getting ready for the concepts, terminology, and sources that the speaker might utilize. Learn to detect the organizational patterns which are used in packaging oral messages, and "get up" physically, emotionally, and mentally for listening. Effective listening is up to you.

EFFECTIVE NOTETAKING

Listening skills are used in conjunction with notetaking skills. Since a typical debate consists of a plethora of individual arguments, and since any single argument's outcome might prove crucial in determining the final outcome of a debate, the advocate cannot rely on memory alone as a tool to provide a reliable record of either side's arguments. Instead, the advocate must listen for and write down each opposing argument's label, warrant or explanation, and support (the citation as well as a synopsis of the evidence). Then the advocate must inscribe his or her own responses. In this way effective listening facilitates complete, accurate, and efficient notetaking.

The procedure for notetaking is designed to provide a systematic record of each argument's ebb and flow during the course of a debate. This process is referred to as *flowing.* The arguments are inscribed on special paper, which must be wide enough to accommodate a complete, horizontal transcript of all the responses made by opposing speakers regarding a particular argument. A legal pad—or art pad—is uniquely suited for this task. An individual piece of this paper is called a *flow sheet;* the entire pad, or tablet, is termed a *flow pad.* The completed transcript of a debate, which includes all of the arguments in a debate and consists of multiple pages, is designated *the flow.* It constitutes an unofficial record of the debate.

The Purpose of a Flow

A complete and accurate record of a debate is an indispensable tool for effective advocacy. Most essential debate functions would prove to be impossible without the aid of a flow.

During a debate the flow serves the advocate in a variety of ways. It consists of a record of the opponent's arguments (ideally consisting of each argument's label, warrant and backing) and the responses to those arguments. First, it facilitates initial refutation. The flow helps the advocate to know what arguments must be answered, it serves as a record of his or her responses to those arguments, and provides an excellent tool to insure proper organization and maximum efficiency during the actual presentation.

Second, the flow constitutes an accurate record of the debate. If the advocate knows precisely what his or her opponent said and did not say in the initial speeches, then it is possible to guard against unreasonable rhetorical manipulation in subsequent speeches.

It is common for advocates, regardless of the setting, to attempt to cast a debate in the most favorable light. Most do so via selective emphasis in the rebuttal periods. Selective emphasis is good advocacy. However, some speakers engage in excessive manipulation of arguments in rebuttals, at times deliberately. An accurate flow is the best defense against distortive practices. In the same vein, the advocate can use the flow to spot and exploit contradictions in an opponent's position. In debates on the topic "that the Federal Government should guarantee employment opportunities for all U.S. citizens in the labor force," it was not uncommon to hear opponents of the resolution argue in one speech that the present system was expanding employment opportunities, and then, in a subsequent speech, that employment, and higher income, caused increased mortality. Contradictions can be pinpointed on the flow.

Third, a flow makes argument synthesis possible, and thus unlocks the key to effective rebuttal speeches. Arguments evolve during the course of a debate, changing form from one speech to the next. Indeed, some extension completely alters the nature, direction, and implications of individual arguments. The flow aids micro-evaluation; it serves as a tool for the advocate, enabling him or her to follow the path of individual arguments throughout a debate. In addition, the flow facilitates macro-evaluation; it

FIGURE 6-1

1AC
C1. Indonesia devastates E. Timor
    A. Suffering/death
        Edwards, CR—82
        "200T, one-third
        of population
        has perished"

functions as a record of all arguments, enabling the advocate to sort out and evaluate the ramifications of all arguments presented during a debate. Advocates, who are the most formidable during the rebuttal speeches, utilize their flows to maximize argument synthesis.

Finally, the flow constitutes a tool for the evaluation of individual arguments and of an entire debate. At the conclusion of a debate, the flow can be studied in an effort to analyze the effectiveness of particular strategies and the adequacy of responses to individual arguments. A careful examination of the debate flow is one of the most useful learning tools available to the advocate. It enables the debater to pinpoint mistakes, evaluate the potential of approaches that were used, and identify those arguments that require more or better analysis and evidence. In short, the flow holds the key to continued growth in advocacy.

General Procedures

In illustrating flowing procedures and techniques, we will use excerpts from a debate on the topic, "the U.S. should curtail its arms sales to other countries." In this particular debate, the affirmative argued a case variant grounded in the premise that, if the United States stopped arms sales to Indonesia, the latter would cease in its effort to subjugate the people of East Timor. The affirmative contended that the U.S., as Indonesia's primary arms supplier, bears a special responsibility for the human death and suffering and the loss of freedom of the East Timorese.

On a micro level, a flow simply consists of the evolution of an individual argument during the course of a debate. It starts with the initial introduction of an argument into a debate. For example, the affirmative, supporting a cutoff of U.S. arms sales to Indonesia, might argue a first contention that, "Indonesia has devastated East Timor; death and loss of human rights have characterized the Indonesian military incursion. Let's look first at the suffering and death that has resulted. Representative Don Edwards, in the *Congressional Record* of March 1982, reported that, since the Indonesian invasion in 1976, 'the Timorese death toll may exceed 200,000—perhaps one-third or more of the island territory's original population of 700,000'—as a result of the war, and the disease and starvation that accompanied it." This should be flowed, as depicted in Figure 6-1. The designation, "1AC," identifies the particular speech in the debate; this argument was presented in the "first affirmative constructive" speech. The

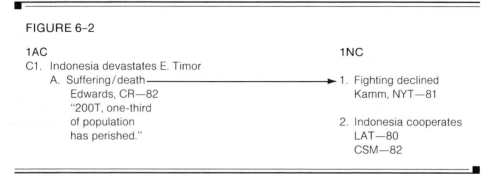

FIGURE 6–2

1AC
C1. Indonesia devastates E. Timor
   A. Suffering/death
      Edwards, CR—82
      "200T, one-third
      of population
      has perished."

1NC
1. Fighting declined
   Kamm, NYT—81

2. Indonesia cooperates
   LAT—80
   CSM—82

abbreviation, "C1," stands for, "contention one," as identified by the speaker. Since the speaker indicated that Indonesia's devastation would be examined in two dimensions, suffering and death, as well as the loss of human rights, an "A" is used to characterize "death and suffering," consistent with proper outlining technique. *The Congressional Record* was abbreviated, "CR."

Symbols and abbreviations—as a form of informal shorthand—should be employed whenever possible to aid flowing. While there is no universal system of shorthand for advocacy, there are common-sense characterizations. Common debate terms are often abbreviated (i.e., "DA" for disadvantage, "TA" for turnaround, "PMA" or "PMN" for plan-meet-advantage or plan-meet-need, "T" for topicality, "PO" for plan objection, "PS" for present system, etc.) Evidence citations are commonly shortened (i.e., "BW" for *Business Week,* "USN&WR" for *United States News & World Report,* "NYT" for *New York Times,* "CR" for *Congressional Record,* "SR" for *Saturday Review,* etc.) Finally, acronyms and symbols found in everyday language can facilitate efficient flowing (i.e., "GNP" for Gross National Product, "$" for dollars, etc.). One caveat should be kept in mind: any system of informal shorthand must make sense to the person using it. After all, a system of shorthand is designed to simultaneously facilitate efficient flowing and instantaneous recall. Unless a system meets both objectives it is of little value to the advocate.

Initially, a negative advocate must examine strategic options (see chapter 11). He or she then might decide to contest the affirmative's significance claim, that the Indonesian invasion resulted in substantial human suffering and death. If so, the flow continues with the initial negative responses to the original argument. In response to the "suffering and death" claim, the negative claims: "First, the fighting has declined," citing Henry Kamm in the *New York Times* in 1981. "Second," the negative argues that, "according to reports in the *Los Angeles Times* and the *Christian Science Monitor,* the Indonesians are now cooperating with outside relief agencies in order to speed assistance to the East Timorese." These responses should be flowed next to the original argument, connected by an arrow, as indicated in Figure 6–2. You should observe the continued use of abbreviations and symbols. In this instance, the designation, "1NC," stands for the "first negative constructive" speech; just the last name of

---

FIGURE 6-3

1AC	1NC
C1. Indonesia devastates E. Timor	

      A. Suffering/death
         Edwards, CR—82
         "200T, one-third
         of population,
         has perished"

---

the primary source is noted; and each of the secondary source references are abbreviated. In addition, each of the two responses are numbered.

Each individual speech should be flowed vertically. The initial presentation can be recorded in order, as presented, in the far left column on the flow sheet. The next speech should be flowed in the adjacent column to the right. If the content of a speech directly clashes with elements of a previous presentation, those responses should be recorded directly adjacent, and an arrow should be used to denote the interconnectedness of the arguments. This is illustrated in Figure 6–2. The negative's claims that, "fighting has declined" and "Indonesia is now cooperating with outside relief agencies to speed assistance," clash with the affirmative's argument on "death and suffering." Hence, they should be flowed directly adjacent to that argument, and connected via arrow.

If the content of a speech does not directly clash with elements of a previous presentation, leave the space adjacent to the original material blank, and record the new content in a separate place. For example, if the negative didn't argue the two points depicted above, instead claiming that, "Indonesia would resent U.S. interference into their affairs, turn to alternative suppliers for their military equipment, and step up the brutality against the East Timorese," then this position should be flowed in a different place, since it does not directly clash with the affirmative's argument that the "Indonesian invasion has devastated East Timor." Affirmative responses to this negative argument should be flowed adjacent to it, regardless of when (in what order) they are presented in the affirmative's speech. Figures 6–3 and 6–4 illustrate these points. The temptation is to flow the speaker's arguments consecutively, ignoring the importance of argument interrelationships. This, of course, makes the flow very difficult to use. If a position does not directly clash with a previous argument, it must be flowed separately, as in this case. In Figure 6–4, "PMA–1" stands for "plan-meet-advantage one," designating the particular class, or family, of argument and the standing within that class. Again, observe the use of abbreviations. Evidence citations are designated by last name, and year of publication. If the evidence is especially important, a synthesis of it should be inscribed. More information, such as source qualifications, might be indicated if it appears significant. Subsequent affirmative responses, which clash with the plan-meet-advantage, should be flowed to its immediate right.

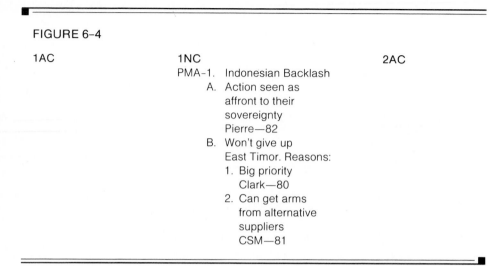

FIGURE 6–4

1AC	1NC	2AC
	PMA-1. Indonesian Backlash	
	A. Action seen as affront to their sovereignty Pierre—82	
	B. Won't give up East Timor. Reasons:	
	1. Big priority Clark—80	
	2. Can get arms from alternative suppliers CSM—81	

On a macro level, a flow consists of a complete record of a debate. It includes all arguments which are presented during the course of a debate. Case arguments contest and bolster the rationale for change, as presented in the initial affirmative presentation. They should be flowed, each speech assuming one horizontal column. In team debate, a case flow consists of seven columns, as illustrated in Figure 6–5. Lincoln-Douglas, or one-person debate, is characterized by fewer individual speeches than team debate. Hence a case flow involves only five columns, as shown in Figure 6–6.

Case arguments are initiated and organized by the affirmative. Counterplans and plan arguments, by contrast, are initiated and organized by the negative. Plan arguments, in particular, attack and defend the course of action recommended by an affirmative. They should be flowed on separate pages, each speech requiring one vertical column. If the negative presents plan attacks in the first constructive speech, those arguments should be flowed in seven columns in team debate, as depicted in Figure 6–7. They should be flowed in four columns in Lincoln-Douglas debate, as illustrated in Figure 6–8.

If the negative introduces plan arguments in the second constructive speech, they should be flowed in four or five columns. The placement of the affirmative's plan determines whether a four- or five-column approach is desired. Some prefer to have

FIGURE 6–5

First Affirm. Construc. Speech	First Negative Construc. Speech	Second Affirm. Construc. Speech	First Negative Rebuttal Speech	First Affirm. Rebuttal Speech	Second Negative Rebuttal Speech	Second Affirm. Rebuttal Speech

FIGURE 6-6

First Affirmative Constructive Speech	First Negative Constructive Speech	First Affirmative Rebuttal Speech	First Negative Rebuttal Speech	Second Affirmative Rebuttal Speech

the plan displayed in a column adjacent to the negative's plan attacks; others flow the plan at its point of origination (i.e., usually on the case flow, at the point delivered). A five-column approach is depicted in Figure 6–9.

Finally, negative generic positions, including topicality arguments, alternative-mechanism approaches (counterplans) or counter-warrant defenses, should be recorded on separate paper. For purposes of flowing, negative generics should be treated in precisely the same manner as negative plan arguments (see illustrations above).

Flowing Technique

There are no "instant cures" for deficient flowing. However, the advocate's attention to proper technique, coupled with diligence and practice, will steadily enhance flowing prowess. We will identify those techniques that contribute to effective flowing.

Flow the Labels.   We recommend that the advocate start small. Initially, strive to flow the labels of all arguments that are presented. Although this precludes an evaluation of the warrants and backing for each opposing point, it minimally provides a complete record of a debate; hence, refutation can occur. Once this level of proficiency is attained, go on to the next stage.

Flow Citations.   The next step is to attempt to flow citations for each piece of evidence and for any examples that are used to support or illustrate an argument. The advocate who is able to flow all argument labels, citations, and examples can accomplish most of the functions of refutation.

Flow a Synopsis.   When the second step is mastered, attempt the final stage: strive to flow a synopsis of all crucial evidence and explanations which are provided. This stage represents optimal proficiency.

FIGURE 6-7

First Negative Construc. Speech	Second Affirm. Construc. Speech	Second Negative Construc. Speech	First Negative Rebuttal Speech	First Affirm. Rebuttal Speech	Second Negative Rebuttal Speech	Second Affirm. Rebuttal Speech

---

FIGURE 6–8

First Negative Constructive Speech	First Affirmative Constructive Speech	First Negative Rebuttal Speech	Second Affirmative Rebuttal Speech

---

The less-experienced advocate often finds it difficult to make sound choices regarding arguments because only a fraction of an opponent's presentation can be inscribed (regardless of flowing proficiency). This problem is magnified since choice is an on-going process—a continuing responsibility of the advocate as he or she listens to and flows arguments. The uncertainty involves what to include and exclude. Argumentative maturity, which is a product of experience, is the only sure solution to this problem. Nonetheless, you should bear in mind the stages delineated above; they constitute a systematic approach to flowing which can minimize the role of choices.

Consider Other Techniques. Other techniques are a matter of individual preference. Since each speech is flowed in a separate column, is it necessary to draw lines to set up columns? The answer is that it doesn't really matter. Some advocates set up columns on their flow sheets before a debate, while others demarcate columns during a debate. Still others find it unnecessary to draw lines at all. Is it helpful to flow alternate speeches with a different color pen to set them apart? Some find this procedure helpful; others do not. Is there a rule of thumb concerning the vertical spacing of arguments during a speech? Generally, allow ample room. Compact vertical flowing conserves paper, but it can render a flow virtually worthless. If, for example, an affirmative advocate flows his or her initial constructive speech compactly, while a negative opponent decides to concentrate his or her attack on a few select points of the affirmative's case, instead of responding in a more proportional fashion (this is usually an effective negative strategy), then the affirmative's flow might well be rendered useless for all subsequent speeches. Hence, ample vertical spacing is wise.

Flow All Speeches. Finally, we recommend that advocates flow all speeches in a debate. In Lincoln-Douglas debate this goes without saying. In team debate, the last affirmative and negative rebuttalists must flow all speeches. They have the responsi-

---

FIGURE 6–9

Affirmative Plan	Second Negative Constructive Speech	First Affirmative Rebuttal Speech	Second Negative Rebuttal Speech	Second Affirmative Rebuttal Speech

---

bility to synthesize and selectively extend any or all of the arguments, regardless of the speech of origin. However, it might appear that the first affirmative and negative advocates, who complete their own speaking responsibilities before their colleagues, do not need to flow the last rebuttals. We disagree. All speakers should maintain an accurate flow throughout the debate. First, each advocate should assist his or her colleague in rebuttal preparation. In team debate, there are no argument specialists. Because arguments interrelate and overlap, the responsibilities of individual speakers must do likewise. The advocate, who has completed his or her own speaking responsibilities, should continue to flow the debate, evaluate argument outcomes, and assist in synthesis. Second, a flow of the entire debate is a prerequisite to evaluation. If an advocate expects to make an informed judgment about the debate, a complete flow is essential. Furthermore, if the flow is to assist learning and preparation, a complete transcript is essential in order to remember how one's opponent has responded to a particular argument.

Maximization of flowing technique requires patience and hard work. One thing is clear: effective notetaking is an indispensable tool in the process of advocacy; and there is *no* surer method to enhance one's flowing proficiency than constant practice. A sample flow of a complete debate follows. We have chosen a full debate on the topic, "the U.S. should curtail its arms sales to other countries." This particular debate focused on U.S. arms sales to Indonesia. The affirmative argued that the U.S. should stop arms sales to Indonesia in an effort to halt the latter's subjugation of East Timor. The negative maintained that affirmative significance claims were exaggerated; neither Indonesia nor the U.S. is responsible for conditions in East Timor; the Timorese support union with Indonesia; U.S. arms sales to Indonesia facilitate important strategic objectives; curtailing U.S. arms sales to Indonesia will fail to accomplish a favorable alteration of Indonesian policy and might precipitate a backlash toward East Timor; and curtailing U.S. arms sales is, on balance, an undesirable policy position.

Figure 6–10 illustrates arguments which clashed with the rationale for change offered in the first affirmative constructive speech. Figure 6–11 depicts arguments which originated from new positions, presented in the second negative constructive speech.

Developing an understanding of listening and notetaking techniques is the first step, but understanding alone will not assure competence. These tools of advocacy must become internalized so that they become almost second nature. Continual practice is the only sure route toward mastery of these techniques.

PROFICIENT ORGANIZATION OF MATERIALS

The proficient organization of materials is another essential tool of advocacy. Chapters 4 and 5 examined the procedures and techniques which are used to gather evidence and to organize it in briefs and blocks for use in a debate. This section will focus on organizing these materials to facilitate their rapid retrieval during a debate. We will stress the need to utilize a system of organization, and will suggest specific techniques for proficient organization of materials.

FIGURE 6-10

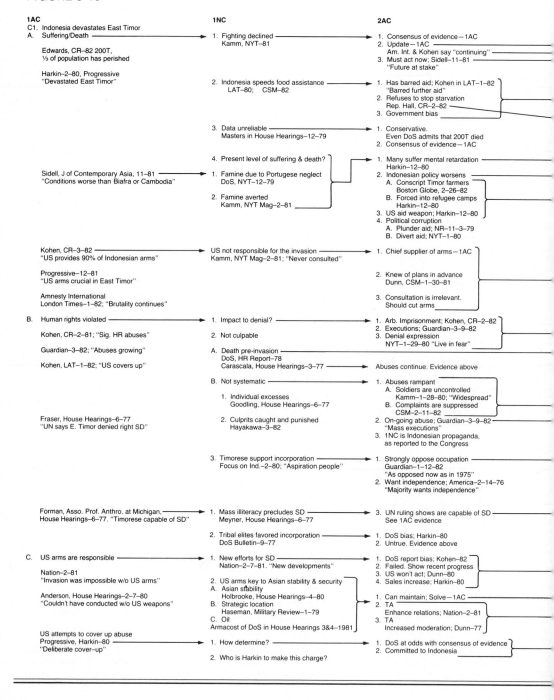

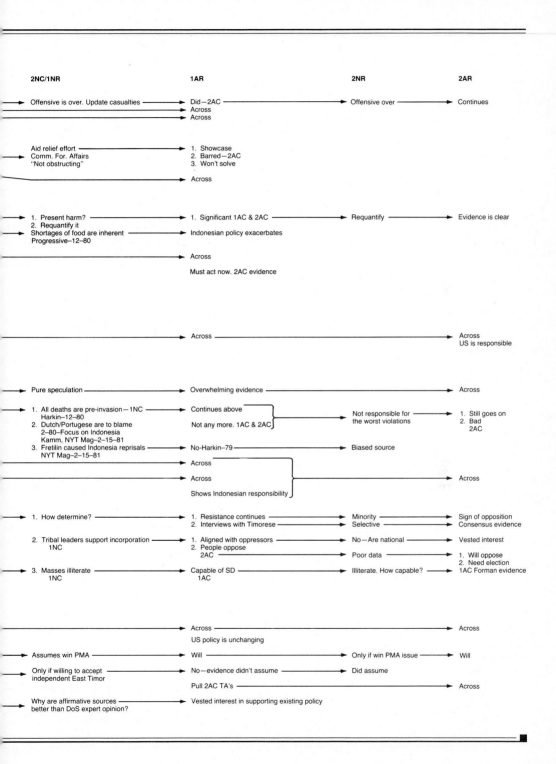

2NC/1NR	1AR	2NR	2AR
Offensive is over. Update casualties	Did—2AC Across Across	Offensive over	Continues
Aid relief effort Comm. For. Affairs "Not obstructing"	1. Showcase 2. Barred—2AC 3. Won't solve Across		
1. Present harm? 2. Requantify it Shortages of food are inherent Progressive—12–80	1. Significant 1AC & 2AC Indonesian policy exacerbates Across Must act now. 2AC evidence	Requantify	Evidence is clear
	Across		Across US is responsible
Pure speculation	Overwhelming evidence		Across
1. All deaths are pre-invasion—1NC Harkin–12–80 2. Dutch/Portugese are to blame 2–80–Focus on Indonesia Kamm, NYT Mag–2–15–81 3. Fretilin caused Indonesia reprisals NYT Mag–2–15–81	Continues above Not any more. 1AC & 2AC No-Harkin–79 Across	Not responsible for the worst violations Biased source	1. Still goes on 2. Bad 2AC
	Across Shows Indonesian responsibility		Across
1. How determine?	1. Resistance continues 2. Interviews with Timorese	Minority Selective	Sign of opposition Consensus evidence
2. Tribal leaders support incorporation 1NC	1. Aligned with oppressors 2. People oppose 2AC	No—Are national Poor data	Vested interest 1. Will oppose 2. Need election
3. Masses illiterate 1NC	Capable of SD 1AC	Illiterate. How capable?	1AC Forman evidence
	Across US policy is unchanging		Across
Assumes win PMA	Will	Only if win PMA issue	Will
Only if willing to accept independent East Timor	No—evidence didn't assume	Did assume	
	Pull 2AC TA's		Across
Why are affirmative sources better than DoS expert opinion?	Vested interest in supporting existing policy		

FIGURE 6-10 (Continued)

1AC	1NC	2AC

Plan
1. Administration Board oversees
2. Mandates
   A. Stop US sales to Indonesia
      for one full year
   B. Resume sales if conditions are met:
      1. Cessation of HR abuse in Timor
      2. UN supervised elections for SD
3. Funding GFRs
4. Enforcement via DoJ Fines & imprisonment
5. Intent

C2. US will militate fighting/repression → 1. Invasion occurred even w/o US arms → 1. No. Consensus evidence
   Atlantic Monthly–7–82   See 1AC
   2. Can't be sure. Failed to cut arms

A. Directly → 2. Won't surrender Timor for US arms → 1. Totally dependent on US arms
   Weatherbee, Strategic Review–Fall–1980   Ramos-Horta, CSM–1–30–81
   Sidell, J of Contemporary Asia–11–81   2. Two suppliers; Meyner, Hearings–77
   "US arms are instrumental"   3. Embargoes fail empirically → 3. Threats fail
   NYT–80   Immediate cuts work
   Nation–2–81   (no time to sub.)
   "Could not do so w/o US arms"

   Anderson, House Hearings–2–7–80
   "Can't w/o US aid"

   Harkin–12–80, Progressive → 1. Must balance HR → 1. Need consistency; Pringle–80
   "We have moral obligation"   A. Generally; NYT–1–2–77
   B. Strategic goals at stake–see above   2. Enhance US image; Pierre–82

B. Via leverage → 1. No US leverage → 1. DoS bias
   Works   2. US has leverage
   Harkin–12–80, Progressive   A. Generally   Chomsky & Herman–79
   "Pressure can & should be brought bear"   Holbrooke, House Hearings–6–80
   "Don't have real leverage"   3. Indonesia is totally dependent
   Chomsky and Herman–1979   B. Will fail on East Timor issue   Ramos-Horta, CSM–1–30–81
   "US can use influence to end atrocities"   C. Overestimate US influence in matter   4. Clear consensus of evidence
   Pringle of Foreign Service–1980   1AC
   CSM–1–30–81   "The day is past . . ."
   "Firm commitment to SD could
   bring peace & freedom"   2. Threshhold for use of US leverage?

   3. Arms provide US influence–Pierre–82 → Yes–But must cut arms to exercise

   PMA–1. Backlash

   A. Action seen as affront to their sovereignty
   Pierre–82   1. Propaganda; Pringle–80

   B. Won't give up   2. 1AC & 2AC; PMA evidence
   Timor–Reasons:

      1. Big priority; Clarke–80

      2. Can get arms from alternate suppliers   1. Are dependent; Ramos-Horta above
         CSM–81
      2. Who will supply?

         A. Won't buy from Soviets
            LaRouque–5–80

         B. UN nations oppose Indonesia on Timor issue
            Kamm, LAT–1–7–82

      3. US aid is key
         Anderson, House Hearings–2–7–80

2NC/1NR	1AR	2NR	2AR

Occurred w/o arms
1NC
Can be—see below

Now—Other willing suppliers—below —————————————→ Across
                                    Across —————————————————————————→ Across

All efforts failed ————————————— No—Past efforts only threats; as ——→ Failed   Plan is different
1NC   such, provided a warning   from past efforts

                                  Plan curtails immediately

Need balanced policy ————————————→ Bankrupt policy ————————————————→ Ignores US security interests

TA—Hurt US image   Strengthen our relations—2AC ————→ Hurts—1NR   1. 2AC evidence
A. In Indonesia; Pringle—80   Enhance US image   No—1NR   2. No impact
B. As reliable ally; Bennet—3–23–77

No leverage
A. 1NC evidence   1. Dependence is total ————————————————————————————————→ Across
B. Additional support   2. Consensus of opinion ————————————→ 1NR evidence ignored
   WSJ–2–6–80; Pringle—80

No consensus shown ——————————————————————————————————————→ Across

Across ———→ Across

Across ———→ Across

No—would lose leverage then ——————→ Indonesia will respond ————————→ No   Consensus evidence
Anderson—80   1AC & 2AC

1. No; NYT–1–2–77
   W. Post–11–15–79
2. Will pay the price of cutoff
   Weatherbee in Strategic Review—Fall–1980   1. Assumes only threat; ———————→ No; evidence is clear ————→ Wrong assumption
3. Will turn to other suppliers   immediate cutoff will work
   Weatherbee—80; "US sanctions   2. Indonesia is totally dependent ——→ 1. Assumes PS ————————→ Dependent
   turn country to other suppliers"   Ramos-Horta, CSM–1–30–81   1AR
                                                 3. Need US aid   2. Weatherbee evidence good
                                                    Chomsky & Herman   1NR
                                                    "Whats & needs US assistance
                                                    in its military reequipping"

Not inherent—characterizes
past patterns   Position assumes no ————————————————→ Pull 1NR evidence
1. Demand remains   affirmative solvency
   Rep. Darwinski, CR–3–29–79
2. Buyers market; Nueman & Harkavey–79
   "buyers' market"   1AC & 2AC evidence is specific   Pull 1NR evidence
                                  and denies argument

1. Will surrender alliance with US ————————————————————————————————→ Will surrender the alliance
   Lipsky in FA–78   on this issue
   "If US presses HR, will surrender
   the partnership"
2. Soviets will sell
   Harkavey, The New Geopolitics–79
   BW–3–10–80; Pierre–82

1. No restraint—hasn't affected
   US policy

Cutoff ends influence ————————————→ 1. No—Solvency evidence better
DoS, Arms Transfer Policy–7–77   2. DoS biased
"Diminish influence"   3. 1AC & 2AC evidence

FIGURE 6-11

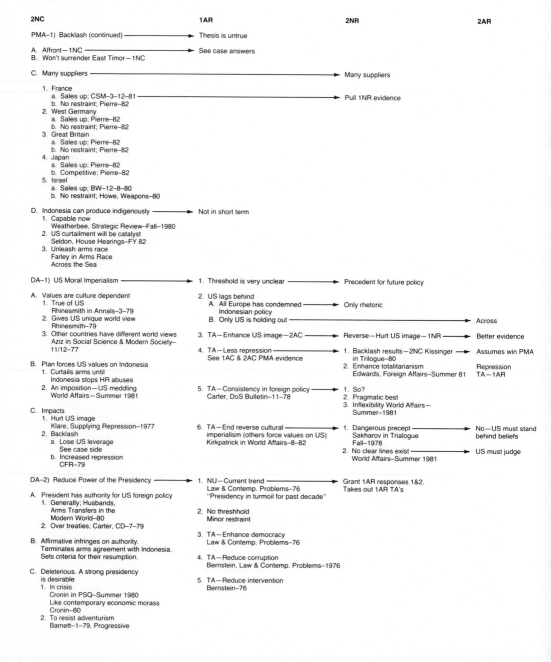

2NC	1AR	2NR	2AR

PMA–1) Backlash (continued) ──────────▶ Thesis is untrue

A. Affront — 1NC ──────────▶ See case answers
B. Won't surrender East Timor — 1NC

C. Many suppliers ──────────────────────────────▶ Many suppliers

   1. France
     a. Sales up; CSM–3–12–81 ──────────────────────▶ Pull 1NR evidence
     b. No restraint; Pierre–82
   2. West Germany
     a. Sales up; Pierre–82
     b. No restraint; Pierre–82
   3. Great Britain
     a. Sales up; Pierre–82
     b. No restraint; Pierre–82
   4. Japan
     a. Sales up; Pierre–82
     b. Competitive; Pierre–82
   5. Israel
     a. Sales up; BW–12–8–80
     b. No restraint; Howe, Weapons–80

D. Indonesia can produce indigenously ──────▶ Not in short term
   1. Capable now
     Weatherbee, Strategic Review–Fall–1980
   2. US curtailment will be catalyst
     Seldon, House Hearings–FY 82
   3. Unleash arms race
     Farley in Arms Race
     Across the Sea

DA–1) US Moral Imperialism ──────────▶ 1. Threshold is very unclear ──────▶ Precedent for future policy

A. Values are culture dependent   2. US lags behind
   1. True of US   A. All Europe has condemned ──────▶ Only rhetoric
     Rhinesmith in Annals–3–79   Indonesian policy
   2. Gives US unique world view   B. Only US is holding out ──────────────────────────────▶ Across
     Rhinesmith–79
   3. Other countries have different world views 3. TA—Enhance US image — 2AC ──────▶ Reverse — Hurt US image — 1NR ──────▶ Better evidence
     Aziz in Social Science & Modern Society–
     11/12–77   4. TA—Less repression   1. Backlash results — 2NC Kissinger ──▶ Assumes win PMA
                     See 1AC & 2AC PMA evidence   in Trilogue–80

B. Plan forces US values on Indonesia   2. Enhance totalitarianism   Repression
   1. Curtails arms until   Edwards, Foreign Affairs–Summer 81 TA — 1AR
     Indonesia stops HR abuses
   2. An imposition — US meddling   5. TA—Consistency in foreign policy ──────▶ 1. So?
     World Affairs — Summer 1981   Carter, DoS Bulletin–11–78   2. Pragmatic best
                                        3. Inflexibility World Affairs—
C. Impacts   Summer–1981
   1. Hurt US image
     Klare, Supplying Repression–1977   6. TA—End reverse cultural ──────────▶ 1. Dangerous precept ──────────────▶ No — US must stand
   2. Backlash   imperialism (others force values on US) Sakharov in Trialogue behind beliefs
     a. Lose US leverage   Kirkpatrick in World Affairs–8–82   Fall–1978
       See case side   2. No clear lines exist ──────────────▶ US must judge
     b. Increased repression   World Affairs–Summer 1981
       CFR–79

DA–2) Reduce Power of the Presidency ──────▶ 1. NU — Current trend ──────────▶ Grant 1AR responses 1&2.
                                   Law & Contemp. Problems–76   Takes out 1AR TA's
A. President has authority for US foreign policy   "Presidency in turmoil for past decade"
   1. Generally; Husbands,
     Arms Transfers in the   2. No threshhold
     Modern World–80   Minor restraint
   2. Over treaties; Carter, CD–7–79
                                  3. TA—Enhance democracy
B. Affirmative infringes on authority.   Law & Contemp. Problems–76
   Terminates arms agreement with Indonesia.
   Sets criteria for their resumption.   4. TA—Reduce corruption
                                Bernstein, Law & Contemp. Problems–1976
C. Deleterious. A strong presidency
   is desirable   5. TA—Reduce intervention
   1. In crisis   Bernstein–76
     Cronin in PSQ–Summer 1980
     Like contemporary economic morass
     Cronin–80
   2. To resist adventurism
     Barnett–1–79, Progressive

Importance of a System of Organization

Time is the most precious of all commodities in debate. As an opponent speaks, many tasks require the advocate's attention—almost simultaneously. The following demands are ever-present: listening carefully to one's opponent; flowing all opposing arguments as accurately and thoroughly as possible; selecting the strongest overall position and the most effective responses to each opposing argument; gathering the briefs and evidence which are needed to support specific responses; and completing the flow in preparation for one's speech.

Given these and other demands, the advocate must minimize the time and thought required to complete rote tasks, such as the retrieval of briefs and evidence. If a substantial effort is required to locate a particular brief or a specific piece of evidence, the advocate will be hard-pressed to effectively execute his or her other tasks. Hence, it makes good sense to adopt, utilize and maintain a system of organization of briefs and evidence.

Common Organizational Systems

There is no universal system for organizing briefs and evidence. Experienced advocates develop personal hybrid methods, involving unique adaptations of one or more common organizational formulas. What is important is that you utilize a system; it makes no difference whether the system conforms to some accepted pattern.

Choose an organizational pattern that meets your needs. Some circumstances call for a relatively simple pattern, while others dictate a more sophisticated system. Some debates are casual. Topics are announced on short notice, and the research requirements are minimal. In this case, the advocate may simply arrange the materials by topic headings and place them in file folders, each with an appropriate title. Other debates are quite formal. Topics are announced well in advance, and research requirements are substantial. Contemporary intercollegiate debate fits this mold. In this instance, the advocate must develop an intricate organizational system to assure quick retrieval of necessary briefs and evidence from a myriad of materials.

Generally, briefs should be titled and organized in folders with the folders appropriately titled and organized in a file according to subject headings. Evidence should be recorded on notecards (see chapter 4) and stored in a box or drawer, subject headings separated from each other by tabbed file guides. Is there a particular system for organizing briefs and evidence? There is a wide variety of systems to choose from. We recommend the following two organizational schemes. You should select the one which best suits your needs.

Topical System.   A topical, or issues, organizational system is perhaps the most popular. This system finds its origins in the issue content of the particular resolution which is the focus of debate. To utilize this system, you should first classify material as either affirmative or negative. Then, divide negative material according to the potential affirmative cases embodied in the resolution. Second, organize material in terms of broad issue headings, both substantive (significance, inherency, alternative proposals, efficacy, and disadvantages) and theoretical (topicality, generic rejection of the propo-

---

FIGURE 6-12

NEGATIVE
SALES TO INDONESIA
  SIGNIFICANCE
    Death and Suffering
      Data Deficiencies
      Current Trends
      Invasion Causality
        Not US Fault
        Fretilin
      Famine Causality
        Portuguese to Blame
        Farming Practices at Fault
        Indonesia Not Cause
      PS Solves
        Food Aid
          Gets to Needy
          Indonesia Facilitates
        Resettlement

---

sition, etc.). Finally, subdivide the broad issue headings into smaller units, continuing this process until all specific issues are separated. Use the same pattern for both brief and evidence files.

An excerpt from a file on the topic that, "the U.S. should significantly curtail its arms sales to other countries," illustrates this system (see Figure 6–12). As a caveat, note that this illustration represents only a small component of a complete file. It contains only one affirmative case variant (U.S. arms sales to Indonesia), only one broad issue (significance), and only part of one component of that issue (death and suffering). A complete file would include affirmative and negative, negative indexing based on affirmative case possibilities, all of the broad substantive and theoretical issue headings, and all of the specific issues within each broad category.

Decimal System. Well-researched advocates who participate in formal debates may require a more sophisticated organizational system. The decimal system of filing is much more intricate, well suited to more demanding circumstances.

The decimal system classifies material in precisely the same manner as a topic (or issues) organizational system. It is unique only in that it titles each heading using a decimal coding system in place of the written labels characteristic of the topic system.

Three numerals are placed to the left of a decimal. The first digit designates a general division of materials. Each advocate is free to select his or her own categorization. The following example simply illustrates one possible breakdown of the "curtail

FIGURE 6-13

400 NEGATIVE
410 SALES TO INDONESIA
   412 SIGNIFICANCE
      412.1 Death and Suffering
         412.11 Data Deficiencies
         412.12 Current Trends
         412.14 Invasion Causality
            412.141 Not US Fault
            412.143 Fretilin
         412.15 Famine Causality
            412.151 Portuguese to Blame
            412.153 Farming Practices at Fault
            412.155 Indonesia Not Cause
         412.17 PS Solves
            412.171 Food Aid
               412.1711 Gets to Needy
               412.1713 Indonesia Facilitates
            412.173 Resettlement

U.S. arms sales" topic. Items under the first integer might include: general definitions, 1; the advocate's own affirmative case areas, 2 and 3; generic case possibilities within the resolution, 4, 5 and 6 (i.e., sales to specific countries, 4 and 5; generic sales, 6); generic efficacy arguments, 7; generic disadvantages, 8; generic counterplans and counter warrants, 9.

The second integer provides an opportunity to identify broad areas within the general categories (i.e., arms sales to Indonesia, 410; arms sales to Pakistan, 420; arms sales to Israel, 430; etc.). The third numeral classifies general issues (i.e., topicality, significance, inherency, alternative proposals, efficacy and disadvantages) within a particular affirmative case area. Digits can be added to the right of the decimal, as needed, to continue the process of subdividing issues. Figure 6–13 illustrates this approach, using precisely the same classifications as in Figure 6–12.

Of course each brief and/or evidence card should be coded according to its placement in the file (regardless of whether a topical or decimal system is used). In this manner the advocate will be able to efficiently refile the materials upon the conclusion of a debate.

SUMMARY

Effective listening, accurate and efficient notetaking, and the proficient organization of materials are indispensable tools in argumentation and advocacy. Unfortunately, very few people are even minimally proficient in these skills. Studies indicate that the average person listens at a 25 percent effectiveness level. The same person has a limited capacity for accurate and efficient notetaking, and possesses limited organizational skills.

This chapter examined the role and importance of listening, notetaking, and organizational skills in advocacy, and suggested specific techniques to optimize individual proficiency. These competencies are the tools of the advocate's trade. They must be understood, and then internalized, to start the student on the road toward mastery.

Notes

[1]Interview with Lyman K. Steil, "Secrets of Being a Better Listener," *U.S. News & World Report,* May 26, 1980, pp. 65–6.

[2]George Comstock, *Television in America* (Beverly Hills: Sage Publications, 1980). p. 30.

[3]Ralph G. Nichols, "Listening Is A 10-Part Skill," *Nation's Business,* July 1957, p. 56.

[4]Ralph G. Nichols and Leonard A. Stevens, *Are You Listening?* (New York: McGraw Hill Book Company, 1957), pp. 12–13.

[5]As quoted in Andrew D. Wolvin and Carolyn Gwynn Coakley, *Listening* (Dubuque: Wm. C. Brown Company, Publishers, 1982), p. 9.

[6]Wolvin and Coakley, p. 88.

[7]See: Sanford E. Gerber, "Dichotic and Diotic Presentations of Speeded Speech, *Journal of Communication,* 18 (1968), 272–82; Grant Fairbanks, Newman Guttman, and Murray S. Miron, "Effects of Time Compression Upon the Comprehension of Connected Speech," *Journal of Speech and Hearing Disorders,* 22 (1957), 10–19; David B. Orr, "Time Compressed Speech—A Perspective," *Journal of Communication,* 18 (1968), 288–92; and James MacLachlan, "What People Really Think of Fast Talkers," *Psychology Today,* November 1979, pp. 113–17.

[8]Wolvin and Coakley, p. 88.

[9]Kent R. Colbert, "Speaking Rate of N.D.T. Finalists from 1968–1980 (Editor's Corner)," *Journal of the American Forensic Association,* 18 (1981), 73–76.

[10]Florence I. Wolff, Nadine C. Marsnik, William S. Tacey and Ralph G. Nichols, *Perceptive Listening* (New York: Holt, Rinehart and Winston, 1983), pp. 155 and 158–59.

CHAPTER SEVEN

EVIDENCE

Evidence is defined as a statement made in an argument which is intended to provide the substance or supporting material needed to prove a claim being advocated. Evidence may consist of facts, examples, statistics, an authority's testimony of opinion, or truisms, to mention a few of its many possible forms.

The probative weight of evidence depends on the nature and purpose of the argument which it is intended to prove. Different fields of argument have their own preferred types of evidence, and observe different rules for determining the relevance and strength of evidence. For instance, in a trial, the testimony of witnesses makes up the bulk of evidence in the case to be considered by the judge and jury. There are well defined legal rules governing the admissibility of evidence and its degree of credibility once admitted to the trial. In a theological dispute over a doctrinal issue, the advocate must rely on the authority of the Bible and the opinions of recognized commentaries.

Generally, scientific and technical fields prefer empirical evidence such as statistics and facts. More humanistic, philosophical, artistic, and ethical fields draw upon evaluative and rhetorical forms of evidence such as testimony of authorities, narrative examples, analogies, etc. The amount and quality of evidence needed in a given argument is related to the nature of the argumentative situation. A trusted source speaking to a united group of true believers needs little or no evidence to convince them of his or her claim. This textbook, however, is not about argumentative situations limited to one-sided motivational speeches by persuasive speakers. We are interested in studying situations in which there is dispute or controversy, where there is resistance or doubt toward the claim, and where an opposing advocate challenges or questions a claim. In this framework, evidence is obviously an essential component of proof.

It is easy to assume that if a statement appears in writing, it must be true. This view of evidence is naive. Just because a book asserts a statement does not mean that it is true; it merely indicates that the author of that book *thinks* that the statement is true. Whether we should share this viewpoint depends on several factors, such as the qualifications of the author, the type of claim being made, and the reasoning behind the claim. We should not blindly assume a statement is true simply because someone makes it. Instead, we should attempt to formulate our own judgment about the truth of the statement, using the quotation to assist us in reaching this conclusion.

Suppose, for example, that you read an article in a newspaper that suggested a certain musical group was the best in the country. Would you accept this conclusion simply because a newspaper article made the assertion? You might give any of several possible answers, depending on several relevant factors. Only if you believed that the statement about the musical group is true would you accept it without question. Otherwise, if you were not familiar with the group, you might want more information about it. If you knew the group, but thought some other group was better, you would argue with the newspaper's assertion. You would demand further reasons, more evidence. The truth of the statement for you would be based on the reasons provided in the article for the conclusion, as well as a host of other arguments and evidence with which the critic was familiar. In short, a single statement in one article would not be enough to reach a conclusion about a music group; additional *evidence* would be sought before drawing a firm conclusion.

If we are that careful about drawing a conclusion about a music group, how much more caution should we exercise when we argue about nuclear policy, defense spending, health care, poverty, the environment, and other critical issues? Although it may be easy to agree with the first article we read on a topic, that is not a wise method of developing knowledge. We should investigate the reasons behind the evidence and examine the expertise of the individual making a statement before we assign credibility to the evidence. This information tells us how confident we should be in a conclusion. Sometimes, the evidence may be so strong that no other conclusion can reasonably be drawn; in other cases the evidence may be so weak that there is only a slight chance that a given statement is true. The implication for a policymaker is that the amount of confidence one should have in a conclusion depends on the strength of the evidence behind that statement. For these reasons it is important to develop standards for evaluating the strength of evidence used in a debate.

Evidence plays an important role in most conflicts. Both sides will present numerous quotations, examples, and statistics to support their positions. Evidence may frequently be contradictory; one authority may defend one position, another may defend an opposite viewpoint. In these cases, it is important to develop some standard for weighing the evidence. An advocate needs to be able to explain why his or her evidence is superior to the evidence presented by the other side. In addition, a critic needs to develop a method for evaluating the evidence presented in the controversy.

In evaluating evidence it is important to develop a perspective on the role of evidence in argument. Although evidence is important in argument, it should not be viewed as a substitute for analysis and reasoning; instead it should be viewed as a supplement to the reasoning process. The weight to be given to a piece of evidence depends on a wide range of factors, and a responsible advocate should be able to make sound judgments about the quality of evidence.

TESTS OF EVIDENCE

Two Types of Tests

In examining evidence, two standards can be applied. The first standard is universal in nature and applies to all evidence. The second standard is more specific and depends on the varied and individual requirements of evidence in the particular field of argument under consideration. Evidence varies in type: some evidence consists of quotations from experts, other evidence consists of the presentation of examples, and still other evidence consists of statistics. Depending on the nature of the specific evidence, the tests that can be used to evaluate the evidence will vary.

Note that the tests are merely guidelines to use in evaluating evidence. There probably is no "perfect" piece of evidence; instead, evidence varies in strength. These tests should help in determining the strength of the evidence that is introduced in a debate.

Six General Tests

There are six general tests of evidence that can be used to evaluate the adequacy of all evidence. These general tests can be supplemented with additional specific tests, depending upon the type of evidence used to support an argument.

Relevant? First, the advocate should ask if the evidence is relevant to the issue under dispute. Not all evidence on a topic will be useful in an argument. A wise advocate examines all evidence keeping in mind the arguments that it is designed to support. In a courtroom, for example, lawyers examine facts seeking to separate the irrelevant and inadmissible evidence from the relevant evidence. Similarly, in looking at newspapers, books, journals, and documents, the advocate will need to seek out the relevant portions of the material from the irrrelevant.

Adequate? Second, the advocate should ask if there is an adequate amount of evidence to support a conclusion. Important decisions or important conclusions should not be based on a single statement by a single individual; ideally a wide variety of evidence should be used. What is an adequate amount of evidence will vary, depending on several factors. Sometimes, we may be forced to act based on weak information simply because no additional information is available. In other cases, when the decision is important, a high standard for evidence may be warranted. A decision to launch nuclear weapons, for example, probably should not be based upon a rumor that the Soviet Union might be considering a preemptive attack; stronger evidence would be needed.

There are a number of factors to consider in determining whether an advocate has enough evidence: (1) *The importance of the issue.* Generally, the more important the issue, the more evidence required to support that position. For example, more evidence would be required to support a drastic change in our defense policy than would be required to demonstrate a need to repair a road. (2) *The quality of the evidence.* The greater the quality of the evidence, the less evidence is needed. If the advocate has strong evidence to support an argument, little additional evidence might be required. On the other hand, if an argument is based on weak, circumstantial evidence, a great deal of information might be needed before an advocate could claim to establish an argument. (3) *The likelihood of conflicting evidence.* If there is little or no conflicting evidence on an issue, not much evidence is necessary. Little evidence is needed to prove that the world is round or that the sun will rise in the morning. On the other hand, if the issue is highly controversial, a greater quantity of evidence is needed. Arguments about whether or not the death penalty deters crime, or whether gun control can decrease deaths would require much research and high-quality evidence, since any credible opponent will have discovered evidence that reaches conclusions opposite those of the advocate. (4) *The salience of the claim to the audience.* If the claim touches on a central belief, and there is resistance to it, more proof is necessary than if it is a peripheral belief. It would take a great deal of high-quality evidence to change a fundamental belief of the audience. If the advocate is defending a position that is not important to the audience, however, less evidence would be required. (5) *The credibility of the advocate.* If the advocate has a high degree of credibility with the audience, less evidence is needed. The President or a member of Congress, for example, can frequently make a persuasive argument without citing large amounts of evidence; the audience will believe their statements simply because of who they are. On the other hand, the same argument, if advanced by a student, might require additional evidence to support it because the student does not have the same degree of credibility.

Consistent?   The advocate should ask if the evidence is consistent with other known evidence. One check that is useful in determining the reliability of a source of evidence is to compare it to other available information. When the forged Hitler diaries were being examined, the test that exposed them as a forgery compared the handwriting used in the diaries with samples of Hitler's handwriting known to be authentic. When the handwriting samples did not match, it was clear that the diaries were forgeries. Similarly, when a person makes a statement or a prediction, it is wise to compare that statement or prediction with other known facts.

This test should be applied with some caution. Simply because one piece of evidence conflicts with other evidence does not mean that it is false; merely that it needs further examination. When Galileo argued the world was round, he was arguing a position that was inconsistent with the positions supported by other experts. That did not mean his position was false, although it did suggest that some caution was warranted before accepting his viewpoints.

Recent?   A fourth question to ask is if the evidence is recent. Generally, the more recent the evidence, the better. Conditions may change over a period of time, rendering old evidence of dubious value. Just as a year-old newspaper would be of little use in discovering what movies are showing or what is the price of a stock, old evidence may not provide us with the information necessary to select the best policy. To discover the strength of troop levels in Europe, or the current level of employment or inflation, recent evidence is critical. The level of pollution in a city may decline over a period of time. New laws or Supreme Court decisions may make old arguments outmoded.

This does not mean that old evidence is never useful. Sometimes, the date of the evidence is irrelevant. If a study demonstrated that pollution was deadly in 1960, presumably it is still deadly today. A newer study would be superior only if it employed superior statistical methods (or if it was based on the lower levels of pollution today), not simply because it was conducted more recently. Similarly, philosophical evidence supporting values is often timeless. Brandeis' defense of the right to privacy in 1890 is just as persuasive today as it was when it first appeared.

In a few cases, old evidence may be superior to new evidence. When one is attempting to discover a historical fact, the closer the evidence is to the actual event, the better the evidence. For example, if we wanted to know what types of problems were faced by Americans living in the 1830's, evidence drawn from the diaries of individuals living during that period of history might be stronger than a textbook about that era. Many distortions may develop between the time an event occurred and when it is finally reported. A recent book may reflect many of these distortions. If a lawyer arguing a case in front of the Supreme Court wants to prove a certain interpretation of the law is inconsistent with the intent of the writers of that law, the best evidence would be statements the framers made when the law was being debated in Congress, not statements by historians stating what the historians *think* the framers of the law thought. The best evidence would be the primary document, not reports on a report about the document. Similarly, in disputes over values, evidence from Plato, Aristotle, and John Stuart Mill can be very useful in suggesting ways of resolving value conflicts.

Acceptable? The fifth question the advocate should ask is if the evidence is acceptable to the audience. Evidence is useful to an advocate only if the audience both understands and accepts it. The evidence should be kept simple. If the audience cannot understand a statement, how can they be expected to use that evidence in making a decision? A complex statistic may provide strong support for a position, but if no one understands the statistic, it will not influence the decision makers.

The audience must also be willing to believe the evidence. There are some positions that can be supported by evidence yet, even after the evidence is presented, the audience still may not believe the position. There are a few individuals, for example, who have argued that a small nuclear war would be a good idea, that unemployment is desirable, or that inflation is beneficial to the country. Most Americans, however, would not believe that evidence without substantial explanation. In addition, the source of the evidence must be acceptable to the audience. For example, the statement "I hold that a little rebellion now and then is as necessary in the political world as storms in the physical," has been found to be almost universally accepted when it was attributed to Thomas Jefferson and almost universally rejected when attributed to Lenin. Reading from *Pravda* is not a wise strategy for most audiences. It is wise to avoid quoting individuals that are not respected by the audience; instead, highly credible sources should be read to support arguments.

Supported? Finally, the advocate should ask if the reasons for a conclusion are included in the evidence. Much evidence is conclusionary; only the conclusions of the author are given without any reasons. A quotation that simply says "gun control is a good (or bad) idea," is conclusionary. No reasons are given in the quotation as to *why* this conclusion is justified. It would be better if the evidence explained why these conclusions are justified, instead of simply presenting the conclusion of the individual quoted. The best evidence presents reasons for a conclusion in a specific manner; not just general conclusions. In this way, the strength of the evidence is easy to determine by examining these reasons.

TESTS OF TESTIMONY

Testimony is defined as evidence which consists of a person's statements or assertions as to what he or she thinks is true. In the accepted usage of argumentation theory, the advocate's own testimony is not generally regarded as evidence, but rather as unsupported assertions that require outside proof. Testimonial evidence, or the quoted assertions made by someone outside the controversy, may be either factual or opinionated. Factual testimony is someone's statement that an event which he or she witnessed is true. This type of testimony may be seen in news reporting, scientific research reports, etc. Eyewitness testimony is the staple of courtroom trials.

Testimony of opinion is someone's statement of a value judgment, a commitment or conviction that something should be true. Opinionated testimony is of little value in controversies over factual issues. It is useful in value-charged controversies to the extent that it clearly articulates the source's attitude toward the subject under discussion, clarifies the reasons for inferences and interpretations regarding the subject, and lends added credibility to the advocate by the weight of the authority vested by the audience in the source of the testimony. Opinion testimony, unlike factual testimony, is inherently personal and subjective.

Whether the testimony used as evidence in an argument is for a factual or a value-loaded purpose, it is important to establish the credentials of the source being quoted. The strength of the testimony is directly related to the degree to which the source of the testimony is perceived by the audience as trustworthy and competent.

Much of the evidence used in arguments consists of quoting statements from experts in the field. It is important that the advocate be cautious in using this type of evidence. Just because a source makes a statement does not mean that the statement is true. From experience, we know that some people tell lies or distort statements. In the courtroom, it is not unusual to find witnesses to the same act describe it in different ways, depending upon their interest in the case. Similarly, individuals who testify about public policy will sometimes present distorted statements. In order to use testimony effectively, it is important to understand and develop methods for weighing the strength of testimonial evidence. The reliability of this type of evidence depends on several factors.

Qualified?

First, it is important to discover if the person quoted is qualified to make a statement on the issue being debated. The strength of testimony depends on the reliability of the individual making the statement. The key to the weight we should give to testimony is the confidence we have in the opinion of the person testifying. To that end it is important that we know the qualifications of the sources supporting a conclusion. A statement on foreign policy by an expert on international affairs should carry more weight than that of a taxi driver. We need to know not only that the person is an expert, but that the individual is an expert on the matter under consideration. A law professor may be qualified to testify about the nature of the law, but that would not make him or her qualified to testify about the economic effects of a tax cut. An economist may be qualified to discuss economic policy, but not the desirability of a medical practice. In short, in order for a person's statements to warrant serious consideration, the person should be an expert in the field being discussed. To this end, it is necessary to know both the individual's qualifications, and how other experts in the field regard this individual.

The individual should also be capable of observing the event being discussed. Some testimony concerns the details of a specific event. We turn to witnesses to find out about the details of a crime, or to discover when an event actually took place. To evaluate this type of testimony, it might be wise to look at the mental and physical condition of the observer. A tired observer might miss some important details. A biased observer might distort details. Some witnesses are pressured into "seeing" an event in a certain way. In addition, sometimes a "witness" to an event could not physically have seen the event described; in other cases the witness' view may have been unclear due to distance, darkness, or other factors.

Biased?

Second, the advocate should ask if the witness is biased. A biased witness can be defined as a person with an interest in the outcome of a dispute. Some individuals may benefit if a certain policy is adopted. They can be expected to support a position, not necessarily because they think the position is true, but because it is in their interest to support the position. A member of the President's cabinet, for example, can be expected to say he or she supports the administration's policies even if that individual does not, simply because attacking the policies may result in being fired. A member of the National Rifle Association can be expected to oppose gun control simply because of his or her membership in that organization.

Testimony from biased individuals should be relied on with caution because the testimony is often based more on the role of the individual than on an objective evaluation of the facts. The biases of an individual can cause the individual to distort information, either intentionally or unintentionally. If we think that something is true, we tend to focus our attention on facts that support our conclusions. Democrats would tend to view a Democratic President in a favorable light, while Republicans would view the same President in an unfavorable light. A policeman viewing a riot, for example, may be biased in assigning the blame to the protesters, while the protesters might think the actions of the police against them were the real causes of the riot.

This does not mean that biased testimony has no merit. All individuals have some biases, although some biases are stronger than others. In addition, some biases occur after a person researches a topic. Anyone who intensively researches a subject will tend to form an impression about the issues involved in the topic. A person might research civil liberties and, after objectively looking at the evidence, decide to join a civil liberties action group. If this type of testimony were ignored, then that of most experts would be ignored. The key is to ask if the bias exists because of the role of the individual, as opposed to the individual's impartial examination of the evidence.

One case where biased testimony may be desirable is when the testimony is reluctantly given. In our roles, there are certain attitudes that are expected of us. We expect the military to ask for more money. We expect members of a President's cabinet to support the President. A criminal is expected to claim that he or she is innocent. When people testify in a manner that is inconsistent with what is expected, that is called reluctant testimony. In these cases, the bias helps the evidence. If a general testified that the military required larger appropriations, we would discount the testimony. Yet if the same general asked for *smaller* appropriations, the testimony would be given more credibility since it is contrary to our expectations based on the individual's role.

Most Recent?

A third issue to examine in evaluating testimony is to ask if the statement is the source's most recent position. Many experts will alter their view on a subject as they discover more about it. Many philosophers will defend one position as a youth, only to modify their views as they come into contact with new ideas. As new studies are conducted or new theoretical paradigms are developed, scientists may change their minds on many issues. For these reasons, it is important that the advocate watch out for changes (gradual or sudden) in the views of experts.

EVALUATING STUDIES

In the last part of the twentieth century, numerous problems have been the subject of extensive studies by governmental agencies, private groups, and scholars. These studies have been used by advocates to support various positions. We use the term *study* here in a broad sense; it refers to a systemic attempt to gather and organize information on a topic. The study may conduct independent experiments on the subject (as was the case with the Coleman study on the effect of integration on education), or the study may simply reflect a synthesis of existing information. In examining a study, there are several factors to consider.

Who Conducted?

It is important to know who conducted the study. The study will often reflect the bias of the individual who conducts the study. A study by the Tobacco Institute on the effects of smoking will probably conclude that cigarette smoking is not harmful. The bias of a group will affect the types of materials that are read, as well as the design of any experiments that are conducted. In addition, sponsorship pressures may be placed on those who conduct a study. For example, when President Nixon appointed a commission to study marijuana laws, he announced that if the commission supported the legalization of marijuana, he would ignore the report. It was not surprising that the commission did not reach that conclusion, given that announcement. Often, studies are funded by organizations and interest groups that have a bias on the topic. These agencies tend to fund only research that will support their views. Those commissioned to conduct this research may feel pressure to reach conclusions that the funding agencies would like (especially if they want additional funding in the future). This pressure is not exerted by all funding agencies, and not all researchers give in to these pressures, but it is useful to know whether these sponsorship pressures create uncertainty about the independence of the researcher.

It is also important that the individuals conducting the study be knowledgeable about the subject matter of the study. The conclusions of the study are acceptable only if we think that the reasoning process and expertise of those conducting the study should be relied upon. Thus it is important to know the credentials of those who conduct the study.

How Conducted?

It is also important to understand how the study was conducted. Consider the typical "blue ribbon" commission report authorized by the President. Usually, a commission is appointed when the President feels he needs expert information on a current issue where the nation's political feelings are strongly divided. Their study could be based upon a very brief review of material, or it could consist of a lengthy analysis of everything on the topic. It is critical that, before we accept the findings of a commission, we know how the commissioners conducted their research. What material did they look at? Was there a sincere effort to obtain valid, independent, scientific facts? Who did they talk with? How long was the study conducted? How much support did the study have? Did all members of the study listen to all the evidence? These questions all address issues that are important factors in evaluating reports of commissioned investigations. Some commissions provide excellent information, but other commissions may fail one or more of these tests.

What Assumptions?

Third, it is important to know the assumptions of the studies. Some studies make certain assumptions about the world *prior* to the study. For example, a study on the energy crisis might make the assumption that future conservation will only increase at a certain rate. Based upon that assumption, it might suggest that we need to build a certain number of nuclear reactors in the future. If that assumption is inaccurate, however, the conclusion of the study is almost worthless. For another example, in recent hearings before the banking subcommittee of Congress, a witness from the home-lending agencies urged support for adjustable rate mortgages (ARM's) which permit them to increase or decrease mortgage interest rates on existing home loans. Their projections were based on the past *ten* years' increase in housing prices, but only the past *two* years' fluctuations in home loan interest rates! As a result, their conclusion was that home buyers could expect their home value to increase greatly in the future, but their interest rates would remain fairly stable. If those assumptions were reversed, the home values would show a stagnating trend, while interest rates would be widely increasing. Neither method, however, would be reliable, since different units of time (ten years vs. two years) were being compared.

STATISTICS

Statistics may be defined in two ways, each of which contributes to an understanding of the role of numerical and quantitative statements as evidence. First, statistics can be viewed as a methodology, or a way of thinking about and manipulating large aggregates of facts. In science, laboratory workers and engineers must be trained in statistical methods in order to make sense of large collections of information. In this definition of statistics, the confidence we place in scientific findings is rooted in the data according to correct statistical methods. For example, we ask the government to provide free inoculations to all citizens at risk when the Center for Disease Control declares the threat of a new epidemic of influenza, because we trust that agency to know how to gather reports of the disease and how to interpret whether or not we are on the verge of an epidemic. In principle, the view of statistics as a sophisticated method of thinking tells us whether causal relationships are observed between and among the elements of a system being studied. If the method of reasoning from the statistics is appropriate, then it enables us to make predictions of the outcomes of the situation under study.

Second, statistics as evidence may be defined as the result or product of some statistical method—that is, the quantitative findings stated as a figure, percentage, rate, or other numeric assertion. Often, we are told that 55 million adult Americans smoke cigarettes, or the President enjoys a 42 percent popularity rating, or the unemployment rate is 6.2 percent. In this sense, statistics are merely an accumulation of facts stated as a total or average. In principle, this form of evidence is similar to the use of examples. Statistics, viewed as collections of examples, illustrate the significance or scope of a problem.

Statistics have become an important part of contemporary arguments. Few arguments take place that do not rely, at least in part, on statistics. We use statistics to measure economic progress, the popularity of movies, the quality of an education, and many other things. Auguste Comte once remarked that "there is no inquiry which is not finally reduced to a question of numbers." Although this may be somewhat of an exaggeration, it is true that statistics play an important role in many of our arguments. To evaluate these arguments effectively, an advocate must have some concept of the nature of statistics. While it would be impossible to cover all the issues related to statistics in one chapter, this section will attempt to outline some of the major issues related to reasoning with statistics.

Initially, it is important to recognize that not all numbers are the result of a statistical method of study. Some individuals estimate or even fabricate numbers carelessly without attempting to verify the number. Crowd estimates by police authorities often consist of such "guesstimates." A person may say that "there were ten thousand people at the concert," without verifying the number. The statement should serve the same function as if the person said "there were many people at the concert," but somehow people consider the first statement as sounding more authoritative. To say there were 3,586 wars in the last century (a figure pulled out of thin air) sounds more authoritative than the statement that there have been "many" wars in the last century. People would assume that the first figure, because of its precise number, was arrived at in some scientific method, when in reality there was no systematic method used to reach that figure. Even scientists have been known to speak in statistical hyperbole. Barry Commoner once wrote that the involuntary risk of pollution to health is 10,000 times more significant than a comparable risk taken voluntarily. In academic debates, that figure was often quoted to establish the significance of affirmative cases that attempted to solve the harms of environmental pollution. In reality, Commoner could not have devised an accurate method of comparing the relative magnitude of voluntary and involuntary harm. He was merely expressing his personal judgment in a graphic turn of phrase. These types of "statistics" appear frequently in the literature. Politicians will often cite "statistics" that were created for a specific speech. Before we treat a number as a statistic, then, we should know how the individual citing the number calculated that figure. Only then do we know how much credibility to assign to a statistic.

A number of factors make properly used statistical evidence valuable. Strong statistical evidence will employ precise methods in measuring what is being studied. Good statistical procedures have evolved from years of testing and analysis to the point where they reflect a rigorous method of testing knowledge. These procedures often reflect an objective way of looking at a problem, and they will produce the same or similar results, regardless of who conducts the experiment.

Disadvantages of Statistics

The use of statistics in argument is not without its critics. Some individuals have suggested that statistics are easily distorted and frequently misused. Three criticisms of statistics are sometimes mentioned:

1. Statistics emphasize the quantifiable. In the attempt to convert information into numbers, much desirable information is ignored. For example, in evaluating students, it is easy to measure their intelligence through tests and grades, but it is difficult to measure other factors. How does one quantify hard work? How does a teacher numerically measure how pleasant a student is? How do you measure personality? Can honesty or integrity be assigned numerical values? In all these cases, statistics are of little use in measuring these important qualities. Unfortunately, if a school principal is forced to quantify the advances made during a year, it is easy to point to easily quantified skills (such as those measured by the SAT), instead of the harder to quantify characteristics. Similarly, it is easier to measure the price of a product than it is to measure the quality of a product, so economic measures often weigh costs of goods more than quality. As a result, many have suggested that the emphasis on statistics may cause us to ignore the non-quantifiable in favor of the quantifiable. While some observers have suggested that the objectivity provided by statistics is a desirable trait, since it does permit the objective measurement of quantifiable data and thus makes

the first step toward technology, others have noted this objectivity hides the necessity for subjective choice in making decisions.

2. A second problem with statistics is experimenter bias. Experimenters often approach a study with certain expectations about the result. They will assume that the experiment will confirm certain conclusions which are grounded in theory. This is proper. However, there is always the danger that, as a result of these expectations, the experimenter may subconsciously manipulate the experiment in such a way that it confirms his or her preconceived conclusions. This effect is sometimes called the Rosenthal effect, after Robert Rosenthal, who conducted several experiments involving graduate students who were requested to conduct experimental studies. Some of the students were told to expect one result; others were told to expect the opposite result. Rosenthal discovered that the results of the experiments often corresponded to the student's expectations.[1] This was not because of any conscious attempt to distort the statistics, but because of the nonverbal behavior of the individuals conducting the studies. To minimize this effect, some experimenters (especially in medicine) use a "double blind" method of conducting an experiment, keeping the purpose of the experiment secret from both the participants in the experiment and those individuals conducting the experiment.

This bias can influence the study in other ways. In conducting a study, experimenters often are forced to make certain judgments about how the study should be conducted. The experimenter must decide how to measure something, what group of individuals to study, or what statistical tools to use. These choices are often made in a manner that supports the anticipated results. There have been several studies of governmental statistics, for example, that have concluded that the design of governmental statistics is often such that it makes the administration look better than if alternative statistical designs were used.[2] Similarly, some critics have noted that a study may demonstrate no effect of a teaching technique (or of a drug), not because the technique or drug has no effect, but because the experiment was poorly designed or because it used crude measurement techniques.

3. Some statistics are falsified. The previous attack on statistics assumed that researchers were honest individuals who produced distorted statistics, not out of any conscious desire to mislead the public, but through an unconscious choice of statistical methods and through unconscious nonverbal behavior. Unfortunately, not all researchers are honest. A small number of researchers, under pressure to publish articles and books, will make up statistics. In the early 1980's, for example, scientists at two of the most prestigious universities in the country were caught manufacturing results of studies that either were never conducted or were tampered with by the experimenter. One prominent British scientist published several studies on the importance of heredity in determining intelligence that were based on alleged experiments that never took place. Even Isaac Newton distorted a few astronomical readings to support his theory of gravity.[3] While the majority of statistics are the result of honest research, the problem of fabricated statistics is significant enough to cause us to exercise caution in using figures.

These reservations about statistics do not mean that statistics are of no value. The criticisms just presented apply to isolated statistical studies, not to the vast bulk of published research reports. These limitations do suggest, however, that it is important to look at the source of the statistic as well as the way it was reached before we can evaluate it. Some researchers may be competent and unbiased, while others may be biased and inexperienced. In addition, many published studies (especially those published in journals) are reviewed by outside experts, which helps to minimize errors. Important studies are also frequently replicated and examined by other experts in the field; this helps screen out weak studies. These checks are effective, however, only if the advocate relies on statistics from high-quality sources and if the advocate seeks out additional information about the statistic that could confirm (or deny) the conclusions of the studies.

Advantages of Statistics

There are many good arguments in favor of using statistics. Statistics are often superior to other types of evidence. Many suggest that, even if statistics are flawed, they may provide a view of the world that is superior to other ways of discovering the truth. All evidence has some weaknesses; this is no reason to reject statistical evidence. At least statistics attempt to view a problem in an objective manner with some common guidelines for methodology agreed upon by most social scientists.

Second, even if statistics are inaccurate, that does not mean that a statistic is useless. We should attempt to discover the direction of the inaccuracy of a statistic before we determine if it is useless. For example, in the 1970s, there were several studies conducted that attempted to discover the relationship between air pollution and health. One major study was attacked by many as having several methodological faults. While several of these attacks were valid, some observers noted that these attacks did not undermine the basic thesis that air pollution was harmful since the methodological problems caused their study to *underestimate* the problem of pollution; these attacks simply proved that the problem was greater than the study indicated.

A third defense of statistical reasoning suggests that, even if individual studies have problems, the combination of multiple studies, each with different problems, can help support a conclusion. Even if each individual study may suffer from a random problem, the probability of several different types of studies independently reaching the same poor conclusion is unlikely.[4] This would not be the case if all the studies had the same type weakness, but it would suggest that even experiments with some methodological problems can be of some marginal use when part of a larger body of studies using multiple methodologies. The divergent methodologies act as "checks and balances" for each other, resulting in a more reliable view of the world.

Types of Statistics

Up to this point, we have assumed that there is a single type of statistic, but there are many different ways to reach a statistical conclusion. Depending on the type of statistic that is used, different tests should be applied. While there are numerous complicated statistical methodologies that are used in the literature on public policy, four types of statistics are especially common in debate: descriptive statistics, surveys, models, and experimental designs.

Descriptive Statistics   A descriptive statistic attempts to measure (or describe) some characteristic. The consumer price index, gross national product, IQ score, SAT and ACT scores, and FBI crime statistics are all types of descriptive statistics. These statistics all attempt to define the scope of a given set of phenomena. The United States census is a descriptive statistic, based on a count of all citizens. Every decade, it compiles demographic statistics about how many people live here, where they live, their ages and sex, what they do for a living, and a host of other countable details.

The first question one should ask about descriptive statistics is, what is the basis for the statistic? What do these numbers mean? For example, when the FBI publishes its annual report, many of its "successful prosecutions" are for interstate auto thefts, not the more serious crimes. For some airlines, the number of flights that arrived "on time" includes flights that arrived merely 15 minutes late. The definition of a term used in the statistic may not correspond with the common meaning of the term.

The second test of a descriptive statistic is to examine if the measure is used consistently. Often the basis for a statistic may change over a period of time. For example, the unemployment statistic has referred to different things at different times. Sometimes military veterans are considered unemployed when they leave the military; at other times they are not considered in the statistics. Similar problems arise in comparing life expectancy rates. Some countries (like the United States) include infant deaths in determining the average life expectancy; other countries do not include infant deaths in their calculations, resulting in a higher life expectancy. To ensure a consistent measurement, many statistics include procedures to correct for changing measurements. Many statistics measuring the success of movies, for example, will adjust the money figures for inflation in an attempt to make the comparisons more accurate.

One measurement that is frequently misused is the "average." In reality, there are three different ways to measure the "average" of something. The *mean* is the arithmetic average; it is reached by adding together all the units, and dividing the total by the number of units being measured. The *median* is the middle number; half of all of the items being measured will be larger than this figure; half will be smaller than this figure. The *mode* is the figure that appears most frequently. For example, if nine (9) families had individual incomes of $15,000, 2,000, 2,000, 2,000, 1,700, 1,500, 1,500, 700, and 600, the mean income would be $3,000 ($27,000/9); the mode would be $2,000 (since three families have that income); and the median income would be $1,700 (since four families earn more than that amount and four earn less than that amount). All of these "averages" are legitimate; which "average" is best depends upon what the advocate wants to do with the "average."

A third test of a descriptive statistic is to ask whether the measurement is valid. Does the number have any relationship to anything? The LSAT and GRE tests, for example, theoretically measure the ability of individuals to survive law school and graduate school, yet several studies have suggested that, at least in the past, these tests have not been a reliable measure of the success of those who have taken the test; i.e., there seems to be little relationship between the scores of these tests and performance in law or graduate school.

Surveys   A survey, or a poll, is a systematic attempt to generalize the characteristics of a sampling of individuals to a larger population. For example, the Gallup poll asks people how they feel about issues of public policy, and then predicts what the American population as a whole feels about the issues. Various television rating systems predict the number of people who watched specific programs based on the viewing habits of a few individuals.

There are several tests for surveys based on sampling methods. First, the number of individuals who are selected for the sample must be large enough to allow a conclusion to be reached. If the experimenter merely asks one or two individuals about a topic, no conclusion can be reached about the general population. Instead, the experimenter needs to ask a reasonably large number of people about the topic before any general conclusion can be reached (the exact number of individuals who need to be surveyed depends upon a variety of factors, including the size of the population being studied).

Second, the sample must be representative of the population being studied. It is important that the individuals questioned reflect the general population. In order for the small sample to reflect the attitudes of the broader population of interest to the experimenter, the sample must have similar characteristics to the larger population. A survey on agricultural policy conducted in rural Iowa, for example, might reflect the opinion of the population of rural Iowa, but it would not reflect the opinion of the population of the entire country. If an advocate wished to discover the attitude of the country on an issue, this survey would be of little use (although it would be useful if the advocate wished to know the attitude of individuals in the specific rural area covered by the poll). The classic example of a poor survey was the *Literary Digest* poll of 1936, which predicted that Franklin Roosevelt would lose the election (he won by a land-slide). The survey was conducted on a random sample, drawn from telephone books. Unfortunately, 1936 was during the Depression, and millions of people did not have phones. More importantly, those individuals who did not have phones (and thus who were not surveyed) were the poor, who voted overwhelmingly for Roosevelt.

Third, the survey questions must be fair. It is important that the questioner phrase the questions of the survey in a fair manner. A question, "Do you favor diverting money from wasteful defense programs to help feed poor Americans?" will result in a different response than the question, "Do you favor diverting money from our underequipped military to help support welfare chiselers?" although both questions address the issue of military vs. domestic spending. The phrasing of the question can influence the type of response received. A more neutrally worded question (for example, should the federal government make the largest increases in military or domestic spending?) might produce more accurate results. One poll, conducted in the 1960s, asked graduating high school seniors if they planned to attend college. Those who said no were then asked why they were not attending college. They were given two choices: they were not attending college because they could not afford college; or they did not attend college because they did not have the intellectual capability to attend college. Not surprisingly, more seniors attributed their failure to attend college to lack of funds than to stupidity. The result was based on the design of the questions.

Finally, the respondents must honestly answer the questions. One assumption behind all surveys is that if a person says they believe in X, they really do believe in X. Unfortunately, many people may lie to questioners, either intentionally or unintentionally. If a survey asked about church attendance, for example, many individuals may suggest they attend church more frequently than is really the case. Similarly, people may say they read more books and watch higher-quality TV programs than they really do. Additionally, many people feel compelled to express an opinion on a subject regardless of the strength of their opinion (or even if they do not have an opinion). Some surveys take this into account, both by including questions designed to tell if the subject is truthful, and by permitting the respondent to indicate how strongly he or she feels about an issue. How serious this problem is may depend on the subject matter of the question, but it could distort the results of some polls. Fortunately, more sophisticated polls have developed methods to minimize these problems with polling. Not all polls will employ these statistical methods to minimize error; for that reason it is important to look at the reputation of the organization that conducts a poll before assigning credibility to its survey.

Models A model is an attempt to project the operation of a system by creating an idealized structure of the relevant factors affected by the policy. In statistical methods a model is the basis for a *computer simulation.* For example, many economists will develop "models" of the economy and use these to predict the future growth of the economy. In looking at a model, it is important to analyze the assumptions of the model. What factors are being considered? What does the model consider to be important? For example, there have been several models that have attempted to predict the safety of nuclear power plants. Many of the studies that predict that nuclear power is safe assume that the emergency core cooling system will be successful, even though there is some evidence that this assumption is invalid. If the assumption is proven to be false, the entire model would have to be changed.

Computer simulations and models that attempt to analyze many variables are very complex. Trying to integrate multiple elements can produce significant errors. In such a complex model, a few small errors can have a much greater effect on the final conclusions than a single large error, since the model uses exponential multipliers. When the computer model integrates a great number of variables, and the process being analyzed is very complex, the likelihood of a few small errors creeping in is very high. The simpler the model, the more likely it is that an important variable will be overlooked.

A second way to evaluate a model is to examine its past reliability. Has this model been accurate in the past? If so, there is some reason to trust it. This test does have some limitations, however. For example, many econometric models (models of the economy) were extremely accurate during the 1960s, when the economy was relatively simple (some have argued that economic predictions could have been made with a slide rule during that period). When the economy became more complex in the 1970s, with forces such as the energy crisis hindering economic growth, the old models were no longer very accurate, and new models needed to be developed.

Controlled Experiments   An experiment is a test of a scientific hypothesis which predicts that one or more variables are responsible for one or more outcomes. The objective of the experimental test is to manipulate the variable or variables of choice in order to maximize treatment outcomes while controlling other variables in order to minimize competing influence. The purpose of a scientific experiment is to test whether a theory is an accurate account of phenomena. Testing hypotheses by means of experiments is the heart of the scientific method.

Experiments in education, psychology, communication, and other social sciences use random selection and assignment of subjects to groups. The groups are treated uniquely and then compared to assess treatment outcomes. Suppose, for example, we wanted to measure the effectiveness of a new drug on headaches. We might take subjects with headaches and divide them into two groups. One group would receive the drug and the second group would receive a placebo (an unmedicated facsimile). Then we would compare the results observed in these two conditions to test whether subjects who received the drug recovered from headaches faster than those who did not. In this case, the group which received a placebo serves as a benchmark which allows us to assess treatment effects.

There are some questions that should be asked about an experiment like this. First, are the subjects in the study typical? In order to generalize from the study to a broader group of people, the individuals in the study must be similar to the broader population. Some have criticized studies in psychology, for example, because they were conducted mainly on college students enrolled in introductory psychology courses, and these students may have different characteristics than other segments of the population (although there are some studies suggesting this is not a major problem). Similarly, many have suggested that changes in management practices that were effective in Japan may not work in America since our economic and business systems are different from those in Japan.

Second, is there a benchmark to facilitate assessment of treatment effects? One way to accomplish this is to use a control group which consists of subjects who are not exposed to the treatment. For example, there are many studies suggesting that a college education helps individuals become more confident. These studies compare the self-esteem of individuals before and after they attend college, and they note that people are more confident in themselves when they graduate than when they entered college. There are serious problems with this type of study. The most obvious flaw is that the students' self-confidence may have improved even with no college education. If the students had worked or joined the military instead of going to college, their confidence may have increased (maybe even more than if they had gone to college). This problem could be minimized by comparing the self-confidence of both the students and non-students at the time the choice is made to attend college to the confidence of both groups four years later. If the people who went to college have greater self-confidence than those who did not, this would give a more accurate test of the beneficial effect of college on self-confidence.

Another problem with this experiment exists even with the addition of a control group. The assumption is made that the students who go to college have similar characteristics to their peers who do not. This assumption is questionable. Students who go to college may, on balance, be more interested in learning, smarter, and have other characteristics that distinguish them from those students who do not go to college. To eliminate this problem, the characteristics of the control group must be the same in all critical ways as the characteristics of the experimental group. This situation is often difficult to create, because it implies experimenter power to *assign* persons randomly drawn from a population either to attend or not to attend college for four years. Such a procedure is the only sure way to have a comparable set of individuals in the test group and the control group. Such a procedure is obviously impractical in the real world.

WEIGHING EVIDENCE

Often the basis of a disagreement consists of conflicting evidence. One advocate will cite evidence supporting one point; the opponent will read evidence suggesting the opposite view is correct. An effective advocate must be able to make sense of this competing evidence. This should be done by weighing the quality of the evidence, not by simply counting the number of quotations introduced. While the amount of evidence supporting an argument may sometimes be relevant (for example, if the evidence for one side stems from a single source which is inconsistent with the consensus of authorities), the quality of the evidence is a more important factor in determining the strength of the argument. So far, we have discussed ways of evaluating evidence in order to assist this weighing. In addition, as will be discussed in the next chapter, it may be useful to look at the *reasons* given by the individuals quoted in weighing the evidence. Evidence with reasons is better than conclusionary evidence. There are other guidelines that may assist the weighing of evidence.

Initially, the advocate should be sure that the evidence he or she uses conflicts with the opponent's evidence. Sometimes evidence that seems to conflict is not contradictory. For example, evidence that the number of traffic accidents is declining does not deny evidence that 55,000 people die each year from accidents. Evidence that says early detection of illness would save lives does not contradict evidence that we cannot detect certain illnesses early. In these cases, the relative strength of the evidence is less crucial to the argument's validity since the sources of the evidence do not disagree with each other; they are making statements about different issues. The principle is that it is important to be clear on the meaning of the evidence to make sure that the evidence does in fact contradict.

In decision making, it is also important to understand that not all issues can be resolved clearly. As indicated in chapter 2, when discussing the effects of policies we cannot always be sure of our claims, hence we must deal in probabilities. The fact that different bits of evidence on an issue conflict may indicate that there is still uncertainty regarding the issue. Experts of equally high repute may sincerely disagree. In this case, it might be worthwhile for an advocate to admit that the evidence on an issue is conflicting, and then to discuss the implications of this uncertainty. For example, the Food and Drug Administration has developed a policy that, if uncertainty over the safety or efficacy of a new drug exists, it should be kept off the market until adequate testing permits us to be more sure about it. The presumption is that the risks of undesirable effects of a drug are too great to permit the drug to be sold. In law, on the other hand, if there is uncertainty about guilt, an individual is set free. There is a presumption of innocence in our court system. In those cases where the evidence conflicts, then, it may be useful to identify standards for resolving issues when there is uncertainty. As we have discussed, each major arena of human argumentation has its own accepted or presumed criteria for making decisions in the face of uncertainty.

USE OF EVIDENCE IN DEBATE

There are additional guidelines for the use of evidence in academic debate. Initially, it is important for the advocate in an academic debate setting to have support for all major arguments that he or she advances. While some advocates may think that their arguments are clearly accurate, frequently these "obvious" positions are challenged by the opposing debater, and this forces the advocates who initiate the argument to provide support for their position. The general rule to follow is that "the advocate who asserts must prove."

In addition, it is important for every debater to provide documentation for all evidence introduced into the round. As we discussed in chapter 4, advocates should have complete citations available for all the evidence read. When presenting evidence in a debate, the advocate should also indicate to the judge where the evidence is from. This should include, at a minimum, the name of the source, the source's qualifications, and the date of the evidence. Some judges prefer more detailed evidence citations.

SUMMARY

The effective advocate needs to be able to understand how to evaluate the strengths and weaknesses of different types of evidence and reasoning. Evidence is frequently used in arguments to support positions. It is important to understand that the quality of different pieces of evidence will vary. In order to be able to weigh the evidence accurately, it is important to look at the source of the evidence, the reasoning behind it, and the wording. Similarly, in order to evaluate statistics it is necessary to have an understanding of the philosophy of statistics, as well as the weaknesses of statistical proof.

The key to evaluating evidence, whether expert testimony, statistic, or example, is to ask how much confidence a rational person should have in the support material. This should help the advocate both in weighing evidence and in selecting the best material to support an argument.

Notes

[1]Robert Rosenthal, *Experimenter Effects in Behavioral Research* (New York: Appleton-Century-Crofts, 1966).

[2]David Zarefsky, Erwin Chemerinsky, and Alan S. Loewinsohn, "Government Statistics: The Case for Independent Regulation—A New Legislative Proposal," *Texas Law Review,* 59 (1981), 1223–46.

[3]William Broad and Nicholas Wade, *Betrayers of the Truth* (New York: Simon & Schuster, 1982).

[4]See Eugene J. Webb, Donald T. Campbell, Richard D. Schwartz, and Lee Sechrest, *Unobtrusive Measures: Nonreactive Research in the Social Sciences* (Chicago: Rand McNally, 1966), pp. 1–34.

CHAPTER EIGHT

REASONING

Reasoning is the process of inferring a conclusion or conclusions from evidence presented in a debate. Reasoning is an important element of the decision-making process. A complete analysis of any system will examine several interrelationships between the components of the system. In order to evaluate the nature of these relationships and to predict the effect of various policies, it is important to be able to distinguish between facts or predictions that are supported by strong arguments and those that are poorly supported. For this reason, the advocate should acquire a thorough understanding of the nature of reasoning.

There are three major approaches to the study of reasoning. The first approach involves developing a model of argument in order to understand the nature of reasoning. The second approach is constructive: it attempts to identify forms of correct reasoning, and then develops an understanding of what makes this reasoning correct. The third approach to reasoning (the study of fallacies) is critical in nature: it identifies types of argument, and then attempts to discover what it is about these types of reasoning that makes them inadequate.

These three approaches will be discussed in this chapter. We will begin by examining a model of argument. Next, we will discuss four major types of reasoning: causal reasoning, sign reasoning, reasoning by example, and reasoning by comparison. Finally we will examine the nature of fallacies and analyze some of the more common fallacies.

TOULMIN'S MODEL OF ARGUMENT

Before discussing specific types of argument, it might be helpful to develop a general outline of the nature of arguments. One of the most influential argumentation theorists in the twentieth century is Stephen Toulmin, currently at the University of Chicago. In *The Uses of Argument*,[1] Toulmin suggested that the traditional ways of

FIGURE 8-1

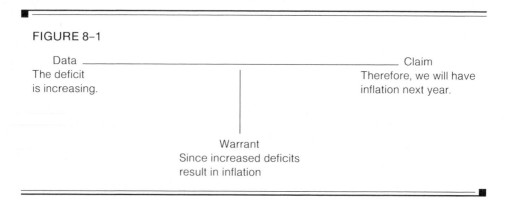

looking at argument were inadequate in explaining how argument worked in ordinary discourse. He then proposed a model of argument to help explain the process of arguing.

To understand this model of argument, let's analyze a simple argument. Suppose an advocate makes the following argument: "Next year we will have inflation, since the deficit is increasing." At first glance, this argument seems to have two parts: a conclusion ("next year we will have inflation") and support for that conclusion ("the deficit is increasing"). Toulmin calls these two components of an argument the *claim* and the *data*. The claim is the statement that the advocate hopes to establish. The data is the evidence, facts, or reasoning used to support the claim.

While this argument seems relatively simple, it involves a great deal more. The question any individual analyzing the argument must ask is, How does the advocate get from the data to the claim? How can one assume that, given the truth of the data, the claim necessarily follows? To answer this question, Toulmin introduces a third element to his model, the *warrant*. The warrant is the assumption that permits the reasoner to move from the data to the claim. In our example, the data "the deficit is increasing" justifies the claim "we will have inflation next year" *only* if we assume that increased deficits result in inflation. This assumption would be the warrant in our argument. The initial model of argument, then, would look like Figure 8–1; we move from the data to the claim through the use of a warrant.

The data consists of the raw material that forms the basis of the argument; the warrant includes the shared understandings of an argumentative community concerning when an inference is justified. Before filling in the rest of the model, it would be useful to examine the warrant in more detail. The warrant is the key to effective argumentation. If we use accurate warrants, our arguments will be strong; weak warrants doom our efforts to failure. The question becomes, Where do these warrants come from?

To answer that question, Toulmin introduces another concept, that of an *argument field*. An argument field (sometimes called a discipline) is a collection of individuals who share common goals and common standards for argument. For example, physics could be considered one field, biology another field. Toulmin suggests that each field of argument has its own type of reasoning. Reasoning in law, for example, is different from reasoning in medicine, which is different from the type of reasoning that takes place between artists.

There are two types of warrants. *Field invariant warrants* apply to all fields of argument. The last part of this chapter will analyze some of these. *Field variant warrants* apply only to arguments that take place within a field. Many forms of reasoning, according to this perspective, are field variant. Arguments that are effective in one field may not be effective in other fields. Suppose, for example, that we wanted to demonstrate that a certain individual committed a murder. In the field of law, evidence from eyewitnesses, fingerprints, photographs, and lab tests could all be useful. This material would act as data, and the rules of evidence would help determine the standards for evaluating this evidence. Suppose, however, we were arguing, not in a court of law, but in an English class. To "prove" that a character in a novel committed a crime, we might point to the physical features of the character, the weather when the character is introduced, and so on. This type of support material, while worthless in a court of law, could be very persuasive in the field of English literature. The reason for this distinction is that in the field of literature, there are certain rules for inference that permit us to move from this type of evidence to a conclusion. Similarly, when we debate about the causes of death, arguers in the field of medicine will use different types of evidence and different warrants than those in sociology because the two fields have different standards for evaluating evidence.

To understand how warrants function in arguments, Toulmin introduces three other components of argument. The *backing* is the support for the warrant. In our example of the debt causing inflation, we might support our warrant by drawing from the field of economics, noting that members of that field tend to support our warrant (that deficits tend to cause inflation). We might also note that there is historical evidence to support our warrant. The backing helps us strengthen the warrant.

The *rebuttal* (or *reservation*) can be defined as the exception to the warrant. Few warrants are unconditional; there are often exceptions to the rules established by the warrants. A full understanding of the warrant requires that we understand those situations in which the warrant does not support an inference.

Finally, the *qualifier* indicates the amount of certainty that we have in a claim. As discussed in chapter 2, not all decisions are reached with the same degree of certainty. We can support some conclusions (or claims) with a great deal of certainty—others with only tentative approval. Ideally, the qualifier should be consistent with the warrant, backing, and reservation. The stronger the warrant, the more forceful the qualifier can be; the weaker the warrant, the less certain the qualifier. The full argument would look like the one in Figure 8–2 on page 132. Using our earlier example, a full argument would look like Figure 8–3 on page 133.

It is important to recognize that the full argument implied by Toulmin's model will rarely be presented in an argument. Often the warrant and other parts of the model are unstated. This does not mean that the model is not of any use to the advocate. The model can help the advocate identify unstated assumptions by an opponent. These

132 • REASONING

FIGURE 8-2

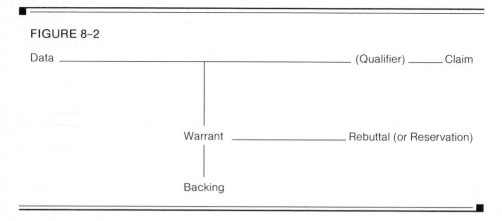

Data ——————————————————— (Qualifier) ———— Claim

Warrant ————————————— Rebuttal (or Reservation)

Backing

assumptions can then be brought out in the open and refuted. In addition, the model can be used by the advocate to analyze his or her own arguments, either to improve the arguments or to help anticipate opposing arguments.

In order to make these evaluations, however, it is important to understand the nature of some of the field invariant warrants that are frequently used in arguments. There are certain types of reasoning that occur with a great deal of frequency in argument. These types of reasoning have been studied extensively, and certain guidelines have been developed for them. The next section of this chapter will explore some of the warrants commonly used in arguments concerning public policy.

Causal Reasoning

Causal reasoning is the process of making an inference about the dynamic relationship that exists between the components of a system. Of all the types of reasoning, causal reasoning is most relevant to policy systems analysis, which is used in governmental and corporate decision making. Causal reasoning is based on analyzing the ways in which separate elements of a system interact and affect one another. There is a strong presumption that there is a binding relationship between different elements that make up the system, and that changes in one or more of the elements will produce direct or indirect changes in the others in a systematic, predictable way. For example, when a person argues that higher governmental spending *causes* inflation, that individual is using causal reasoning. Causal relations should be distinguished from correlations. A correlation exists when two events are associated with each other. Causality implies more than simply that two events are associated with each other; it implies that one event led to the existence of the other. For example, some observers have noted that there is a close correlation between stock market prices and the league affiliation of the year's Super Bowl winner. While the two may correlate with each other, it is unlikely that there is a causal relationship between the two. While correlation is necessary for causation to exist, by itself correlation does not establish a causal relationship.

FIGURE 8-3

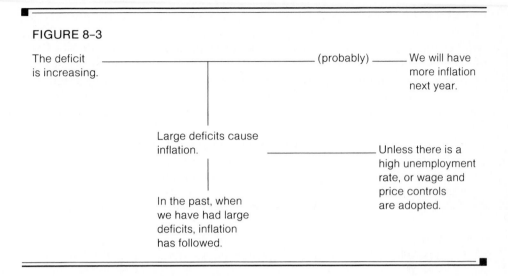

The deficit is increasing. —————————— (probably) ——— We will have more inflation next year.

Large deficits cause inflation.

—————————— Unless there is a high unemployment rate, or wage and price controls are adopted.

In the past, when we have had large deficits, inflation has followed.

Causal reasoning is a very complex type of reasoning. The true cause of an event often cannot be directly observed; it must be inferred from a set of facts. This is particularly true in matters of human motives and action, and in issues of public policy. Economists disagree about the causes of unemployment and inflation. Historians disagree about the causes of war. Psychologists disagree about the causes of human behavior. All of this disagreement takes place because we cannot "see" causal relations. As important as causal argument is to advocacy, we must settle for less than certain conclusions about causal relationships.

The logical requirements for a cause-effect relationship to exist are that the cause must be both necessary and sufficient to produce the effect. A necessary cause is a cause without which the effect will not take place. A sufficient cause is a cause that, by itself, will produce an effect. In order to identify the causal structure of a problem and prevent its undesirable effects, we must analyze which causes are necessary to produce an effect. In order to ensure that a desired effect will occur, it is important to identify the *sufficient* causes of a condition. There are some things to look for in examining causal arguments.

First, is the causal relationship logical? Ask about the nature of the link connecting the different elements of a system. These should be directly related before we decide that a causal relationship exists. In arguing that cigarette smoking causes cancer, medical scientists do more than just note that there is a correlation between smoking and cancer; they attempt to explain logically why the relationship exists. Similarly, causal arguments attempting to predict that a proposed policy will result in a specific effect should include reasons to explain why such a relationship could be expected to exist. The thrust of this line of causal analysis is to demonstrate a necessary link between cause and effect.

Second, is the imputed cause significant enough to produce the effect? While two items may be logically related, it is possible that the relationship is not strong enough to cause an effect in some cases. For example, while increased governmental spending may cause inflation, that does not mean if the government increases spending by $200 million (a tiny percentage of the total federal budget) for a school lunch program, we are doomed to inflation. In the nature of systems analysis, there may be a minimal degree or threshold of causal influence before an effect may result. Here, the thrust of the argument is to determine whether there is a *sufficient* cause to produce the alleged effect.

We have emphasized in this book that there are often multiple causes of an effect, or a single cause may produce multiple effects. In many situations it is difficult to determine precisely what event causes another, or what proportion of an effect may be attributed to a given cause. For example, one theory to explain the causes of World War I points to the assassination of Archduke Francis Ferdinand of Austria-Hungary as the immediate cause of the war. Other theories point to secret treaties, or to increased international tensions as the cause of the war. In retrospect, all these reconstructions probably have a point. There are numerous causal factors related to any war. The assassination, by itself, was not a sufficient cause of War War I; other conditions had to exist before that single action could trigger worldwide violence. On the other hand, it is arguable whether the tensions would have eventually led to a war; some catalyst or "spark" was necessary, whether it was the assassination or some other event.

Third, we should ask if there is a counteracting cause. While two events may be causally related, there may be some way to disrupt this relationship. For example, increased governmental spending may generally lead to inflation, but this relationship can be eliminated if, in addition to increasing governmental spending, we also increase taxes or adopt price controls. In these cases, we can try to intervene to prevent the causal relationship.

Finally, we should ask if a third cause produces both the cause and the effect. Sometimes the reason two events always happen at the same time is because a third event independently causes both observed events. For example, some people have suggested that arms races cause wars. They note that in a majority of the cases where nations have engaged in arms races, the nations have ended up in war. Another explanation for this correlation is that both arms races and wars are caused by a third event: the existence of tensions between countries. When countries oppose each other, they tend to build more weapons. It is argued that this hostility, not the arms race, causes war.

Sign Reasoning

Reasoning from a sign is the process of making an inference about causal relationships on the basis of some extraneous symbol. Sign reasoning is illustrated by the concept of circumstantial evidence. Like a causal argument, reasoning from sign is constructed as an "if . . ., then . . ." pattern. Unlike causal reasoning, the antecedent sign represents only a clue or indicator that a consequential relationship must exist. The sign is used as an association device, not a correlation or causal link; the sign is not directly connected with the phenomenon which it suggests. The sign reasoning pattern is to causal reasoning what the analogy is to the process of reasoning from example. While it superficially looks like causal reasoning, the logical connection is much weaker. Yet, like the analogy, sign reasoning can be useful in explaining and simplifying arguments that are very technical and complex. In many situations, sign reasoning is as near to causal argument as the evidence allows. The whole area of attitudinal motivations for political behavior can only be established by means of signs, since attitudes themselves are intangible and cannot be studied directly in order to establish their link to behavior.

For example, when leaves fall off trees, that is a *sign* of autumn. The leaves falling off a tree do not cause autumn; they merely act as an indicator that autumn has arrived. When we see a flag at half mast, we consider that to be a sign that someone important has died. If we want to find a good roadside cafe, we look for one with a lot of trucks parked around it. Similarly, we often read about the warning *signs* of cancer, or *signs* of trouble in a marriage.

In examining sign reasoning, we should look at three things. First, are the sign and the conclusion logically related? There should be some reason to think that the sign is an indicator that something else exists. The adage, "where there's smoke, there's fire," an example of sign reasoning, makes sense only because there is a logical connection between the two events.

Next, we should ask whether the sign is invariably assigned to a certain meaning, or if there are exceptions. Leaves falling off a tree may be a sign of autumn, but it may also be a sign that the tree has died. At the University of Texas, when the tower is lit up in orange, that is normally a sign that the athletic teams have won a contest. But on occasion the tower is bathed in orange light because a faculty member has won an honor. The sign's importance in these cases is ambiguous; there may be other explanations for the sign.

Finally, we should ask ourselves if the sign reasoning is cumulative. By this, we mean that the more signs that are available to support a conclusion, the more confidence we should have in it. For example, many political commentators use sign reasoning to support a conclusion that a politician is (or is not) running for an office. If a politician hires a speech writer, for example, that is a sign that the politician is thinking about campaigning. The more of these signs a person can point to (for example, if the politician also increases the number of speeches given, alters voting behavior, etc.), the stronger the sign reasoning will be.

A sign is a weak form of argument but a strong mode of persuasion in some situations. Causal relationships are difficult to prove in a scientific laboratory, and it is even more difficult in human or political situations. In political systems, often the only evidence available consists of what people say or do. These can only be indirect indicators or signs of their inward feelings and values. If the basic issue in dispute is a nonfactual resolution of value, the advocate is well advised to recast the abstract resolution of the asserted value into a more concrete situation, which can be readily understood as an indication or sign of the value's existence. For example, "the military policy of the current United States administration is immoral," was a recent resolution debated in the Oxford Union. The opposing advocates translated this abstract resolution into specific policies or situations, such as nuclear weapons proliferation, or intervention into Latin American countries, in order to strengthen their cases. These situations were then cited as signs of the morality or immorality of the administration's policy. Together with the analogy and testimony of authoritative opinion, sign reasoning is a major source of support for value-oriented claims.

Reasoning by Example

An example is defined as one member of a larger group or population, cited to serve as proof regarding the group as a whole. An example may be a single instance, illustration, case study, or fact. Sometimes, an advocate may wish to use examples to support a position. In selecting these examples, the advocate should look out for four characteristics of a good example. First, the example should be typical of the group or population it is supposed to exemplify. When using an example, the advocate attempts to reach a general conclusion. The advocate suggests that, since something was the case in one example, it is true of the rest of the group. This type of conclusion can be drawn only if the examples given are typical. To argue that the lack of zoning did not stop Houston, Texas from becoming a thriving metropolitan area may be a poor example since many things about Houston make it an atypical city (for example, the presence of the oil industry, NASA, and deed restrictions). Similarly, drawing a conclusion about a graduating class by looking only at the top students would not lead to a reliable conclusion.

Second, the advocate should ask whether negative examples exist. If a debater presents one positive example, it can be undermined if the other side can present cases where the opposite was true. When the Model Cities program was enacted in the 1960s, examples were cited of cities where the concept was successful, but these examples were undermined by the mention of cities where the concept failed to live up to expectations. Given the presence of both positive and negative examples, few conclusions could be drawn about the Model Cities policy in general.

Third, the advocate should ask whether the examples cover a critical period of time. Sometimes, in order to examine an example adequately, we need to look at it over a period of time. For example, in examining the effect of strip mining for coal on the environment, some have pointed to examples of areas where the mines were reclaimed and crops were growing where at one time coal had been mined. Critics of this position argue that these examples are not valid since, while reclamation may work in the short run, after several years erosion caused by the mining can eliminate the success of the reclamation. Thus the example ignores the long-term effects of the problem.

Finally, the advocate should ask whether significant details have been left out when presenting the example. The presentation may reflect the bias of the advocate, and as a result, the advocate may leave out critical information. An advocate may present an example where an anti-crime program worked, neglecting to add that while the program was being adopted, the unemployment rate in the city also declined, so it is impossible to tell whether the drop in crime was a result of the new program or the decrease in unemployment (or both).

Reasoning by Analogy

Reasoning by analogy is defined as the process of comparing a known example as evidence with an unknown example which you are attempting to explain and clarify. As in English literature, an analogy is primarily used to make an idea clear by showing how it is similar to something else. If an advocate supports a new proposed policy, a similar program already in effect in another country might be cited to show that since it works there, it might also work in the United States.

Reasoning by analogy is similar to reasoning by example, but it differs in two important respects. The two forms of reasoning both take a known example as the point of departure. But while the process of reasoning by example is aimed at proving a general conclusion about the whole group or category, the process of reasoning by analogy is merely aimed at comparing a known example with the unknown for the purpose of making it clearer. Since this is a rhetorical purpose rather than a substantive proof, the analogy may be either literal or figurative, as long as it succeeds in clarifying or simplifying the unknown.

In disputes over empirical or factual issues, literal analogies are generally more acceptable than figurative analogies. If the items are similar enough to show that the unknown and known examples are relatively interchangeable, the analogy functions as a reason by example. In practice, the unknown example being compared is rarely identical to the known example, otherwise there would be no need for an analogy to clarify it. In disputes over intangible, abstract, evaluative issues, however, the figurative analogy is frequently used. In moral and ethical reasoning, many of the most profound doctrines people live by are based on common stories, parables, and other forms of analogies. There is no literal analogy possible for clarifying the realm of the spirit, so we rely on figurative analogies such as biblical references that compare the person's relationship to the church with the child's relationship to the parents, or the sheep's relationship to the shepherd. Not only are religious symbols clarified by analogies, but political ones are as well. Who can forget the climactic episode in the Watergate hearings when White House counsel John Dean testified that he had told President Nixon that the cover-up had become a "cancer on the Presidency"?

There are two main tests for reasoning by analogy. First, the two items being tested must be similar in nature. The thesis of reasoning by analogy is that, if two things are similar, what worked with the one will work with another. If we reason that a mass transit system used in Atlanta should work in Houston we must assume that these cities are similar in size, traffic patterns, existing transportation systems, and so forth. As a matter of fact, transportation officials in Houston made such a comparison, and concluded that Atlanta's system would not work in the larger, more sprawling area to be served in Houston.

The second test for reasoning by analogy is suggested by the first: the differences between the two examples being compared must not be critical. While no two objects being compared can be identical, they must not be different in ways that are critical to the comparison being drawn. For example, some business consultants have suggested that management techniques that are successful in Japanese corporations should be used in the United States. To support this argument, it is noted that Japan and the

United States are similar, in that both countries are industrialized and they compete for international trade. Since the management techniques work in Japan, it is reasoned, they should work in the United States. The problem with this argument is that, while Japan and the United States are similar, the two countries differ in critical ways. The cultures of the two countries are vastly different. This factor must be considered any time two countries are being compared. In addition, the relationship between the worker and the company is different in Japan, where many workers stay with a company for their entire careers. The turnover is much higher in the United States. This is a critical difference affecting the comparability of management techniques in companies operating in Japan and in the United States.

These tests of the adequacy of an analogy almost always disclose logical weaknesses in this type of reasoning. Since the analogy is primarily used for the purpose of clarifying an unknown example, by definition the unknown example is unfamiliar to the audience. If that were not true, if the audience had no uncertainty about the unknown example being advocated, there would be no reason to introduce an analogy to begin with. As a result, it is relatively simple to look at an analogy and discover numerous areas where the examples being compared are dissimilar. The asserted comparison thus breaks down. For this reason, an analogy is often labeled "the weakest form of argument." Nevertheless, it is a powerful rhetorical tool for clarifying and simplifying an unknown, complex, abstract concept or argument in a way that is consistent with the advocate's perspective. Its logical weakness may be offset by its psychological, persuasive impact when used effectively.

Reasoning by analogy plays an important role in the field of law. Much of legal reasoning involves comparing an individual case with prior cases in order to discover the rules that define the law in the area studied. These prior cases constitute a legal precedent to apply to the case at hand. In several areas of law, there are hundreds of cases, which are grouped in a manner that makes sense. For example, if a lawyer is attempting to discover the current view of the law governing free speech, he or she would consult all the previous cases involving that topic. The lawyer would then attempt to distinguish the characteristics found in all the cases upholding a person's right to speak from other characteristics in those cases upholding the right of the state to prohibit individuals from speaking. This is a complex process; often initial rules are proposed only to be rejected when a new case is discovered that does not conform to the proposed rule. Once the essential characteristics of those cases on each side have been located, the lawyer decides which group the immediate case falls into. In essence, this process of deciding case law based on precedents from past decisions is reasoning by analogy: This case is like previous known cases. Reasoning by analogy is much more rigorously governed in the judicial arena than in any other forum of human dispute because the legal rules are very strict.

This type of reasoning can also apply to non-legal situations. In attempting to predict the actions of a nation, for example, it might be wise to begin with two clear examples: one where the nation acted in an aggressive manner, and one where the nation acted peacefully. The advocate then attempts to develop initial guidelines for distinguishing these two situations. Why did the nation act one way in one situation, and another way in the other situation? Once the initial guidelines are developed, additional examples of the nation's actions are examined, and the guidelines are then modified to account for the new information. This process continues as more and more examples are studied until finally a clear set of guidelines is created explaining how the nation behaves. The more situations covered by the final "rule," the better the rule.

FALLACIES

Until two or three decades ago, the traditional approach to the teaching of argumentation emphasized formal logic as the ideal theoretical model for understanding reasoning and for applying rationality to human decision making. Formal logic equaled rationality, which equaled reasonableness. To those who took such a limited, literal approach to argumentation as being equated with formal logic, it followed that any argument which violated the rules of formal logic was irrational (or at least irrelevant), and hence was a fallacy. Thus the traditional approach to reasoning, based on formal logic, defined a *fallacy* as any violation of formal logical rules.

According to this definition of fallacy, most of the arguments found in the real world disputes are invalid. Most informal reasoning, political argumentation, religious discourse—in fact, just about any rhetoric outside the scientific laboratory—fails to conform to strict logical rules. The traditional approach condemned all practical decision-making methods. It is not difficult to compile a lengthy list of fallacies to be "corrected," i.e., cast into formal logical reasoning patterns, if possible, or rejected as invalid.

During the past few decades, this view of fallacies has undergone a change. Numerous philosophers, influenced by C. L. Hamblin's book, *Fallacies,*[2] have noted that the description of fallacies in numerous popular works has been very superficial. While a fallacy has traditionally been defined as a type of argument that seems to be sound but is not, the exact nature of fallacies has proved to be elusive to students of reasoning. Often the examples given to illustrate fallacies have either been too simplistic, or they have been examples of arguments that could be valid under certain circumstances. There has been much discussion of what it means to call an argument a fallacy, as well as what constitutes a fallacy. As a result of the renewed interest, numerous fallacies have been examined systematically, and fewer and fewer arguments have been found to be of *no* utility to an advocate.

We wish to propose a modification of the traditional view of fallacies. From our perspective, a fallacy is a type of argument, establishing a degree of probability, containing a generic weakness.[3] There are two implications of this view: it sees the fallacy as an argument designed to establish probability, and it focuses the attention of the advocate on a generic weakness of the fallacy. Each of these two features should be examined before we discuss specific types of fallacies.

While a fallacy cannot support a claim that aims at demonstrating an absolutely certain conclusion, it may be of some use where the conclusion only requires a degree of probability, not certainty; especially where there is no other information available. For example, it is traditionally a fallacy to accept a conclusion simply because everyone agrees with it (the bandwagon). However, if an individual was in a new city, and was looking for a place to eat, it might make sense to eat at a restaurant that many people thought was good. In this case, the decision is not based on certainty, but in the absence of additional information, the decision could be termed reasonable. On the other hand, to base a decision on the wisdom of DNA research (a decision with significant implications) on the opinion of a few lay individuals could be disastrous. Fallacies may be useful when there is no alternative source of information relevant to a decision, where the decision is of limited significance, and when probability is the goal of argument.

The second characteristic of a fallacy is that it is an argument with a *generic weakness*. By generic weakness, we mean a potential flaw that is common to that type of reasoning. Whether this weakness is fatal to the argument will depend on two factors: if the generic weakness is applicable to a specific argument, and the type of conclusion that is being drawn. The applicability of the generic weakness to a specific argument should be discussed in the specific advocacy situation. The advocate who feels that an opponent has made a fallacious argument can present the generic weakness of that argument; the defender of the argument can explain why the generic weakness does not apply to this specific argument. Labeling an argument a fallacy does not end an argument; it begins an argument by attacking its weakness. In some cases these generic weaknesses may be fatal; in other cases they can be answered.

What is important, then, is to understand the nature of the generic weaknesses and conditions in an argument that make it a fallacy. This will permit the advocate to determine whether an argument is fatally flawed as to its function in support of a claim. In addition, it will help an advocate attack fallacious arguments. A fallacious argument may frequently be worthless, but at the same time (especially if a low level of probability is the goal of argument and no other support is available), the fallacy might be useful. An examination of some of the more common fallacies will support this view.

Hasty Generalization

The fallacy of hasty generalization is defined as making an unwarranted leap from insufficient or atypical examples to a broader, general conclusion. An individual who meets one person from New York City who has a certain characteristic and then decides that *all* people from New York City share that characteristic commits the fallacy of hasty generalization. This is why stereotyping whole categories of people by racial, ethnic, sexual, or other groupings, based on a few personal encounters, is irrational.

The weakness of this type of argument should be clear. A broad conclusion cannot be reliably drawn from a single case. As we discussed in the section on reasoning by example, an adequate number of examples should be used to support a generalization. A single example may be atypical, or negative examples may exist. Relying on a limited number of examples for a conclusion can be risky.

On the other hand, there are times when it may be necessary to rely on a limited number of examples. There may be some cases in which a large number of examples do not exist, so we must cautiously draw conclusions from a limited supply. For example, in predicting the effects of United States military intervention in other countries, there are relatively few specific examples to draw from when making a generalization. Similarly, in the social sciences there are a number of theorists who advocate the use of single case studies, suggesting that we can find out more about certain aspects of psychology and sociology by investigating a few cases in great depth, instead of looking at numerous cases superficially. While this type of reasoning will not lead to certainty, it may be the best source of information in some situations.

The hasty generalization is a perfect example of the new approach to the interpretation of fallacies. By definition, any generalization must rely on a certain number of examples that is less than the total population being generalized about. If the number of examples is insufficient to support the conclusion, then the argument is considered to be fallacious. But what number of examples constitutes a "sufficient" number? The traditional view of fallacies offers no guidance, and most likely would label most generalizations as invalid on the basis of the strict rules of formal logic. The new "generic weakness" view of fallacies analyzes whether the specific claim being advocated requires more examples, and/or whether the claim being supported is asserted to be relatively certain or tentative. Thus, the same generalization argument based on examples may be either valid or fallacious, depending on its conformity with these criteria of usage in different argumentative situations.

Ad hominem

The *ad hominem* argument is defined as an attack on the character of a speaker instead of the speaker's arguments. The Latin term means "against the man." The classic case of the *ad hominem* argument is calling an opponent names instead of attacking his or her arguments. For example, in a political debate, a speaker might ignore the arguments made by an opponent, arguing instead that the opponent is a dishonest person. Instead of explaining why an argument is poor, an advocate might call the opponent incompetent. Someone might argue that an opponent is defending a position just because of self-interest. Other advocates call their opponents "communists" or "radicals" in order to dismiss their arguments instead of taking the time to explain the weaknesses behind their positions.

This type of argument is usually irrational. Even stupid, dishonest, and biased individuals can make good arguments. We should evaluate an argument on the strength of the evidence supporting the position, not by the nature of the person making the argument. On the other hand, sometimes attacks on a speaker are warranted. In a courtroom, for example, attacks on the credibility of a witness may be very relevant in determining if a statement by that witness should be believed. Similarly, in evaluating the credibility of evidence, we look at the qualifications of the author of the evidence. In a political campaign, it could be argued that some (but not all) attacks on the character of an advocate could be relevant. The point is that the legitimacy of an *ad hominem* attack depends upon whether the character of the individual has any reasonable relationship to the credibility of the arguments (or, in the case of the politician, to the decision faced by the audience). Unless the attack has some relevance, it should be avoided.

In academic debate, students are presumed to be equally inexpert and equally honest. *No* personal attacks on opponents are permitted, except to make a charge of evidence fabrication. In that exceptional instance, the charge may not be made trivially or in passing. Students are expected to keep the discussion focused entirely on the substantive issues and not on their opponents' personalities.

Post hoc, ergo propter hoc

This fallacy is defined as the false or mistaken attribution of a causal relationship where none exists. The Latin term may be translated, "After that, therefore because of that." The *post hoc* fallacy suggests that, because one thing followed another, the first event *caused* the second event. An example of this fallacy would be the following argument: after the football season begins, the temperature drops; therefore football causes cold temperatures. This is not a very strong position. The relationship between the two events could be coincidental. As discussed in the section on causal reasoning, while it is necessary to prove two things are related in time to prove a causal relationship, by itself this does not prove a causal relationship.

From the viewpoint of policy systems analysis, the *post hoc* fallacy is the most important fallacy to recognize. A system consists of a set of components bound together in a set of interlocking relationships. These relationships are invariably of a causal or correlational type. Systems planning and decision making depend on the assumption that it is possible to predict the outcomes of policy changes introduced into the system. For systems analysis to be effective, it is essential that the analyst has a clear and accurate grasp of the real relationships that exist between and among the system's components. To be fooled by the fallacy of *post hoc* in systems analysis is to be misled into making erroneous predictions of probable effects of changes in the system, or of failing to anticipate effects that will occur. Decision making is always difficult in a complex system, as in government at the federal level. There are always multiple goals, relationships, and components. There is rarely a straightforward, single-cause, single-effect closed system. Potential intervening variables and confounding variables always occur in policy decision making. What the *post hoc* fallacy comes down to is *incomplete* systems analysis that causes the decision maker to overlook certain important components or relationships or to overemphasize others, and therefore miscalculate the predicted outcomes resulting from the chosen alternative.

Appeal to Authority

Authoritative testimony is neither fallacious nor valid, in and of itself. In a dispute over a factual issue, empirical evidence is a better means for resolving the issue, although an acceptable authority's conclusionary opinion may serve to confirm or reinforce a claim proved through other means. In a dispute regarding a value judgment or an opinionated issue, it should be recalled that such claims are neither literally true nor false, and reasonable persons can hold opposite opinions in sincerity and good faith. Proof of a value claim may well place heavy reliance on the testimony of an authority. In either instance, whether on an empirical issue or an opinionated issue, it is preferable that any authority used to support a conclusion should meet high standards. The decision to accept a statement by an authority should be based on numerous factors, including the qualifications of the authority, the reasoning given by the authority, our ability to make an independent judgment about the issue, and so on. It is a fallacy, generally speaking, to rely solely on the opinion of one source for a position on a case, to introduce testimony from any source who may be biased, incompetent to testify, or untrustworthy for other reasons. The advocate should be cautious about accepting evidence from authorities uncritically; the blind acceptance of authority can be disastrous.

Appeal to Tradition

The appeal to tradition suggests that since we have done something a certain way in the past, we should continue to do so in the future. People argue that we should not modify the curriculum in a school because there have always been certain requirements; since they have worked in the past, they should work in the future. This theory has a great deal of appeal. The idea that traditions should be upheld is a value shared by many. Even traditional debate textbooks talk about a "presumption" that we stay with existing programs until they are shown to be inadequate (the systems view of presumption avoids this fallacy, since it bases presumption on risk analysis). The reasoning behind this view of presumption is quite similar to the fallacy of tradition.

The weakness of this argument is simple: just because we have always done something in a certain way does not mean that it is the correct way. Society is constantly changing; it may be desirable for us to alter our policies to reflect the new changes. Even the court system which relies on precedents (meaning, on tradition) recognizes the need to overturn old cases when they become outmoded. The point is that we should decide what to do on the merits of the alternatives, not simply because we have done something a certain way in the past.

Bandwagon

The bandwagon fallacy is the argument that, since everybody thinks something is true, it is true. Frequently newspapers and magazines will publish opinion polls describing what the majority of Americans think about an issue. This is used to support the acceptance or rejection of the issue. Certainly in a democracy there are some issues that should be decided by a popular vote. In addition, there is something to be said for the notion that "when in Rome, do as the Romans." A new resident in a community may wish to conform to the norms until he or she develops a familiarity with the rules of the community.

The problem with this type of reasoning is that the public can be wrong. On many issues, the public does not know all the facts, and may change its mind if more information were available. Some issues transcend public opinion. The structure of our government is such that certain issues (for example, those rights in the Constitution and the Bill of Rights) are held to be beyond the will of a temporary majority of individuals. President Kennedy ignored the polls when he enforced the Civil Rights

Act, saying that a moral issue of such magnitude could not be measured with a thermometer. The way to discover the truth is not to take a poll, but to examine the evidence and reasoning that support a conclusion.

Slippery Slope

The slippery slope fallacy is defined as the assumption that if we do something, we commit ourselves to doing other, similar actions. For example, some opponents of Medicare suggested that, if we adopted the program, we would end up with a socialistic economy. Opponents of deploying troops in Central America argued that, if we sent advisors to that nation, the net result would be a massive military intervention.

The problem with the slippery slope fallacy is that it is fatalistically "all-or-nothing." It assumes that an action, once taken, irrevocably commits you to the next step, and then on to the next. In fact, most policy actions are easily divided into a series of smaller, discrete stages which can be taken on a tentative, incremental basis. More critics of government charge that there is a lack of follow-through, rather than a slippery slope of escalating actions in a policy area. Not every interpersonal contact results in intimate friendships; not every business decision leads to fortune or to ruin. If the government passes a new law in a given area of social concern, it need not escalate inevitably into that area. Laws can be, and have been, limited in scope and even repealed on occasion.

There are, however, some cases where this type of argument may be valid. It can be argued that taking an initial step, while not *logically* committing someone to a second step, might create *psychological* pressures to act. The argument against sending even a small number of troops into other countries is that once those troops are there, a psychological momentum is created, leading to future escalation. In addition, it can be argued that taking the first step in a new direction can be very important. Once we justify the initial action, it becomes a precedent to justify future actions that are similar in nature. A cigarette smoker attempting to give up smoking may be able to justify "cheating" once and smoking a cigarette. However, once the initial cigarette is smoked, it becomes easier to justify smoking another, and then another. Similarly, many civil libertarians suggest that if we violate a right once, it becomes easier to violate that right a second time and to violate even more rights after that. The best defense against the erosion of our rights is to combat it when it starts, not after it has gained momentum. Since a rule was violated once on someone's behalf, those wishing to violate the right will argue that it is unfair not to violate it again on someone else's behalf. The result of this type of reasoning is that soon no right is held sacred, and frequent violations of rights can be justified by referring to past actions that have violated rights.

We do not wish to argue that pressures can never be resisted; we merely note that they are real and should be considered by advocates. There is another type of fallacy called *special pleading* in which an advocate suggests that an exception should be made to a rule in this specific case. A senator might argue that we should raise the budget ceiling just this once for a new spending program. The problem with this argument is that it may lead to a snowball, where everyone asks for an exception to a rule. Unless a clear principle can be developed to distinguish between acceptable and unacceptable exceptions, this type of reasoning could destroy the original rule.

Straw Argument

A straw argument is an argument an advocate refutes which is not relevant to the debate. For example, if an opponent has a strong argument that an advocate cannot beat, the advocate might choose to ignore that argument and argue against another argument that he or she can defeat. In a debate over gun control, for example, if a pro-gun control advocate suggests that gun control might eliminate accidents, his or her opponent might ignore this argument and instead argue that gun control does not reduce crime, an argument that is irrelevant to accidents. Obviously whether or not an argument is a straw argument depends upon whether it is, in fact, relevant to the issues in the debate. Similarly, in a court, a lawyer who argues that a law is a bad one is attacking a straw argument, since the question in the court is not whether the law is wise, but if the law applies to the case before the court.

REASONING AND VALUES

One especially complex area of reasoning is the issue of how we apply reasons to value conflicts. Many of our arguments concern values; we argue about whether a decision was just; we argue about which team is the "best" team; we argue about what is the "good life." While arguments about values are common in our society, there is only a limited amount of agreement about how value disputes should be resolved.

Most theorists agree that, in resolving arguments about values, there are two major issues: the definitive issue, and the designative issue. The definitive issue asks what is meant by the value being debated. What is meant by "good," "just," or "fair"? The designative issue asks if the facts conform to the definition established in the definitive issue.

For example, suppose two individuals were arguing about which music group was the "best." There would be two issues the advocates should address. The definitive issue would ask what is meant by the "best music group." Does "best" mean most popular? Most influential? Most respected by the critics? The loudest? Depending upon the answers to these questions, different groups will emerge as the best.

The designative issue simply asks which group meets the criteria developed in resolving the first issue. If by "best" we mean the best-selling group, then the designative issue would concern which group has sold the most records. If by "best" we mean the most influential, this stage would be devoted to deciding which group has influenced the public more than any other.

The implication of this view of argument is that most of the debates over values concern different definitions of key terms in the debate. If one set of definitions is used, a value may be affirmed; if another set is used, then the value would be rejected. For this reason, resolving definitions in value disputes is critical. The meanings of some terms may depend upon the philosophical view taken by the advocate. Terms such as "just" and "fair" have specific meanings in different philosophical systems. For this reason, one way to resolve disputes over values would be to defend a philosophical system (such as those discussed in chapter 2) and then to apply that system to the terms used in the resolution. Similarly, one can resolve definitional problems by appealing to the goal of the field in which the dispute takes place. For example, in determining whether a judicial decision was "just," the goals of the legal field could be used to resolve conflicts over the meaning of the term.

SUMMARY

An understanding of the nature of reasoning is important to the advocate. This understanding can not only assist the advocate in discovering weaknesses in the position advanced by an opponent, but it can also help the advocate develop the strongest possible case. Once the advocate has discovered the best possible evidence and the best possible arguments to support a position, it is necessary to organize that material effectively. The nature of this process will be discussed in the next chapter.

Notes

[1]Stephen Toulmin, *The Uses of Argument* (Cambridge: Cambridge University Press, 1958).

[2]C. L. Hamblin, *Fallacies* (London: Methuen & Co., Ltd., 1970).

[3]Walter Ulrich, "In Defense of the Fallacy," *Argument and Social Practice: Proceedings of the Fourth SCA/AFA Conference on Argumentation*, J. Robert Cox, Malcolm O. Sillars, and Gregg B. Walker, eds. (Annandale, VA: Speech Communication Association, 1985), pp. 110–26.

PART THREE

PROCESS
OF
ADVOCACY

CHAPTER NINE

AFFIRMATIVE CASE CONSTRUCTION

Policy systems debate consists of a comparison of alternative courses of action. It requires at least two principals, one to make a claim (the affirmative) and another to rebut it (the negative). The affirmative advocate must initiate argument on behalf of a particular policy thesis; this constitutes the presentation of the affirmative's case (position). Then the affirmative must defend that policy position against any and all negative attempts to rebut it; this involves a defense of the affirmative's case.

This chapter will introduce the student to affirmative advocacy. Special emphasis will be placed on the initial affirmative position. First we will explore the nature of affirmative advocacy, and then we will describe and explain its fundamental burdens. The advocate will want to construct the strongest possible affirmative position. Therefore we will focus on those theoretical and practical considerations which support the selection, construction, and presentation of the affirmative's case, including case selection criteria, organizational options, and the essential ingredients of a strong first affirmative constructive speech. Chapter 11 will examine the special nature of affirmative advocacy and will explore the strategies and tactics involved in defending an affirmative position.

NATURE OF AFFIRMATIVE ADVOCACY

In formal policy debate the resolution determines affirmative and negative ground. A debate resolution is a statement, usually phrased as a declarative sentence, which embodies a controversy over one or more proposed courses of action (policy options). The resolution is the focus of controversy between opposing advocates. The affirmative must advocate the resolution while the negative must oppose it. Because the resolution plays a central part in advocacy, we will begin this chapter with a brief discussion of the role, function, and implications of the resolution.

The Debate Resolution

The resolution should clearly define the basis for argument. Disagreement, if channeled productively, can be an asset. The decision-making schemes utilized in government and business often employ formal disagreement to test alternative courses of action. Irving Janis, for instance, has observed that an effective decision-making process includes the role of "devil's advocate," one or more persons assigned to argue against the dominant position.[1] This method was used by President John F. Kennedy during the Cuban Missile Crisis.

Disagreement, when unchanneled, often results in nothing more than petty bickering. It is undisciplined and unproductive. Unfortunately, most informal argument is of this type. As a result, the term "argument" often carries a disdainful connotation.

A resolution organizes and directs formal disagreement into productive channels. It constitutes a statement of controversy which clearly defines the basis for argument. A resolution is a simple sentence which clearly defines affirmative and negative ground.

A resolution might be worded as a statement of fact, value, or policy. The use of the policy resolution has traditionally distinguished American forensic debate. A policy resolution requires the affirmative to argue for the adoption of a particular policy (or direction of policy). Contemporary high school and collegiate debaters have argued for and against such policy resolutions as, resolved that: "the federal government should implement a program which guarantees employment opportunities for all United States citizens in the labor force"; "the United States should significantly curtail its arms sales to other countries"; "all United States military intervention into the internal affairs of any foreign nation or nations in the Western Hemisphere should be prohibited"; "the federal government should significantly strengthen the guarantee of consumer product safety required of manufacturers"; "the federal government should establish minimum educational standards for all elementary and secondary schools in the United States"; and so on.

The rapid growth of membership in the Cross-Examination Debate Association at the collegiate level and the emergence of Lincoln-Douglas debate at the high school level have resulted in the increased use of the value resolution in American forensics. The value resolution requires that the affirmative argue for the superiority of a particular value disposition.

We believe that the distinction between policy and value resolutions is largely a matter of emphasis. As we discussed in chapter 2, most policy resolutions involve important value controversies. Policy should not be examined in a vacuum. Instead, a decision maker should establish a hierarchy of values. Whether it is desirable to strengthen consumer product safety depends on the relative standing of two conflicting values: should the federal government strive to maximize citizen safety (protecting citizens from an overzealous profit motive of companies, or, protecting citizens from themselves) or to promote American free enterprise? Whether it is desirable to prohibit United States military intervention in the Western Hemisphere depends on the prioritization of conflicting values: should the United States commit itself to arresting the spread of communism or to promoting other aims, including human rights, the principle of self-determination, or the goal of peace?

Similarly, values cannot be intelligently examined in a vacuum. Making effective choices from among conflicting values requires that we apply them to specific scenarios. Or, in Charles L. Schultze's words: "We cannot simply determine in the abstract our ends or values and the intensity with which we hold them. We discover our objectives and the intensity that we assign to them only in the process of considering particular programs or policies. We articulate ends as we evaluate means."[2] Whether economic growth is more important than environmental quality depends on the specific context. Few decision makers would opt for growth or environmental quality as absolute ends. Instead, they would evaluate the context. For instance, rational decision makers would reject environmental restrictions aimed at controlling a minor pollutant if those restrictions carried a strong probability of sharply curtailing economic growth and unemploying millions of American workers. Conversely, such decision makers would adopt environmental restrictions designed to eradicate a major pollutant which threatened all human life, especially if such restrictions were likely to have only minor economic consequence. In short, policy resolutions involve value controversies, whereas value resolutions entail the application of values to policy scenarios.

Division of Ground

What does it mean to advocate the resolution? It means that the affirmative advocate argues on behalf of a course of action that falls within the confines of the resolution.

The resolution distinguishes affirmative and negative ground. It differentiates those courses of action which are potentially available to the affirmative from those potentially available to the negative. For example, the resolution that "the United States should significantly curtail its arms sales to other countries" requires that an affirmative, utilizing any one of a variety of possible warrants (including generic and/or specific country rationales), argues for a substantial reduction in United States arms sales to other countries. The key demarcating terms in this resolution are "significantly curtail" and "arms sales." The affirmative must choose its position within the confines imposed by the specific wording of the resolution. The negative must select its position outside of the confines of the resolution (i.e., the negative can select from options which fall short of the resolution—which "curtail," but do not "significantly curtail"—or those which go beyond the resolution—which focus on United States foreign military assistance, etc.).

A resolution should provide as much balance as possible between affirmative and negative terrain. Sometimes advocates will be in a position to provide input concerning the wording of a debate resolution. At other times they will not. In either event, advocates must understand the ramifications of the wording of a resolution.

The nature of the resolution determines affirmative and negative terrain; as such, it has a significant impact on advocacy. The division of ground between affirmative and negative is a zero sum affair insofar as an increase in affirmative ground stems directly from a proportional decrease in negative ground.

Broader resolutions expand affirmative ground and reduce negative ground. The scope of the terrain opens up—or closes off—affirmative and negative tactical options. For example, the resolution that "the federal government should adopt a national program of public works for all unemployed citizens," requires an affirmative advocate to support a specific course of action. By contrast, this resolution affords maximum flexibility for the negative advocate since he/she is free to select a position from the broadest possible terrain (i.e., the negative can defend anything with the exception of a national program of public works for all unemployed citizens).

It is possible to increase the affirmative's latitude by broadening the resolution, rewording it to read that "the federal government should fundamentally alter its present economic policies." This alteration in wording allows an affirmative to select from a wide variety of possible positions. An affirmative could argue in support of a balanced federal budget, work requirements for welfare recipients, an increase or decrease in the money supply, wage and price controls, a program of public works for the unemployed, or any number of other positions. As a result, affirmative options are increased and its burdens reduced. By contrast, the negative advocate is constrained by the broader resolution. The negative will find it difficult to advocate any position without trespassing onto affirmative terrain. Thus, negative options are restricted and its burdens enhanced.

Emphasis on *Should*

It is the obligation of an affirmative advocate to demonstrate the desirability of the resolution. Policy resolutions contain the word *should* to focus attention on the nature of the affirmative's burden. The affirmative must demonstrate simply that its policy is desirable—that it *should* be adopted. The affirmative is under no obligation to prove that its policy *would* be adopted.

The resolution that "the United States should adopt a nuclear freeze" illustrates this distinction. The question posed by the resolution is clear. Should the United States adopt a nuclear freeze? In order to answer this question, advocates must debate the relative merits of a nuclear freeze. The word *should* in the resolution is intended to direct attention to the overall desirability of this proposed action. It requires that advocates argue the substantive issues embodied in this resolution. Who would benefit militarily from a nuclear freeze? Would a nuclear freeze reduce or increase the chance of nuclear war? What impact would a freeze have on the proliferation of nuclear weapons? If the United States initiated a unilateral nuclear freeze, would the Soviet Union follow our lead? And so on. The word *should* directs attention to those considerations which determine whether or not the proposed course of action is desirable.

To focus the attention in a debate on what should be done, the debate community has developed the concept of fiat. Fiat is the temporary suspension of relevant political variables in order to foster a more complete comparison of effects. Fiat is the embodiment of the term *should* in a resolution. It is another way of saying that the proper focus of debate is whether or not a particular course of action *should* be adopted. *Fiat redirects our attention from questions of* would *to questions of* should. The affirmative must simply demonstrate that its position—and therefore, the resolution—is comparatively advantageous over the negative's position. If the affirmative were required to prove that its recommended policy *would* be adopted, the focus of the debate would shift from a consideration of the superior policy to the mundane issue of whether existing congressional and executive support could be mustered on behalf of the plan.

Affirmative and negative advocates invoke fiat to direct attention away from questions surrounding implementation to the issues concerning desirability. For example, under the resolution that "the United States should significantly curtail its arms sales to other countries," an affirmative advocates that U.S. arms sales to Israel should be stopped; that Israel, as a result of its settlements on the West Bank, refusal to consider an autonomous Palestinian state, and invasion of Lebanon, is the most significant impediment to a Middle East peace. Furthermore, the affirmative maintains that the United States could utilize its arms sales as an effective lever to move Israel off center on these issues and facilitate a lasting peace in the Middle East. Fiat assumes that if this course of action was desirable, it would be enacted. Otherwise, debate would surely be bogged down on plan implementation questions. Does United States public opinion support a stoppage of arms sales to Israel? Would Congress, which historically has proved to be a staunch supporter of Israel, adopt the measure? Would the President concede to such legislation? Is a government curtailment, which encompasses public as well as private sales, a constitutional action? Such questions, while important practical and political concerns, divert the advocate's attention. Fiat assumes that if a particular action is desirable, then it ought to be initiated.

BASIC AFFIRMATIVE BURDENS

The basic burdens of affirmative advocacy for a policy resolution are grounded in the essential features of the various argumentation paradigms (we discussed paradigms in chapters 1 and 2). The affirmative's burdens are essentially the same, regardless of which paradigm is employed. However, there are subtle differences in the composition of the basic burdens, and in the role that basic burdens play in decision making.

The basic affirmative burdens include:

1. TOPICALITY. Does the proposed policy fully meet the jurisdictional requirements imposed by the resolution?

2. SIGNIFICANCE. What potential benefits (problem alleviated or advantage gained) would stem from the adoption of the proposed policy?

3. INHERENCY. What features of the present system contribute to the problem? Can present system failings be remedied short of systemic change?

4. SOLVENCY. Will the proposed policy secure the potential benefits (solve the problem or gain the advantage)?

5. DESIRABILITY. Is the proposed policy generally desirable? Will it produce harmful side effects? Do these side effects offset affirmative significance?

The affirmative advocate will want to construct and defend its position so as to meet each of these basic burdens. In this way the affirmative can advocate a case which meets the requirements of any and all of the argumentative paradigms depicted in chapters 1 and 2.

Topicality

Topicality poses a jurisdictional question. It seeks to determine whether the affirmative advocate has stayed within appropriate bounds. Or, more specifically, does the affirmative position fully meet the jurisdictional requirements imposed by the resolution? If not, the affirmative position should be rejected.

Topicality's importance stems from the essential functions which the resolution performs. First, it provides the topic for discussion. Debate cannot take place without a topic, framing the nature of the dispute. Indeed, advance notice of the topic is a prerequisite to substantive debate. Without it, the advocates would have no idea how to go about research and preparation, and the chances for an intelligent exchange would be limited. A second related function of the resolution is to divide the ground between the advocates. Both functions are crucial. An agreement on topic and on the demarcation of terrain between the advocates—which presuppose an agreement on critical terms—is a prerequisite to intelligent argument. Topicality, because it serves these vital functions in debate, is an *a priori* issue.

Topicality's *a priori* nature can be illustrated by a judicial analogy. In judicial decision making, the question of jurisdiction (a procedural issue) is usually considered independently from the question of case merit (a substantive issue). The same is true in debate. Because the resolution restricts jurisdiction, the issue of topicality must be resolved before substantive issues can be considered.

The affirmative has the right to define terms. This does not mean that the affirmative is free to adopt Humpty Dumpty's dubious linguistic approach, as when he told Alice, "When I use a word, it means just what I choose it to mean—neither more nor less." The negative retains the right to challenge affirmative definitions.

The affirmative's right to define terms is defended on two grounds—the first, pragmatic; the second, analogical. The pragmatic basis appears reasonable. The affirmative is charged with the responsibility of defending the resolution; it must present an interpretation of the resolution in the first constructive speech. Therefore, the affirmative ought to be able to define the terms as part of the justification for its interpretation. The affirmative's right to define the terms of the resolution is also based on a legislative process analogy. According to this analogy, authors of a bill have the initial right to define the critical terms of the legislation so as to clarify its intent; thus, the affirmative advocates should have the initial right to define the important terms of the resolution.

In order to ascertain whether an affirmative is topical one must look to the plan and not to the advantages. The affirmative's plan is the sole repository of topicality. This means that while the course of action advocated by the affirmative must fall within the confines of the resolution, the affirmative has complete latitude to focus on any of the advantages which stem from that course of action—whether or not they *appear* to be relevant to the content thrust of the resolution. The resolution calls for action; not for the results of action. Hence, to fulfill the resolution, some action must be initiated, and this action is embodied in the plan. Any affirmative advantage, which results from the adoption of a topical plan plank, can be advanced as a potential benefit of the resolution.

Significance

Significance is the measure of the potential benefits (problem to be overcome or advantage to be gained) which would stem from the adoption of the affirmative proposal. As we have seen, a policy resolution embodies a mandate for change. The first question which the affirmative must address in support of any resolution is, why change? This is a fundamental affirmative requirement. It constitutes the essence of any rationale in favor of change. As a result, significance is an undisputed affirmative burden, irrespective of paradigmatic considerations.

How much significance is necessary to justify change? This question must be answered in the context of a given debate. Generally, the affirmative's significance requirement varies in direct proportion to the risks associated with the proposed change. If your best friend argues that you style your hair a different way, you may be willing to adopt his or her suggestion on the basis of scant support for a relatively insignificant benefit (i.e., perhaps your friend argued that the proposed hair style makes you look more mature). By contrast, if your friend argues that you quit school and invest your modest savings in a joint business venture, you would require strong support on behalf of significant benefits. The same rule of thumb applies in more formal decision-making scenarios.

In order to demonstrate significance, an advocate must either indicate that a need or problem exists which is important enough to require action, and/or that one or more advantages can be accrued through change. For example, under the resolution that "the federal government should establish minimum educational standards for all elementary and secondary schools," the affirmative might argue for the adoption of interdistrict busing of elementary and secondary school students. In this instance the affirmative could establish significance by (1) indicating that a need, or problem exists (i.e., the educational attainment of minority schoolchildren is deficient); (2) demonstrating that interdistrict busing is advantageous in comparison with the present system's approach of various combinations of inaction, magnet schools, and intradistrict busing (i.e., interdistrict busing maximizes school integration; and that minority students optimize school achievement in integrated educational settings); or (3) proving that a need, or problem, exists (i.e., the educational attainment of minority schoolchildren is deficient) and in addition that interdistrict busing is superior to the present system's approach (i.e., promotes racial harmony via shifting the burden of integration from a prejudiced and insecure population of lower and lower-middle class whites to a more tolerant and secure group of middle and upper-middle class whites).

The affirmative advocate must do two things to establish significance. First, the affirmative must demonstrate that the value it seeks to promote is important. As we previously noted, policy resolutions involve important value controversies. Affirmative benefits stem from the accelerated promotion of one or more basic values. The affirmative advocate must indicate that the value it seeks to promote is important, and/or is more important than competing values. The interdistrict busing example above is illustrative. In this instance, an affirmative advocate must demonstrate the importance of equal educational opportunity in order to establish significance. In addition, the affirmative may have to prove that equal educational opportunity is a more important value than a variety of competing values, including local control (the value that underpins the neighborhood school), cultural homogeneity (the value that supports homogeneous residential patterns and makes possible *de facto* segregation), and others. If equal educational opportunity is unimportant, or is less important than competing values, then the affirmative cannot establish significance.

Second, the affirmative must provide a quantitative or qualitative measure of significance. A value might be important, but that alone is not sufficient. The affirmative must demonstrate that the value manifests tangible impact. For example, there must be a means to translate equal educational opportunity into definitive terms. One way is to provide actual data on comparative educational attainment of white and non-white students. The affirmative could cite relative test scores, dropout rates, the proportion of students who continue their educations beyond high school, etc., in order to show what might be gained from the proposed change. The affirmative must both justify and measure the value that it seeks to promote in order to establish significance.

Inherency and Solvency

Policy systems analysis is the best tool for clarifying the affirmative's inherency and solvency burdens. Inherency addresses present system or non-resolutional solutions to the problem; solvency deals with affirmative solutions.

Inherency. Inherency constitutes a search for a sometimes elusive causality. If the problem is caused by the present system, then an affirmative plan which replaces that system with an alternative may be able to solve the problem by eliminating its cause.[3] Inherency attempts to answer the question, *why* is one system more likely than another to maximize the desired goal? What makes one system more efficacious than another?[4]

The affirmative should strive to identify those features of the present system that contribute to the problem. Inherency attempts to answer the causal question. This burden represents a search for blame. If the present system causes or contributes to the problem, then a change in the present system may ameliorate the problem. If not, there is no reason to alter the present system.

A recent policy controversy illustrates inherency's causal function. During the period of 1979 to 1981 the United States suffered from double-digit inflation. People were concerned about the problem, which soon developed into the most salient national issue, according to public opinion polls. A clear consensus developed that inflation was a significant problem. The question of inherency, however was less clear. Interest soon surged in support of a constitutional amendment to require a balanced federal budget. But did federal deficits cause the problem? If deficits were responsible for the 1979–81 inflation spiral, then a constitutional amendment which eliminated annual federal deficits might have been the appropriate solution to inflation. The crucial question was whether or not the annual federal deficits were to blame. If they were not, then the adoption of a constitutional amendment, while an interesting symbolic gesture, would have had little impact on the rate of inflation. The question of inherency is thus important because it uniquely calls attention to the question of blame.

To establish inherency the affirmative advocate must demonstrate that the *attitudes* and *structures* that characterize the present system cause or contribute to the problem. Attitudes embody the philosophy or perspective of the present system.[5] They are sometimes difficult to discern because the present system often works at cross-purposes, committing its energies and resources in the pursuit of diverse, often conflicting objectives.[6] For example, the present system provides price supports to tobacco farmers and invests resources to campaign against cigarette smoking; it negotiates agreements which set automobile tariffs at levels which benefit foreign producers and enacts a bail-out of the tottering Chrysler Corporation; it is committed legislatively to the often conflicting goals of full employment and price stability (the economists' Phillips Curve is based on the assumption that full employment and price stability represent competing alternatives); it promotes free enterprise and passes legislation which regulates business activities.

How does one discover the true colors of the present system? It is not an easy task. However, patterns are discernible. The existence of certain programs and the absence of others often provide a pattern. Objectives spelled out in the preamble of various legislative initiatives can provide valuable clues. Individual components of the present system cannot be intelligently examined in a vacuum. Search first for the broader philosophical perspective that characterizes the totality of the present system; then view the specific programs or structures. This two-pronged approach to inherency will prove to be the most productive.

Solvency.   The affirmative's thorough examination of the underlying causes of the problem simultaneously results in a strong inherency and solvency position. If the problem has been correctly diagnosed, and particular features of the present system are identified as causal or blameworthy, then the affirmative has taken a first strong step toward solvency. While proper inherency analysis doesn't guarantee solvency (i.e., one or more features of the present system may be correctly identified as being at fault, but the affirmative's proposed solution may prove to be no better), it is an important first step. Indeed, it is a prerequisite to solvency. In the inflation example above, if federal government deficits were incorrectly identified as the underlying cause of inflation, then there are two possible ramifications. There is no assurance that the problem is ingrained in existing structures. Thus, inflation may subside *even without* the action proposed by the affirmative. On the other hand, there is uncertainty whether the affirmative's proposal, a constitutional amendment to require a balanced federal budget, would affect the inflation problem. In short, both the issues of permanence and solvency remain in doubt.

Desirability

The final affirmative burden is desirability. The affirmative advocate must demonstrate that benefits outweigh costs—that net case significance more than offsets net disadvantage impact. We have already discussed the elements involved in net case significance. Net disadvantage impact concerns the costs or consequences of the adoption of the affirmative's proposal. Despite all affirmative efforts to establish significance, the affirmative must also adequately refute the disadvantages or consequences associated with the adoption of its proposed course of action. In policy debate this burden is characterized by the equation: net benefits are greater or less than net costs.[7] If an affirmative proposal would yield greater disadvantages than advantages— if the right side of the policy equation outweighed the left side—then that proposal should be rejected outright. Disadvantages are discussed in greater detail in chapters 10, 11, and 12.

CASE SELECTION CRITERIA

In some ways it is easier to argue in support of something than against something. The advocate starts on his or her terrain on the affirmative. Cases can be chosen, research accomplished, and tactical options selected which optimize the affirmative's position.

The first step in optimizing affirmative advocacy is to select the strongest possible affirmative position. As we indicated previously, affirmative terrain consists of all possible case options. An affirmative advocate must exercise an intelligent choice among the case possibilities that lie within affirmative terrain. This section will provide case selection criteria, consisting of four broad elements, to facilitate an effective affirmative case choice.

Validity

The first of the criteria to be used in case selection is validity. An affirmative advocate should carefully examine a potential position for its validity. This enhances the likelihood that the position will be able to stand up to negative scrutiny. In addition, advocates usually find it much easier to defend a position in which they believe.

There are two important dimensions of validity which should be used in evaluating a case for possible use. Initially, *the position should be generally regarded as true. If it isn't, the case variant has limited potential,* because negative advocates will be able to uncover the position's flaws as they conduct additional research. Conversely, if it is regarded as true, then additional research will benefit the affirmative. Affirmative advocates should select a position which carries the potential for maturation. Such a position will grow stronger over time, able to withstand the increasing breadth and depth of negative scrutiny. This is essential for success on the affirmative.

This leads directly to the second dimension of validity: adequacy (measured in terms of breadth and depth) of the available evidence to support the affirmative position. Some affirmatives are tempted to ground their cases on one or two key sources, even though their conclusions run against the grain of the dominant research in an area. These positions could be valid, but cannot be verified via a consensus of the available evidence. There are a myriad of examples of this problem in forensic debate. We will offer just one. On a recent high school resolution "that the federal government should initiate and enforce safety guarantees on consumer goods," some affirmatives advocated that the federal government require all cigarettes manufactured in this country to be self-extinguishing, thus diminishing the hazard of fires which start from careless smoking. The limited research in support of the self-extinguishing cigarette posed two problems for affirmatives. First, it was difficult to sustain an intensive research effort. The more the advocates investigated the issues surrounding self-extinguishing cigarettes, the more the evidenciary advantage shifted to the negative. Second, any affirmative advocating self-extinguishing cigarettes proved to be especially vulnerable to the negative position to delay action until further study could be conducted (the study counterplan position will be considered in more detail in chapter 10). This negative position maintains that it would be premature to act now. Instead, we should require a systematic and rigorous investigation to determine if action is warranted. Against an affirmative position, which is grounded in one or two sources, this appears to be a wise alternative.

Ease of Meeting Affirmative Burdens

The second criterion for affirmative case selection involves the ease of meeting basic affirmative burdens. Since the affirmative advocate's success depends on his or her ability to sustain argumentation on topicality, significance, inherency, solvency, and desirability, it makes sense to evaluate case prospects in terms of these basic burdens.

An affirmative position should be topical. The advocate will not want to risk the targeted receiver's rejection of the affirmative position on jurisdictional grounds, yet this is a common temptation in forensic debate. We advise that the advocate exercise good judgment in case selection. Although it may be possible for well-researched affirmatives to find evidence to prove that almost any position is topical, this approach will not suffice with all critics. Some judges view topicality in more intuitive terms. Select an affirmative position which all critics can accept. There is simply no good reason to risk the receiver's wrath on the basis of questionable topicality. Select an affirmative case which is intuitively *and* argumentatively topical.

An affirmative position should clearly meet the burdens of inherency and solvency. The affirmative advocate would be advised to take a strong position in both areas. Ensure, for instance, that the affirmative position can adapt to the full spectrum of inherency standards. The affirmative must be able to demonstrate inherency— whether the judge believes that the very presence of the problem in question is sufficient proof of the present system's culpability, or whether the critic thinks that an affirmative must indict all relevant present system structures germane to the problem. Similarly the affirmative must be prepared to prove solvency unequivocally. The analysis of the solvency claim should be supported by a variety of expert sources, individuals who are well respected in their areas of expertise. In addition, affirmative solvency should be supported by methodologically sound study evidence and empirical examples. For instance, if an affirmative argues in support of a national mass media campaign to reduce the incidence of cigarette smoking, the advocate should attempt to bolster his or her solvency claim with studies indicating that mass media campaigns can change people's attitudes and behavior, and with specific examples where mass media campaigns reduced the incidence of cigarette smoking (i.e., the Stanford Heart Disease Prevention Program Three Community Study). Both steps are important in optimizing the affirmative position, as we will explain in chapter 11.

Net Comparative Advantage

To meet the third case selection criterion, simply choose an affirmative position with a substantial net comparative benefit. This brings into play the interrelationship between the affirmative burdens of significance and desirability. Affirmative advocates should carefully examine the potential benefits and costs of a prospective position. An optimal case possibility yields the highest ratio of significance to disadvantages. This is the heart of policy systems analysis.

Reasonableness

The fourth criterion to be used in case selection is reasonableness. Affirmative advocates should select a position which targeted receivers (those persons who will pass judgment on the affirmative) will find reasonable. This increases the probability that those receivers who constitute the *immediate and secondary* target audience will eventually accept the advocate's position. This task often isn't as easy as it appears. As a result of an ever-expansive mass media coverage, it has become increasingly difficult for political advocates to select a case which is appropriate for both the immediate and secondary receivers.

It is short-sighted to select an affirmative position based on unrealistic expectations about the audience. Such a miscalculation is a common error, especially on the part of forensic advocates, who sometimes choose a case based on the standards of the most liberal elements in the critic population. Such case selection is misguided, since forensic advocates must defend their affirmative cases before a broad spectrum of critics. A position which a segment of critics would find unreasonable is more of a liability than an asset.

ORGANIZATIONAL OPTIONS

It is the affirmative's responsibility to initiate clash in a debate. This is the function of the first affirmative constructive speech which offers a rationale for change grounded in the particulars of the affirmative's case. The initial affirmative presentation should be scripted in advance of an actual debate. Since the affirmative must initiate clash, it can construct its first speech in advance of a debate, taking care to select each analytical, evidenciary, and rhetorical component so as to generate the optimal impact on the receiver.

How should an affirmative organize those elements in the initial speech? This section will examine organizational strategies for the first affirmative constructive, describing and evaluating three distinct packaging options.

Problem-solution, comparative advantage, and goal and criteria are common but quite distinct packaging options for the first affirmative constructive speech. We will examine each option, using specific case variants to illustrate the various organizational alternatives. The advocate should select the option that is best suited for his or her specific case.

**FIGURE 9-1   PROBLEM-SOLUTION OR NEED APPROACH
SINGLE CONTENTION**

INTRODUCTION

Affirmative Plan

CONTENTION: U.S. Military Intervention in Latin America Increases the Chances of Superpower War

- A. U.S. Is Militaristic in Latin America
    1. Militarism Is the Cornerstone of U.S. Policy toward Latin America
        a. This Is the Legacy of the Monroe Doctrine
        b. The Reagan Administration Supports This
    2. Current U.S. Involvement in Latin America
        a. Assistance & Advisers in El Salvador
        b. Covert Operations Against Nicaragua
        c. Implied Threats Against Cuba
- B. U.S. Involvement Increases the Chance of War
    1. Local Wars Can Escalate to Regional Wars
    2. Cuba and the USSR Are Likely to Respond
    3. Nuclear Confrontation Is Possible
- C. Nonintervention Is a Superior Policy
    1. U.S. Can Protect Interests in Latin America via Alternative Means
    2. Nonintervention Will Be Reciprocated
        a. By Cuba
        b. By the USSR
    3. Nonintervention Reduces the Chance of War

Problem-Solution Approach

Problem-solution, or need case, remains the most common organizational approach in standard speeches of advocacy. It was the most popular organizational package for the first affirmative constructive speech in forensic advocacy until the late 1960s, when the comparative advantage option surpassed it.

As the name implies, this option calls for the complete delineation of the problem, or need, prior to a consideration of the solution. The problem or need is presented in the form of contentions.

A single contention might embody the entire need, as illustrated in the outline of an affirmative case in support of the resolution that "All United States military intervention into the internal affairs of any foreign nation or nations in the Western Hemisphere should be prohibited," in Figure 9-1. In this instance, the affirmative argued that U.S. military intervention in Latin America is extensive. The U.S. provides overt assistance, including military sales and aid in addition to advisers, to the unpopular Samoza government in El Salvador; employs covert methods against the Sandinista government in Nicaragua; and has increased the level of belligerence directed at Castro's Cuba. Such intervention is counterproductive. U.S. activities in Central America have spurred an escalation of hostilities in the area and threaten to provoke a major confrontation with Cuba. If that happens, the U.S.S.R. will be inevitably drawn into a conflict with the United States. The affirmative further maintained that the only way to avert this "drift into war" scenario is for the United States to initiate a pledge of non-intervention into the internal affairs of any nation or nations in the Western Hemisphere. In addition, the affirmative claimed that such a pledge would reduce Cuban adventurism and precipitate a reduction in tensions with the Soviet Union, which might serve as a catalyst to American and Soviet disarmament negotiations. Careful examination of Figure 9–1 reveals that a single contention contains the affirmative's significance, inherency, and solvency. In this example, the plan was presented early in the first affirmative constructive speech because the single contention included the affirmative's solvency. This is one of only two hard and fast rules with regard to the plan's placement in a debate. The other is the obvious need to present the totality of the affirmative's position, including the plan, in the constructive (as opposed to the rebuttal) speeches.

The affirmative may wish to employ multiple contentions to develop its need. This approach allows the advocate to place distinct case components within separate contentions. For instance, harm, inherency, and solvency might be developed as separate contentions. When the advocate uses multiple contentions he or she should place the affirmative plan after the significance and inherency contentions but prior to the solvency contention.

Multiple contentions contribute to clarity by providing distinctive packaging for each of the affirmative case elements. But on the other hand, in focusing on the individual components of the case, multiple contentions can divert attention from the interrelationships which characterize the whole affirmative position. In short, emphasis on the parts can serve to obscure the whole. Figure 9–2 on page 162 depicts the same affirmative case elements, but organized so as to illustrate the use of multiple contentions.

The advantage of the problem-solution approach lies in its simplicity. It is a logical mode of assembling ideas, consistent with the receiver's expectations that discussion of the problem should precede consideration of solutions. As such, this approach facilitates maximum clarity.

Comparative Advantage Approach

The comparative advantage approach draws its roots from Aristotle. In his *Rhetoric,* Aristotle noted that when a consensus exists as to ends (in any scenario in which debate prevails as an appropriate tool for decision-making, there is more apt to be agreement than disagreement regarding ends), advocates should focus their attention on the most "expedient" means of attaining them.[8] Englishman David Ricardo coined the phrase "comparatively advantageous" when in 1817 he and Adam Smith advocated that a nation's economic interests were better served via specialized production in those areas of maximum efficiency than by the domestic production of all commodities for the purpose of maintaining economic self-sufficiency. This notion was dubbed the "Law of Comparative Advantage."[9]

The comparative advantage approach focuses on the relative desirability of the affirmative's plan. The affirmative must continue to meet the same basic burdens (i.e., its topical change must be significant, inherent, solvent, and desirable), but this mode

---

FIGURE 9–2   PROBLEM-SOLUTION OR NEED APPROACH
MULTIPLE CONTENTIONS

INTRODUCTION
CONTENTION 1: U.S. Policy in Latin America Is Militaristic
    A. Militarism Is the Cornerstone of U.S. Policy toward Latin America
        1. This Is the Legacy of the Monroe Doctrine
        2. The Reagan Administration Supports This
    B. Current U.S. Involvement in Latin America
        1. Assistance & Advisers in El Salvador
        2. Covert Operations Against Nicaragua
        3. Implied Threats Against Cuba
CONTENTION 2: U.S. Involvement in Latin America Increases the Chance of War
    A. Local Wars Can Escalate to Regional Wars
    B. Cuba and the USSR Are Likely to Respond
    C. Nuclear Confrontation Is Possible
Affirmative Plan
CONTENTION 3: Nonintervention Is a Superior Policy
    A. U.S. Can Protect Its Interests in Latin America via Alternative Means
    B. Nonintervention Will Be Reciprocated
        1. By Cuba
        2. By the USSR
    C. Nonintervention Reduces the Chance of War

---

of packaging shifts attention from the problem to the solution. An affirmative, using this approach, claims that its proposal is superior to alternatives, and therefore should be adopted.

Any affirmative case can utilize this packaging mode. It differs from the problem-solution or need approach simply in emphasis. Figure 9–3, employing the same case variant as characterized the previous examples, illustrates the comparative advantage organizational option.

The comparative advantage organizational approach has surged in popularity in forensic advocacy. Its main attraction is that it focuses attention on the whole affirmative position, thus facilitating the comparison between policy alternatives.

Goal and Criteria Approach

A goal and criteria approach focuses on the value which the affirmative seeks to optimize. As we observed previously in this chapter, most policy resolutions involve important value controversies. The need or comparative advantage approach contains an implicit alteration of values. The goal and criteria cases differ from the other approaches only in that they direct attention to the reprioritization of values at the outset.

An affirmative position on the resolution that "the federal government should

FIGURE 9-3   COMPARATIVE ADVANTAGE APPROACH

INTRODUCTION

Affirmative Plan

ADVANTAGE: NONINTERVENTION REDUCES THE CHANCE OF WAR

A. U.S. Policy in Latin America Is Militaristic
1. Militarism Is the Cornerstone of U.S. Policy toward Latin America
   a. This Is the Legacy of the Monroe Doctrine
   b. The Reagan Administration Supports This
2. Current U.S. Involvement in Latin America
   a. Assistance & Advisers in El Salvador
   b. Covert Operations Against Nicaragua
   c. Implicit Threats Against Cuba
B. U.S. Involvement Increases the Chance of War
1. Local Wars Escalate to Regional Wars
2. Cuba and the USSR Are Likely to Respond
3. Nuclear Confrontation Is Possible
C. Nonintervention Is a Superior Policy
1. U.S. Can Protect Interests in Latin America via Alternative Means
2. Nonintervention Will Be Reciprocated
   a. By Cuba
   b. By the USSR
3. Nonintervention Reduces the Chance of War

establish a comprehensive program to significantly increase the energy independence of the United States," depicts the goal approach. This affirmative argued that the United States must make a strong commitment to the goal of energy independence. It maintained that energy self-sufficiency is an important objective. On the one hand, it holds the key to maximum economic growth and full employment. In addition, it is the best safeguard of world peace, since superpower competition for Middle East oil is one of the most probable scenarios for conflict. This goal approach is shown in Figure 9–4.

Some view the criteria and goal cases as functional equivalents.[10] We maintain that there is a subtle distinction between the two approaches. A goal case calls attention to the value that the affirmative seeks to enhance, whereas the criteria approach places the emphasis on the standards that ought to be utilized en route to a particular goal. For example, the goal of the federal government in taxing citizens and corporations is to raise the revenues that are needed to fund the government's activities. The standard which should be used to measure the success of the Internal Revenue Service in achieving this goal is its efficacy in collection. However, some argue that an important criterion in revenue collection is fairness or equity. The critical emphasis should not be whether the IRS is able to collect on taxes due, but whether the taxing scheme functions in an equitable manner, collecting taxes according to ability to pay. This position shifts the emphasis used to evaluate the tax system. If, for instance, large corporations or wealthy individuals are able to exploit "loopholes" in the tax laws to

---

FIGURE 9-4   GOAL APPROACH

INTRODUCTION

Affirmative Plan

GOAL: It Is Desirable for the U.S. to Be Independent from Foreign Energy Producers
  A. Energy Independence Is Important
     1. America Is Presently Dependent
     2. U.S. Energy Dependence Is Harmful
        a. GNP and Unemployment
        b. Most Likely Scenario for U.S./U.S.S.R. Confrontation
  B. Present System Policies Fail to Maximize U.S. Independence from Foreign Energy Producers
     1. U.S. Is Committed to Oil
     2. U.S. Oil Supplies Limited
     3. Alternatives Are Thwarted
  C. Affirmative Maximizes the Goal of U.S. Independence from Foreign Energy Producers

---

avoid their fair share of taxes, then the tax system has failed to maximize this criterion. Thus, the criteria approach would call attention to the federal government's taxing capacity more in terms of equity in collection; the goal approach would emphasize its success in collection. Of course, the goal and criteria approaches could be employed in tandem, the former emphasizing a particular goal and the latter concentrating on the method of attaining that goal.

A Matter of Emphasis

The problem-solution, comparative advantage, and goal and criteria approaches are more similar than different. The differences between them are largely cosmetic (i.e., a matter of emphasis in packaging). An affirmative position must contain essentially the same elements, regardless of packaging. These elements include: significance (the extensiveness and severity of the problem), inherency, and solvency. In addition, the affirmative change must be topical and affirmative benefits must outweigh costs, although these elements are not normally addressed in the first affirmative constructive speech. The point of departure between approaches is based on: (1) the order in which the elements are presented (a function of emphasis), and (2) a semantic difference (a function of approach). We have illustrated the functional similarity of the problem-solution and the comparative advantage organizational approaches in Figure 9-5 and Figure 9-6. Note that each approach utilizes the same basic elements. However, these elements are packaged differently.

   As we observed previously, most affirmative positions involve important value controversies. This is true regardless of the organizational approach which is chosen to package the affirmative's case. Whether the affirmative seeks a fundamental or minor

---

FIGURE 9–5   PROBLEM-SOLUTION APPROACH

Contention
    The Problem
        Extensiveness
        Severity
    Inherency
Plan
Solvency or Plan-Meet-Need

---

value reprioritization in the process of advocating that this nation should "strengthen the guarantee of consumer product safety," "regulate mass media communication," "guarantee employment opportunities for all United States citizens in the labor force," "establish minimum educational standards for all elementary and secondary schools," etc., the need, comparative advantage, or goal and criteria approaches are all quite similar. The differences between them are more cosmetic than substantive. These approaches simply constitute different modes of presenting an affirmative position.

THE INITIAL AFFIRMATIVE POSITION

A strong initial affirmative position is the foundation for effective affirmative advocacy. The affirmative advocate can either capitalize on the strengths of the initial constructive presentation or pay the price for omissions or weaknesses in all subsequent speeches in the course of a debate.

Some debaters mistakenly assume that the first affirmative constructive is the least important speech in a debate, since it precedes the initiation of clash by the negative. This is a mistaken impression. The initial affirmative speech determines the

---

FIGURE 9–6   COMPARATIVE ADVANTAGE APPROACH

Goal (stated or implied)
Plan
Advantage
    Significance
        Extensiveness
        Severity
    Inherency or Uniqueness
    Solvency or Plan-Meet-Advantage

parameters for all subsequent clash. As a result, it may be the most important speech in a debate, because it provides the argumentative anchors that form the basis for all subsequent refutation. It also generates first impressions, which are important in all communicative settings.

In this section we will examine the crucial elements which are involved in the building of a strong initial affirmative position, including: definition of the terms of the resolution, case construction, case wording, and plan construction.

Defining Terms

As we noted previously in this chapter, the affirmative has the right to define the terms of the resolution. This is an important responsibility. It serves to clarify the resolution, thus facilitating a clear demarcation of affirmative and negative ground.

The demarcation or division of terrain is critical, since it controls an advocate's argumentative options. For example, the resolution "that the federal government should significantly strengthen the regulation of mass media communication in the United States," is on its face ambiguous with regard to the phrase, "mass media communication." Does "mass media communication" simply constitute the print and electronic media? Mass media communication authorities might disagree. They would observe that mass media communication does not function in isolation. Instead, it usually works in conjunction with interpersonal communication. Indeed, all effective mass media communication campaigns feature both mass media and interpersonal elements. Thus, a more restrictive interpretation of "mass media communication" would severely hamper an affirmative on the "regulation of mass media communication" resolution. For instance, if the affirmative sought to enlist the mass media in the pursuit of one or more public health objectives (to improve nutrition or prenatal care, to reduce the incidence of alcoholism, smoking, or drug use, or to stress the importance of regular exercise), it must offer and defend a more expansive interpretation of "mass media communication," which includes mass media and interpersonal—otherwise the affirmative's solvency prospects are limited. Similarly, if "mass media communication" includes only the print and electronic media, then negative counterplan possibilities (incorporating an interpersonal communication strategy) are bolstered.

An affirmative advocate should exercise his or her right to define the terms of the resolution in an effort to control the argumentative terrain. This should be done in the first affirmative speech. One way of accomplishing this is to use specific definitions of critical terms. Where are such definitions found? An obvious starting point is the dictionary; then encyclopedias, which contain more substantive definitions. The *International Encyclopedia of the Social Sciences* is extremely useful. This source, and other similar publications, use articles by authors in the field to define terms. In addition, the advocate may look for legal definitions. Since the function of topicality bears a resemblance to the judicial practice of interpreting statutes, court definitions may prove most appropriate. Legal definitions may be found in *Black's Law Dictionary, Words and Phrases, Corpus Juris Secundum,* and by scrutinizing individual court cases.

The types of definitions noted above are general in nature; they do not consider the field or context in which they are used. To find definitions which are specific to the subject under consideration, one may look for specialized or "topic-specific" dictionaries. They are extremely useful, though not available on every topic. Examples include the *Dictionary of Business and Scientific Terms,* the *Dictionary of American Government,* and the *Thesaurus of ERIC Descriptors.* Finally, and most important, substantive definitions are found in general research. These are perhaps the best definitions. They often are field-specific and include clarification. For example, in debating the resolution "that the United States should establish uniform rules governing the procedure of all criminal courts in the nation," some advocates turned to the *Georgetown Law Journal's* definition of "criminal procedure." The *Georgetown Law Journal* provides an annual comprehensive review of all published criminal procedure divisions. This project classifies all specific procedural issues under generic headings, including "investigation and police practices," "preliminary proceedings," "trial," "sentencing, parole, and probation," "review proceedings," and "prisoners' rights." This constitutes an excellent field-specific interpretation of the phrase "criminal procedure."

Although we recommend specific, well-researched definitions, there are two additional approaches to the task of defining terms. Both of these approaches rely on the affirmative's plan to interpret the resolution. First, the affirmative can offer its proposed policy as one of many examples of the resolution. The affirmative advocate thus suspends consideration of individual terms until the negative challenges his or her general interpretation. Second, the advocate can utilize the affirmative plan as an operational definition of the resolution—the affirmative's plan *is* the resolution. An affirmative advocate should avoid this approach. Since one affirmative plan normally constitutes only a portion of affirmative terrain, an operational definition serves to constrict affirmative and enlarge negative terrain.

Case Construction

Obviously the initial affirmative presentation must meet all of the basic burdens described previously in this chapter. The affirmative must demonstrate significance, inherency, and solvency; show that the affirmative position is generally desirable (i.e., that benefits exceed costs); and be prepared to prove that the net desirability of the affirmative position stems from topical plan provisions.

These basic burdens are the strategic focus of affirmative advocacy. Significance, inherency, and solvency must be addressed in the first affirmative constructive speech. Each of these basic burdens may be delineated in components within a single contention, or in separate contentions (see Figures 9–1, 9–2, and 9–3). Although the affirmative should make sure that its net desirability stems from topical plan provisions, topicality is normally not raised as an issue by the affirmative in the initial speech. The thrust of the initial affirmative position establishes one component of net desirability—benefits. The other component—costs—is usually initiated by the negative.

Solvency warrants special emphasis at this time. *Solvency may be the most critical component of the first constructive speech.* The affirmative advocate must provide sound analysis as well as strong evidenciary backing in support of the position's solvency. Even in the face of a compelling need, if the proposed course won't solve the problem, then there is no justification to act. A strong solvency position serves the affirmative advocate in another fashion. A solid initial solvency position offers tremendous potential for exploitation in subsequent affirmative speeches, since the first affirmative constructive solvency evidence can be used to preempt negative plan-meet-need arguments and to lay the foundation for turnarounds against negative disadvantages. We will discuss these strategies in some detail in chapter 11.

An affirmative, advocating a curtailment of U.S. arms sales to Indonesia on the topic that "the United States should significantly curtail its arms sales to other countries," illustrates the potential of a strong initial solvency position. The sample flow in Figures 6–10 and 6–11 depicts this scenario. The affirmative argued that the U.S. should stop arms sales to Indonesia in an effort to halt the latter's subjugation of East Timor. Among the strongest negative arguments against this position are: first, that curtailing U.S. arms sales to Indonesia will fail to alter Indonesian policy, and second, that this action would precipitate a backlash against the United States, possibly aggravating the situation in East Timor and generally hurting U.S. strategic objectives in Asia. Yet the initial affirmative speech indicated that a curtailment would work; that Indonesia would be unable to continue the campaign in East Timor without U.S. arms (Sidell in the *Journal of Contemporary Asia,* November 1981; *Nation,* February 2, 1981; Anderson in House Hearings, February 7, 1980; and Harkin in the *Progressive,* December 1980), and therefore that U.S. arms can exert substantial leverage to alter Indonesian policy toward East Timor (Chomsky and Herman in their 1979 book and the *Christian Science Monitor,* January 30, 1981). Most negatives will be unable to directly contest the analysis and evidence which underpin the solvency position. Yet, unless they do, this analysis and evidence can be utilized in subsequent affirmative speeches to refute the aforementioned negative positions.

The affirmative advocate must do two things to optimize the initial solvency position. First, the affirmative advocate must utilize strong analysis and evidence in the first constructive speech to provide a sound analytical and evidenciary grounding for the solvency position. Ideally the supporting evidence should include the testimony of experts who explain why the proposed course of action would work, studies which support the affirmative's claim, and empirical verification.

The affirmative advocate must then ensure that the plan both alleviates the harms and overcomes the inherencies. Sometimes affirmative advocates are overzealous in establishing significance, resulting in the inability of the plan to eradicate the problem. More often, however, affirmatives fail to overcome their own inherency analysis, thus paving the way for a strong negative plan-meet-need argument.

In overcoming traditional structural inherency, the affirmative must either alter existing structures or replace them in order to overcome the barrier to solvency. For example, on the topic "that the federal government should strengthen the regulation of mass media communication in the United States," some affirmatives argued that strong federal action is needed now to ensure that the impending boom in cable television is controlled in the public's interest. These affirmative advocates maintained that on the one hand, existing regulation via the Federal Communication Commission and the Federal Trade Commission ensured the primacy of profit over public interest, and furthermore, that the commercial exploitation of cable television is assured in the absence of federal legislation providing for specific government regulation. Affirmative plans overcame these barriers by providing for an independent federal control over cable television. Federal regulation was proposed to reinstitute the common carrier obligation struck down in the court's ruling in *FCC* v. *Midwest Video* in 1979, including the requirement that cable operators provide community access channels to be owned and operated by municipalities, and turn over a percentage of their profit to provide complete cost coverage on access channels; prohibit all future cross-ownership of cable and other media; and limit the size of cable companies. Since the inherencies were based on both the absence of a public interest mandate for cable as well as the weakness of existing regulation, grounded as it is in a strong commercial orientation, the plan offered a specific mandate for both the provision and funding of access channels.

Overcoming attitudinal inherency is more intricate. Attitudinal inherency is based on an unwillingness on the part of key policy makers or the general public to support the course of action advocated by the affirmative. Attitudinal inherency is usually used in conjunction with structural indictments. Indeed, many theorists maintain, and we concur, that pure structural inherency is a ruse. Structures do not exist in a vacuum (i.e., they do not originate or sustain themselves on their own). Instead, attitudes underpin structures.

The resolution that, "All United States military intervention into the internal affairs of any foreign nation or nations in the Western Hemisphere should be prohibited," offers an interesting case in point. Structural inherency appears obvious: there are no laws which prohibit United States military intervention in the Western Hemisphere. The War Powers Act offers some limitation on the executive's discretion to commit American forces abroad, but it falls far short of actually prohibiting military intervention. Yet, if inherency's function is to answer the causal question, the absence of a law prohibiting military intervention in this hemisphere is insufficient to explain why the United States is presently intervening. Why has the United States increased its military assistance to the government of El Salvador? Why has the Reagan administration approved the use of American military advisors in support of El Salvadoran forces? Why has the United States stepped up covert activities directed against Sandinista-run Nicaragua? Why did Congress authorize the Symms Amendment, which reaffirmed United States hostility toward Cuba? In this case structural inherency offers practically no clue as to why the United States is intervening in the hemisphere. Instead, the observer must look to the attitudes of policy makers with regard to military intervention. The historical attitude of the United States supports pro-interventionist policies in the Western Hemisphere. It has been more than a century since the United States proclaimed the Monroe Doctrine, which articulated our special interests in this hemisphere. Since that time numerous American Presidents have militarily intervened into the internal affairs of various nations in Latin America. In addition, the attitude of the Reagan administration favors pro-interventionist policies in the Western Hemisphere. The President strongly supports United States action to arrest the spread of communism. This combination of historical and contemporary attitudes explains both the absence of a prohibition on U.S. military intervention as well as the stepped-up use of military intervention during the Reagan presidency. Thus, inherency includes both structural and attitudinal components.

In an effort to achieve solvency, an affirmative advocate must go beyond structures; he or she must come to grips with the attitudes which underpin structures. How can an affirmative solve for attitudes? One way is to alter attitudes. However, this approach is uncertain at best. Although laws can change attitudes (some credit the 1964 Civil Rights Act with precipitating a change in the prejudicial attitudes of many Americans toward blacks), we recommend a more certain solvency approach. The best approach is to alter structures to preclude attitudes. In the case of prohibiting military intervention in the Western Hemisphere, there are several possible approaches. The War Powers Act could be tightened to prevent the President from authorizing military assistance or deploying American troops without the consent of the Congress; laws governing the authorization, funding and use of covert military operations could be strengthened; or a blanket prohibition could be adopted which required a formal declaration of war prior to the commitment of U.S. military assistance or forces on foreign soil in this hemisphere. In each instance, structures must be altered to circumvent the attitudes of policy makers.

Elevating the locus of responsibility for policy is the most common means of overcoming attitudes which stand in the way of domestic policy changes. This is a long-standing strategy for coping with resistance to policy objectives. Since the New Deal era, in issue arena after issue arena, resistance to policy changes have been overcome by shifting the locus of responsibility to a higher plane, thus diluting opposition. On the topic "that the federal government should establish minimum educational standards for all elementary and secondary schools," many affirmatives supported a requirement for sex education in all schools; others argued that the public, or their elected representatives, should not be allowed to exercise censorship of schoolbooks or materials. In both instances affirmatives constructed inherency positions grounded in attitudes (i.e., citizens and school officials oppose sex education or favor censorship of schoolbooks). The affirmative didn't attempt to alter these attitudes to achieve solvency (an unlikely prospect). Rather, they sought to insulate the schools from the attitudes by shifting responsibility from local school boards to the Federal government. Citizen attitudes might remain as firm against sex education or in favor of school censorship, but it no longer mattered. By shifting the locus of responsibility to a higher plane, the affirmative could argue that those attitudes could no longer affect public policy on these issues.

Case Wording

The first affirmative constructive speech must be clear and concise. It should also be persuasive. We will focus attention on these wording functions. Other considerations are less important.

The first task in drafting the initial affirmative speech is to construct a detailed outline of the affirmative position, much like the samples provided in Figures 9-1, 9-2, and 9-3. The outline forms the organizational skeleton of the speech. The remaining steps in composing the speech involve placing meat on the bones of the skeleton by providing for narrative development of each of the elements contained in the outline. We recommend that the advocate adhere as closely as possible to the structure embodied in the outline of the affirmative position. This insures that it will be possible to distinguish clearly between and delineate the interrelationship of the separate components of the case. This approach to the drafting of the initial speech commits the affirmative to a defense of clearly delineated components of a case.

The major affirmative claims constitute contentions. Each must be worded carefully and developed fully. The wording for contentions in the first affirmative constructive forms the themes which are used for subsequent refutation, and eventually, for packaging a decision scenario. Therefore, contentions should be worded to enhance clarity, persuasive impact and credibility. Each contention must be properly developed. This will usually require a number of individual points in support of the contention. Each individual point requires adequate development as well. We recommend that the advocate internalize a simple four-step process to use in developing each point, consisting of the following elements: (1) label, (2) explanation, (3) support, and (4) delineation of impact. This process is used to develop individual points in the sample first affirmative constructive speech later in this chapter. We will discuss the use of this process in more detail in Chapter 11.

The affirmative advocate should invest the time in the first affirmative constructive speech to achieve maximum persuasive impact. A few techniques serve this end well. Effective introductions enhance ethos, preview the speech, and generate attention and interest. Select wording to enhance clarity and persuasiveness. Tell the affirmative story with a touch of literary flair. Incorporate elements of philosophy and history, and a reasonable dose of humor in the first affirmative constructive speech. Such efforts yield positive results. They enhance the ethos of the speaker and make the affirmative's case more interesting and persuasive. Finally, strive to optimize the delivery of the first constructive speech for full persuasive impact.

Plan Construction

Policy systems analysis hinges on the affirmative's proposal of a specific policy. The plan embodies a specific policy position. As a result, the affirmative plan is the focus of policy debate. Its provisions are the source of both affirmative benefits and costs. Whether a resolution should be affirmed depends on the relative desirability of a particular proposal. Affirmative plans take various forms. They range in import and intricacy all the way from simply worded proposals put to any one of the small and innocuous organizations which pervade the American scene, to detailed pieces of legislation placed before Congress. In each instance, however, the plan constitutes the centerpiece of policy disputes.

Topical Provisions. An affirmative plan consists of topical and enabling provisions. Topical provisions directly adopt the resolution. If a resolution indicated that "all United States military intervention into the internal affairs of any foreign nation or nations in the Western Hemisphere should be prohibited," a plan's topical provisions would contain the prohibition. If a resolution mandated that "the federal government should significantly strengthen regulation of mass media communications in the United States," the plan's topical provisions would specify the nature of the strengthened regulation of mass media communication. And if a resolution required that "the United States should significantly curtail its arms sales to other countries," the plan's topical provisions would specify the nature of the arms curtailment. In short, the plan's topical provisions contain the thrust of the resolution's mandate.

Enabling Provisions.   Enabling provisions allow the plan to function. These include such essential plan functions as administration, funding, and enforcement, in addition to more incidental features such as phase-in, education, continued research and development, review, and affirmative intent. Enabling provisions are not topical in their own right, but are essential to the enactment of the resolution. As such, they are legitimate features of an affirmative's plan.

Administration, funding, and enforcement are indispensable in accomplishing the resolution's mandate. Plan administration consists of the infrastructure to oversee and direct the attack on the harm. Such infrastructure might already exist, consisting of a present public or private structure. In this case an affirmative advocate could charge such structure with the responsibility of plan oversight and implementation. More often, however, the affirmative has launched an indictment against existing structures as part and parcel of its inherency analysis. In this instance the same structure should not be used to administer the affirmative's plan. Instead, a new structure must be created in order to assure effective plan oversight and administration. For example, on the resolution, "that the United States should significantly curtail its arms sales to other countries," an affirmative could argue a strong inherency position that President Reagan, his inner circle of advisers, and the Department of State are staunch pro-sales advocates. Thus, it would be unwise to utilize the Department of State to administer an arms sales prohibition because plan circumvention would be virtually assured. Instead, an affirmative advocate should create an independent board or commission in the plan to oversee and implement the mandate.

If the affirmative opts to create a new board or commission to administer the plan, it will need to consider questions with regard to its size, composition, powers and checks. Poorly conceived affirmative boards and commissions can become the target of negative plan arguments.

Plan funding insures sufficient resources to accomplish the affirmative's mandate. Two dimensions warrant special attention: funding adequacy and desirability.

Funding adequacy refers to whether there are sufficient revenues to provide for the topical and enabling mandates of the plan. Sometimes the topical plan provisions require substantial revenues. For example, the resolution that "the federal government should establish a comprehensive program to significantly increase the energy independence of the United States," required substantial tax revenues. Most affirmatives indicted the private sector for its unwillingness to take the lead in the development of alternatives to fossil fuels (the private sector was chided for its conservative and short term profit orientation). As a result, affirmatives charged the federal government with the responsibility to develop alternative energy sources, and at considerable public cost. At other times the topical plan provisions require minimal revenues. The resolution that "all United States military intervention into the internal affairs of any foreign nation or nations in the Western Hemisphere should be prohibited," makes practically no demand on public or private resources.

Additionally, a plan's enabling provisions inevitably warrant adequate funding.

Provisions for a board or commission, enforcement, research and development, and possibly education require modest revenues.

The affirmative advocate must provide sufficient revenues. This can prove to be a troublesome requirement since the advocate must specify a particular funding source and defend its desirability. Whether an affirmative advocate chooses to fund the plan from increases in personal income tax, corporate income tax, various excise taxes, or deficit spending, he or she opens the door to negative arguments against the plan's funding provision. As a result, some affirmatives fund the plan via general federal revenues (not specifying a particular funding source) while others use a combination of more esoteric sources, which they may not be able to defend adequately, but which they hope the negative will not be able to attack specifically.

We recommend that affirmatives either designate a particular revenue source, or utilize general federal revenues, and prepare to defend their choice against possible negative arguments. The question of funding is an important issue and should not be taken lightly. It is, after all, the principal reason why government must exercise choices. Some theorists suggest that argumentation on funding can distract from the more essential issues concerning the resolution's desirability.[11] We believe this view is simplistic. Government and individuals face a similar malady. In an era of scarcity income is finite, and some very difficult choices must be made with regard to spending options. Neither government nor individuals can purchase all of everything that they desire. This economic fact of life has been driven home during the Reagan presidency.

Plan enforcement prevents obstruction of the plan's mandate. An affirmative advocate may utilize existing laws, penalties, and agencies, or create entirely new ones, in an effort to insure compliance with the plan's mandates. A single criterion— efficacy—should guide the advocate in this decision. If existing enforcement mechanisms will work, use them. If not, devise new mechanisms. For example, the sample affirmative case, shown in Figure 9–7, called for the creation of a special congressional watchdog committee to insure compliance with the plan's mandates.

Finally, a variety of incidental features enable the plan to function and are thus essential to the mandate of the resolution. The plan may require a phase-in period. A phase-in is particularly helpful if the plan constitutes a broad mandate for a substantial change. The plan may require an education provision, especially if solvency depends on a change in public attitudes. For example, a federal program of energy conservation is doomed in the absence of supportive public attitudes (as President Carter's conservation initiative revealed). The affirmative's plan will need a provision for continued research and development in the event that either the problem or the solution involve technological ramifications. For example, affirmatives arguing for the resolution "that the federal government should adopt a comprehensive program to significantly increase the energy independence of the United States," might choose to commit America to a greater mix of passive alternatives (especially conservation and solar), claiming advantages based on the superiority of passive alternatives over fossil fuels. Nonetheless, their plans should continue—even accelerate—research and development in all energy sectors to maintain future options. For the same reason such affirmatives would be wise to include a plan provision for periodic review. Both the research and development and periodic review provisions minimize the dangers of

FIGURE 9–7 SAMPLE FIRST AFFIRMATIVE CONSTRUCTIVE SPEECH

The United States is committed to a policy of military intervention in Latin America. The Reagan administration has provided military assistance and advisors in support of the government in El Salvador, authorized the use of covert operations against the government of Nicaragua, and launched an invasion to overthrow the government of Grenada. As a response to these events we support the resolution that, "All United States military intervention into the internal affairs of any foreign nation or nations in the Western Hemisphere should be prohibited." The United States' commitment to military intervention in the region is an unqualified mistake. We propose to erase the errors that have been made, for, as in the *Antigone* of Sophocles, "All men make mistakes, but a good man yields when he knows his course is wrong and repairs the evil." Thus, we support the adoption of the following plan as one example of the resolution:

I.   MANDATE: All U.S. military policy shall be altered as follows with all conflicting legislation being superceded. The United States will adopt and adhere to a military nonintervention policy into the internal affairs of foreign nations in the Western Hemisphere. All military intervention into the internal affairs, defined as "the covert or overt commitment of U.S. military forces within the territory of another country," shall henceforth be prohibited. The policy will be available to the Soviet Union for their signature, creating a nonintervention pact.

II. ENFORCEMENT: A congressional watchdog committee shall be established. It will be provided with adequate funding and staffing so as to insure compliance with plan mandates. Congress will be assured access to information relevant to military decisions. Normal judicial procedures will be utilized to prosecute violators of the plan's mandate.

III. FINANCING: Any needed funding will be provided through general federal revenues.

IV. INTENT: Affirmative speeches shall serve to clarify plan intent. Any plan provision found to be unconstitutional or nonjurisdictional shall be severed. This policy shall serve as a precedent for legislation dealing with the Eastern Hemisphere.

The adoption of the affirmative proposal yields one compelling advantage.
ADVANTAGE: REDUCE THE CHANCE OF WAR.

The propensity for the United States to engage in military activities in the Western Hemisphere is indicated in subpoint *A: United States' Policy Is Interventionist.*

The passage of the Symms Amendment in August 1982 provided a legislative green light for United States military intervention in Latin America. Illinois Senator Charles Percy observed at the time that, ". . . (the) Symms resolution might indeed be the first blundering, stumbling step toward U.S. military intervention in Latin America."

There is every indication that Senator Percy was correct in his prognostication. The March 16, 1982, issue of *U.S. News & World Report* warned that stepped-up U.S. involvement in El Salvador (a $25-million increase in military aid coupled with an increase in U.S. military advisors to 54) is ". . . just the beginning of a massive escalation of the U.S. presence." The commitment of advisors is the first step toward deeper involvement, as the *Central America Report* warned in December 1982: "The shift toward U.S. direct military involvement became evident in 1981 when Green Berets dressed in camouflage were seen patrolling the Honduran border with El Salvador. In March 1982 approximately 100 U.S. military personnel were stationed in the country." Although the President insists that the advisors are in no immediate danger, he authorized that hostile fire pay be allocated to the U.S. personnel in the area. This clearly indicates the danger surrounding the deployment, as the journal *Inter-American Economic Affairs* observed in the Fall 1981 issue: "A request to designate El Salvador as a hostile-fire area was approved in early 1981 and then reversed to avoid the impression that the United States had combat forces in El Salvador. However, we found the hostile fire pay has been paid to most of the U.S. army personnel in El Salvador on an individual monthly certified basis. The overall extent and continuous nature of these payments indicates that the Department of Defense virtually treats El Salvador as a hostile fire area."

Furthermore, U.S. actions directed against Nicaragua are ominous. The *New York Times* reported on August 5, 1982 that the joint U.S. and Honduran military maneuvers along the Nicaraguan border have increased tensions in the region. In addition, the Reagan Administration's decision to approve paramilitary operations against the government of Nicaragua threatens the peace. Indeed, Michael Barnes, Chair of the House Foreign Affairs Subcommittee on Inter-American Affairs, called the plan, "a virtual declaration of war against Nicaragua." Finally the U.S. invasion of Grenada illustrates the willingness of the Reagan Administration to use overt military intervention in this hemisphere.

Regrettably such interventionist tendencies can only result in a scenario laced with bloodshed, as we establish in *B: U.S. Involvement Increases the Chance of War.* Once the United States has committed advisors to a nation, we have an inherent obligation to protect them. This obligation could eventually require direct U.S. intervention, as Louisiana Senator Russell Long warned in 1981: "I'm sure (Reagan) doesn't intend to involve us in a war there any more than President Lyndon B. Johnson or (Dwight D.) Eisenhower intended to involve us in a war in Vietnam. But once you get our military people in a situation where they can get killed or where you end up with a choice between massive intervention on the one hand and humiliating withdrawal on the other, what are you going to do? Greater involvement then may become inevitable." Senator Long is not alone in expressing just such fears. Forty-eight members of Congress earlier last year sent a plea to President Reagan to terminate his policy and withdraw U.S. advisors. Their rationale was outlined before the Subcommittee in Inter-American Affairs in March of 1981: "There is a good chance that introduction of military advisors will increase the risk of one or more American casualties, forcing the U.S. either into another Vietnam or a humiliating withdrawal, either of which would weaken the U.S. position around the world."

The El Salvadoran conflict has already begun to mirror our actions in Vietnam, as the Center for American Policy observed in 1982: "The parallels with Vietnam are striking (in El Salvador): the same inflated rhetoric and forecasts of the dire consequences of defeat; the same problem of a central, narrowly based and repressive government backed by the U.S.; and the same progression of involvement from a little military aid to military advisors, then more aid and advisors until the U.S. finds itself in the midst of a war from which there seems no escape save for defeat, which is unacceptable."

Not only does the United States risk involvement in another Vietnam, but U.S. advisors independently risk escalation of the conflict. For example, escalation of the fighting in El Salvador corresponds to the commitment of U.S. advisors. The *El Salvador Bulletin* reported this in August 1982. "The recent intensification of the war—marked by the return of U.S.-trained Salvadoran troops and officers . . . and . . . the involvement of U.S. advisors in military operation centers and battlefronts as reported to the *New York Times* on June 25—has contributed to the further regionalization of the Salvadoran war." Further, such maneuvers could ignite a regional war, as *MesoAmerica* warned in November 1982: ". . . the joint (U.S. and Honduran) maneuver could accidentally ignite a real war." Finally, any direct intervention by U.S. troops will guarantee a prolonged conflict in the area. Michael Klare of the Institute of Policy Studies concluded in 1981 that, ". . . any U.S. intervention could result in a conflict on a much larger scale and at a much higher level of violence than that experienced in Vietnam. Such an encounter would be inherently dangerous—risking, as it does, confrontation with the U.S.S.R. and escalation to thermonuclear war."

The inherent risks involved in our deploying of advisors and troops mandate a saner and safer course of action. Thus we conclude *C: Nonintervention Is A Superior Policy.* Obviously, a prohibition of U.S. military forces would preclude the risk of escalation to superpower confrontation, as Michael Klare, previously qualified, noted in September 1982: "The only way we can prevent an interventionary war fought with conventional weapons from escalating into a nuclear war is by preventing the interventionary war in the first place."

Mere rhetoric on the part of President Reagan as to nonintervention is not a sufficient safeguard against actual troop deployment. In fact, reliance on verbal self-restraint was condemned by the Committee on U.S.-Latin American Relations in a comprehensive study of U.S. intervention in the Western Hemisphere. The study, completed in 1975, concluded that: "Verbal commitments to stop interventionist practices are necessary but not sufficient. International pledges through treaties and multilateral declarations are also helpful but are unlikely to add much to national commitments."

Further safeguards against inappropriate governmental activities should be built into U.S. governmental machinery. In order to be efficacious in a changing world, a policy of nonintervention must not allow for exceptions. This necessity for credibility was explained by University of California Political Science Professor Gertov in his book, *U.S. Against the World,* in 1974: "If proscriptions against unilateral intervention are to have meaning, they must be enforced with respect to 'good' and 'bad' governments and 'progressive' and 'reactionary' movements. Nor should they leave open the alternative of intervening where success is likely and U.S. interests are clearly at stake." Furthermore, to allow a flexible interventionist policy subjects the lives of others to a game of international politics, as Gertov continued: "When the risks and costs of intervention are weighed, human life becomes totally politicized. The achievement of political and military objectives invariably has priority in American policy making over prospects of destructiveness as was the case, for example, in the Congo, Vietnam, Nigeria/Biafra, and Bangladesh." Such reasoning led the Committee on U.S.-Latin American Relations to conclude in favor of the resolution that, "all United States military intervention into the internal affairs of any nation or nations in the Western Hemisphere should be prohibited." The Committee concluded: "The U.S. should refrain from unilateral military interventions in Latin America, and covert U.S. interventions in the internal affairs of Latin American countries should be ended."

Professor Gertov provided empirical support for the desirability of a blanket prohibition on U.S. military intervention in this hemisphere. After examining all previous U.S. interventions in the Western Hemisphere, he concluded that the harmful results of U.S. involvement dictate that U.S. policy should be based on those past failures. He stated in 1974 that: "The lessons for future decisions on revolution abroad should come from unsuccessful interventions; those that have achieved U.S. objectives in the short run do not advance American interests in the long run, and in fact retard them."

As we indicated at the outset of this speech, ". . . a good man yields when he knows his course is wrong and repairs the evil." We believe that the present course, which relies heavily on U.S. military intervention in this hemisphere, is wrong. Military intervention is simply an option which should be ruled out. To repair the evil of the current course we urge the adoption of the resolution.

policy lock (see chapter 10). An intent plank provides for continued clarification of plan mandates throughout affirmative speeches.

Enabling provisions allow the plan to function. They are not topical in their own right but they are legitimate *because* they are essential to the enactment of the resolution. By contrast, an illegitimate plan provision is not topical but contributes to affirmative benefits.[12] Such a provision is illegitimate because it is not essential to the enactment of the resolution. The distinction that separates enabling provisions from illegitimate plan planks is equated to the difference between workability and solvency. Workability concerns the plan's capacity to function or operate while solvency deals with the benefits of the plan. The notion of benefits includes the aggregate of affirmative impacts, regardless of origin. Thus, preempting a plan disadvantage contributes to affirmative benefits, and, if accomplished via a non-topical plan provision, should be considered as illegitimate. A plan provision, though non-topical, is legitimate if it contributes to workability, but is illegitimate if it contributes to solvency.

Figure 9–7 contains a first affirmative constructive speech on the topic, "that all United States military intervention into the internal affairs of any nation or nations in the Western Hemisphere should be prohibited." Note the specificity of the plan's provisions.

SUMMARY

It is the affirmative advocate's responsibility to initiate argument on behalf of a particular policy thesis; this constitutes the presentation of the affirmative's case (position). This chapter introduced the student to the initial affirmative position, including: the nature and function of affirmative advocacy, the ramifications of essential affirmative burdens of advocacy, and the theoretical and practical considerations which underpin the selection, construction, and presentation of the affirmative's case. Chapter 11 will explore the strategies and tactics involved in defending an affirmative position.

Notes

[1] Irving L. Janis, *Group Think: Psychological Studies of Policy Decisions and Fiascoes,* 2nd ed. (Boston: Houghton Mifflin Company, 1982), pp. 266–68.

[2] Charles L. Schultze, *The Politics and Economics of Public Spending* (Washington, D.C.: The Brookings Institution, 1968), p. 38.

[3] David Zarefsky, "The Role of Causal Argument in Policy Controversies," *Journal of the American Forensic Association,* 13 (1977), 179–81.

[4] Bernard L. Brock, James W. Chesebro, John F. Cragan and James F. Klumpp, *Public Policy Decision-Making: Systems Analysis and Comparative Advantages Debate* (New York: Harper and Row, Publishers, 1973), p. 157.

[5] Zarefsky, p. 185.

[6] Tom Goodnight, Bill Balthrop and Donn W. Parson, "The Problem of Inherency: Strategy and Substance," *Journal of the American Forensic Association,* 10 (1974), 231.

[7]Brock, et al., p. 80.

[8]Aristotle, *The Rhetoric of Aristotle: An Expanded Translation with Supplementary Examples for Students of Composition and Public Speaking,* trans. Lane Cooper (New York: D. Appleton and Company, 1932), pp. 34–35.

[9]Jahangir Amuzegar, *Comparative Economics: National Priorities, Policies, and Performance* (Cambridge: Winthrop Publishers, Inc., 1981), p. 126.

[10]Karen Rasmussen and Daniel DeStephen, "Building Cases," in *Decision by Debate,* Douglas Ehninger and Wayne Brockriede, 2nd ed. (New York: Harper & Row, Publishers, 1978), pp. 186–88.

[11]J. W. Patterson and David Zarefsky, *Contemporary Debate* (Boston: Houghton Mifflin Company, 1983), p. 206.

[12]Cole Campbell, *Competitive Debate* (Chapel Hill: Information Research Associates, 1974), p. 155.

CHAPTER TEN

NEGATIVE
CASE
CONSTRUCTION

While the affirmative in policy systems debate must initiate argument on behalf of a particular policy thesis or proposition, the negative must contest the affirmative's position. The negative advocate can accomplish this in one of three ways: direct refutation of affirmative claims; constructive argument on behalf of a particular policy position or positions, which warrants a rejection of the resolution; or some combination of these approaches. Regardless of the approach chosen, the negative advocate must defend critical components of that position against any and all affirmative attempts to rebut it; this constitutes a defense of the negative's case.

This chapter will introduce the student to negative advocacy. Special emphasis will be placed on the elements of negative case construction—on the selection and implementation of strategic choices which constitute a negative position in a debate. We will examine in some detail the theoretical and practical considerations which underpin the selection and construction of individual negative argumentative options. Chapter 12 will explore the strategies and tactics involved in defending a negative position.

While a negative position consists of some combination of strategic elements, a strong position involves the optimal melding of strategic options. It would be both impossible and strategically self-defeating for a negative advocate to argue all of the argumentative options available to him or her. Instead, the negative advocate must make wise choices from among available options.

STRATEGIC OPTIONS: THE STAPLES

Direct refutation constitutes a systematic assault upon the claims of the affirmative's case. The negative advocate using direct refutation attempts to respond to all of the claims advanced by the affirmative. This was once the traditional approach to negative advocacy. Indeed, direct refutation grew out of and hit its peak during the dominance of the stock issues paradigm in debate. As indicated previously, this paradigm required that the affirmative construct and defend its position so as to meet fully each of a series of burdens, including topicality, significance, permanence, solvency and desirability. As long as stock issues prevailed as the dominant paradigm, the negative's responsibility appeared obvious: to attempt to undermine one or more of the affirmative's stock issue claims. This was best accomplished via straight refutation against those claims.

Contemporary Role of Direct Refutation

The ascendency of policy systems debate changed this. Policy systems debate features a comparison of alternative courses of action. Thus, the negative's use of straight refutation alone is seldom sufficient to defeat an affirmative.[1] Direct refutation can usually do no more than minimize an affirmative's claim and *may* contradict more promising negative positions.

For example, in debating the resolution that, "the federal government should strengthen the guarantee of consumer product safety required of manufacturers," an affirmative might argue that the guarantee of consumer product safety would be significantly strengthened if air bags were installed in all passenger vehicles manufactured in the United States. The affirmative could claim that thousands die each year and hundreds of thousands are injured in highway accidents; the current air bag option now provided by automobile manufacturers has failed—and will continue to fail—to significantly increase air bag installations because the public is not safety oriented. Present government efforts to require air bags have been met by persistent opposition, first by manufacturers and then by an unsympathetic administration; and studies demonstrate that mandatory use of air bags would reduce highway deaths by as much as 47 percent, injuries by as much as 26 percent.

Consider the limited potential of straight refutation. A negative might be able to reduce affirmative significance, but minimally. It is a fact that thousands die, and hundreds of thousands are injured, each year in traffic accidents. A negative could make inroads against affirmative inherency, but not substantially. Consumers simply won't purchase air bags; and the present system has dragged its feet on this issue for nearly a decade. The negative might attack affirmative solvency, claiming that air bags will not save as many lives as studies have suggested. Yet, even the most conservative studies indicate that air bags will achieve a substantial reduction in automobile deaths and injuries.

Furthermore, direct refutation alone constitutes a de facto commitment to existing policy. As Allan J. Lichtman and the late Daniel M. Rohrer observed, "Inevitably, the rejection of one policy or course of action means the adoption of another policy or course of action. Even doing nothing or suspending judgment is a form of action and thus a policy."[2] Others have claimed that direct refutation involves a suspension of judgment in lieu of sufficient justification; that deliberation precedes action.[3] Yet, policy deliberation seldom functions in a vacuum, absent operational commitments. Any decision to suspend judgment is simultaneously a de-facto commitment to existing policies.[4] This realization calls attention to the weakness of direct refutation. If the negative can do nothing more than minimize affirmative significance, inherency and/or solvency, what has it to offer? In the absence of additional negative positions, the rational policy analyst would surely choose the more desirable affirmative alternative. In short, the use of direct refutation can minimize but not single-handedly defeat an affirmative's claims.

Nonetheless, the selective use of straight refutation continues to play an indispensable role in negative advocacy by complementing other strategic options. For instance, direct refutation has two uses which ought to be strategic staples in the negative's tactical arsenal: first, minimization of affirmative significance; second, erosion of affirmative solvency.

The negative advocate should focus direct refutation on significance and solvency in almost every debate. This attention is warranted for two reasons. First, significance and solvency constitute undisputed affirmative burdens. Negative inroads in these areas are viewed as important by virtually all critic judges. Second, negative attacks against affirmative significance and solvency are relatively safe. This is not the case with many other strategic options which carry substantial risk. As we will explain in chapter 11, it is possible for an affirmative advocate to reverse, or turn, negative defenses of present system programs and alternative proposals as well as negative plan disadvantages. By contrast, significance and solvency attacks cannot backfire on the negative.

Additionally, it is in the negative's best interest to attempt to neutralize affirmative solvency claims. As we introduced in Chapter 9 and will stress in Chapter 11, the affirmative's initial solvency analysis and evidence provides the footing for subsequent responses to negative efficacy and disadvantage attacks. The negative advocate who ignores affirmative solvency evidence does so at his or her own risk.

Minimizing Significance

As previously explained, the affirmative must do two things to establish significance: demonstrate that the value it seeks to promote is important, and provide a quantitative or qualitative measure to indicate the impact of the value. For example, under the resolution that, "the federal government should establish minimum educational standards for all elementary and secondary schools in the United States," affirmatives might argue for the adoption of inter-district busing of elementary and secondary school students. In order to establish significance the affirmative advocate might argue two points: first, establish the relative importance of equal educational opportunity; and second, decide current inequality of educational opportunity by comparing actual data such as test scores and dropout rates of white and non-white students.

The negative should respond to both arguments. First, the negative advocate can contest the affirmative's value. As we noted previously, policy resolutions involve important value controversies. Affirmative benefits stem from the accelerated promotion of one or more basic values. Yet, movement along a continuum toward one value represents simultaneous movement away from an alternative value.

The negative should challenge an affirmative value reprioritization on two counts. First, the negative advocate should isolate and scrutinize the affirmative's value claim. Where a value claim is vulnerable, use direct refutation against it. For example, an equal educational opportunity which is achieved by thwarting high-ability students in order to benefit low-ability students loses much of its appeal. It means a mediocre educational experience for *all* students. Second, prepare to argue that alternative values are more important. The inter-district busing example is again illustrative. The negative could argue that local control (the value that underpins the neighborhood school), cultural homogeneity and others are more important than equal educational opportunity. The impairment of competing values, if more important than an affirmative value, offers a potent source for negative disadvantages.

Second, the negative advocate can dispute the impact of the affirmative's value. In the example above, the affirmative attempted to prove significance by comparing the educational attainment of white and non-white students as indicated by their relative test scores and their dropout rates.

The negative can argue against the tangible impact of the affirmative's value in the following manner. First, evaluate the analysis and evidence used in support of the affirmative claims. Apply the standards and tests developed in Chapter 7, "Evidence," Chapter 8, "Reasoning," and Chapter 13, "Refutation and Rebuttals." If an affirmative claim appears suspect, attack it. Second, carefully examine the suggested causalities. The affirmative must demonstrate a significant correlation between its value variable and its impact variables. In the inter-district busing example, the affirmative assumes that unequal educational opportunities result in lower test scores and higher dropout rates. But what of other important variables? The negative advocate will want to test the correlation between non-white performance and alternative variables such as socio-economic factors, language barriers, and the student's home environment.

Contesting Solvency

To establish solvency the affirmative must isolate the correct causal variables. Sound analysis and evidence are needed for the solvency position. The affirmative must insure that the plan solves or alleviates the harms by acting to effectively overcome the inherency.

It is imperative that the negative advocate contest initial affirmative solvency analysis and evidence as vigorously as possible. The sample flow on the topic, "the U.S. should curtail its arms sales to other countries," illustrates this need (see Chapter 6). The affirmative argued that the U.S. should stop arms sales to Indonesia in an effort to halt the latter's subjugation of East Timor. The negative argued that Indonesia would not give up Timor; furthermore, it could easily procure armaments elsewhere. As a result, the negative claimed that the affirmative plan would fail to alter Indonesian policy; indeed, it might precipitate a backlash toward East Timor. The negative documented these claims well.

However, the affirmative was able to refute this position by exploiting the solvency analysis and evidence in the initial speech. This example shows why the initial affirmative solvency position must be contested via direct refutation. The strategic importance of the negative attack on the solvency evidence goes beyond the attempt to deny any advantage to the affirmative case. If the negative advocate can effectively neutralize—or even weaken—affirmative solvency claims, then he or she undermines potential affirmative responses to subsequent negative solvency and disadvantage attacks.

STRATEGIC OPTIONS: TAKING THE OFFENSIVE

The negative advocate should use direct refutation to minimize affirmative significance and weaken affirmative solvency in almost every debate. Nonetheless, direct refutation is a defensive posture; no more than a holding action. It can minimize, but cannot defeat, an affirmative's claims.

Thus, the negative advocate will want to use direct refutation in combination with offensive strategic options. Fortunately, negative offensive options are many and diverse. The trick is to make wise choices from among available options—to fashion an optimal combination. This section will examine the theoretical and practical considerations which support the selection and construction of the negative's offensive argumentative options. We will focus our attention on the following areas: a defense of the present system; minor repairs, and both hypothetical and conditional counterplans; the standard or traditional counterplan; efficacy attacks; plan disadvantages; generic positions; and topicality.

A Defense of the Present System

The affirmative must prove that the problem that it has delineated actually exists in the present system; that it is permanent. This burden represents the search for blame. To establish permanence the affirmative advocate must demonstrate that the attitudes and structures that characterize the present system cause, or contribute to, the problem.[5]

The negative may choose to contest an affirmative's inherency. The philosophy and programs which constitute the present system have traditionally played an important role in the negative's tactical arsenal. However, there are substantial risks associated with this negative approach which must be carefully weighed.

Strategic Risks. The present system usually features a slow and deliberate approach to change. This stems from the need to pursue diverse and often conflicting values. The present system seeks employment and price stability; personal liberty and security; free enterprise and occupational and consumer protection; increased farm income and low consumer food prices; and so forth. And it establishes a variety of programs in the pursuit of each of these conflicting goals. A maze of goals and programs exists in the present system's approach. The result is confusion over ultimate aims. If the present system *appears to be* working at cross purposes, then it is.

The slow and deliberate pursuit of diverse and conflicting goals results in two notable shortcomings. First, the potential of the present system to predict efficacy (to demonstrate a reasonable probability of success on affirmative terms) is mixed at best. The policy systems approach demands a comparison between the efficacy of present system options and an affirmative alternative.

The affirmative advocate, however, is in the best position to demonstrate probable efficacy—to predict solvency—for his or her proposal. Prediction carries a built-in affirmative advantage as a result of the single-mindedness of most affirmative approaches. An affirmative plan moves with a singular purpose in the pursuit of a specific objective. However, the present system cannot, which results in an unfair comparison. Instead, the present system must wrestle with conflicting objectives and limited resources. It lacks the necessary consensus to move with haste toward some special interest group's valued goal. The affirmative is thus in a better position to demonstrate probable efficacy for its proposal—a result of affirmative single-mindedness, which is secured via fiat.

A second shortcoming, which stems from the decision-making system employed by the present system, is readily apparent. The slow and deliberate pursuit of diverse and conflicting goals makes it easy for an affirmative to prove perversity in terms of some "pet" affirmative objective. It also lays the groundwork for the dangerous inherency turn-around. Simply put, it is easy for an affirmative to show that a component of the present system prevents an optimal solution to—or exacerbates—a particular problem. If the allegation is that the present system works at cross-purposes, then it is clearly guilty. That is, after all, the nature of the system, and it is guilty of being precisely what it is supposed to be. The essence of the problem is that the present system chooses not to pursue absolute goals. It chooses not to commit its energies and resources in the pursuit of a particular value in a vacuum. In policy arena after policy arena, this is the only reasonable explanation as to *why,* in David Zarefsky's words, "presumably good people tolerate evil."[6]

A Strategic Approach to Inherency.   We are *not suggesting* that the negative advocate abandon a defense of "What is." Rather, *we advocate a deliberate and strategic use of this argument variant.* The following guidelines should assist the negative advocate in capitalizing on inherency's potential assets while avoiding its risks.

1. The negative should argue inherency *only if* that position is valid. As with affirmative case selection, there are two important dimensions of validity. First, the negative's position should be true. Second, its position must be supported by sufficient breadth and depth of evidence. If the negative's inherency position fails either test, there is a good chance that it will further the affirmative's—and not the negative's— position. The affirmative case on the resolution that, "all United States military intervention into the internal affairs of any nation or nations in the Western Hemis-phere should be prohibited," illustrates this guideline (see Figure 9–3). The affirma-tive's inherency position was that militarism has been, and continues to be, a corner-stone of U.S. policy toward Latin America. Furthermore, the affirmative claimed that current U.S. military intervention in the region is extensive. The U.S. provides overt assistance, including military sales and aid in addition to advisors, to the unpopular Samoza government in El Salvador; employs covert methods against the Sandinista government in Nicaragua; and has increased the level of belligerence directed at Castro's Cuba. The negative would be foolish to attempt to contest this affirmative's inherency claims. This example fails both of the aforementioned tests. The affirma-tive's inherency claims are fundamentally true; furthermore, they are easily documen-

table. As a result, a negative inherency defense is sure to be beaten outright, or turned, by the affirmative.

2. The second guideline is an obvious but often overlooked precondition. Simply put, a strong negative inherency position consists of a defense of present system programs in conjunction with the direct refutation of initial affirmative inherency analysis and evidence. Thus, the negative should utilize both approaches—or neither one. If the negative attempts to defend present system programs, without simultaneously refuting the initial affirmative inherency position, then the affirmative advocate can defeat the negative's argument by simply extending the inherency analysis and evidence that was in the initial speech. Thus, it is imperative that the negative advocate contest the initial affirmative inherency position if he or she intends to defend present system programs.

3. We strongly encourage the negative advocate to exploit the strengths of the present system's incremental approach to change. The slow and deliberate pursuit of diverse and conflicting goals produces two notable benefits. The first stems from the values which are slighted in the tradeoff noted previously. There are well defined consequences which stem from single-minded pursuit of absolute values. These result from the competing values, and the programs which promote them, which are undermined as a consequence of the affirmative's reprioritizing. Affirmative movement along a continuum toward a desirable goal represents the simultaneous movement away from some equally desirable value.[7] For example, the price of increased security is a restriction of individual liberty (as anyone who has experienced the inconvenience of current airport security arrangements knows full well); the cost of price stability is high unemployment; the price of tax relief is government deficits and/or reduced government services; and so on. Notwithstanding affirmative claims that their plan produces *only* benefits, any attempt to reprioritize basic values produces both good and bad results. A single-minded shift along a continuum, especially a large shift, carries with it the potential for grave consequences. These must manifest themselves as significant disadvantages.

A second strength which stems from the present system's incremental approach is that it is more adaptive. The present system's lack of single-mindedness is, in essence, a strength. This strength manifests itself in two ways. On one hand, present programs are better tailored to multiple causation. As indicated previously, inherency's chief role involves prediction; this is a function of plan analysis. Causality is vital in the effort to determine the probability of competing alternatives. Yet, most problems are terribly complex, almost defying a precise determination of causality. Indeed, it is doubtful whether one can identify a single causal variable for most social, political and/or economic problems. As political scientist Thomas R. Dye has observed, "Most of society's problems are shaped by so many variables that a single explanation of them—or remedy for them—is rarely possible."[8] This, in large part, explains the multiplicity of present system approaches.

Indeed, most contemporary approaches are directed toward symptoms, as opposed to causes. Hence, poverty is attacked via programs to increase the purchasing power of the poor (i.e., income maintenance, food stamps, low income housing, etc.). These efforts ignore the causes of poverty. Similarly, crime is approached in terms of law enforcement efforts. These ignore the causes of crime. As a result, it is easy to show that variables, other than those isolated by an affirmative, are in part responsible for the harm in question. Of course this does not mean that the present system has the potential or the resources to solve the problem. This was the traditional application of inherency's causality function. Rather, it probably means that an affirmative solution is not well-tailored to the problem. Hence, affirmative solvency, its probability of success, may be diminished.

In addition, the present system's more adaptive approach is safer. Multiple programs in the pursuit of multiple objectives take on the form of an indefinite sequence of policy moves. As a result, mistakes can be observed early and corrected.[9] The deliberate pursuit of multiple approaches in the pursuit of multiple objectives facilitates adjustment. In contrast, an affirmative's swift and single-minded pursuit of a single goal allows much less room for self-correction. In fact, all too often the scope of affirmative change renders self-correction virtually impossible. Thus, the risk dimension of the calculation which multiplies risk times impact takes on added importance. If the affirmative has miscalculated—if the proposed plan does result (despite evidence to the contrary) in unintended consequences—potential remedies may be rendered impotent. This is not the case with an incremental approach to change which leaves more room for adjusting to unanticipated consequences.

It is out of this quagmire of confusion that a defense of "What is" derives new strength. The approach of the present system involves the slow and deliberate pursuit of diverse and conflicting values. It stands in stark contrast to most affirmative plans which feature the swift and single-minded pursuit of one goal. The present system's approach manifests known shortcomings concerning prediction and perversity. Yet, this generic approach also features unique strengths which the negative advocate can exploit.

4. The final guideline is that the negative advocate must fully understand and internalize the relationship between two seemingly diverse positions: a defense of the present system and plan disadvantages. A decision to defend present system programs carries with it important ramifications for potential plan disadvantages. These ramifications must be carefully examined prior to a final decision on negative positions.

Plan disadvantages stem from one of three phenomena: some are generic to the resolution; others result from the movement toward solvency; still others stem from the implementation of a specific affirmative proposal.[10] A negative advocate's defense of present system programs will usually contradict plan disadvantages of the first two variants. This is always true if the resolution embodies a direction of change. Such resolutions focus a debate on what we term "the solvency gap"—a measure of the increment which separates the present system from the affirmative's plan. Both systems pursue some accepted goal, but the resolution mandates that the affirmative pursue it to a greater degree.

The resolution that, "the federal government should significantly strengthen the guarantee of consumer product safety required of manufacturers," illustrates this problem. If the negative argues that the present system can solve the problem—that it can increase consumer product safety—then how can it advocate plan disadvantages which are generic to the resolution, or which stem from the movement toward solvency? Such disadvantages would have no unique grounding since both the present system and the affirmative's plan endeavor to increase consumer product safety. Of course the negative may still argue disadvantages which result from the unique way in which the affirmative attempts to achieve solvency. For example, if the negative position regarding consumer product safety policy employs a market strategy in contrast to an affirmative's regulatory approach, then the negative can still argue plan disadvantages grounded in the evils of federal regulation of manufacturers.

The intricate relationship between a defense of the present system and plan disadvantages will be clearer after we have discussed two subsequent subjects: plan disadvantages (later in this chapter) and the negative position (in chapter 11).

Alternative Proposals: Initial Steps

Negative advocates may argue alternative proposals to an affirmative's plan. Some involve minor modification of present system structures; these are termed "minor repairs." Others feature more substantial alterations in present system mechanisms; these are labeled "conditional and hypothetical counterplans." We do not believe that these positions constitute strong strategic options. They occupy ephemeral ground between two definitive negative positions: a defense of the present system and the standard counterplan. As such, they can prove to be difficult to defend.

Minor Repairs.   Sometimes the present system, as constituted, remains a small change away from being able to eradicate the problem. In such circumstances the negative advocate might propose that small change. However, an important criterion should be borne in mind when considering this alternative. The negative minor repair is an appropriate option *only if* the philosophy and general structures of the present system are fundamentally sound. For example, on the topic that, "the federal government should significantly strengthen the guarantee of consumer product safety required of manufacturers," some affirmatives maintained that existing Consumer Product Safety Commission standards on certain product classes were too weak; others claimed that standards didn't extend to some product classes. Some negatives responded with minor repairs, arguing for a specific strengthening and/or extension of CPSC standards. This is an appropriate and potentially effective use of the minor repair position.

All negative minor repairs must meet three basic burdens: non-topicality, viability, and desirability.

Obviously a negative minor repair cannot be topical. Yet, as indicated in Chapter 9, the wording of contemporary policy questions makes it difficult for the negative to argue a minor repair without crossing the threshold into affirmative terrain. Increasingly resolutions are worded as statements of increment or degree; they call for an agent (usually the federal government) to do something more—or less—than is currently being done in a particular area. This makes it difficult to argue a minor repair. If the negative advocate supports an extension of the status quo, and if the minor repair is viable (i.e., if the modified present system would be able to pursue the goal in question as well, or nearly as well, as the affirmative), then he or she has achieved the mandate of the resolution, crossing into affirmative terrain.[11]

The negative minor repair must constitute a viable alternative to the affirmative's plan. Viability consists of three elements. First, the negative must make a commitment to a specific mechanism. Second, the negative must also prove efficacy (show that the mechanism can solve the problem). Third, the negative should demonstrate a propensity to solve the problem. It is not enough that the minor repair have potential. The negative should be prepared to show that the mechanism's potential can be unleashed. This can be accomplished via: (1) showing a trend toward solvency, or (2) invoking fiat to catapult the mechanism toward solvency.

Finally, the negative minor repair must prove to be a desirable alternative to an affirmative's plan. This is a function of net benefit as opposed to net cost. The negative advocate must be prepared to argue the unique benefits of the minor repair; in addition, the negative must be on guard against the inherency turnaround argument which focuses on the consequences of the repair.

Conditional and Hypothetical Counterplans. Some theorists maintain that conditional and hypothetical counterplans are synonymous. We perceive a distinction between the two. A conditional counterplan commits the negative to a specific policy. It differs from the standard counterplan only in that the former specifies circumstances for use. A specific condition acts as a trigger, invoking the counterplan. Also, the conditional counterplan option is appropriate only when small changes are sought. For example, a negative advocate might want to defend the present system with modifications (i.e., an extension of coverage, an increase in funding, etc.), but be unable to demonstrate propensity. Thus, instead of using a minor repair, which presumes propensity, the advocate can turn to the conditional counterplan, which does not. Once the conditional counterplan is advanced, it must be defended in much the same manner as the standard counterplan position, which we will examine next.

The hypothetical counterplan commits the negative to nothing. It has no independent function except as illustration—especially in bolstering a negative topicality position. For instance, on the resolution that, "the federal government should significantly strengthen the regulation of mass media communications in the United States," some affirmatives argued cases grounded in an expansive interpretation of "mass media communications" (i.e., to improve nutrition or prenatal care, to reduce the incidence of alcoholism, smoking, or drug use, etc.). Such interpretations featured both mass media *and* interpersonal communications elements. The topicality of the former is obvious; of the latter is questionable. Many negatives contested affirmative topicality, claiming that the interpersonal component was illegitimate, and using a hypothetical counterplan to illustrate their position.

Alternative Proposals: The Standard Counterplan

Sometimes the negative advocate will want to go beyond a defense of existing alternatives. Following careful investigation and thought about the problem area, the negative may conclude that the evil is significant and that nothing short of a major change will solve it. In this instance the negative may propose the creation of new structures or the assignment of new functions to existing structures. This constitutes the negative standard counterplan position.

Description.   The negative counterplan is an alternative to the resolution. Its role and function vary according to paradigm. For the traditional critic judge, the counterplan constitutes a substitute for the resolutional mandate; it attempts to solve the same harm. For the hypothesis testing judge, it is a way of supporting the null hypothesis; it proves that the resolution is false. And, for the policy systems critic, the counterplan represents a mutually exclusive and superior alternative to the affirmative's plan.

In the right circumstances, the counterplan position is an excellent vehicle to permit the negative advocate to shift from a defensive to an offensive posture in a debate. As we will discuss in greater detail in chapter 11, the affirmative advocate enjoys formidable intrinsic advantages over his or her negative counterpart. First, the affirmative has the advantage of initiating clash in a debate. Cases can be chosen, research accomplished, and tactical options selected which optimize the affirmative's position. The affirmative advocate can literally control the argumentative terrain, maneuvering the negative in a direction toward tactical options based on affirmative strengths and negative weaknesses. Second, the increased emphasis on hard data drawn from empirical research has resulted in a lopsided comparison between courses of action advocated by the affirmative and the negative. Because most empirical social science research carries a strong bias in favor of the research hypothesis being considered, affirmative advocates will inevitably be able to locate more empirical support for their position than negative advocates will be able to uncover against it.

The negative counterplan position can minimize this disparity. First, it allows the negative advocate to seize the initiative in a debate. The counterplan functions much like an affirmative position. It allows the negative advocate to wrest control of the argumentative terrain from the affirmative, maneuvering the affirmative toward tactical options based on negative strengths and affirmative weaknesses. Second, the counterplan can constitute a pro-hypothesis position. Thus, the negative can also capitalize on the pro-hypothesis bias in contemporary social science research.

Negative speaker functions take on an affirmative aura in a counterplan debate. Of course the first negative constructive speaker may still attack the affirmative's case in traditional fashion. In handling the counterplan, however, the first negative constructive speech resembles the first affirmative constructive speech. The first negative constructive speaker presents the counterplan, shows that it is non-topical and competitive, possibly lays the argumentative footing for a continued claim to presumption, and develops the advantages to the counterplan. The first negative rebuttal speaker may elect to extend his or her original case attacks. However, in arguing the counterplan position, the first negative rebuttal speech functions much like the second affirmative constructive speech. The first negative rebuttal speaker extends the counterplan position in the face of affirmative attacks (just as the second affirmative constructive speaker normally extends the affirmative case in the face of negative attacks).

The second negative constructive speech may change very little. The second negative constructive speaker is free to attack the affirmative's plan. However, the second negative constructive speaker must additionally assume some responsibility in defending the counterplan position. This advocate should answer any second affirmative constructive plan objections to the counterplan or render assistance to the first negative as is needed. Naturally the burdens on the second affirmative rebuttal speaker increase in a counterplan debate.

Criteria for Use. The negative counterplan can be a viable negative strategic option—in the right circumstances. However, there are times when the counterplan position is the wrong argumentative choice—in spite of the strategic advantages cited previously. The trick is knowing when to utilize the negative counterplan option. The negative advocate should carefully consider two criteria in evaluating the appropriateness of a counterplan approach.

The first criterion is that the substantive conditions must be suitable. The negative advocate should consider using the counterplan position when he or she is the best prepared to contest the merits of an affirmative's case. Unfortunately, advocates are usually the most tempted to initiate the counterplan option when they are the least prepared to contest an affirmative's case. Inappropriate use of the counterplan inevitably backfires. It often plays right into affirmative hands, and it always produces mediocre calibre argumentation. So, inappropriate use has earned a bad reputation for the counterplan among some critics. The negative should consider a counterplan position if: (1) ample research has been completed on the affirmative case variant; (2) all strategic options have been carefully thought through; and (3) the counterplan appears to be the strongest possible position.

The counterplan option is especially appropriate when the present system confronts a no-win scenario. Such a scenario includes two dimensions. First, if no efficacy can be shown for present system mechanisms; that is, if the thrust of the present system holds no promise. Second, if existing present system trends preclude the best plan disadvantage arguments. This circumstance is not uncommon. If the present system lacks viability, the negative advocate should wisely elect not to defend it. Nonetheless, the present system can continue to plague the negative because the direction of the system may preempt potential disadvantages.

For example, an affirmative position to increase nuclear power generation in support of the resolution that, "the federal government should establish a comprehensive program to significantly increase the energy independence of the United States," places the negative in a no-win scenario. On the one hand, present nuclear power generation does not contribute substantially to U.S. energy independence. Hence, it would be futile for the negative advocate to attempt to offer the existing nuclear option as a vehicle to achieve energy independence. On the other hand, the negative cannot effectively argue significant plan disadvantages which stem from the consequences of nuclear power generation (i.e., risk of nuclear accidents such as core meltdown, waste disposal difficulties, and so on). In essence, the present system acts as an albatross on the negative. Many nuclear power facilities already exist; still more are on the drawing board. Hence, the negative cannot demonstrate a unique risk to increased nuclear power generation even if it could prove that the nuclear alternative is unqualifiedly bad. The counterplan position provides a way out of this no-win scenario. The negative could counterplan, phasing out nuclear power generation (reversing the trend of the present system). This places the negative advocate in a position to maximize his or her plan disadvantage arguments.

Naturally the counterplan strategy is only appropriate when the argumentative conditions are suitable. This second criterion for use carries two implications. On the one hand, the conditions must prove right for the advocate. The advocate considering the counterplan position should think through a number of important questions. Do I know how to argue counterplan theory? Can I substantively extend the counterplan position against all possible affirmative arguments? Am I capable of handling the additional coverage demands of the typical counterplan debate? Am I skilled in rebuttal issue selection? In addition, the conditions must be appropriate for the critic judge. The negative must determine whether the judge is receptive to a counterplan position. The counterplan is a viable position only if all parties are capable and amenable.

Theoretical Burdens.   A solid theoretical foundation is a prerequisite to success in arguing the negative counterplan position. This presupposes both an understanding of and a capacity to apply counterplan theory in the debate round. The advocate who hasn't mastered the theory would be ill-advised to argue the counterplan position. It is much like playing with fire in advocacy; the unskilled advocate is likely to get burned. As we will demonstrate in Chapter 11, most affirmative wins against counterplan positions stem directly from negative theoretical failings.

Four theoretical issues loom large in counterplan debates. The first three are absolute conditions for acceptance of a negative counterplan.

First, a negative *counterplan must be non-topical.* This is true because a topical counterplan provides a reason for the critic judge to accept the resolution. The resolution distinguishes affirmative and negative ground, differentiating those arguments which are potentially available to the affirmative from those potentially available to the negative. The affirmative, and only the affirmative, must uphold the resolution! There are no circumstances in which the negative may usurp this obligation.

A handful of contemporary theorists have contested this requirement. They maintain that the non-topicality requirement poses an unfair burden on the negative; that contemporary resolutions are often so expansive as to preclude viable negative counterplan positions.[12] We have previously discussed the implications of broad resolutions. Because the division of ground between affirmative and negative is a zero-sum affair, broader resolutions tend to expand affirmative terrain and to reduce negative terrain. This results in an increase in affirmative tactical options and a reduction in negative options. In such circumstances, the negative counterplan option is often foreclosed. For example, the resolution that, "the United States should establish uniform rules of procedure for its criminal courts," epitomizes this problem. The affirmative can choose from among a myriad of excellent case possibilities; the negative, by contrast, has severely limited counterplan prospects.

Furthermore, these theorists argue that the competitiveness standard (see below) alone is enough to assure sufficient clash between affirmative and negative advocates. Therefore, the necessity of a non-topicality requirement is moot.[13]

We disagree with this position. While it is true that more expansive resolutions tilt the tactical advantage toward the affirmative, the most appropriate solution is to compose more balanced resolutions. In addition, the resolution serves to divide the terrain; this in turn facilitates clash. Counterplan non-topicality and competitiveness requirements are additive—together they promote the probability of negative clash. Without the non-topicality burden, the temptation would be too great for negatives; many would turn their affirmative cases into counterplan positions, using an increased quantity of weak pseudo-arguments (artificial arguments) to fulfill the competitiveness requirement. This would substantially reduce clash.

Arguing the non-topicality of the counterplan is not easy. The negative advocate must defend non-topicality on an analytical and evidenciary level against potentially well-prepared affirmative opponents. Furthermore, the negative must win the non-topicality issue cleanly. Because non-topicality is a dichotomous issue requiring an all-or-nothing judgment, if any doubt remains, the critic judge may well discard the counterplan.

The second theoretical condition is *competitiveness*. A negative counterplan must be a reasonable substitute for the affirmative proposal. Allan J. Lichtman and Daniel Rohrer have observed that, "... the logic of comparative advantages and of contemporary decision theory indicate that policy argument is an attempt to select the best policy from the range of available options."[14] The counterplan competitiveness standard ensures that the comparison of alternative policies will prove meaningful. In this manner, competitiveness guarantees clash between opposing advocates.

In policy systems debate two tests—or standards—are most commonly used to assess the competitiveness of a negative counterplan position. The counterplan must pass just one of these tests.

The first test is mutual exclusivity. Could the two policies exist simultaneously? Or, in the words of Lichtman and Rohrer, "Adoption of a counterplan must be tantamount to rejecting the policy system offered by the affirmative ... If two policies cannot coexist, a decision-maker must choose between them."[15]

The following examples illustrate the mutual exclusivity test. Some affirmatives argued for a federal mandate to require interdistrict busing of public school students in support of the resolution that "the federal government should establish minimum educational standards for all elementary and secondary schools in the United States." These affirmative advocates claimed that the educational attainment of minority school children is deficient, interdistrict busing is the vehicle to accomplish school integration, and minority students optimize school achievement in integrated educational settings.

Of course negative non-resolutional terrain is expansive. Thus, a myriad of negative counterplan possibilities exist, but very few of these could muster competitiveness. A negative advocate could counterplan that the United States adopt a nuclear freeze. This option is clearly non-topical, but it is obviously not mutually exclusive. That is, a nuclear freeze policy is not a substitute for a federal mandate for interdistrict busing of school children. The two policies can exist simultaneously. Hence, there is no basis for clash. Alternatively the negative could counterplan with various strategies to increase the educational attainment of minority students. For example, the negative could provide incentives for states to target minority districts to receive a heavier share of their educational expenditures, provide bilingual instruction, and so on. These options might appear competitive at first glance. After all, they do at least address the affirmative's problem area. However, these counterplan possibilities do not constitute substitutes for interdistrict busing. It is quite possible to adopt various efforts to increase minority achievement *and* to mandate interdistrict busing. Thus, such positions are not mutually exclusive to the affirmative's plan.

A mutually exclusive alternative *forces a choice* between two courses of action. For example, the resolution that, "all United States military intervention into the internal affairs of any foreign nation or nations in the Western Hemisphere should be prohibited," requires an affirmative to stop U.S. military intervention in the hemisphere. If the affirmative argued that the United States should cease all military activities—while the negative offered a counterplan to increase United States military efforts—on behalf of the Samoza government in El Salvador, then a clear choice *must* be made. It is simply impossible to simultaneously decrease *and* increase U.S. military presence in El Salvador. The negative's counterplan option is quite obviously a mutually exclusive alternative. Most instances, however, are not this clear cut.

The second test for competitiveness is on-balance superiority. This involves a comparison of the net benefits of the affirmative's plan and the negative's counterplan. Lichtman and Rohrer describe this test as follows: "A counterplan is also competitive with an affirmative plan if simultaneous adoption of both the counterplan and the affirmative plan, though possible, is less desirable than the adoption of the counterplan alone."[16] This test forces clash between the two policy positions at the point of comparative desirability. If it is better to adopt the counterplan alone, then it is a viable substitute for the affirmative's proposal.

An affirmative position to promote the standardization of North Atlantic Treaty Organization forces and equipment in support of the resolution that, "the United States should significantly increase its foreign military commitments," illustrates this competitiveness test. A negative could counterplan that the United States initiate a Graduated Reduction In Tension (GRIT) strategy to improve relations with the Soviet Union. The counterplan consists of a unilateral step to reduce superpower tensions (the step could take varied form: a force reduction, an arms negotiation concession, etc.). The affirmative could respond, charging that the negative counterplan is not competitive. The affirmative would claim that the counterplan is not mutually exclusive; that the U.S. can initiate a GRIT strategy *and* at the same time take steps toward NATO standardization. In this instance, the negative can concede mutual exclusivity, arguing instead that the adoption of both policies is less desirable than the adoption of the GRIT position alone. The GRIT strategy requires that a clear signal be sent to an adversary; this is accomplished via the counterplan action. However, the affirmative's NATO standardization position inadvertently transmits an opposite signal; it provides belligerent cues to the Soviets. At this point the focus shifts to the question of comparative desirability. Is the affirmative's NATO standardization policy more or less desirable than the negative's GRIT position? If GRIT is the more significant policy, and since GRIT's success requires a clear signal whereas the simultaneous adoption of GRIT and NATO standardization transmits a mixed signal, it is better to adopt the GRIT position alone than the GRIT position in conjunction with the NATO standardization policy. In this instance the counterplan position meets the on-balance superiority test. Thus, it is a competitive alternative.

The third theoretical condition is *justification;* namely, there must be some reason to adopt the counterplan position instead of the affirmative alternative. This requires that the negative advocate: (1) win a unique advantage to the counterplan (i.e., the GRIT position reduces superpower tension with a variety of concomitant benefits); and/or (2) win a unique disadvantage against the affirmative's plan—one that applies to the plan but not to the counterplan. Justification is measured in terms of net benefit. That is, the net desirability of the negative's counterplan position must exceed the net desirability of the affirmative's position.

In short, the negative advocate must demonstrate that his or her counterplan position is non-topical, competitive, and superior to the affirmative's position. If the advocate is successful on all three counts, then the counterplan position will win. If the negative fails on even one test, however, then the affirmative will prevail.

A fourth theoretical issue is *presumption.* In a counterplan debate does presumption lie with the affirmative or with the negative? This question is a bone of contention among theorists. The traditional perspective holds that, since the negative abandons its traditional ground in a counterplan debate, presumption shifts to the affirmative. Thus, the burden is on the negative to demonstrate the superiority of its position.[17] By contrast, the hypothesis tester maintains that presumption always remains against the resolution in accordance with the premise that, "He who advocates must prove."[10] Thus, the burden is still on the affirmative to prove that the resolution is true.

The policy systems paradigm requires the locus of presumption to be evaluated based on the circumstances unique to a particular debate. It holds that presumption should not be assigned arbitrarily to one side or the other. Rather, it is grounded in the basis of presumption, which is potential risk. Risk is a function of the scope of an advocate's proposed change; the larger the change, the greater the risks.[19] This explains why presumption rests with the present system—thus with the negative—in traditional debates.

Determining presumption in a counterplan debate is no different; it is determined by assessing comparative risk potential. Presumption rests with the policy which embodies less change, and therefore less risk. Of course, the assignment of presumption is a point of contention in a debate. For example, if an affirmative advocate argued for the adoption of a NATO standardization policy, and his or her negative counterpart responded with a GRIT counterplan position, both sides have a right to contest the locus of presumption. In this instance, however, based on the risk potential standard, it would appear that presumption will ultimately rest with the affirmative's policy. Taking steps to increase the effectiveness of NATO constitutes a moderate departure from the status quo; adopting the GRIT strategy represents a more significant change.

Variants.   Most negative counterplan options are specific to the topic. Some, however, are generic in nature. Three of the most common generic variants are grounded in alternative agents, the antithesis of the resolution, and further study. We will briefly describe each of these counterplan positions.

The *alternative agent counterplan* is a common option on most resolutions. This counterplan position offers a substitute for the agent of change specified in the resolution; it then argues that the alternative agent is more desirable. For example, on the resolution that, "the federal government should establish minimum educational standards for all elementary and secondary schools in the United States," many negatives argued that the states—as opposed to the federal government—are a superior agent of change in education. As with most alternative agent counterplans, non-topicality is one of the trickiest issues. In this example the critical question is whether uniform and concurrent state action constitutes *de facto* federal action? There are strong arguments for and against this thesis.

An antithesis of the resolution counterplan mandates movement in the opposite direction of the resolution. It provides clear lines of clash, placing the negative in a position to maximize its plan disadvantages. It is especially appropriate when the present system confronts a no-win scenario. The nuclear power generation example on page 190 on the resolution that, "the federal government should establish a comprehensive program to significantly increase the energy independence of the United States," depicted the use of this counterplan variant.

The *study counterplan* calls for systematic investigation prior to action. The study option maintains that decision makers should delay action, at least until the results of additional investigation are available. The study counterplan constitutes a contemporary rendition of the traditional straight refutation negative. It functions much like a risk disadvantage; it suggests that decision makers should proceed cautiously in the face of uncertainties. However, the study counterplan is a more attractive option than the straight refutation position. It mandates an initial step (to investigate thoroughly the problem in question). This step may lead to subsequent substantive measures. The study position, in short, offers the hope that something will be done on behalf of the problem.

We recommend, however, that negative advocates exercise caution in using the study counterplan option. This position presents two difficulties. First, the study counterplan is appropriate only if there is a genuine need for additional information. The negative advocate should use this strategic option *only:* (1) if limited affirmative data has been provided, and/or (2) if the negative is in a position to offer strong straight refutation against affirmative reasoning and data (especially on efficacy), and (3) if study is likely to produce useful information. It is a futile effort to argue a study counterplan position when the negative advocate is unable or unwilling to attack affirmative data. Such an approach primarily serves to undermine negative credibility. Second, it is difficult to defend competitiveness of the study counterplan. Most affirmatives include provisions for study in their plans. Thus, the key question asks: Is it better to study and then act, or to act and then study? The negative advocate must provide a convincing rationale that further investigation is imperative prior to action. Otherwise the best course of action is simultaneously to adopt the plan in order to treat the problem and study.[20]

Figure 10–1 depicts the counterplan position. We have chosen a study counterplan which was argued against an affirmative position to phase out United States military intervention on behalf of the Samoza government in El Salvador on the resolution that, "all United States military intervention into the internal affairs of any foreign nation or nations in the Western Hemisphere should be prohibited."

FIGURE 10-1   STUDY COUNTERPLAN POSITION

COUNTERPLAN

I.   An independent research and analysis association shall be established. Specialists in the fields of international politics, Latin American studies, military policy, diplomacy, history and political science will be selected to be members of the association.

II. The independent research and analysis association will accomplish the following mandates:

   A. Undertake a systematic investigation of political and military conditions in El Salvador. Evaluate the costs and benefits of continued U.S. military intervention on behalf of the Samoza regime.

   B. Upon completion of its investigation the recommendations of the study group shall be proposed as a policy and submitted to U.S. decision makers and to the public. Steps A and B must be completed within two years.

   C. A national referendum process shall be established for the sole purpose of determining the future direction of U.S. policy toward El Salvador. A majority decision will be binding upon decision makers.

   D. All arguments and data relevant to the conclusions of the association will be disseminated to the general public through mass media channels.

   E. The association will be provided adequate funds, staff and facilities to carry out its mandates. Funding will be provided via general federal revenues. Any relevant information shall be made available to the association on request.

III. Anyone found guilty of violating or subverting the counterplan's mandate or intent shall face fines and prison terms. Enforcement will be via existing procedures.

IV. Negative speeches shall serve to clarify questions of counterplan intent.

OBSERVATION I: NON-TOPICALITY

   A. The counterplan does not prohibit U.S. military intervention.

      1. A potential prohibition is problematic; we don't know what the association will recommend.

      2. If a prohibition did finally result from the counterplan's mandate, it would be at most an indirect effect. The counterplan simply mandates study and referendum.

   B. Indirect or effects topicality is an illegitimate standard. It destroys negative ground which exists opposite the resolution since many actions might indirectly reduce the likelihood of U.S. military intervention (i.e., reducing defense spending, increasing foreign aid appropriations, etc.).

OBSERVATION II: COMPETITIVENESS

   A. Net benefits. Better policy results from adequate, reliable and extensive analysis. The study must precede action in order to preclude the possible consequences of non-intervention.

   B. Mutually exclusive. A policy maker can't adopt a policy and then study to determine if that policy should be adopted. An effort to evaluate whether a policy of non-intervention is desirable must precede the enactment of a policy of non-intervention.

   C. One standard is sufficient. Just as the affirmative has to present only one standard for justification, the negative has to offer only one reason why both the affirmative's plan and the negative's counterplan cannot be adopted.

OBSERVATION III: SOLVENCY—A BETTER POLICY
(we will use only a skeleton outline from this point)
    A. Adequate data is crucial for good policy
    B. Insufficient, or conflicting, data results in poor policy decisions
        1. Quick-fix solutions fail
        2. Poor policies result
    C. El Salvador policy must be studied
        1. There is insufficient information now
        2. Existing information is unreliable
            a. Information from the left is ignored
            b. Government propaganda is accepted
            c. Specific sources are bad
                i. AWC, ACLU and LAO
                ii. Wire service reports
                iii. Rights organizations
        3. Other studies dispute claims of affirmative
    D. Study is the best available policy
        1. There is no risk to delaying a decision
        2. Study will yield the better policy
OBSERVATION IV: ADVANTAGE—ENHANCE DEMOCRATIC PROCESS
    A. Participation is essential for democracy
        1. Knowledge is critical to democracy
        2. Process and policy are key to democratic decision making
    B. Counterplan enhances democratic values

Solvency Attacks

The affirmative must demonstrate that its particular proposal will solve the problem or accrue the advantages as argued in the initial affirmative presentation. An affirmative assumes the burden to prove efficacy for its position. As we indicated previously, the negative ought to use direct refutation to contest initial affirmative solvency analysis and evidence. This is the first step in undermining or weakening the affirmative solvency position. It is important, but it is nonetheless a defensive strategy. Initial inroads ought to be supplemented with a negative offensive attack on the affirmative's solvency position. This is the role that the negative's plan-meet-need (PMN) or plan-meet-advantage (PMA) arguments must play. The PMN continues the process of diminishing affirmative significance.

While all solvency arguments are designed to diminish affirmative significance, the absolute PMN goes even further. This rare but potent argument takes out all affirmative solvency. At this point (barring any affirmative turnarounds of negative positions) a debate is over. The absolute solvency argument, however, is rare. The standard efficacy attack is normal fare. It too is a strong position if it contributes to the minimization of affirmative significance.

Solvency arguments come in one of four basic designs. Each entails a mode of analysis—a way of viewing an affirmative's proposal.

Workability. The first variant is the workability argument. It concerns the mechanics or specific provisions of an affirmative's plan. A good workability argument can prove most damaging to an affirmative position; a mediocre one is a waste of time.

The negative advocate should systematically scrutinize an affirmative's plan in the following areas in search of potential workability arguments. First, look for mechanical and administrative deficiencies, sometimes called "plan flaws." Does the plan provide for administrative support, sufficient expertise, a viable revenue source, and so on? Affirmative fiat does not obviate plan workability considerations. As indicated in chapter 9, fiat assumes that if a particular action is desirable, then it ought to be initiated. It directs attention away from petty questions surrounding plan implementation to the issues concerning desirability. Of course, significant plan mechanical and administrative deficiencies are germane to the question of desirability. For instance, if an affirmative called for the adoption of a $40-billion Federal employment program in support of the resolution that, "the federal government should implement a program which guarantees employment opportunities for all United States citizens in the labor force," and if the plan's $40-billion price tag fueled another round of double-digit inflation or resulted in significant reductions in other spending initiatives (i.e., health care, defense, etc.), then the proposal's mechanical features substantially diminish the plan's desirability. Thus, an affirmative may fiat a specific plan feature, but it cannot fiat workability. For example, an affirmative may fiat funding of the plan; however, it cannot fiat the adequacy or the desirability of the revenue source. An affirmative may fiat personnel to administer the plan, but it cannot fiat the availability of sufficient expertise. The negative advocate must attempt to hold an affirmative opponent accountable for the mechanical and administrative workability of the plan.

Second, the negative should carefully examine plan enforcement provisions. Utilizing the affirmative's plan and the cross-examination periods as vehicles for information, the negative advocate should determine the means and the adequacy of affirmative enforcement. With such information in hand, the negative can accurately appraise the potential of workability arguments and plan disadvantages which stem from an affirmative's enforcement. Bear in mind that affirmative enforcement needs are dependent upon both the total sweep of its change and the nature of its inherency. The negative advocate should make sure that an affirmative's enforcement provisions are sufficient to overcome its inherencies (both structural and attitudinal).

Finally the negative will want to discover whether an affirmative's plan has any precedents—successful or not. This is an important area for negative research and subsequent argument development. If a particular plan has successful precedents, then the affirmative should be able to provide strong empirical documentation in support of its solvency. This places the negative in a difficult situation. If the negative is not prepared to contest affirmative documentation via straight refutation, then it might be best to forego all efficacy attacks against the affirmative position. Conversely, if a particular plan has been tried and has failed, then the negative can turn to a tremendous store of empirical documentation to bolster its efficacy attacks. Either way, a careful consideration of plan precedents is crucial.

Alternative Causality. The second solvency argument design is alternative causality. It attempts to assess an affirmative plan's success in eradicating the important causes of the problem in question. If the problem has been incorrectly diagnosed, then the affirmative's proposed solution may prove to be wholly inadequate. The 1979–81 policy controversy over possible solutions to double-digit inflation illustrates this PMN variant. Many argued in support of a constitutional amendment to require a balanced federal budget. We know now that federal government deficits were not the primary cause of the 1979–81 bout with inflation. During the first two years of the Reagan presidency, federal deficits soared to record high levels and yet the rate of inflation plummeted. Thus, if a Constitutional amendment to require a balanced federal budget had been initiated, it would not have uniquely slowed inflation (of course *it may have* triggered a major economic depression, as the amendment's opponents claimed).

Many affirmative plans are prone to this PMN variant as a result of oversimplification. The important economic, political, and social problems of our time involve speculative and multiple causation. Yet, due to time constraints, affirmative advocates are forced to isolate a limited number of causes which can be solved via relatively simple plan mechanisms. However, such efforts to simplify complex issues are suspect. The negative should isolate and identify alternative causal variables; then indicate the impact of each upon the affirmative's harm.

Circumvention. Another PMN variant is the circumvention argument. It concerns the potential to escape from—or thwart—the affirmative's mandate. This argument assumes that those individuals or groups which are hostile to the affirmative's policy position (possibly the same ones identified in the affirmative's initial inherency position) will not knuckle under. Instead, they will exploit plan loopholes, refuse compliance and attempt to counteract the plan's mandate. Affirmatives who develop superficial inherency positions—ones that indict present system structures while glossing over underlying attitudes—pave the way for the negative circumvention argument. Structures do not function in a vacuum; it is the presence of attitudes which makes possible the emergence and development of structures. Thus, hostile atittudes are likely to remain and, unless an affirmative can change them or render them inactive, to manifest themselves in new ways in a post-plan environment.

The circumvention argument requires three steps. First, motivation must be shown. Motivation consists of hostile attitudes directed against the plan. Sometimes the affirmative will provide the motivation in its initial inherency position. In most cases, however, it is the negative that must offer the analysis and the evidence to establish motivation. Second, the means of or vehicle for circumvention must be demonstrated. How will the hostile attitudes manifest themselves? What mechanisms are operable channels to thwart an affirmative's mandate? This step is an important one; it makes or breaks the circumvention argument. Finally, the impact of the circumvention argument must be indicated.

Plan-Meet-Need Disadvantage. The plan-meet-need disadvantage argument is a hybrid. It simply combines a solvency attack with a plan disadvantage (which we will consider next), arguing that an affirmative's plan will fail to ameliorate and/or

---

FIGURE 10-2   PLAN-MEET-NEED DISADVANTAGE

PMN DA: NEGOTIATIONS HOLD NO PROMISE
   A. No potential exists for negotiations
      1. The Left won't negotiate
         a. Rebel leaders refuse
         b. Splintering precludes
         c. Empirically in 1979
      2. Government won't negotiate
         a. Far Right refuses
         b. Splintering precludes
   B. If parties agreed to negotiate, no political solution is possible
      1. Extremists preclude solution
         a. Seek a military victory
         b. Will sabotage process
      2. Even Department of State admits limited potential for negotiations
   C. Negotiations will strengthen the Left
      1. Negotiations legitimize Left
      2. Left will use negotiations to fuel a complete military victory

---

aggravate the problem. We will provide an example on the resolution that, "all United States military intervention into the internal affairs of any nation or nations in the Western Hemisphere should be prohibited," to illustrate the structural composition of the plan-meet-need disadvantage. The affirmative argued that the United States should phase out its military intervention on behalf of the Samoza government in El Salvador; that this would produce a political, as opposed to a military, solution to the current civil strife by motivating all parties to the negotiating table. The plan-meet-need disadvantage claims that: (1) the parties won't negotiate; (2) if they did, they couldn't agree on a political settlement; and (3) if they could, the left would emerge as the most powerful faction. Figure 10-2 depicts the structure of this argument.

The negative's solvency position continues the process of diminishing affirmative significance. The position consists of two dimensions: straight refutation against initial affirmative solvency analysis and evidence in conjunction with an offensive attack on the affirmative's solvency position. We will examine the strategic and tactical dimensions of the solvency position in chapter 12.

Plan Disadvantages

Plan disadvantages focus on the consequences of the adoption of an affirmative proposal. The abbreviated version of the policy equation posits that: net case significance is greater or less than net disadvantage impact. Most standard negative argumentative options—including straight refutation, extratopicality, defense of the present system, minor repairs, conditional counterplans, and efficacy attacks—concentrate on affirmative benefits. Indeed, absent plan disadvantage arguments, the affirmative advocate is in a most enviable position. The advocate assumes the role of a mythological bearer of gifts—a policy systems Santa Claus—who is able to bestow positive impacts oblivious to other consequences.

The plan disadvantage argument depicts affirmative costs. It redirects attention to the real world where the principle of scarcity prevails. Scarcity precludes policy systems omnipotence; it presupposes the need to make hard choices. Scarcity means that there can be no positive impact without negative impact; no benefits without costs; in essence, no "free lunch." Thus, the plan disadvantage attempts to establish an offsetting or countervailing impact. As such, this position is the most important option in the negative's tactical arsenal.

Basic Requirements.   The basic requirements of the plan disadvantage are similar to those of an affirmative advantage.

The first requirement is *uniqueness*. The negative advocate must demonstrate that the plan disadvantage inheres in—is unique to—an affirmative's proposal. This constitutes the link of the plan disadvantage. The link embodies the thesis of the disadvantage; it ties an affirmative's plan to a particular consequence. We will illustrate this requirement with a common plan disadvantage on the resolution that, "all United States military intervention into the internal affairs of any foreign nation or nations in the Western Hemisphere should be prohibited." In this instance the negative argued a "Red Spread" disadvantage against an affirmative position which called for a generic ban on all future U.S. military intervention in this hemisphere. How does a blanket prohibition of United States military intervention in the hemisphere trigger the "Red Spread" disadvantage? The answer, and the thesis of this disadvantage, is that the threat and actual use of United States military intervention deters and arrests communist expansion in Latin America. If the United States adopted a policy of non-intervention in the hemisphere, then Soviet- and Cuban-backed communist insurgencies would envelop Latin America.

The second requirement is *significance*. The negative must prove that the plan disadvantage embodies serious consequences. Two steps are involved. Initially, the negative must demonstrate that the value which the affirmative plan undermines is an important one. All policy questions embody values in conflict. All affirmative plans alter value hierarchies. Just as affirmative benefits stem from the accelerated promotion of one or more basic values, affirmative consequences result from the values slighted in the tradeoff. In short, value reprioritization cuts both ways. In addition, the negative must provide a quantitative or qualitative measure of significance. A value might be important, but that alone is not sufficient. The negative must demonstrate that the value manifests tangible impact. In the example above, any one or more possible impacts of the "Red Spread" disadvantage might be developed. The negative could argue that communism tramples individual rights of speech, assembly, worship and thought; terrorizes segments of the population; and spreads like a cancer to envelop all surrounding countries.

Figure 10–3 depicts the structure of the disadvantage argument. We have chosen a "Red Spread" disadvantage which was argued against an affirmative position to phase out United States military intervention on behalf of the Samoza government in El Salvador.

FIGURE 10-3   PLAN DISADVANTAGE

DA: BAN ON U.S. MILITARY INTERVENTION WILL FUEL COMMUNIST EXPANSION IN THE HEMISPHERE (RED SPREAD)

- A. Soviets & Cubans fuel revolution
  - 1. Generally
    - a. Soviets are expansionist
    - b. Seek maritime hegemony
  - 2. In El Salvador
    - a. Soviets encourage Cubans
    - b. Cuban role is instrumental
      - 1. Cuba supplies rebels
      - 2. Cuba provides proxies
    - c. El Salvador guerrilla effort is controlled by avowed Marxists
- B. The elimination of the U.S. presence in El Salvador will result in communist gains
  - 1. El Salvador will go communist
    - a. Is on the brink now
    - b. U.S. holds the key
  - 2. Central America will go communist
    - a. The threshold is now
    - b. El Salvador is pivotal
- C. Communist gains guarantee repression
  - 1. Suspension of basic freedoms
  - 2. Domestic repression and death
- D. Further Communist gains in the region will prove to be disastrous for the U.S.
  - 1. Undermines the credibility of U.S. policy commitments on a worldwide basis
  - 2. Assures complete communist hegemony

Analytical Basis.   Plan disadvantages stem from one of four basic phenomena. Each entails a mode of analysis—a way of viewing an affirmative's proposal.

The first variant of plan disadvantage is generic. This type stems from the debate resolution itself. In this instance, the thrust and direction of the affirmative's specific approach is irrelevant. The resolution itself triggers the plan disadvantage.

This could occur in one of two ways. First, the value thesis of the resolution may provide grounds for the disadvantage. For example, the resolution that, "the federal government should significantly strengthen the guarantee of consumer product safety required of manufacturers," embodies a clear value thesis that government should increase regulation of manufacturers in order to enhance consumer protection. This value thesis is all-encompassing. It will manifest itself *regardless of the particular case approach* an affirmative chooses. Thus, the negative can argue plan disadvantages based on the evils of increased government regulation of manufacturers (i.e., reduced productivity, erosion of business confidence, etc.). Second, the agent specified in the resolution may serve as the source of the disadvantage. For example, the resolution, "the federal government should establish minimum education standards for all elementary and secondary schools in the United States," commits all affirmatives to a federal mandate in education, regardless of any particular affirmative's case approach. Thus, the negative can argue plan disadvantages based on the evils of federal—as opposed to state—action in the education sphere (i.e., flexibility, innovation, control, etc.).

The second type of plan disadvantage occurs as a result of the movement toward solvency. Its impact is proportional or inverse, depending on the nature of the specific argument. On one hand, if the disadvantage's impact is proportional, then it gains momentum as the affirmative's plan moves toward maximum solvency. For example, if an affirmative called for the increased use of coal as a domestic energy source in support of the resolution that, "the federal government should establish a comprehensive program to significantly increase the energy independence of the United States," the negative could argue various consequences. The affirmative's plan will require increased domestic coal production. Yet, deep mining has historically proven to be injurious to workers while strip mining scars the environment. In addition, the plan mandates the increased use of coal as an energy source. But, coal generates more air pollution than alternative energy sources. These consequences, of course, are small initially, but they increase as the affirmative mandate moves toward maximum solvency.

On the other hand, if the disadvantage's impact stems from the vacuum created from the point of plan implementation to maximum solvency, then its impact dissipates during that interim. This is an especially effective argument when coupled with a negative solvency position. For example, if an affirmative mandates a graduated reduction in oil imports in conjunction with a national commitment to alternative fuels in support of the "energy independence" resolution above, the negative could argue that energy shortages will cripple American economic performance. This consequence occurs at plan implementation; it dissipates as energy alternates gear up to fill the gap.

The third class of plan disadvantage stems from the implementation of the affirmative's mechanism per se. The disadvantage's impact is immediate. This variant may be the most common of the four types; in part as a result of its link potential. Since this disadvantage stems directly from the affirmative's plan, greater care is often shown in establishing the argument's link.

If the affirmative's significance or solvency are future oriented, this mode of plan consequence is especially valuable since its impact multiplies from the point of implementation. In this instance, the affirmative benefit is delayed; but consequences are immediate. For instance, almost all affirmative programs which "significantly increase the energy independence of the United States" will necessitate financial outlays of tens of billions of dollars. Such enormous expenditures could produce a myriad of evils: they could set off a new round of double digit inflation by placing significant pressure on the money markets; they could spur further cuts in fragile federal social expenditures; and so on. Energy independence occurs in the intermediate or long-term future; the consequences of increased federal outlays are immediate.

The fourth variant of plan disadvantage results from policy interrelationships. Action along a single, narrow front inevitably spills over into other policy sectors.

These spillovers constitute decision costs, usually the loss of valued programs, which must be carefully evaluated.

Any affirmative decision to act has a direct and often significant impact on seemingly non-competitive policy domain. The essential premise of this position is that all inputs (resources) involved in a decision to act are scarce. As a result, any commitment to act in pursuit of one objective will reduce the total pool of inputs, making less available for some future action.[21]

Three priority considerations are relevant in any affirmative attempt to accelerate the promotion of a particular value. First, financial priorities. It is based on a scarcity of government revenues (whether real or perceived). Financial priorities assumes that public funds are scarce; that in an era of tight budgets and so-called "taxpayer revolt," the government must make critical decisions with respect to existing and proposed public programs. In essence, it assumes that any new funding priority would be enacted only at the expense of existing programs.

The second priority consideration is social priorities. It involves the scarcity of good will, or, at least of a passive tolerance. The thesis is that change carries the potential for social cleavage. New programs, especially moral mandates which lack broad-based popular support, strain the social fabric and risk thwarting alternative changes. Moral mandates are the most dangerous. They can significantly retard social welfare programs and endanger individual rights by increasing the political vulnerability of their proponents. Finally, political priorities can force valued programs to be cut or lost altogether. Political coalitions make policy via a complex mosaic of give-and-take which places a premium on compromise. An affirmative mandate which circumvents the coalition-building process results in political tension which sets in motion the wheels of both a circumvention plan-meet-need argument and a political priorities disadvantage. This risk is greatest when policy choices are the most controversial.[22]

Affirmative plans also have indirect and often significant impacts on seemingly non-competitive policy domain. Policy adoption produces symbolic impacts which can propel, or impede, present system programs.

Policy impact is an encompassing phenomenon. It is a measure of *both tangible and symbolic effects* (what changes in the environment result from public policy adoption). Current attempts to assess or weigh public policy impact fall short because they virtually ignore symbolic outcomes.[23] Yet, these are important. In the international sphere, the symbolic impact of a nation's economic, military or foreign policy is often the most definitive result.

Political scientist Murray Edelman claims that all government measures provide "condensation symbols" which generate substantial impact upon receivers.[24] In some instances government policy adoption may serve to reassure groups, thwarting a promising reform impetus. Once assured by a highly heralded policy adoption, the public accepts the policy claims and becomes quiescent.[25] Thus, reform policies can immobilize the very groups that are the most active in pressing for change. Public policy—regardless of its intent—serves to quell reform attitudes. This has clearly been the result of most anti-trust legislation, some civil rights laws, and the work of various regulatory agencies, among them the Federal Communication Commission, the Federal Energy Office, and others.[26]

Generic Positions

Generic arguments are based on genus—a sub-division within an entire class, or the entire class itself. All of the negative positions discussed in this chapter could be developed as generic arguments. In short, an argument's grounding—and not its type—distinguishes the generic from other positions.

The most common form of generic argument is grounded in the essence of the debate resolution itself. Thus, if a resolution calls for "the federal government to guarantee employment opportunities for all United States citizens in the labor force," the negative could develop generic approaches based on: the federal government as agent (i.e., a states counterplan, a private associations counterplan, a financial priorities disadvantage, and others); the notion of a guarantee (i.e., an inflation disadvantage based on impairing fiscal policy as a tool to militate business cycles and others); and the mandate for increased employment (i.e., a stress/mortality disadvantage based on the research of Joseph Eyer and others). If a resolution mandates that, "all United States military intervention into the internal affairs of any foreign nation or nations in the Western Hemisphere should be prohibited," the negative could argue generic positions based on: the United States as agent (i.e., a symbolic cues disadvantage such as undermining the START position or fueling Russia/China rapprochement and others); or the resolution's requirement of non-intervention (i.e., a "Red Spread" disadvantage, a humanitarian intervention counterplan, and so on).

The Counterwarrant. One of the more controversial strategic options in contemporary debate is the counterwarrant. The counterwarrant is grounded in the resolution as opposed to the affirmative's particular example of the resolution. It consists of a generic rationale for the rejection of the resolution. As such, the counterwarrant is a more rational attack from the point of view of hypothesis testing as opposed to policy making.

The negative, in arguing the counterwarrant, focuses clash on the representativeness of affirmative examples.[27] Thus, while an affirmative may argue on behalf of a particular example of the resolution, the negative can challenge the affirmative's example as atypical, offering alternative examples as reasons to reject the resolution. For instance, if an affirmative argued for implementation of the recommendations of the Senate Select Committee on Nutrition, yielding an advantage of reducing mortality and morbidity which result from poor diets in support of the resolution that, "the federal government should guarantee comprehensive medical care for all United States citizens," the negative could argue one or more counterwarrants. The negative would claim that the affirmative example was not representative of the resolution. This position assumes that the examples must be generalizable; that a person can infer on the basis of the affirmative's example that the resolution is true.

The negative could argue a representative example (or examples) which denies the validity of the resolution. For instance, the negative may argue that a guarantee of "comprehensive medical care for all citizens" would: (1) result in a sharp increase in unnecessary medical procedures (including x-rays, surgical procedures, medication, etc.), or (2) produce severe economic consequences due to the enormous federal expenditures which would be required to implement such a program. Thus, the negative would claim that the resolution should be rejected—in spite of the potential validity of the affirmative's position.

Appropriateness of Generic Arguments.   Generic positions are among the most controversial of negative strategic options. Indeed, some critic judges are more hostile to generic arguments than they are to bad arguments, believing the former to constitute the worst case of the latter. We maintain that no particular argument mode innately constitutes good or bad argument. Generic argument shares the same potential with every other argument mode to be *either* good or bad. The appropriateness of the negative counterwarrant position depends on the generalizability of the affirmative's plan and case to the resolution as a whole: the counterwarrant is an appropriate negative option when the affirmative's plan and case is unrepresentative of the resolution; it is an inappropriate option when the affirmative's position is representative of the resolution.[28] We will discuss standards to evaluate the legitimacy of the generic counterplan and the generic disadvantage in chapter 11. The negative advocate will want to apply these standards to determine the appropriateness of a particular generic position.

Topicality

Topicality is one of the few issues that most critics agree has an absolute impact. Whereas most issues in debate are resolved in relative terms, topicality is an all-or-nothing proposition calling for a dichotomous judgment. As such, it is a potent negative option.

As we explained in Chapter 9, the affirmative has the right to define terms, but the negative retains the right to challenge the affirmative's definition(s). This poses a sticky question. How does the negative advocate demonstrate the superiority of his or her definition(s) over the affirmative definition(s)? The answer lies in the nature of the topicality argument itself. It is not sufficient simply to challenge an affirmative interpretation of the resolution. Instead, a negative advocate must offer a properly developed topicality argument.

The essential ingredients of a topicality argument include the following elements. First, standards for evaluating topicality should be delineated. Without such standards, the critic judge has no basis to select one definition over another. The standards underpin the evaluation, and thus play a critical role in determining the outcome of a topicality argument. It is important that the negative provide these criteria for evaluation. Second, the negative must demonstrate that the affirmative's interpretation fails to meet the standards. The first and second steps must be well integrated. It doesn't do much good to present standards if the reasons as to why the affirmative is not topical are not grounded in those standards. Needless to say, these reasons must be carefully articulated. Finally, a mention of the impact of the topicality argument is warranted, though it need not be elaborate.

Standards obviously hold the key to topicality. They function as perceptual lenses for the evaluation of this argument genre. A negative advocate's success in arguing topicality thus presupposes a mastery of the standards.

Macro Perspective.   While standards underpin an evaluation of topicality, they do not function in a vacuum. In order to evaluate standards of topicality, a broader macro perspective is required. A macro perspective functions as a tool to evaluate the appropriateness of competing topicality standards.

"Reasonableness" was once the dominant macro perspective. However, it afforded maximum latitude to affirmative advocates. As a result, reasonableness has been challenged by "the better definition" as a superior macro view. Proponents claim that the latter more effectively restricts affirmative latitude.

Reasonableness is based on the presumed value of variety as a source of educational enrichment in debate, and on the ambiguity of the English language. The latter justification is more compelling. It suggests that words are uncertain, and that since meaning stems from usage, meaning is open to interpretation. As a result of this ambiguity, there is no one "correct" interpretation of a debate resolution. Indeed, there may be different interpretations of a word or group of words—all of which are equally reasonable.

Although reasonableness gained wide acceptance, it poses its own ambiguity. What does it mean to be reasonable? The term itself defies precise definition. This prompted James J. Unger to observe that: "It [reasonability] is far too vague and lacking in substance to offer anything more than a set of individualized, biased, and even emotional standards which must vary from judge to judge, debate to debate . . . reasonability as a limitation upon definitional excess is both ineffective and counterproductive."[29]

The "better definition" alternative was initially offered as a superior standard of topicality. Yet, it is more than a standard; it is a vehicle to facilitate the evaluation of competing standards. The better definition perspective is best described by Unger, in his words:

> . . . in order to defeat the topicality of the affirmative approach the negative must be prepared to engage in a three-step process. (1) The negative must offer a clear alternative definition of terms or a clear alternative standard of application of same. (2) The negative must demonstrate the superiority of its interpretation to that of the affirmative. This would be accomplished through a two-fold process of comparison. First, the relative linguistic and policy support which each approach commands would be assessed . . . Second, the relative forensic support available must also be assessed. (3) The negative may be called upon to demonstrate that the affirmative plan cannot comfortably fit under its own definitional approach. Once having accomplished all three of these steps the negative may legitimately claim that for the purposes of this debate the affirmative case no longer meets the terms of the resolution as most accurately therein interpreted, and thus it should be rejected.[30]

There are two ways to view the relationship between "reasonableness" and "the better definition." One way is to consider the two to be competing perspectives to facilitate an evaluation of standards of topicality; they are alternative lenses for the viewing of standards. The other way is to view the latter as a refinement of the former; the "better definition" is a means to direct and shape the notion of "reasonableness."

Specific Standards. A negative advocate's success in arguing topicality presupposes a mastery of the various standards of topicality. This entails both understanding and application. We will briefly describe and evaluate a sampling of the most common standards in policy systems debate.

The first standard is *grammatical structure.* Interpreting a debate resolution involves more than simply determining the meaning of individual words. A resolution, much like any sentence, must be understood in terms of its grammatical structure. If the grammatical structure were rearranged, an entirely different meaning would result from precisely the same words.[31] Thus, the grammatical pattern of a debate resolution must be maintained and strictly observed in order to derive the correct meaning from the words which constitute the pattern.

In this fashion the grammatical structure acts as a limitation on the possible interpretations of the resolution. This is especially true of modifiers which help determine the meaning of the headword. Modifiers play an important role in determining meaning. Negative advocates must carefully scrutinize affirmative interpretations for possible misuse of modifiers. In the resolution that, "the United States should significantly curtail its arms sales to other countries," the placement of the word "significantly" in the sentence indicates its function; it modifies "curtail," the action mandated by the resolution, and not "arms sales," the object of that action. Hence, the affirmative must "significantly curtail" a mandate relative to the totality of U.S. arms sales. This is a more imposing burden than a requirement that the affirmative "curtail . . . significant arms sales."

Another possible grammatical error involves the misclassification of the words of the resolution, i.e., using a noun as an adjective. The proper classification of words cannot always be determined by viewing the word apart from its use in the sentence because the English language includes many words which, when used differently, belong to two or more classes. Jerome Frank refers to the false assumption that each symbol has but one use as the "one-word, one-meaning fallacy."[32] It is only when words are placed in a sentence that proper classification is possible.

A second standard is that the *definitions of individual terms must not contradict.* Terms may not be defined to mean opposites. This is a common mistake, especially when an affirmative utilizes its plan to illustrate its interpretation of the resolution. Any time an affirmative proposal contains provisions which accomplish opposite objectives, and those provisions illustrate one of the terms of the resolution, then the affirmative is guilty of this mistake.

This is not an acceptable practice for two reasons. First, it is important to be able to evaluate the topicality of individual plan planks. The plan is not implemented as the net result of the separate planks; on the contrary, each plank is implemented to comprise the whole. Evaluation of extra-topicality presupposes the distinctiveness of individual plan planks. Second, negative ground is lost. If the affirmative can simultaneously disestablish and establish or curtail and increase, then it has rendered the important action word in a debate resolution to be all-inclusive. The result is that the negative loses ground which exists opposite the mandate of the resolution.

A third standard, the *context of word use and phrasing,* serves as an ideal complement to grammatical structure. Context implies that a phrase is greater than the mere sum of its individual parts. Meaning is a function of word use, and words change their meaning as context varies. Hence, dictionary definitions of individual words may or may not reveal the optimal interpretation of those words in a debate resolution.

The context of word use and phrasing clarifies the meaning of important word groups, i.e., "minimum educational standards," "mass media communication," "foreign military commitments," "foreign trade policies," etc., that are often found in debate resolutions. An accurate interpretation of individual components of word groups cannot be determined in any other manner than by examininig the context in which those words appear. One troubling question, however, comes to mind. What is the origin of a contextual definition? The answer, of course, lies in the patterns and usage of individual words.

The fourth standard is *context of the field*. It assumes that meaning is field dependent; that words and phrases are best interpreted by experts in the field or discipline where the words are commonly used.[33] Hence, the "powers of labor unions" should be determined by labor relations experts, "foreign military commitments" by foreign policy and military specialists, "minimum educational standards" by education theorists and practitioners, and so forth. We would go beyond simply claiming that field context is a useful standard for evaluating topicality. We maintain that the strict adherence to field is *essential* to policy systems advocacy.

Field context is not unreasonably confining. The definitions of experts in a particular field often vary considerably, sometimes more than standard dictionary definitions. On any question, and in any field, one is sure to find disagreement among theorists and practitioners.

The fifth standard is that an affirmative interpretation *must not unreasonably limit or delimit* the topic. As we have previously indicated, one of the most important functions—perhaps the most important—of a debate resolution is to distinguish affirmative from negative ground. Since the total available terrain is a constant, its division is a zero-sum affair; any increase in affirmative ground can only result from a comparable decrease in negative ground, and vice versa. A resolution should not be so narrowly construed so as to limit the affirmative to one and only one plan, disallowing all other possible interpretations, but on the other hand, a resolution should not be so loosely construed that any and every conceivable claim automatically supports the affirmative side.

The superior means of determining whether an affirmative interpretation adequately limits is to examine the remaining negative ground. An affirmative interpretation must leave the negative with adequate ground, measured in terms of strategic options. If, for example, the affirmative's definition makes it impossible to counterplan, that definition must be suspect. It is an essential element of fairness that the negative should be able to choose from among various strategies in opposing the topic. The affirmative has the advantage of focusing the resolution; the negative deserves an opportunity to oppose the resolution in the manner it chooses.

The sixth and final standard for the evaluation of topicality is the *intent of the framer(s) of the resolution*. High school and collegiate resolutions are composed by topic committees, distinct entities which utilize a process consisting of research,

---

FIGURE 10-4   DIRECT AND INDIRECT EFFECTS

DIRECT EFFECT
    Step One (Plan)
    Step Two (Topical Result of Plan)
INDIRECT EFFECT
    Step One (Plan)
    Step Two (Non-Topical Result of the Plan)
    Step Three (Topical Result of the Plan)

---

deliberation, refinement, and adoption. In the final stage, debate coaches choose among the topics which survive the initial screening. During the screening phase the topic committee may develop assumptions as to the meaning of a resolution. The intent standard holds that those assumptions ought to serve as a guide for debaters in interpreting the resolution.

Intent serves as a useful guide to interpretation in the judicial arena. For instance, a strict constructionist believes that the intent of the framers is the most compelling basis for an understanding and interpretation of the meaning of the Constitution. There is, however, an important difference between the judicial arena and competitive debate: judges have a legislative record to facilitate their determination of intent; debaters do not. In competitive debate there is no objective means of determining the intent of the framers of the resolution. Furthermore, the framers aren't clairvoyant; they function with a limited sense of *possible* affirmative interpretations; hence, *there is no intent* in most instances. It is when coaches and debaters begin to probe a topic beyond the surface exploration of the framers that questions of interpretation arise for which intent can offer no assistance.

Direct Versus Indirect (Effects) Topicality.   The affirmative must be directly topical; the plan must have a direct topical effect. The critical distinction is between "direct effect" and "indirect effect." The resolution calls for some action which is topical, i.e., which has a direct topical effect. A direct effect implies that an action operates "proximately" to produce an outcome, absent the presence of an intervening variable. This differs from an indirect effect which is mediated. In essence, all topicality is by effects. However, legitimate topicality is by direct effects.

Indirect effects constitute an illegitimate affirmative topicality claim for a variety of reasons. First, as previously indicated, the affirmative's plan is the repository of topicality; indirect effects move the locus of topicality to the advantages. This shift carries several implications. Topicality loses its position as an *a priori* issue. Topicality is an independent consideration. It requires adjudication prior to an evaluation of the merits of the case. The use of indirect effects, however, changes this. Topicality becomes a subordinate issue; it is dependent on the outcome of the efficacy of the plan. Thus, topicality becomes an uncertain issue, dependent upon other issues which admit degree.

Second, indirect effects delimit, thus restricting negative ground. If the securing of an advantage is what makes an affirmative position topical, then affirmative ground expands significantly. Finally, extra-topicality would become a moot issue. The topicality of portions of the plan would be irrelevant. All that would be required is that the plan produce a topical result; an affirmative could choose to include provisions in its plan, without regard to their topicality.

Guidelines for Arguing Topicality.   The negative advocate must be reasonable in handling topicality. When should topicality be argued? Certainly not against every affirmative case, or even most cases. Overusing topicality saps its potential as a voting issue. Also, topicality arguments which have limited applicability to a particular affirmative approach lack credibility. When topicality is argued the setting should be appropriate and the issue should be pursued seriously.

Finally, the topicality argument itself should be reasonable. Standards that are too restrictive, so that practically no affirmative could meet them, are not well received. Indeed, an otherwise questionable affirmative interpretation may gain credibility as the result of unreasonable negative topicality standards.

SUMMARY

It is the negative advocate's responsibility to contest the affirmative's position. The negative advocate can accomplish this via direct refutation of affirmative claims, constructive argument on behalf of a particular position or positions which warrants a rejection of the resolution, or a combination of these approaches. This chapter introduced the student to negative advocacy, placing special emphasis on the elements of negative case construction—on the selection and implementation of strategic choices which constitute a negative position in a debate. We examined the theoretical and practical implications which underpin the selection and construction of individual negative argumentative options, including direct refutation to minimize significance and contest efficacy as well as a variety of offensive strategic options such as a defense of the present system; minor repairs and both hypothetical and conditional counterplans; the standard or traditional counterplan; efficacy attacks; plan disadvantages; generic positions; and topicality. Chapter 12 will explore the strategies and tactics involved in defending a negative position.

Notes

[1]Bernard L. Brock, James W. Chesebro, John F. Cragan and James F. Klumpp, *Public Policy Decision-Making: Systems Analysis and Comparative Advantages Debate* (New York: Harper & Row, Publishers, 1973), pp. 136–37.

[2]Allan J. Lichtman and Daniel M. Rohrer, "The Logic of Policy Dispute," *Journal of the American Forensic Association,* 16 (1980), 239.

[3]See: Craig A. Dudcak, "Direct Refutation in Propositions of Policy: A Viable Alternative," *Journal of the American Forensic Association,* 16 (1980), 234; and John S. Gossett, "Counterplan Competitiveness in the Stock Issues Paradigm," in *Dimensions of Argument: Proceedings of the Second Summer Conference on Argumentation,* ed. George Ziegelmueller and Jack Rhodes (Annandale: Speech Communication Association, 1981), pp. 571–73.

[4]Lichtman and Rohrer, pp. 239–40.

[5]David Zarefsky, "The Role of Causal Argument in Policy Controversies," *Journal of the American Forensic Association,* 13 (1977), 184.

[6]Zarefsky, p. 184.

[7]David Braybrooke and Charles E. Lindblom, *A Strategy of Decision: Policy Evaluation as a Social Process* (New York: Macmillan Publishing Co., Inc., 1970), p. 85.

[8]Thomas R. Dye, *Understanding Public Policy,* 3rd ed. (Englewood Cliffs, NJ: Prentice-Hall, Inc., 1978), p. 16.

[9]Braybrooke and Lindblom, p. 123.

[10]Michael Pfau, "A Systematic Approach to Opposing Policy Change," in *Advanced Debate, 3rd ed.,* David A. Thomas and Jack Hart (eds.), (Lincolnwood, IL: National Textbook Company, 1987), p. 44.

[11]John F. Schunk, "A Farewell to 'Structural Change': The Cure for Pseudo-Inherency," *Journal of the American Forensic Association,* 14 (1978), 148.

[12]Ed Panetta, "The Resolutional Counterplan: A Gentleman's Agreement," paper presented at the Speech Communication Association annual convention, Washington, D.C., 13 November 1983.

[13]Panetta.

[14]Allan J. Lichtman and Daniel M. Rohrer, "A General Theory of the Counterplan," *Journal of the American Forensic Association,* 12 (1975), 72.

[15]Lichtman and Rohrer, "A General Theory of the Counterplan," pp. 74–75.

[16]Lichtman and Rohrer, "A General Theory of the Counterplan," p. 76.

[17]Austin J. Freeley, *Argumentation and Debate: Reasoned Decision Making,* 5th ed. (Belmont, CA: Wadsworth Publishing Company, 1981), p. 211.

[18]J. W. Patterson and David Zarefsky, *Contemporary Debate* (Boston: Houghton Mifflin Company, 1983), p. 215.

[19]Lichtman and Rohrer, "The Logic of Policy Dispute," p. 244.

[20]For a consideration of additional limitations of the study counterplan position see: Thomas J. Hynes, Jr., "Study: Hope or False Promise," *Journal of the American Forensic Association,* 16 (1980), 192–98.

[21]John D. Steinbruner, *The Cybernetic Theory of Decision: New Dimensions of Political Analysis* (Princeton: Princeton University Press, 1974), pp. 16–17.

[22]Charles L. Schultz, *The Politics and Economics of Public Spending* (Washington, D.C.: The Brookings Institution, 1968), pp. 46–47.

[23]Mayer N. Zald, "Politics and Symbols: A Review Article," *The Sociological Quarterly,* 7 (1966), 85.

[24]Murray Edelman, *The Symbolic Uses of Politics* (Urbana: University of Illinois Press, 1964), p. 7.

[25]Edelman, p. 155.

[26]Joseph R. Gusfield, *Symbolic Crusade: Status Politics and the American Temperance Movement* (Urbana: University of Illinois Press, 1976), p. 182.

[27]James W. Paulsen and Jack Rhodes, "The Counter-Warrant as a Negative Strategy: A Modest Proposal," *Journal of the American Forensic Association,* 15 (1979), 207.

[28]Jack Rhodes, "A Defense of the Counter-Warrant as Negative Argument," in *Dimensions of Argument: Proceedings of the Second Summer Conference on Argumentation,* ed. George Ziegelmueller and Jack Rhodes (Annandale: Speech Communication Association, 1981), p. 486.

[29]James J. Unger, "The Words of a Debate Proposition and the Debate Subject Matter: Friends or Foes," paper presented at the Speech Communication Association annual convention, Anaheim, Cal., 14 November 1981, p. 4.

[30]Unger, pp. 4–5.

[31]Paul Roberts, *Patterns of English* (Chicago: Harcourt, Brace & World, Inc., 1956), p. 12.

[32]Jerome Frank, *Courts on Trial: Myth and Reality in American Justice* (New York: Antheneum Press, 1970), p. 299.

[33]Donn W. Parson, "On Being Reasonable: The Last Refuge of Scoundrels," in *Dimensions of Argument: Proceedings of the Second Summer Conference on Argumentation,* ed. George Ziegelmueller and Jack Rhodes (Annandale: Speech Communication Association, 1981), p. 540.

CHAPTER ELEVEN

AFFIRMATIVE STRATEGIES AND TACTICS

Initiating argument on behalf of a particular thesis or proposition—presenting the case or position—is the first phase of affirmative advocacy. The second phase involves a defense of the affirmative's position against any and all negative attempts to rebut it. This chapter will focus on the second phase, systematically examining the strategies and tactics which constitute the basis of effective affirmative advocacy. Affirmative strategies involve a macro perspective of a debate; they focus on debate as a whole entity. Affirmative tactics constitute a micro perspective by concentrating on the individual components of a debate.

Initially, we will explore the intrinsic advantages of affirmative advocacy. The thrust of this chapter, however, will concern the strategies and tactics of affirmative refutation. Specifically we will examine the task of affirmative case extension, strategic responses to all standard negative argumentative positions, and affirmative rebuttal tactics. These areas embody the heart and soul of affirmative advocacy.

INTRINSIC ADVANTAGES OF AFFIRMATIVE ADVOCACY

Intuitively it might appear easier to argue against—as opposed to in favor of—almost any proposition. Indeed this was once the case. Until recently the placement of presumption against all debate propositions provided a clear edge to the negative advocate. Today, despite the placement of presumption, that negative edge has eroded considerably. In all contemporary policy debate an affirmative advocate enjoys formidable intrinsic advantages over his or her negative counterpart. This is especially true in forensic debate where affirmatives usually win approximately 60 percent of all championship caliber debates. The affirmative advocate must understand these intrinsic advantages in order to exploit them.

Controlling the Argumentative Terrain

The affirmative has the advantage of initiating clash in a debate. Cases can be chosen, research accomplished, and tactical options selected which optimize the affirmative's position. This is the first step in controlling the argumentative terrain.

The next step involves selecting tactical options so as to maintain control over the argumentative terrain throughout the course of a debate. This is an important objective. If an affirmative can dictate the terrain, it can control the debate. If not, it is at the mercy of events in the round.

Controlling the argumentative terrain is not an easy task. Effective negative advocates will seek to wrest control from the affirmative. Indeed, this is a prerequisite to successful negative advocacy.

It is up to the affirmative to exercise control over the argumentative terrain. The affirmative must assume the initiative from the start, maneuvering the negative in a direction toward tactical options based on affirmative strengths and negative weaknesses. The affirmative can exercise tactical control via various methods. First, the advocate can construct the plan in such manner as to preclude certain negative positions (involving inherency, solvency, disadvantages or alternative solutions), while inviting others. Some negative positions are troublesome; an affirmative will want to avoid them if possible. Other negative positions fuel the affirmative's position; an affirmative will want to encourage these.

Affirmative choices on the proposition that, "all United States military intervention into the internal affairs of any foreign nation or nations in the Western Hemisphere should be prohibited," illustrate this method. Some affirmatives maintained that the United States—from the time of the Monroe Doctrine to the present—has exhibited a strong propensity for military intervention into the affairs of nations in this hemisphere; nonetheless, United States military intervention seldom achieves the end for which it was intended, and as a result of Soviet and Cuban presence, carries substantial risks, especially that United States involvement might trigger regional and/or superpower escalation.

One common negative position involved a disadvantage based on the thesis that a prohibition of United States military intervention would remove the only barrier to communist incursion, thus fueling communist takeovers throughout the hemisphere.

Some affirmatives sought to avoid this argument. They defined military intervention as "the covert or overt commitment of United States military forces within the territory of another country," and constructed their plans so as to prohibit the commitment of United States troops in the hemisphere while allowing for foreign military sales and assistance. Thus, they argued that the disadvantage doesn't apply since United States foreign military sales and assistance are sufficient to arrest communist spread in the hemisphere.

Other affirmatives chose to invite the disadvantage. They defined military intervention as "the overt or covert use of troops, advisors, or military assistance within the territory of another country," and constructed their plans so as to prohibit the broad sweep of United States military intervention. Such affirmatives sought to debate the communist spread position. They were prepared to argue that the thesis of the disadvantage is reversed: that it is United States intervention which drives popular leftist movements into the hands of the Soviets and the Cubans. Thus, they argued that the affirmative prohibition would arrest communist spread, thereby turning the impact of the argument against the negative.

Second, the affirmative can select argument responses in such a manner as to preclude certain argument positions, while inviting others. An example, using the same proposition and case scenario as depicted above, illustrates this tactic. Another common negative position against a prohibition on "all United States military intervention into the internal affairs of any foreign nation or nations in the Western Hemisphere" was nuclear proliferation. The thesis of this argument was that an abandonment of the United States security guarantee in the hemisphere would cause some nations (particularly Brazil and Argentina) to develop indigenous nuclear capability.

Some affirmatives chose to attack this position at its link, arguing that the thesis of the disadvantage was untrue: that Latin American nuclear proliferation is inevitable in time, and that a United States disposition for or against military intervention in the Western Hemisphere has no impact on the decision of potential proliferants. Other affirmatives chose to grant the link or thesis of the disadvantage, concentrating their responses on the issue of whether proliferation is good or bad. Such affirmatives maintained that proliferation results in a reduction in conflict in the international system by making the risks of war intolerable.

All affirmative arguments—those embodied in the initial presentation and those made in response to negative positions—should be selected on the basis of a specific tactical purpose. This enables the affirmative advocate to determine the argumentative terrain, and thus exercise effective control in a debate.

Exploiting the Affirmative Bias in Contemporary Research

Contemporary policy argument practices have grown more evidence-oriented in recent years. This is largely the result of an information explosion which has been making inroads for two decades, especially in the social sciences. The burgeoning number of social scientists and the increased emphasis on empirical and original research, coupled with a sharp increase in the number of conduits for their findings, have produced a wealth of information which was simply not available just a few years ago.[1]

The proliferation of information has produced an increased dependence upon the subject area expert or specialist. As Irving Kristol has commented, "We live in a world dominated by expert opinion. If you want to say something, you try to find someone who has a claim to expert opinion to back you up."[2]

Furthermore, debate—like academe—is currently enamored with hard data drawn from empirical research (and there is an abundance of same). This has produced two impacts on contemporary advocacy.

First, evidence has assumed increased importance in argument. Receivers increasingly expect that advocates will ground their claims in hard data. Naturally, this expectation varies with the argument context.[3] An example drawn from the field of business illustrates this point. On the one hand, corporate decision makers demand that claims are backed with hard data. An executive, making a case that a firm should change its marketing approach, must support all claims with ample substantive backing. On the other hand, a corporate advertising appeal will probably rely more on image than substance to develop its claims. The argument context determines what is appropriate backing.

An expectation that advocates will support their claims with expert opinion or empirical data governs contemporary forensic advocacy.[4] Argument critics continue to admonish advocates that, "... evidence is technically designed to *support* arguments ... not substitute for them."[5] This position has much traditional appeal. Nonetheless, there is a notable trend, in academe and in debate, for the advocate's arguments to be subsumed by his or her evidence. For better or for worse, the unmistakable trend evident throughout the social sciences is that "the data is the argument."

A second impact uniquely benefits affirmative advocates. Namely, the increased emphasis on hard data drawn from empirical research has resulted in a lopsided comparison between courses of action advocated by the affirmative and the negative. An affirmative's mandate is usually more obscure—it is, more often than not, untested outside of the social scientist's "laboratory." Thus, one must extrapolate the benefits and consequences of an affirmative proposal from limited experiences. Often a small experimental program serves as the practical grounding for an affirmative's plan. In such circumstances the affirmative advocate holds a built-in edge since experts involved in such research efforts often develop vested interests on behalf of their programs and their research theses. At other times there is no plan precedent *per se,* just a body of theoretical material. This too is authored by so-called experts with a perspective toward a particular position.

In both instances there will be ample documentation in support of affirmative benefits, but less offsetting evidence on affirmative consequences. Bakan, McNemar, Popper and others have persuasively argued that the "verification" emphasis in existing research stratagems results in a significant pro-hypothesis bias.[6] The alternative to verification is falsification, which gets much less attention in journals. As a result, most empirical social science literature carries a strong bias in favor of the research hypothesis being considered. In short, an affirmative advocate will find much more pro-hypothesis data than anti-hypothesis data on most social science issues. This benefits affirmative advocates who most frequently argue pro-hypothesis positions. The bottom line is that affirmative advocates will inevitably be able to locate more empirical support for their position than negative advocates will be able to uncover against it.

The present system's structures, in contrast, are tested under fire. The status quo includes known and often controversial elements. Its imperfections are readily documentable. Thus, any comparison of consequences between an affirmative proposal and present system mechanisms is inevitably one-sided.

The affirmative has the enviable task of advocating an ideal condition. If the negative chooses the strategic option of defending the present system, it is stuck with the existing condition. This comparison produces an affirmative bias. Affirmative advocates will want to exploit the bias of contemporary research in selecting and defending their positions.

TASK OF AFFIRMATIVE CASE EXTENSION

Affirmative case extension involves all attempts to advance—or provide for further development of—the original affirmative position. Case extension occurs in all affirmative speeches but is the single overriding characteristic of the second affirmative constructive speech. Responses made in this speech set the tone and tenor for all subsequent affirmative case extension.

In most instances case extension requires that an affirmative advocate utilize direct refutation of negative attacks in conjunction with an emphasis and further elaboration of uncontested first affirmative constructive positions. Sometimes case extension involves the introduction of additional affirmative positions. Yet, affirmative case extension involves much more than this. Obviously it requires the mastery of specific case extension techniques. But, in addition, it demands the internalization of a strategic perspective to frame argument choices. Internalization is achieved when the advocate is able to frame argument choices automatically in strategic terms.

Case Extension Techniques

Effective case extension is the essence of the second affirmative constructive speech. But exactly what is *effective* case extension? The answer to this question is important since it determines the manner in which the advocate approaches this task.

Perhaps the best way to answer this question is to examine what effective case extension *is not*.

First, the processes of answering arguments for the sake of answering arguments, or covering the flow (getting to every opposing response) for the purpose of covering the flow, do not necessarily produce effective case extension. It is quite possible to answer every negative argument and still lose a debate. Indeed, some advocates lose debates precisely because of a decision to systematically answer each opposing argument. Usually a direct tradeoff exists between breadth and depth of coverage. There are many instances when not all opposing arguments need to be answered; when just a few opposing positions need to be refuted well. The primary task of extension is to carry the major issues of topicality, significance, inherency, solvency and desirability.

Second, stalemating opposing arguments *does not* result in effective case extension. Stalemating produces an argumentative draw. Yet, some opposing arguments demand responses which do much more than stalemate; other arguments don't require an answer at all. The trick is to *provide a sufficient response*—no more and no less.

The key to effective case extension is that the affirmative assume the initiative in crucial argument areas, thus keeping the negative on the defensive. The affirmative accomplishes this via on-point and substantive case extension. These refutation techniques answer arguments in such a manner that an opponent's analysis and evidence from previous speeches can be of no value in subsequent speeches.

Direct-clash, or on-point, refutation is important. It requires that an advocate respond to each point raised by an opponent in a particular argument sector, so as to "take out" the underpinning analysis and/or evidence. This method preempts an opponent's ability to use constructive analysis and/or evidence in subsequent speeches.

An opponent is forced into the difficult position of providing substantive second and/or third line extension—or losing the particular argument.

An example on the topic, "the U.S. should curtail its arms sales to other countries," illustrates this technique. The affirmative argued that the United States should stop arms sales to Indonesia in an effort to halt the latter's subjugation of East Timor. The affirmative maintained that Indonesia has devastated East Timor, resulting in the death of nearly one-third of the East Timorese population. The negative argued that Indonesia is presently providing food assistance to East Timor to avert further famine. This argument, if emphasized by the negative in subsequent speeches, could damage the affirmative's position because it signals a change in Indonesian policy toward the East Timorese. The affirmative advocate must stop this claim in its tracks with on-point refutation. He or she could update the negative, arguing that Indonesia has reversed its policy, barring further food aid. In addition, the affirmative advocate could indict the negative evidence, pointing out that it consists of Indonesian government assertions passed on via the American press. Both responses are on-point. As a result, the negative advocate cannot resurrect this claim in subsequent speeches short of refutation against the specific affirmative arguments.

Too many advocates utilize indirect clash with an opponent's claims. Indirect clash involves an ill-advised "lump-and-dump," approach to refutation. It constitutes a mindless grouping of an opponent's arguments followed by a series of general responses. This technique is usually ineffective unless the advocate can isolate common assumptions underlying a group of arguments.

We do not recommend a "lump-and-dump" approach for two reasons. First, indirect clash fails to put to rest negative claims. Direct-clash refutation does terminal damage to a claim; it has no further potential short of additional substantive extension. Indirect clash merely renders a claim dormant; it can be resurrected in subsequent speeches with no more effort than is required to call attention to it. Second, an indirect approach obscures clash. Direct clash makes the damage done to an opponent's argument evident—even to the casual observer. Indirect clash obscures issue outcomes. It results in a stalemate of affirmative and negative evidence (inevitable since it has not been directly refuted), which forces the critic to intervene personally in order to sort out the conflicting claims.

Substantive extension is equally important. It requires the advocate's claims to be developed fully, backed by sound analysis and/or strong evidence. The alternative to substantive extension is a press (a question or challenge) or an assertion (an unsupported claim). These are purely defensive tactics. They constitute nothing more than a holding action. Effective case extension requires that the affirmative advocate seize the initiative. Substantive extension is the technique to achieve this tactical end.

Thesis/Perspective

Effective case extension requires that the affirmative advocate establish and maintain a clear thesis or perspective. This process starts in the first affirmative constructive speech with the careful wording of affirmative contentions.

Case wording establishes the themes which are used for subsequent refutation. The use of case themes facilitates affirmative advocacy.

FIGURE 11-1   AFFIRMATIVE CASE THEMES

Introduction

CONTENTION 1: U.S. Policy in Latin America is Militaristic
  A. Militarism Is the Cornerstone of U.S. Policy toward Latin America
    1. This Is the Legacy of Monroe Doctrine
    2. The Reagan Administration Supports This
  B. The U.S. Is Now Involved in Latin America
    1. Assistance & Advisors in El Salvador
    2. Covert Operations Against Nicaragua
    3. Implied Threats Against Cuba
CONTENTION 2: U.S. Involvement in Latin America Increases the Chance of War
  A. Local Wars Escalate to Regional Wars
  B. Cuba and USSR Are Likely to Respond
  C. Nuclear Confrontation Is Possible
Affirmative Plan
CONTENTION 3: Nonintervention Is a Superior Policy
  A. U.S. Can Protect Its Interests in Latin America via Alternative Means
  B. Nonintervention Will Be Reciprocated
    1. By Cuba
    2. By the USSR
  C. Nonintervention Reduces the Chance of War

We will illustrate the potential use of case themes with an affirmative case on the resolution that, "All United States military intervention into the internal affairs of any foreign nation or nations in the Western Hemisphere should be prohibited." The affirmative argued that U.S. military intervention in Central America is extensive. Furthermore, such intervention is counterproductive. It has spurred an escalation of hostilities in the region and threatens to provoke a major confrontation with Cuba and with the Soviet Union. The affirmative further maintained that the only way to avert this "drift into war" scenario is for the United States to initiate a pledge of military nonintervention into the internal affairs of any nation or nations in the hemisphere. In addition, the affirmative claimed that such a pledge would reduce Cuban adventurism and precipitate a reduction in tensions with the Soviet Union which might serve as a catalyst to American and Soviet disarmament negotiations. Affirmative themes are embodied in the contentions above (see Figure 11–1).

First, affirmative themes provide an indispensable organizational tool for categorizing and viewing opposing arguments. For example, if the negative directly challenges Contention 1–B, arguing that current United States military intervention in Central America is designed to deter Cuban adventurism, the affirmative should mentally categorize this response within the confines of contention 3. The affirmative may or may not actually relocate the response for the purpose of refutation; regardless, the affirmative will employ the analysis and supporting evidence in contention 3 in the process of evaluating this negative response.

Second, affirmative themes provide an excellent perspective which can be used to dismiss and/or refute negative responses. The previous example illustrates this. Contention 3 contains the analysis and evidence to refute the negative claim that United States intervention deters Cuban adventurism. The United States can protect its interests in Latin America via arms sales, military and economic assistance, and diplomacy. These means can deter Cuban adventurism; troops are simply not required. Furthermore, a United States policy of nonintervention would be reciprocated. Thus, the affirmative policy ushers in an entirely new policy scenario. It is current interventionist policy which results in Cuban adventurism, and the negative claim is an indictment of present policy. The new policy scenario solves Cuban adventurism.

Third, case themes facilitate affirmative advocacy by providing standards to appraise affirmative and negative arguments. This is important for two reasons. On the one hand, it encourages the advocate to view a debate in holistic terms. This is a prerequisite to effective affirmative advocacy, as we will demonstrate next. On the other hand, it provides a means by which the advocate can package the debate on affirmative terms for the critic judge. For example, a debate on prohibiting "U.S. military intervention . . . in the Western Hemisphere . . ." can be evaluated in terms of a limited number of basic questions. Are we intervening? Is our intervention good or bad? Do the benefits of nonintervention outweigh the costs? In this manner, a myriad of specific arguments can be sorted and evaluated. Furthermore, this can be done on affirmative terms.

Thus, affirmative advocates are advised to establish, maintain and exploit an affirmative thesis or perspective. This is an indispensable feature of effective case extension. In addition, the use of affirmative themes facilitates affirmative control over the argumentative terrain.

A Holistic View

The affirmative advocate must maintain a holistic view of the debate round. A holistic view constitutes "the big picture;" it demands that the affirmative advocate examine all argumentative variables—all possible affirmative and negative positions, every potential response to individual negative arguments, and each strategic option—in terms of their potential impact on the final outcome of a debate.

A holistic view is a macro perspective of a debate round. A macro perspective requires that the advocate view a debate as a whole entity. It pieces together individual arguments to form a composite picture. By contrast, a micro perspective focuses on the individual components of a debate. It concentrates on specific arguments as ends in themselves.

Mastering a holistic view is not an easy task. Indeed, most advocates languish at a micro level, totally consumed in the myriad of individual arguments which comprise the nuts and bolts of a debate. Such advocates never see the forest as a result of all of the individual trees. Their plight is an understandable one; after all, specific argument extension is an especially demanding task. Nonetheless, such a perspective is short-sighted. It places the advocate at the mercy of events in the round; all too often, it plays right into the hands of an opponent.

A holistic view is a strategic perspective. It requires that the affirmative advocate think through all argumentative options in terms of their broader ramifications. It involves careful planning for rebuttals. Most advocates view a debate in chronological and segmented fashion, taking it speech by speech from the first constructive to the last rebuttal. This chronological approach results in minimal control over the evolution of arguments during the course of a debate. We recommend the opposite approach. The advocate should view a debate in reverse order, starting with the last rebuttal speeches and working backwards to the initial speeches. This *reverse mapping* approach affords maximum control over argument development. It is the only way to insure that all positions, specific responses and strategic decisions are made on the basis of their long-term rebuttal ramifications.

A holistic view presupposes that each individual response could impact multiple argument sectors. It is not uncommon for a single affirmative response to one negative position to affect affirmative response options against other negative positions.

Affirmative response choices on the topic, "the federal government should initiate and enforce safety guarantees on consumer goods," illustrate this notion. The affirmative maintained that the federal government should ban the sale and possession of handguns. The affirmative argued that the possession of handguns inevitably results in thousands of deaths each year from accidents and homicides, and that a legal prohibition, coupled with financial inducements and attrition, would eventually eliminate the supply of handguns.

This example will focus on two particular negative positions: (1) a solvency argument based on the thesis that the plan will fail because citizens will not turn in their handguns; and (2) a plan disadvantage grounded in the assumption that, since a national handgun ban would cost the federal government billions, important federal social programs would have to be cut in order to finance the plan.

The best affirmative response against the negative solvency position is that the combined force of law and financial inducements work. Baltimore paid a $50 bounty to get people to give up their guns. In the first seven days, 7,095 firearms were surrendered to authorities at a cost of $330,000. The best affirmative response against the negative plan disadvantage is that the cost would be small. Perhaps you can see the difficulty which the affirmative faces. If the affirmative argues that, "financial inducements work," against the solvency position, then it cannot reasonably maintain that, "plan cost will be small," in response to the plan disadvantage.

An affirmative, relying exclusively on a micro view, would probably go with both answers, evaluating potential responses to each negative position in isolation. This is the all too common micro approach to argument—a one-response-at-at-time and one-speech-at-a-time method of affirmative extension. Such an approach renders argument outcomes chancy at best. Whenever an affirmative advocate fails to strategize beyond a particular response in a particular speech, he or she relinquishes control over the argumentative terrain, often playing right into the hands of the negative opponent. The advocate, employing a holistic perspective, would assess the broader implications of individual extensions.

The affirmative advocate should utilize this holistic view in all phases of debate: in weighing strategic options; determining which positions to advance; deciding on

FIGURE 11-2   PROCEDURE FOR RESPONDING TO STRAIGHT REFUTATION

Indicate the affirmative theme (or sub-theme). Handle each negative response in this manner:

Note the response;
Provide refutation.

Tie back to the affirmative theme (or sub-theme).

specific responses to individual negative arguments; and evaluating the interrelationships among arguments (which is important in order to sort out and evaluate the sum total of all arguments presented during a debate) in the rebuttal periods. There will be further emphasis on and illustration of the holistic perspective later in this chapter and again in chapter 12.

STRATEGICALLY RESPONDING TO NEGATIVE POSITIONS

Although the mastery of case extension techniques, the utilization of an affirmative thesis or perspective, and the adoption of a holistic view are essential components of affirmative advocacy, there is more to the story. Indeed, no treatment of affirmative advocacy would be complete without examining strategic responses to all standard negative argumentative positions. Thus, this section will focus on affirmative responses to the most common negative positions including: straight refutation, topicality, alternative proposals (both inherency arguments and counterplans), efficacy attacks, and plan disadvantages.

Straight Refutation

Straight refutation has traditionally been the most common negative position. It consists of direct-clash refutation against each of the claims made in the initial affirmative speech.

There are three tactical imperatives in dealing with a straight refutation position, two of which were featured in the previous section of this chapter.

First, the advocate must maintain and exploit affirmative case themes. Negative straight refutation can sorely test an affirmative advocate's resolve to maintain case themes and perspective. In responding to straight refutation it is not uncommon for an affirmative advocate to become so engrossed in the myriad of specific negative arguments that affirmative themes are inadvertently abandoned. This problem can be avoided if the affirmative advocate will learn to use a simple procedure in responding to straight refutation, as depicted in Figure 11-2 (note that refutation starts and ends with the affirmative themes). This procedure makes the case theme the focal point of affirmative refutation. This is important, as we indicated previously.

A second tactical imperative is to respond with on-point and substantive extension. This puts the affirmative in command of the debate, keeping the negative on the defensive. There is simply no good reason for an affirmative advocate to respond to negative straight refutation with presses or assertions. This accomplishes nothing worthwhile. Indeed, it can prove disastrous because it backs extension into the rebuttal periods where there is less time to provide substantive responses. The affirmative advocate *should be able to* outextend a negative opponent on its own case. If the affirmative position is a valid one, then the weight of argument and evidence will prevail in the end. Hence, if the affirmative responds substantively, it is unlikely that a negative using straight refutation will be able to remain abreast of affirmative extension.

Third, the advocate must develop an awareness of and strive to maximize the available time. Awareness is a mindset. It must manifest itself during preparation for advocacy. This involves two dimensions. First, the advocate should prioritize responses on all briefs. This guarantees that the most important arguments will always be presented, even if time constraints seriously impinge. Second, the advocate should learn the precise length of responses on all briefs. This is best accomplished by having someone flow and time all responses during a practice session. Awareness must also manifest itself during the course of a debate. This requires that the advocate make an intuitive estimate—prior to each speech—as to the length of time that will be needed to refute each of the opponent's positions, *and* monitor his or her performance during the speech.

Awareness is also a tactical component of advocacy. The affirmative advocate should strive to maximize economy and efficiency of expression. Equally important, the affirmative advocate must avoid the temptation to overkill negative arguments. Most affirmative coverage difficulties stem from a misallocation—as opposed to an insufficiency—of available time. As indicated previously, the trick is to provide a sufficient response; no more and no less.

Topicality

If the affirmative advocate has selected a reasonable case position (one that targeted receivers are likely to accept), understands the theoretical intricacies of topicality, and has thoroughly researched and briefed the issue, then a negative opponent should experience very little success with this argument variant. Two factors combine to produce an affirmative bias on topicality. The affirmative advocate should exploit these factors in responding to a negative topicality argument.

First, the negative must win this issue on the affirmative's ground. The affirmative should prepare to defend the topicality of its position with case-specific arguments and evidence. The negative, by contrast, will usually attempt to adapt generic arguments and evidence to the affirmative's case, often with limited success. Whenever case-specific and generic arguments and evidence compete, the former inevitably prevail.

Second, on topicality, presumption rests with the affirmative. We observed in chapter 10 that presumption generally lies with the negative on the basis of least risk.

Topicality, however, is a jurisdictional question. As such, the notion of least risk does not apply in assigning presumption. Instead, on the issue of topicality presumption rests with the affirmative as a result of the maxim that, "He who advocates must prove."

Nonetheless, presumption shouldn't be taken for granted. The affirmative advocate must initiate and vigorously defend its right to presumption since it is an integral feature of the affirmative's tactical arsenal against the negative topicality position.

Presumption can be defended on two counts. First, an affirmative can invoke a court analogy. Since legislation is presumed to be constitutional until such time that it is effectively challenged in the courts, affirmatives can claim that their plan should be presumed to be topical. Second, since the negative is afforded general presumption, the affirmative should be granted the right to define terms, including the presumption that its definitions are topical. This constitutes a substantial benefit. On the one hand, the negative cannot simply challenge or press the affirmative's topicality. Rather, the negative must develop a substantive position. On the other hand, in the event of a tie, the affirmative is topical. It is not enough for a negative advocate to cast some doubt—to stalemate—on the topicality of the affirmative's plan. Instead, the negative must win the argument conclusively.

It would appear difficult for a negative to win topicality. The affirmative advocate would appear to hold all the cards. On the one hand, he or she can select a case which is intuitively and argumentatively topical. Furthermore, topicality carries an affirmative bias. Nonetheless, some affirmative advocates will fall victim to the negative topicality position—inevitably as a result of insufficient mastery of topicality standards. An affirmative advocate's success in arguing topicality presupposes an understanding and application of the various standards of topicality. Standards underpin evaluation and thus play an integral role in determining the outcome of a topicality argument. Specific standards were discussed in chapter 10.

Alternative Proposals

Negative advocates may offer alternative proposals to an affirmative's plan. Some involve existing or modified present system structures. These alternatives constitute the negative inherency position, once a staple in the negative's tactical arsenal. Others involve the creation of new structures or the assignment of new functions to existing structures. These alternatives constitute the negative counterplan position.

The negative's use of alternative proposals constitutes a classic illustration of the systems perspective in debate. When a negative offers alternative approaches, it tacitly concedes that the affirmative position overcomes presumption. At this point the question is not whether something should be done, but what should be done. A traditional systems debate involves a direct comparison of affirmative and negative alternatives.[7]

Inherency Attacks.   The negative will contend that the problem does not inhere in the present system—that it is not permanent. Thus, the negative may suggest that existing mechanisms or modified present system structures (minor repairs) can solve the problem. For example, on the "prohibit all United States military intervention

... in the Western Hemisphere" resolution, some negatives argued that Congress could use the War Powers Act to constrain presidential initiation of overt or covert intervention in the hemisphere. Other negatives supported a strengthening of the War Powers Act to achieve the same end.

In responding to present system mechanisms or minor repairs, the affirmative advocate should focus his or her analysis and arguments in three areas: topicality, efficacy and desirability.

Negative minor repairs cannot be topical. As we discussed in chapter 10, the negative must select its position from outside the confines of the resolution. Yet, policy questions, which are phrased as statements of increment or degree (i.e., resolved, that some agent should do something more—or less—than is now being done in a particular area), pose substantial difficulty for the negative.

The resolution that, "the United States should significantly curtail its arms sales to other countries," illustrates this problem. This type of resolution places the focus of a debate on what we call "the solvency gap," a measure of the increment that separates the present system from the affirmative's plan. The solvency gap represents the margin between what is topical and what is not topical. When the negative argues for an extension of the present system (for a minor repair), it runs the risk of bridging the solvency gap. If the effort is successful (i.e., if the present system is able to pursue the goal in question as well—or nearly as well—as the resolution), then the negative advocate has crossed the threshold into affirmative terrain. For instance, on the "curtail arms sales" topic, any minor repair which works and succeeds in actually reducing United States arms sales fulfills the mandate of the resolution. The affirmative advocate must be on guard for just such a development, insuring that negative minor repairs are not topical.

A present system mechanism or minor repair must be a viable alternative to the affirmative's plan. Thus, the affirmative advocate should take a negative minor repair to task on three counts. First, force the negative to commit itself to a specific mechanism. If the negative conditionally argues minor repairs, demand a commitment: make the negative support specific mechanisms (and live with the consequences of their choice). The affirmative can elicit a commitment via cross-examination and/or arguing mini-disadvantages (a sharply abbreviated variant of the standard disadvantage, minimally including the thesis of the argument and one impact) against each repair. Second, insist that the negative prove efficacy (show that the mechanism could solve the problem). The negative's minor repair efficacy burden is very similar to the affirmative's case efficacy requirement.

Third, the affirmative advocate should require the negative to demonstrate a propensity to solve the problem. This step is an important one. It is not enough that the mechanism has potential. The negative must be prepared to show that the mechanism's potential can be unleashed. This can be done by: (1) showing a trend toward solvency, or (2) invoking fiat to catapult the mechanism toward solvency. If the negative mechanism meets each of these three burdens, it assumes a position as a full-fledged alternative to the affirmative's plan.

The requirement that the present system mechanism or minor repair constitute a viable alternative to an affirmative's plan is essential. Only then can advocates begin the process of comparing costs and benefits. This comparison inevitably benefits the affirmative. As we indicated earlier in this chapter, the bias in contemporary research produces a one-sided comparison between an affirmative proposal and present system alternatives.

The present system mechanism or minor repair must prove to be a desirable alternative. The affirmative advocate's most effective weapon on the desirability front is a disadvantage which is directed against the present system alternative mechanism. This position involves an extension of the application of cost and benefit analysis from plan to present system domain. It constitutes a disadvantage to the present system. For example, in support of the resolution that, "the federal government should initiate and enforce safety guarantees on consumer goods," some affirmatives argued for mandatory use of protective child restraints in automobiles. Some negatives maintained that increased utilization of standard automobile safety belts was a superior alternative. Affirmatives responded with a disadvantage directed against the safety belt alternative, arguing that it is worse for young children to wear standard safety belts than to ride completely unrestrained. Thus, while the negative maintained the benefits of this alternative, the affirmative utilized a disadvantage to focus on the costs.

If an affirmative advocate fails to exploit this option, a one-sided assessment of policy alternatives will result. A policy systems perspective requires that an affirmative proposal be evaluated in terms of potential benefits versus potential costs. A present system mechanism must be examined using the same lenses. Just as an examination of the affirmative's position is not complete without an exhaustive look at the consequences of the plan, a careful examination of the negative's position demands no less. In the last analysis the superior alternative will offer the most desirable ratio of net benefit as opposed to net cost. In developing the disadvantage against a present system mechanism, be sure to: adapt it specifically to the mechanism in question, and quantify the precise probabilities and impacts.

In summary, the affirmative must defend against negative attacks on the inherency of the problem area. The negative may attempt to show that the problem is not a paramount one, either because the present system has solutions, or because it can be remedied to provide solutions. To extend its inherency position, the affirmative should both refute the negative suggestions and bolster the point that the proposed affirmative system is superior.

The Counterplan Position.   Sometimes the negative will go beyond a defense of existing alternatives. Following careful investigation and thought about the problem area, the negative may conclude that the evil is significant and that nothing short of a major change will solve it. Thus, the negative may propose the creation of new structures or the assignment of new functions to existing structures. This constitutes a counterplan position.

Nothing seems to create greater difficulty for affirmative advocates than a well conceived negative counterplan position. However, if negatives have enjoyed increasing success in arguing counterplans, affirmatives have no one to blame but themselves. In most debates involving standard positions, either the affirmative or negative wins the decision on the basis of superior analysis, evidence and/or skill. By contrast, in most debates featuring a counterplan strategy, either the affirmative or negative loses the decision on the basis of a theoretical or tactical failing. Obviously, the trick is to *avoid losing*. A sound understanding of the theory and tactics of counterplan debating is the best way to achieve this end.

Chapter 10 examined the theoretical basis of the counterplan position. A solid theoretical foundation on counterplans is important to both affirmative and negative advocates. This section will concentrate on the tactics of affirmative responses to the negative counterplan.

It is important for the affirmative advocate to maintain perspective when confronted with a negative counterplan. Two ramifications follow. First, do not abandon the affirmative position. Start with the case structure. If the negative has attacked the case position, use standard case extension procedures. Strive to maintain affirmative themes, provide both on-point and substantive extension, and maximize the available time. If the negative ignores the case, start there anyway. Highlight the important themes, analysis and evidence; provide additional extension as is appropriate.

Second, approach the counterplan from a holistic comparative perspective. A counterplan debate poses a simple choice: the superiority of one plan versus another. Thus, the affirmative's task is quite clear: it must defend its own position as effectively as possible (something that it would have to do in any case), and it must vigorously attack the counterplan position. The question imposed by this scenario is: which proposal is the most desirable? This is a function of each plan's benefits and costs. Benefits stem from a plan's advantages and solvency (the affirmative must defend its advantages and solvency and it must attack the counterplan's advantages and solvency). Costs result from a plan's disadvantages (the affirmative must defend its plan against negative disadvantages and argue disadvantages against the counterplan).

The affirmative advocate must understand and apply counterplan theory. The negative counterplan must meet two theoretical standards. Most affirmative wins against counterplan positions result from the inability of the negative to meet one or both of these standards. First, the affirmative may argue that the negative's counterplan is topical. Although some theorists dispute this requirement, most consider it an absolute standard. We concur. Recall that if the negative supports a counterplan which implements the resolution, then the only choice offered to the critic judge is to accept the resolution regardless of whether the plan or the counterplan is the superior system. The requirement that a counterplan must be non-topical was discussed in chapter 10.

Second, the affirmative can argue that the negative's counterplan is not a competitive alternative. Recall that if the counterplan is merely a supplement or adjunct to the affirmative's plan, rather than a necessary substitute for it, then there is no reason to reject the resolution based on the counterplan's merits. However, there are various standards of competitiveness, and negatives will attempt to claim that one is sufficient to meet this requirement. Hence, the affirmative advocate must be prepared to argue all possible competitiveness standards. Competitiveness standards were examined in chapter 10.

In terms of analyzing the counterplan on its own merits, it is important that the affirmative advocate prepare to initiate and to extend the strongest possible disadvantage arguments against any anticipated counterplan position. As indicated previously, a counterplan debate focuses attention on the comparative benefits and costs of alternative plans. Comparative benefits pose no special problem for affirmatives; they involve standard fare, extending case while refuting solvency attacks and plan disadvantages. The counterplan, however, requires the affirmative to focus on the comparative costs of the negative alternative. This dimension shouldn't, but often does, catch an affirmative off guard. We recommend two solutions. First, research and brief disadvantages against all possible counterplan positions. Second, research and brief second-line extension (affirmative responses to initial negative arguments) and third-line extension (affirmative responses to negative extension of initial arguments) to these positions. Because the affirmative will initiate disadvantages against a negative counterplan in the second affirmative constructive, he or she must be prepared to extend them at least once during the course of a debate. Hence, it is of little value to develop first-line positions without second- and third-line extension.

Finally, the affirmative advocate must be prepared to make hard choices with regard to argument selection. The negative counterplan tactic poses substantial time allocation problems for the affirmative. Hence, maximization of the available time assumes paramount importance in a counterplan debate. Affirmative advocates must be extremely selective in deciding what arguments to initiate in the second affirmative constructive and in choosing those arguments to extend in the rebuttal speeches.

Solvency Challenges

There is no unique tactical approach to guide the affirmative in responding to negative solvency challenges. As indicated in chapter 9, the affirmative advocate must do two things to optimize the solvency position. First, utilize strong analysis and evidence in the first constructive speech to provide a sound analytical and evidenciary grounding for the solvency position. The supporting evidence should include the testimony of experts who explain why the proposed course of action would work, studies which support the affirmative's claim, and empirical verification. Second, insure that the plan both militates the harms and overcomes the inherencies.

If the solvency position is sound initially, it provides an excellent footing for subsequent affirmative responses to negative efficacy attacks. The affirmative advocate is then in a position to capitalize on two negative failings: first, negatives can seldom neutralize initial affirmative solvency evidence (they usually make no effort to do so), and second, the general negative evidence, used to document solvency attacks, is usually not as good as the more specific affirmative evidence. Hence, in responding to the negative efficacy challenge, the affirmative advocate should exploit initial solvency analysis and evidence and provide more of same. This approach will usually prevail.

The sample flow on the topic, "the U.S. should curtail its arms sales to other countries," illustrates this thesis (see chapter 6). The affirmative argued that the U.S. should stop arms sales to Indonesia in an effort to halt the latter's subjugation of East Timor. The negative argued that Indonesia would not give up Timor; furthermore, it could easily procure armaments elsewhere. As a result, the affirmative plan would fail to alter Indonesian policy; indeed, it might precipitate a backlash toward East Timor. The negative documented these claims reasonably well. However, the affirmative was able to refute this position via an effective combination approach. First, it exploited the solvency analysis and evidence in the initial speech. The affirmative had argued that a cutoff of U.S. arms would directly ameliorate the problem since Indonesia would be unable to continue military operations in East Timor without a continued flow of U.S. arms, and would indirectly stop the repression because U.S. arms could be used as a lever to influence Indonesian policy. The negative was unable to refute this evidence. Second, the affirmative provided additional on-point and substantive refutation against the thesis of the negative's position. This combination approach usually constitutes an effective affirmative response to any negative efficacy challenge.

Disadvantages

The plan disadvantage may be the most important argument in the negative's arsenal. Whereas most negative positions concentrate on affirmative benefits, the disadvantage depicts affirmative costs. Since affirmatives will lose policy debates if net costs exceed net benefits, negatives usually place substantial emphasis on disadvantage positions. As a result, affirmative advocates must be prepared to provide the strongest possible responses to all anticipated disadvantages.

Response Options.   To illustrate affirmative response possibilities we will use a common disadvantage on the resolution that, "all United States military intervention into the internal affairs of any foreign nation or nations in the Western Hemisphere should be prohibited." In our hypothetical debate the affirmative case adopted a generic ban on future U.S. military intervention in this hemisphere. The negative responded with a plan disadvantage that a ban on U.S. military intervention would precipitate communist incursions throughout the hemisphere, a disadvantage which is specific to the plan.

A negative disadvantage contains two dimensions: the link and the impact. The link embodies the thesis of the disadvantage. It ties an affirmative's plan to a particular consequence. How, for example, does a blanket prohibition of United States military intervention in the hemisphere trigger communist incursions? The answer, and the thesis of this disadvantage, is that the threat and actual use of United States military intervention deters and arrests communist expansion in Latin America. If the United States adopted a policy of non-intervention in the hemisphere, then Soviet- and Cuban-backed communist insurgencies would envelop Latin America. The impact constitutes the particular evil—*the consequence* of the affirmative's plan. In the example above, any one or more possible impacts of the communist incursion disadvantage might be developed. The negative could argue that communism exacts a horrible price in the host country: it tramples individual rights of speech, assembly, worship and thought; it terrorizes segments of the population; it is sometimes genocidal. In addition, communist gains in one country pave the way for further incursions, as the domino theory has postulated, thus increasingly isolating the United States in a hostile world.

The affirmative may respond to a negative disadvantage in one or more of four ways. First, the advocate may attempt to sever the link, arguing that the thesis of the disadvantage is untrue. In the example above, the affirmative can sever the link by demonstrating that United States military intervention accomplishes nothing; its threat doesn't deter and its use doesn't arrest communist incursions. Second, the advocate may strive to turn the link, arguing that the thesis of the disadvantage is reversed. For instance, an affirmative can turn the communist incursion link by arguing that United States support of right-wing dictatorships in Latin America thwarts peaceful change, thus fueling revolutionary movements. Furthermore, once revolutionary activity begins, United States military opposition plays into Soviet and Cuban hands by forcing insurgent movements to ask Havana and Moscow for support. Thus, the thesis of the negative position is reversed; it is existing policies which produce the consequences of the disadvantage.

Third, an affirmative advocate may attempt to deny the impact, arguing that the impact thesis is untrue. In the example above, the affirmative can deny the impact by arguing that communism does not exacerbate human rights violations, brutalize the host population, or fuel further communist incursions. Finally, the advocate may endeavor to turn one or more of the impacts, arguing that their thesis is reversed. For example, the affirmative could claim that communism is beneficial, that it ends internal strife, promotes an equitable distribution of wealth, fosters indigenous economic and social development, promotes increased awareness and participation in the political process, and so on.

Of course, the affirmative advocate can use any combination of these approaches. Our previous discussion of "a holistic perspective" must be reemphasized, however. The affirmative must carefully examine the strategic implications of each possible position. A holistic perspective requires that the advocate start with the rebuttals, tracing each potential position back through the constructive speeches. Such reverse mapping forces an affirmative advocate to carefully probe for all likely negative responses, and to assess his or her potential to extend on those anticipated responses. Reverse mapping is a process which facilitates a holistic perspective in debate. The following examples depict this process as an affirmative advocate might use it in evaluating strategic options against a negative plan disadvantage. If the plan disadvantage is initiated in the second negative constructive speech (which means that the initial affirmative response to the position must follow in the first affirmative rebuttal), then the affirmative must backtrack through two speeches, as Figure 11–3

FIGURE 11–3   REVERSE MAPPING

1AR: First Affirmative Rebuttal Speech
2NR: Second Negative Rebuttal Speech
2AR: Second Affirmative Rebuttal Speech

1AR   2NR   2AR

FIGURE 11–4   REVERSE MAPPING

2AC: Second Affirmative Constructive Speech
2NC: Second Negative Constructive Speech, or
1NR: First Negative Rebuttal Speech
1AR: First Affirmative Rebuttal Speech
2NR: Second Negative Rebuttal Speech
2AR: Second Affirmative Rebuttal Speech

2AC   2NC/1NR   1AR   2NR   2AR

illustrates. On the other hand, if the plan disadvantage is launched in the first negative constructive speech (which means that the initial affirmative response to the position must follow in the second affirmative constructive speech), then the affirmative must backtrack through four speeches, as Figure 11–4 indicates. Reverse mapping allows the affirmative to ascertain which responses are strong, which responses cannot be sustained in subsequent speeches, and which responses carry the potential to backfire during the course of a debate.

Guidelines.   We will now discuss specific guidelines which might assist the affirmative advocate to use a holistic perspective in examining the strategic implications of possible approaches to a negative plan disadvantage.

The affirmative advocate should attack the link only under the following circumstances: (1) if the link is intuitively suspect, thereby suggesting some potential for this line of argument; (2) if the affirmative can significantly outevidence the negative on this issue, thus avoiding the pitfall of minimizing—but not defeating—the link, thereby still incurring the disadvantage's impacts; and (3) if the affirmative *isn't* planning to defeat the negative's disadvantage by reversing its link or its impact. The disadvantage's link is pivotal. If it falls, the entire position collapses, including any affirmative turnaround impacts. Thus, it is possible for affirmative analysis and evidence on a disadvantage's link to preempt more lucrative responses grounded in a reversal of the link and/or the impact.

Similarly, we recommend that the affirmative attempt to reverse the link only: (1) if the affirmative has both more evidence and better evidence than the negative on this issue; (2) if affirmative evidence is on-point—both to the thesis of the case and to the thesis of the disadvantage. Often affirmative evidence meets the first test but fails the second. This creates a potentially dangerous scenario for the affirmative. Whenever the affirmative attempts to turn a disadvantage, the critic judge *must resolve* the issue. In the scenario depicted above, the judge will be forced to weigh the strength of affirmative and negative evidence, and to make a value judgment on which is superior. The affirmative will want to avoid the perception of a stalemate, which is probable if its evidence is on-point to the thesis of the case but not to the thesis of the disadvantage. In addition, (3) the affirmative should attempt to reverse the link *only if* it isn't planning to defeat the negative disadvantage by denying or reversing its impact.

This is very dangerous terrain. A double turnaround can prove devastating to an affirmative advocate. If, for example, the affirmative reversed the link on the "Red Spread" disadvantage, arguing that a prohibition of United States military intervention would militate the spread of communism; and also reversed the impact of the disadvantage, proving that communism is good, then it has engineered a double turnaround. The affirmative thus contributes to its own undoing, providing a strong reason to reject its own position.

The affirmative advocate should attempt to deny the impact of a disadvantage only: (1) if this position is used in conjunction with arguments which attempt to deny the link or thesis of the disadvantage (this is a very risky strategy when used alone), and (2) if he or she isn't planning to reverse the link or the impact of the disadvantage. If the affirmative denies the impact, then the disadvantage is rendered mute, including any affirmative turnaround impacts.

The affirmative should attempt to reverse the impact of a disadvantage only under the following conditions: (1) if the affirmative is prepared to see the focus of the debate shift from its own case justification to the direction of the impact of the disadvantage. If the negative disadvantage carries more potential impact than the affirmative case, and the affirmative decides to reverse the impact of the disadvantage, then the side that prevails on the disadvantage must also prevail in the debate. In addition, the affirmative advocate should endeavor to reverse the impact of a disadvantage *only:* (2) if he or she has vastly superior evidence; and (3) if the affirmative hasn't argued against the thesis which underpins either the link or the impact of the disadvantage.

The choice is compounded by the possibility of using some combination of these positions. A combination approach makes sense only if the affirmative advocate has carefully examined the strategic implications of each position. Under such circumstances the affirmative advocate may opt to probe the negative defenses for potential weaknesses, holding back the thrust of the affirmative attack until the negative provides one more line of extension. Thus, a combination approach can optimize affirmative flexibility. It is far more common, however, for affirmative advocates to utilize a combination approach for the wrong reasons—not because they have carefully thought the issue through to the rebuttal periods and deduced that a combination approach is the most effective. Rather, because they have first-line analysis and evidence to back the various components of the combination approach. This is the one-response-at-a-time and one-speech-at-a-time micro method of affirmative extension which we indicted earlier in this chapter.

The affirmative advocate should attempt a combination approach only: (1) if he or she has carefully examined the strategic ramifications of each position; and (2) if the advocate desires to maximize flexibility.

The preceding analysis assumes that the negative disadvantage is specific to the affirmative's plan. Other negative disadvantages, however, are grounded in the mandate of the resolution. As such, the "generic" disadvantage is often only tangentially relevant to a particular affirmative's plan. For example, if the resolution calls for "the federal government to guarantee employment opportunities for all people in the labor force," the negative might argue generic disadvantages based on: the federal government as agent (i.e., a social priorities position based on the thesis that increased federal spending will force cuts in valued social programs), the notion of guarantee (i.e., an inflation disadvantage based on the weakening of fiscal policy as a tool to control business cycles), or the mandate for more employment (i.e., an increased stress/ mortality position grounded in the research of Joseph Eyer). When an affirmative advocate responds to a weakly linked, but lengthy, "generic" negative disadvantage with numerous substantive answers (including turnaround extensions against the argument's links and/or impacts), he or she may contribute to legitimizing the negative position.

We recommend that the affirmative utilize a criteria for evaluating the adequacy of a "generic" disadvantage. James J. Unger developed the following standards to assist the affirmative in establishing a threshold of legitimacy. The first is the internal context. Do the sources, used to support the disadvantage agree on the definition and implication of all critical terms? Next, look at the external context. Do the negative sources, used to document the links of the disadvantage, also support the link between the disadvantage and the specific affirmative proposal? The third standard is the subject matter context. Can the negative present at least one subject-matter expert who supports the negative argument in its entirety? Fourth, consider the historical context. If the disadvantage is valid, as linked to the affirmative plan in question, why hasn't such an occurrence resulted from similar actions which occurred in the past?[8] The threshold must be crossed *prior to* a standard assessment of the position. Furthermore, the negative has the burden of proof here. The negative must establish that the disadvantage meets these standards. Only then should the critic attempt to assess the probability and impact of the argument.[9]

AFFIRMATIVE REBUTTAL TACTICS

The advocate should now be prepared to argue the affirmative. We laid out the essentials of the initial affirmative position in chapter 9. We have discussed general and specific affirmative strategies and tactics in this chapter. Thus, the advocate should now be able to construct and extend an affirmative case. Much of the theory and technique covered so far also applies to the affirmative rebuttal speeches. Nonetheless, two additional features of affirmative rebuttal tactics must be pursued at this time: refutation tactics and coverage demands. We will examine rebuttal tactics in greater detail in chapter 13.

Refutation Tactics

Refutation occurs in all affirmative speeches. We have already examined a perspective and specific techniques for refutation. Some additional comments are necessary, however, concerning the tactics of refutation.

In this chapter we have placed particular emphasis on affirmative refutation of specific negative arguments. Preemption is a tactic which assists affirmative refutation. The affirmative advocate can use the preemption to accomplish one of two tactical objectives. First, the preemption can establish the terms or conditions for affirmative/negative clash on a particular argument. For example, in responding to a negative plan disadvantage, the affirmative could initiate a preemption, indicating what the negative must do in order to refute the affirmative responses and thus win the argument. Or second, a preemption can provide anticipatory refutation of negative argument(s). If the advocate expects to hear a specific negative argument, he or she can refute that argument even before the negative has a chance to present it. The value of the preemption is that it initiates clash on affirmative terms.

Of course the process of refutation continues in the rebuttal speeches. The strategies and tactics discussed previously should serve the advocate well in the rebuttals. However, two additional points warrant emphasis.

First, the affirmative must *continue the process of on-point and substantive extension—in those argument sectors that it needs to win, and in those sectors that it can't afford to lose.* Many affirmative advocates seriously err in attempting to extend too much or too little. The optimal approach lies somewhere in between. It presupposes a holistic perspective, which is a prerequisite to intelligent rebuttal choices. Such a perspective makes it possible to determine which argument sectors require additional extension.

Second, the advocate must take care of loose ends or strays. A stray might consist of an individual response (affirmative or negative) in an otherwise "dead" argument sector (an area that was previously contested but, for one reason or another, is no longer germane to the debate outcome) which carries potential ramifications in other active argument sectors. A stray might also consist of a hidden argument—a disadvantage with independent links, or a topicality argument which contains sections (or anticipates responses) that feed other positions in a debate. The affirmative advocate must learn to *recognize and defuse* strays.

Coverage Demands

The exponential increase in the amount of information has complicated decision making in all phases of human endeavor and in contemporary advocacy. This burgeoning of substantive and theoretical issues demands that advocates attempt to cope with far greater breadth and depth in all issue sectors. One result is an increasing premium on coverage in contemporary advocacy. Two techniques to maximize rebuttal coverage are important for the affirmative.

First, the advocate must feel free to drop argument areas. It is not always necessary to cover every argument on the flow: indeed, there are times when it is impossible and other times when it is strategically unsound. *The key to rebuttal success lies in knowing what must be done, doing it well, and leaving the rest.* In the end, the critic judge must be convinced that after all negative attacks are weighed, the affirmative case is still significant, inherent, and the affirmative plan is solvent and desirable. From the systems perspective, carrying these issues will result in proving that the benefits of an affirmative proposal outweigh its costs, more than the present system or any alternative proposals suggested by the negative.

Second, the advocate must become an efficient communicator. This does not entail an increase in speaking rate. Instead, it places the emphasis on speaking efficiency. We encourage all advocates to optimize the techniques of economy of language and argument grouping. These are discussed in some detail in chapter 13.

SUMMARY

Chapter 9 focused on the task of initiating argument—presenting the case or position. This chapter examined the defense of the affirmative's position against any and all negative attempts to rebut it—the strategies and tactics which constitute the basis of effective affirmative advocacy.

Initially we explored the intrinsic advantages of affirmative advocacy. The contemporary affirmative advocate is in an enviable position. The affirmative can initiate and maintain control over the argumentative terrain. Cases can be chosen, research accomplished, and tactical options selected which optimize the affirmative's position. Furthermore, the increased emphasis on hard data drawn from empirical research has produced an affirmative bias. Techniques were examined to enable the affirmative advocate to exploit these intrinsic advantages.

Then we considered the task of affirmative case extension. Case extension requires both the internalization of a strategic perspective to frame argument choices in addition to the mastery of specific case extension techniques. Advocates were advised to use on-point and substantive extension as well as techniques to establish, maintain and exploit an affirmative thesis or perspective. In addition, advocates were encouraged to master a holistic view in all phases of debate: in weighing strategic options, determining which positions to advance, deciding on specific responses to individual arguments, and evaluating the interrelationships among arguments in the rebuttal periods. These are integral components of effective affirmative case extension.

The heart of the chapter focused on affirmative strategic responses to all standard negative argumentative positions, including: straight refutation, topicality, alternative proposals (including inherency arguments and counterplans), solvency attacks, and plan disadvantages. The chapter concluded with a treatment of affirmative rebuttal tactics.

The student should now be ready to engage in affirmative advocacy.

Notes

[1]Alvin Toffler, *Future Shock* (New York: Random House, 1970), p. 31, estimates that the number of scientific journals and articles is doubling every 15 years and that the quantity of scientific and empirical literature is increasing approximately 60,000,000 pages each year.

[2]Irving Kristol, "Is Social Science A God That Failed?" *Public Opinion,* Oct./Nov. 1981, p. 12.

[3]Kathy Kellermann, "The Concept of Evidence: A Critical Review," *Journal of the American Forensic Association,* 16 (1980), 165.

[4]James A. Benson, "The Use of Evidence in Intercollegiate Debate," *Journal of the American Forensic Association,* 5 (1971), 262,

[5]'Fourth Judge Critique: William Southworth, University of Redlands,' "1984 National Debate Tournament Final Debate: Should Any and All Injury Resulting from the Disposal of Hazardous Waste in the United States Be the Legal Responsibility of the Producer of That Waste," edited by John A. Boaz, *Journal of the American Forensic Association,* 21 (1984), 55.

[6]See: David Bakan, "The Test of Significance in Psychological Research," *Psychological Bulletin,* 66 (1966), 423–37; Quinn McNemar, "At Random: Sense and Nonsense," *American Psychologist,* 15 (1960), 295–300; and Karl Popper, *The Logic of Scientific Discovery* (New York: Harper & Row, 1968).

[7]Allan J. Lichtman and Daniel M. Rohrer, "A General Theory of the Counterplan," *Journal of the American Forensic Association,* 12 (1975), 72.

[8]James J. Unger, "The Words of a Debate Proposition and the Debate Subject Matter: Friends or Foes," a paper presented at the Speech Communication Association annual convention, Anaheim, Cal., 14 November 1981, pp. 9–10.

[9]Unger, pp. 9–11.

CHAPTER TWELVE

NEGATIVE
STRATEGIES
AND
TACTICS

The selection and implementation of strategic choices—presenting the case or position—is the first phase of negative advocacy. The second phase involves a defense of the critical components of that position against any and all affirmative attempts to rebut it.

This chapter will focus on the second phase, systematically examining the strategies and tactics involved in defending a negative position. As we indicated in chapter 11, strategies focus on debate as a whole entity whereas tactics concentrate on the individual components of a debate.

Initially we will explore the intrinsic advantages of negative advocacy; then we will discuss the strategy of seizing the argumentative terrain. The thrust of this chapter, however, will focus on the strategies and tactics of negative extension. Specifically we will examine the task of negative case extension, strategically extending all standard negative argumentative positions, and negative rebuttal tactics. These areas constitute the heart and soul of negative advocacy.

INTRINSIC ADVANTAGES OF
NEGATIVE ADVOCACY

In chapter 11 we observed the advantages of affirmative advocacy. They are formidable. Nonetheless, there are advantages of negative advocacy as well. We will explore the role of presumption and flexibility in negative advocacy, which constitute important intrinsic advantages of arguing against—in contrast to arguing for—most propositions.

Presumption

As indicated in chapter 10, there are various perspectives with regard to the locus of presumption in advocacy. The stock issues view is that presumption always rests with existing institutions. Thus, it should be automatically assigned to the negative, barring an abandonment of present system programs (i.e., a counterplan position). The hypothesis-testing view holds that presumption is always positioned against a resolution. Thus, according to those perspectives, presumption is automatically assigned to the negative in all debates.

We subscribe to a third view of presumption. Presumption is based on the risk of uncertainty. Thus, it could be assigned to the affirmative or the negative depending on the circumstances. If an affirmative change entails less risk than a negative alternative (not an uncommon occurrence, especially if the negative argues a counterplan position), then that affirmative should enjoy presumption. More often than not, however, presumption will continue to rest with the negative. This is because the present system's more cautious and adaptive approach is safer. Change occurs in smaller increments. Multiple programs in the pursuit of multiple objectives take on the form of an indefinite sequence of relatively small policy moves. As a result, mistakes can be observed early and corrected.[1] In contrast, an affirmative plan to implement a debate resolution is usually based on the swift and single-minded pursuit of a single goal. Such decisive policy initiatives allow much less room for self-correction. Indeed, often the scope of an affirmative change renders self-correction virtually impossible.[2]

Consequently, the negative advocate is in the best position to claim presumption in a debate round. The policy resolution embodies a mandate for change. The affirmative has no choice in the matter. It must advocate the resolution; as such, the affirmative must always argue in support of change. More specifically, the affirmative must indict the existing policy system for its shortcomings and it must propose and defend a plan to implement a new policy system which embodies changes of a certain magnitude and direction. By contrast, the negative must only oppose the resolution. Although the negative may choose to argue in favor of a systematic change (i.e., it may offer a counterplan alternative), the negative is not obliged to do so. Hence, the negative is in the enviable position of being able to claim argumentative presumption at will.

Presumption affords two advantages. First, it places the burden of proof on one's opponent. Presumption in a debate context is analogous to the presumption of innocence in a court of law. In court, the defendant is not obliged to prove his or her innocence. The prosecution must assume the burden of proof; it must present a prima-facie case or the charge is dismissed. The rationale for the legal presumption of innocence is that it is better to allow a guilty person to go free (as a result of insufficient evidence) than it is to punish an innocent person unjustly. A debate context is similar. If presumption rests with the negative, then the affirmative must assume the burden of proof; it must present a prima-facie case or face certain defeat. The rationale for negative presumption in debate is that it is better to continue with existing policies (absent a compelling reason to the contrary) than it is to exchange them for a new system whose effects may not be known.

Second, presumption serves as a tie-breaker. In the event of an argumentative stalemate, the critic judge should award the decision to the side which advocates the least risky policy; that side should enjoy presumption in the debate.[3] It is important to note that the tie-breaking function of the concept of presumption is not merely an arbitrary rule or convention. The policy systems perspective holds that in the event of an argumentative standoff between advocates of the present system and proponents of an alternative system, there is less risk involved in standing pat with the existing system. Needless to say, the negative advocate should attempt to claim presumption in order to capitalize on these two advantages.

Flexibility

The negative advocate has the advantage of flexibility in a debate. The affirmative faces an unenviable task. The affirmative must prevail on *most of* the argumentative positions that it introduces in a debate. As we indicated in chapter 9, an affirmative advocate must meet the basic burdens of topicality, significance, permanence, solvency and desirability. These constitute fundamental requirements, irrespective of paradigmatic considerations. In the face of such requirements, an affirmative advocate possesses limited maneuverability. An affirmative failing in even a single area can spell defeat. Thus, basic burdens constitute an imposing obligation for an affirmative advocate.

By contrast, the negative advocate enjoys maximum discretion in a debate. First, the negative can decide what facets of an affirmative's position to attack. The negative may opt to contest all, some, or none of the initial affirmative claims. Then the negative can decide how to attack the affirmative's position. Initially the negative can pick and choose from a myriad of argumentative options, and may abandon or bolster such options as a debate progresses. The affirmative advocate, of course, must await the negative's choice and adapt as well as possible. In short, flexibility constitutes a unique and quite imposing advantage for the negative advocate.

SEIZING THE ARGUMENTATIVE TERRAIN

Although the affirmative has the advantage of initiating clash in a debate, the negative is in an excellent position to wrest control over the argumentative terrain from the affirmative, which is a key to successful negative advocacy. It allows the negative advocate to maneuver his or her affirmative opponent in a direction—toward tactical options—based on negative strengths and affirmative weaknesses. This struggle between the affirmative and the negative over the control of the argumentative terrain can prove decisive in most debates.

The negative can seize control of the argumentative terrain in two ways. First, the negative should initiate and defend the strongest possible negative position. This allows the negative to assume the initiative in crucial argument areas, thus keeping the affirmative on the defensive. Second, the negative should select specific arguments from available options on the basis of a clear tactical purpose.

Taking a Position

The position is an embodiment of the negative's strategic approach to a particular affirmative's case. *A position consists of a strategic approach which embodies the central thesis or perspective of the negative with regard to a particular affirmative case.* It is characterized by the particular combination of strategic elements employed by the negative in response to a particular affirmative's case.

Sometimes the position ought to be articulated by the negative advocate during the debate. This is especially important if the negative position is unclear on its face (on the basis of the particular strategic elements chosen). In this instance, the position should be embodied in a clear statement of the negative's thesis—an explicit or implicit explanation of negative strategic choices. At other times the negative position is apparent on its face, requiring no further explanation.

While a negative position consists of some combination of strategic elements, a strong position involves the optimal melding of strategic options. It would be both impossible and strategically unwise for a negative advocate to argue all of the argumentative options available to him or her. Unfortunately, many advocates fail to construct a deliberate and coherent negative position. These advocates pay a substantial price in terms of argumentative dysfunctions.

Selecting Specific Arguments

All elements of the negative position should be selected on the basis of a specific tactical purpose. Some strategic elements weaken or preclude others; some options facilitate others. The negative ignores these argumentative relationships at its peril. Instead, the negative advocate should consciously construct a position, carefully selecting each element from among available options.

Negative choices on the proposition, "that the United States should establish uniform rules of procedure for its criminal courts," illustrate the intricacies of constructing a strong negative position. An affirmative case might establish uniform rules of procedure with regard to pre-trial detention in all courts. Such a case might contend that: the existing system of bail ought to be abolished; that nearly three million people unable to post bail are incarcerated prior to trial annually; that nearly half of these are later found to be innocent of the crimes that they are charged with; that pre-trial incarceration undermines a defendant's right to a fair trial; and that the existing system, in penalizing inability to pay, incarcerates the poor while freeing the dangerous. The affirmative plan might propose that "prediction of dangerousness" should be the only criterion for determining pre-trial detention.

This example is typical of most debates in that the negative must construct a position from among a variety of diverse elements. The difficulty stems from the fact that *individual elements operate synergistically* when combined with other elements. Hence, the potential argumentative relationships must be carefully examined as the advocate attempts to fashion a negative position. Figure 12–1 illustrates an assortment of potential negative arguments against the "abolish bail" affirmative case. Observe the intricacies involved in each of the potential options.

Figure 12–1 illustrates the intricacies involved in negative argument selection. The number of argumentative permutations is substantial. Each negative argument choice carries ramifications for other options. That is, the use of a particular argument may either enhance or diminish other potential argument choices. We will explain the ramifications involved in one argument option per category in an effort to further clarify this point.

Significance Options. Suppose that the negative wants to contest affirmative significance. If the negative advocate chooses to argue that arrest statistics are unreliable, then he or she undermines support for all subsequent claims which depend upon the reliability of arrest data for support. For example, argument option S–1, "arrest statistics are unreliable," weakens options S–3, "bail crime is insignificant," D–1, "increased crime (based on the assumption that detention reduces crime)," and D–2, "increased trial/court congestion."

On the other hand, argument option S–1 fuels options S–2, "attack affirmative studies," and P–2, "can't predict dangerousness (thus no decrease in crime will occur)." Affirmative studies in support of significance and dangerousness claims assume the reliability of arrest data; thus, if the negative advocate can demonstrate that arrest statistics are inadequate, then subsequent negative attacks on significance and dangerousness should be strengthened.

Inherency Options. Next suppose that the negative seeks to argue an inherency position. If the negative advocate opts to support present system efforts to reduce pre-trial detention (which incorporates a modified version of the dangerousness criterion), then he or she makes it next to impossible to indict the dangerousness standard or to argue plan disadvantages which are grounded in the consequences of reduced pre-trial detention. For instance, argument option I–1, "Release on Recognizance (RoR) reforms," weakens argument options P–2, "can't predict dangerousness (thus no decrease in crime will occur)," D–1, "increase in crime (based on the thesis that detention reduces crime)," D–2, "increase trial/court congestion," and D–3, "increase witness intimidation."

By contrast, argument option I–1 facilitates options T–1, "topicality," D–4, "destroy federalism," and CP–1, "states counterplan." Present system RoR efforts complement the topicality argument which presupposes a minimal difference between the present system and the affirmative's plan. In addition, since RoR efforts are uniquely state-level initiatives, negative support for the RoR position bolsters both the federalism plan disadvantage and the states counterplan position.

Solvency Options. What if the negative chooses to attack affirmative solvency? If the negative advocate selects the circumvention plan-meet-advantage argument, he or she can do substantial damage to the affirmative's position. But P–1, "discretion precludes fair trial," weakens argument option I–1, "Release on Recognizance (RoR) reforms." To win circumvention the negative must demonstrate that critical functionaries in the criminal justice system are biased against or are vulnerable to public pressure against pre-trial release and that those functionaries have opportunities to exercise discretion, thus thwarting the affirmative's fair-trial advantage. This option,

FIGURE 12–1   POTENTIAL ELEMENTS OF A NEGATIVE POSITION

Argument Number and Title	Ramifications	
	Choice Weakens: (or precludes)	Choice Fuels:
TOPICALITY		
T–1.　No increase in uniform procedures (affirmative does alter standards but discretion remains)		
SIGNIFICANCE		
S–1.　Arrest statistics unreliable	S–3, D–1, D–2	S–2 & P–2
A. Half arrests unjustified		
B. Bias and falsification		
S–2.　Attack affirmative studies	S–3, D–1, CP–2	P–2
A. Small sample size		
B. No causality shown		
S–3.　Bail crime is insignificant	S–1, S–2	I–1
A. Studies show that less than 5 percent were rearrested—NBS	P–2, D–1, D–3	
B. High risk didn't differ		
S–4.　No court delay causality		
A. Speedy Trial Act decreases	D–2 & D–4	
B. Other causes more important (court space & attorney tactics)	D–2	
INHERENCY		
I–1.　Release on Recognizance (RoR)	P–2, D–1,	T–1
A. Many programs; most states	D–2 & D–3	D–4 & CP–1
B. It's working (most make court appearance; no increase reported in criminal activity during RoR)		
PLAN SOLVENCY		
P–1.　Discretion precludes fair trial	I–1	T–1 & PD–1
A. Prosecutors, judges and juries discriminate		
B. Public pressure biases		
P–2.　Can't predict dangerousness—thus, no decrease in crime occurs	I–1	S–1 & S–2
SOLVENCY/DISADVANTAGE		
PD–1.　Shift to civil commitment (it's worse than time in jail)	D–1, D–2, D–3	
PLAN DISADVANTAGES		
D–1.　Increase in crime (based on the thesis that detention reduces crime)		D–2 & D–3
D–2.　Increase trial/court congestion		D–1 & D–3
D–3.　Increase witness intimidation		D–1
D–4.　Destroy federalism		CP–1
COUNTERPLANS		
CP–1.　States counterplan	D–1, D–2, D–3	D–4
A. Special circumstances		
B. State experimentation		

however, simultaneously undermines the "Release on Recognizance (RoR) reforms" which are based on a structural alteration not unlike the affirmative's. Thus, it is subject to the circumvention argument as well.

On the other hand, P–1 feeds argument options T–1, "topicality," and PD–1, "shift to civil commitment." Both of these arguments are based on the presence of discretion in the criminal justice system. T–1, the topicality argument, claims that discretion denies the resolution's mandate of "uniform procedures." PD–1, the civil commitment solvency/disadvantage option, maintains that the process will not work as the affirmative suggests. If prosecutors and judges cannot jail those defendants that they do not want released prior to trial, they will use civil commitment. Prosecutors and judges have the discretion to seek alternate means to avoid pre-trial release. As such, the negative discretion option feeds both arguments.

Disadvantage Options.   The negative will probably want to argue one or more disadvantages against the affirmative plan. The ramifications here appear positive. D–1, "increase in crime (based on the thesis that detention reduces crime)," enhances argument options D–2, "increase in trial/court congestion," and D–3, "increase witness intimidation." The disadvantage claims increased criminal activity during the period between release and trial coupled with reduced plea-bargaining. Thus, this option enhances the "congestion" and "witness intimidation" argument possibilities.

Counterplan Option.   Finally, the negative might want to advocate a counterplan position. Here the negative advocate selects argument options which encourage state-level reform of pre-trial procedures, and since present state-level reforms have relaxed pre-trial detention requirements, then subsequent negative plan disadvantages grounded in the evils of reduced detention may be rendered non-unique. Thus, CP–1, "states counterplan," impairs argument options D–1, "increase in crime (based on the thesis that detention reduces crime)," D–2, "increase in trial/court congestion," and D–3, "increase witness intimidation." However, CP–1 fuels D–4, "federalism." The state-level counterplan reverses the present trend toward increased federal control, thus strengthening our federal system.

A strong negative position consists of an optimal melding of argument options. Specific strategic elements should be selected to facilitate a sound and coherent perspective on a particular affirmative case. A simple analogy illustrates the common-sense principles at work here. Your wardrobe probably consists of a variety of garments, from summer to winter weight, from casual to formal. In choosing what to wear you do not appraise articles of clothing in isolation. Rather, you evaluate each item in relation to other possible choices in order to coordinate your outfit. Similarly, the negative advocate must carefully select each argument in relation to other potential choices in order to construct the strongest possible position.

Careful argument selection benefits the negative advocate in various ways: it avoids contradictions; it provides a vehicle to wrest control of the argumentative terrain from the affirmative, thus exercising effective control in a debate; and it facilitates argument evaluation—both on the part of negative advocates during the rebuttal periods and the critic judge at the conclusion of a debate.

TASK OF NEGATIVE CASE EXTENSION

Negative case extension involves all attempts to advance or provide for further development of the original negative position. In most instances case extension requires that a negative advocate utilize direct refutation of affirmative responses to original negative arguments in conjunction with an emphasis and further elaboration on uncontested negative constructive positions. As was the case with affirmative case extension, effective negative extension requires both the internalization of a strategic perspective to frame argument choices and the mastery of specific case extension techniques.

A Holistic View

In the same manner as the affirmative, the negative advocate must maintain a holistic view of the debate round. As indicated in chapter 11, a holistic view constitutes "the big picture;" it demands that the negative advocate examine all argumentative variables— *all* possible affirmative and negative *positions, every potential response* to individual affirmative arguments, and *each strategic option*—in terms of their potential impact on the final outcome of a debate.

A holistic view requires that the negative advocate think through all argumentative options in terms of their broader ramifications. It is, in short, a strategic perspective—a macro look at a debate. Instead of languishing in the myriad of individual arguments which comprise the nuts and bolts of a debate, a holistic view focuses on the total picture. It emphasizes careful planning for the rebuttal periods. It is all too easy for advocates to view a debate in a chronological and segmented fashion, taking it speech by speech from the initial constructive to the last rebuttal. A holistic view requires the opposite approach. The skilled negative advocate should approach a debate in reverse order, thinking ahead to the last rebuttal speeches and working backward to the initial ones. This is the only way to insure that all argumentative choices, specific responses and strategic decisions are made on the basis of their long-term rebuttal ramifications.

A holistic view is an indispensable tool for the negative advocate. It can serve as the advocate's guide in his or her efforts to analyze and to argue against an affirmative's position.

Aids Case Analysis. Initially a holistic perspective must guide the negative advocate in analyzing an affirmative's case. Such a perspective constitutes a macro view of an affirmative's position. It includes the following questions: What is the central thesis of the case? What are the explicit and implicit assumptions of the case? What claims must the affirmative win in order to prevail in the debate?

We will illustrate this mode of analysis in examining an affirmative case in support of the resolution that, "All United States military intervention into the internal affairs of any foreign nation or nations in the Western Hemisphere should be prohibited." The affirmative argued that U.S. military intervention in Latin America is extensive. The U.S. provides overt assistance to the unpopular Samoza government in El Salvador, it employs overt and covert methods against the Sandinista government in

Nicaragua, and it has increased the level of belligerence directed at Castro's Cuba. The affirmative further maintained that such intervention is counterproductive. U.S. activities in Central America have spurred an escalation of hostilities in the area and threaten to provoke a major confrontation with Cuba. If that happens, the U.S.S.R. will be inevitably drawn into a conflict with the United States. The affirmative then argued that the only way to avert this "drift into war" scenario is for the United States to initiate a pledge of non-intervention into the internal affairs of any nation or nations in the Western Hemisphere. In addition, the affirmative claimed that such a pledge would reduce Cuban adventurism and precipitate a reduction in tensions with the Soviet Union which might serve as a catalyst to American and Soviet disarmament negotiations.

What is the central thesis of this affirmative case? Clearly the affirmative is claiming that United States military intervention into the internal affairs of any nation or nations in this hemisphere is unqualifiedly bad.

What are the explicit and implicit assumptions of the case? The affirmative is making several statements about the geopolitical environment, including that: there is limited popular support for the non-communist Samoza regime in El Salvador; there is wide popular support for the Sandinista regime in Nicaragua; revolutionary change in El Salvador is inevitable whereas in Nicaragua it is improbable; Central American leftist revolutionary movements are nationalist—not communist—in nature; and U.S. opposition to leftist revolutionary movements drives them to Cuba for support. The affirmative also assumes that: U.S. military force cannot deter the inevitable triumph of leftist revolutionaries in El Salvador, nor can it facilitate success for non-communist revolutionaries in Nicaragua; U.S. military intervention will serve as the catalyst for continued escalation of the fighting in Central America; U.S. military intervention guarantees an increased Cuban presence in Central America; any U.S. military action directed against Cuba will be met by a response from the Soviet Union; and both Cuba and the Soviet Union desire peace in the region and in the world.

What claims must the affirmative win in order to prevail in the debate? To answer this question the negative advocate should look to the central thesis and the explicit and implicit assumptions of the affirmative's case. *In all instances an affirmative must successfully defend the central thesis of the case.* In the example above the affirmative must defend that United States military intervention into the internal affairs of any nation or nations in the hemisphere is unqualifiedly bad. At this point the negative advocate can begin to conceptualize a strategic position. Some argumentative options appear crucial, and others less important. Thus, identification of the central thesis of the affirmative case provides insightful cues concerning critical claims. In addition, the affirmative must successfully defend any and all case assumptions which the negative contests. In short, the negative advocate determines which case assumptions will prove to be critical in a debate. Thus, it stands to reason that the negative advocate can and should exercise discretion in deciding which case assumptions to attack.

Guides Argument Selection.   A holistic view also serves as an indispensable tool for the negative advocate in arguing against an affirmative position. First, a holistic perspective facilitates an emphasis on crucial negative themes. This provides standards to appraise affirmative and negative arguments—a means for the advocate to package a debate on negative terms for the critic judge.

Second, a holistic view plays an important role in initial argument selection and specific argument extension. For instance, a macro view allows the negative advocate to select arguments that will elicit affirmative responses which will facilitate other claims. In other words, a particular argument option can be selected in anticipation of affirmative responses; the negative advocate then concedes the original argument, utilizing affirmative answers to feed a different negative claim.

Negative choices on the resolution, "that the United States should establish uniform rules of procedure for its criminal courts," illustrate this strategy. Figure 12–1 depicted negative argument possibilities against an "abolish bail" affirmative case. Argument options S–4–A, "Speedy Trial Act decreases court delay," and T–1, "no increase in uniform procedures topicality" could be used in this manner.

Argument option S–4–A can be used to facilitate option D–2, "increase trial/court congestion." The Speedy Trial Act employed court streamlining and other methods that were designed to reduce the interval between arrest and trial. This argument option has minimal value in its own right against an "abolish bail" affirmative. Even if the negative could demonstrate efficacy and viability for this present system mechanism, it does not alter the affirmative scenario. Irrespective of the length of court delay, the affirmative will claim that many defendants are incarcerated prior to trial; half of these are later found to be innocent of the crimes that they are charged with; pre-trial incarceration undermines a defendant's right to a fair trial; and the existing system, in penalizing inability to pay, incarcerates the poor while freeing the dangerous.

However, affirmative responses to argument option S–4–A can bolster negative option D–2. In responding to S–4–A, the affirmative might argue that the Speedy Trial Act has failed to reduce the backlog of pending criminal cases, and that court delay undermines American justice (it increases the chances that the innocent will be convicted and the guilty will be acquitted). These responses, of course, fuel option D–2. In D–2 the negative argues that the affirmative plan, in abolishing bail and mandating the dangerousness standard as the only criterion for pre-trial incarceration, will free many defendants who would otherwise await trial in jails; this will reduce the incentive for these individuals to plea-bargain, thus swamping court dockets with additional cases. As a result, the affirmative position exacerbates court delay, impairing justice. In this manner affirmative responses to argument option S–4–A feed option D–2 nicely. On the one hand, these responses indicate that the existing judicial machinery is unprepared to handle an increase in caseload; in addition, they vividly demonstrate the consequences of an increase in delay. Whereas option S–4–A could do only minimal damage to the affirmative's position, argument option D–2 would carry substantial impact in the debate.

In the same vein, affirmative responses to argument option T–1 could facilitate all negative disadvantages (and/or the negative counterplan option). In responding to argument option T–1, the affirmative might argue that its plan of uniform standards represents a substantial departure from the status quo. If so, all disadvantage options take on added uniqueness.

Facilitates Argument Extension.   A holistic view also allows the negative advocate to select answers to affirmative responses against initial negative arguments so as to optimize the negative's position. This is imperative. A holistic view requires that the negative advocate think through all argumentative options in terms of their broader ramifications.

We will illustrate this concept with a negative disadvantage on the resolution, "that all United States military intervention into the internal affairs of any foreign nation or nations in the Western Hemisphere should be prohibited." The scenario involves a negative nuclear proliferation disadvantage against an affirmative position that the United States should terminate all military intervention in this hemisphere because it seldom achieves the end for which it was intended, and as a result of Soviet and Cuban presence, carries substantial risks, especially that this nation's involvement might trigger regional and/or superpower escalation.

While the affirmative faces tough choices in deciding how to respond to this negative disadvantage, the negative's choices are no less difficult. If the affirmative attempted to sever the link, arguing that the thesis of the disadvantage is untrue, that Latin American nuclear proliferation is inevitable in time and that a United States disposition for or against military intervention in the Western Hemisphere has no impact on the decision of potential proliferants, how should the negative respond? Should he or she attempt to refute the affirmative's denial of the link? This strategy makes sense (1) if the negative can outevidence the affirmative on this issue; (2) if the impact of the disadvantage is substantial; and (3) if the negative can prevail in the face of affirmative attempts to reverse the impact of the disadvantage. Or, should the negative abandon this phase of the argument? This approach is reasonable (1) if the negative cannot outevidence the affirmative on this issue, (2) if the impact of the disadvantage is small or moderate, or (3) if the affirmative made no attempt to reverse the impact of the disadvantage. Or, should the negative grant the affirmative responses in an effort to exploit them? This approach is sound (1) if affirmative answers facilitate a stronger negative argument than the disadvantage, or (2) if the affirmative also reversed the impact of the disadvantage and can significantly outevidence the negative on this issue.

If the affirmative attempted to reverse, or "flip," the link, arguing that a prohibition on United States military intervention in the hemisphere would reduce the motivation of those potential proliferants who perceive United States interventionist policy as a threat to their own sovereignty, how should the negative respond? Should the negative advocate attempt to refute the affirmative's reversal of the link? This makes sense (1) if the negative can significantly outevidence the affirmative on this issue, and (2) if the impact of the disadvantage is substantial. Or, should the negative abandon this dimension of the argument? This approach is reasonable (1) if the negative cannot outevidence the affirmative on this issue, and (2) if the impact of the disadvantage is small or moderate. Or, should the negative advocate grant the affirmative responses in an effort to exploit them? This approach is sound (1) if the affirmative has also attempted to defeat the disadvantage by reversing its impact, or (2) if affirmative answers feed another negative argument which is more viable than the disadvantage.

If the affirmative opted to attack the disadvantage at its impact, arguing that the impact thesis of the disadvantage is untrue, that there is no clear relationship between nuclear proliferation and the probability of war, how should the negative respond? Should the negative advocate attempt to refute the affirmative's denial of the impact? This is a good strategy (1) if the negative can significantly outevidence the affirmative on this issue, and (2) if the affirmative has not also tried to reverse the link or the impact of the disadvantage. Or, should the negative abandon this particular phase of the argument? This approach is viable (1) if the negative cannot outevidence the affirmative on this issue, or (2) if the affirmative has mounted a strong challenge against the link of the disadvantage. Or, should the negative advocate grant the affirmative responses in an effort to exploit them? This makes sense (1) if the affirmative advocate also reversed the link of the disadvantage (in this case the negative must concede the affirmative "flip" of the link and the impact), or (2) if affirmative answers fuel a stronger negative argument than this disadvantage.

If the affirmative chose to grant the link or thesis of the disadvantage, concede that there is a relationship between nuclear proliferation and the probability of war, but argue that the impact thesis is reversed, that proliferation is actually beneficial because it dramatically increases the consequences of conflict, reducing the incidence of war and thereby promoting stability in the international system, how might the negative respond? Should the negative advocate attempt to refute the affirmative claim? This is a good approach (1) if the negative can outextend the affirmative on this issue, but even if negative responses are mediocre, (2) the negative advocate may have to make an effort to refute an affirmative attempt to "flip" the impact of the disadvantage unless prior affirmative answers can be used to deny the link or the impact of the argument. Should the negative abandon this dimension of the argument? This makes sense if (1) the affirmative has provided a strong denial of the link or thesis of the disadvantage, and (2) the negative cannot outevidence the affirmative on the reversal of the impact of this argument. In this instance it would be wise to grant the denial of the link and abandon the position. Or, should the negative advocate grant the affirmative responses and attempt to exploit them? This is sound strategy (1) if the affirmative has also reversed the link or thesis of the disadvantage (in which case the negative can grant the "flips" of the link and impact and claim the disadvantage), or (2) if affirmative responses facilitate another negative argument which carries more potential than the disadvantage.

The intricacies of negative argument extension should be apparent. Hence, it is imperative that the negative advocate strategize beyond a specific response in a particular speech. Such a micro perspective often plays right into the hands of an affirmative opponent. The superior approach is to think ahead to the rebuttals, tracing each potential argument back through the constructive speeches. Such reverse mapping forces the negative advocate to probe carefully all potential negative responses in terms of their broader implications.

The negative advocate should utilize this holistic view in all phases of debate: in guiding research efforts; weighing strategic options; determining which positions to advance; deciding on specific answers to affirmative responses to individual negative arguments; and evaluating the interrelationships among arguments (which is crucial in the effort to sort out and evaluate the sum total of all arguments presented during a debate) in the rebuttal periods.

Case Extension Techniques

There is nothing unique about extending negative as opposed to affirmative arguments. The same basic precepts apply to both. As discussed in chapter 11, direct-clash, or on-point refutation, coupled with substantive extension, is the essence of effective case extension. The direct-clash approach requires that an advocate respond to each point raised by an opponent in a particular argument sector so as to "take out" the underpinning analysis and/or evidence. This method forces an opponent into the difficult position of providing substantive second- and/or third-line extension or losing the argument in question. Substantive extension requires the advocate's claims to be fully developed, backed by sound analysis and/or strong evidence. Effective negative extension demands that the negative advocate seize the initiative. Substantive extension is the technique to achieve this tactical end.

STRATEGICALLY EXTENDING NEGATIVE POSITIONS

No treatment of negative advocacy would be complete without a thorough discussion of strategic extension of all standard negative argumentative positions. This section will examine the strategies and tactics of negative extension of standard options, including straight refutation, inherency, alternative proposals, efficacy, plan disadvantages, and topicality.

Straight Refutation

There is nothing particularly fancy about negative extension of straight refutation arguments. There are two tactical imperatives. First, the negative advocate must utilize on-point and substantive extension. This is, of course, easier said than done. Normally the affirmative should be able to outextend the negative on case. If the affirmative position is a valid one, then the weight of argument and evidence will prevail in the end. As a result, second, the negative advocate must learn the selective use of the straight refutation option. On one hand, it is not essential to use direct refutation against all affirmative claims. As we indicated in chapter 10, straight refutation does nothing more than minimize the affirmative position. Unfortunately, minimization carries limited strategic value.[4] The negative advocate should consistently strive to minimize affirmative significance and solvency claims; but little more. Furthermore, it is not imperative to systematically extend on every initial negative point. The negative advocate should attempt to extend only those original arguments (1) which he or she can extend with on-point and substantive responses, and (2) that do meaningful damage to the affirmative's position. The compulsion to extend all initial arguments is sure to frustrate effective negative advocacy.[5]

Inherency and Minor Repairs

We advocate a deliberate and strategic negative attempt to defend "what is." The guidelines discussed in chapter 10 should be internalized in order to assist the negative advocate to capitalize on the potential assets and avoid the risks of the inherency and minor repair argument options. If utilized properly, these argument genre can prove to be a tremendous negative asset; more often than not, however, they constitute a negative albatross. The difficulty is simply that negative advocates are inclined to initiate inherency and minor repair arguments by reflex, without carefully examining their ramifications in terms of other argument options. Hence, it is important to reemphasize the guidelines for arguing inherency (they apply equally well to minor repairs).

The first guideline, and a cardinal rule governing the use of most negative argumentative options, is that the negative advocate should argue inherency or minor repairs only if the position is valid, that is, if it is true and if it can be supported by sufficient breadth and depth of evidence. Second, the negative should defend present system programs or minor repairs in conjunction with the direct refutation of initial affirmative inherency analysis and evidence. The negative, in short, should utilize both approaches—or neither one.

The third guideline is that the negative advocate should exploit the strengths of the present system's incremental approach to change. It involves the slow and deliberate pursuit of diverse and conflicting values. It stands in stark contrast to affirmative plans which feature the swift and single-minded pursuit of a single goal. The present system's deliberative approach features unique strengths which the negative advocate should exploit. And fourth, the negative must fully understand and internalize the intricate relationship between the present system programs/minor repair options and plan disadvantage arguments. A defense of present system programs or minor repairs often precludes specific plan disadvantage variants. Thus, the negative position must be carefully constructed so as to avoid potential contradictions.

The negative advocate should bear in mind two additional "rules of thumb" when considering the minor repair option. First, the minor repair is appropriate only if the philosophy and general structures of the present system are fundamentally sound. That is why a defense of present system programs is so often used in conjunction with the minor repair argument option. Second, all negative minor repairs must meet each of the following burdens: non-topicality, viability and desirability. These were explained at some length in chapter 10.

Alternative Proposals

The counterplan position is an excellent vehicle to permit the negative advocate to shift from a defensive to an offensive posture in a debate. However, it is an intricate position. As a result, many counterplan debates are decided on the basis of a theoretical or tactical failing on the part of the affirmative or the negative.

Such miscues can be avoided if the negative approaches the counterplan debate using a holistic perspective. A holistic view should guide the negative during the constructive speeches in selecting initial argument options and planning second- and third-line extension of all critical arguments. Remember that the counterplan debate poses a simple choice: the comparative superiority of the negative's counterplan versus the affirmative's proposal. This is determined by an examination of each alternative policy's benefits and costs. Benefits are contained in a plan's advantages and solvency (thus, the negative must defend the counterplan's advantages and solvency; it must attack those of the affirmative). Costs are embodied in a plan's disadvantages (the negative must defend the counterplan against affirmative disadvantages and must argue disadvantages against the affirmative's plan).

The rebuttal periods are especially difficult in a counterplan debate. The counterplan position poses substantial time allocation problems for all advocates. It literally adds an additional layer of argument to a debate. Hence, the negative advocate must be prepared to make hard choices with regard to argument selection and emphasis. In most counterplan debates time allocation constraints will begin to impinge in the initial constructive speeches, and by the second negative rebuttal, time may be the single most imposing difficulty. Negative advocates must therefore hone argument selectivity skills as a debate progresses.

Finally, the negative advocate must exercise sound judgment in evaluating the appropriateness of a counterplan approach. First, the substantive conditions must be suitable. Use the counterplan position when *best prepared* to contest the merits of an affirmative's case. Second, the argumentative conditions must be right. The advocate must be fully prepared to understand the intricacies of counterplan theory, and be competent to argue it skillfully, substantively extend the counterplan position, and handle the additional coverage requirements of counterplan debates. In addition, the negative must determine whether the critic judge is receptive to a counterplan position.

Solvency Attacks

The negative's solvency position continues the process of diminishing affirmative significance via straight refutation against initial affirmative solvency analysis and evidence in conjunction with an offensive attack on the affirmative's solvency position. We discussed the basic design of efficacy attacks in chapter 10. We will now examine the strategic and tactical dimensions of the solvency position.

The initial strategic consideration involves the construction of the plan-meet-advantage argument. Three considerations are important. First, plan-meet-advantage arguments require independent construction. This necessitates that the negative advocate ground each solvency argument independently with a unique warrant. Independent construction forces the affirmative opponent to respond separately to each argument (ideally to each argument's component parts). Second, the link or thesis of the plan-meet-advantage argument must be carefully articulated, adapted to the particulars of an affirmative's plan. Third, the label of the plan-meet-advantage argument should accurately reflect its impact. An argument's label is crucial. The label should characterize the nature of the argument and its impact. An argument that is underlabeled may be misevaluated by the critic judge; an argument that is overlabeled may undermine the advocate's credibility.

A second strategic dimension concerns plan-meet-advantage argument selection. Two criteria should guide the negative advocate. First, the negative should strive to avoid choosing solvency arguments which undermine inherency, minor repair or counterplan options. Plan-meet-advantage arguments do not have to be unique (applicable only to the affirmative's plan). However, negative solvency arguments which militate efficacy for both negative and affirmative mechanisms pose a clear contradiction to negative disadvantage arguments. In this instance, the plan-meet-advantage argument takes precedence. Second, plan-meet-advantage arguments should be significant and extendable. If the solvency argument lacks viability, it should be discarded. Furthermore, the negative advocate must clearly articulate the impact of the argument to the critic judge.

The final strategic consideration involves the interrelationship between negative direct refutation of affirmative solvency claims and negative offensive attacks on an affirmative's solvency position. It is simply imperative that the negative mount a strong assault on initial affirmative solvency analysis and evidence. This serves to neutralize or even weaken affirmative solvency claims which in turn undermines affirmative responses to negative plan-meet-advantage arguments. As we illustrated in chapters 9 and 11, the analysis and evidence which underpin initial affirmative solvency claims can prove devastating to negative plan argumentation.

Plan Disadvantages

The plan disadvantage is the most imposing element in the negative's tactical arsenal. It is the primary reason why the plan should be rejected on its merits. While all other negative argumentative variants attempt to minimize affirmative claims, the plan disadvantage constitutes a countervailing claim. Because the plan disadvantage uniquely depicts affirmative costs, the negative *should* win policy debates if it can demonstrate that the net costs of an affirmative's plan exceed the net benefits.

The advocate must construct and implement a strategic approach which recognizes that the plan disadvantage is the most potentially damaging negative argument option. Naturally most affirmative advocates are aware of the plan disadvantage's strategic role. This insures that this argument variant will normally be hotly contested. The following strategic considerations should assist the negative advocate in arguing the plan disadvantage effectively.

Initially, the negative advocate must prepare to shoulder the burden of proof for the plan disadvantage. The basic requirements of this argument are similar to those of an affirmative advantage. The plan disadvantage must be unique to the affirmative's proposal; furthermore, it must embody serious consequences. The negative advocate cannot afford to shirk either of these burdens. Affirmative opponents—if they can do nothing more—will usually challenge the adequacy of a disadvantage's links and impacts.

Second, the negative advocate must pin down affirmative plan provisions and claims. Affirmative advocates sometimes design vague plan provisions in order to foster tactical maneuverability in responding to negative plan disadvantages. Vague plan provisions sometimes permit affirmative evasion of strong negative attacks. Thus, it is important for the negative advocate to restrict the potential maneuverability of an affirmative's plan.

The negative advocate can initiate a number of preventive steps to limit unwarranted affirmative maneuverability. The negative advocate can use cross-examination to pin down unclear portions of an affirmative's plan. Also, the advocate should ask to examine the written draft of the plan if there is any uncertainty over specific features of an affirmative's proposal.

When confronted with an intentionally vague affirmative plan, the negative can initiate a direct attack. For instance, many affirmatives use an "optimal mix of finance mechanisms" to preempt negative plan disadvantages based on the consequences of particular funding alternatives. Needless to say, funding is an important feature of a plan's mandate; significant potential plan consequences stem from the advocate's choice of funding mechanisms. Thus, the negative advocate can—and must—pin the affirmative down to a specific formula. The negative can utilize cross-examination probes designed to ascertain what mix would be used in the face of specific economic conditions—present or future. If the affirmative refuses to commit itself to a designated mix under specific conditions, the negative advocate must be prepared to document the mix that would be used in those circumstances based on the opinions of economic experts. The negative can use these and other preventive measures to pin down an elusive affirmative opponent. This enables the advocate to argue the most appropriate plan disadvantages.

A third strategic concern involves plan disadvantage extension. The negative must prepare to provide the strongest possible answers to all affirmative responses to plan disadvantage arguments. Two implications follow. First, both on-point and substantive extension are absolutely essential. These refutation techniques permit the negative advocate to refute affirmative responses to plan disadvantages in such a manner that the opponent's analysis and evidence from previous speeches can be of no value in subsequent speeches. This allows the negative advocate to maintain the argumentative initiative in this important area.

Also, the negative must employ a holistic perspective to decide which positions to advance and to determine specific answers to affirmative responses to individual plan disadvantages. Negative extension of plan disadvantages is an intricate task. Thus, it is important that the negative advocate strategize beyond a specific response in a particular speech to examine all argumentative ramifications. We previously discussed the intricacies of negative argument extension in illustrating negative response possibilities against affirmative answers to a negative nuclear proliferation disadvantage. figure 12–2 on pages 256 and 257 summarizes the negative plan disadvantage response option criteria. *It should be internalized so as to assist the negative advocate in evaluating potential extensions of any plan disadvantage argument.*

A careful evaluation of strategic permutations is indispensable to effective negative extension of plan disadvantage arguments. In policy debate the plan disadvantage is the *most formidable* argument in the negative's tactical arsenal. Normally it is very difficult for the negative to win a debate without winning a plan disadvantage. But the plan disadvantage is at the same time the *most dangerous* option at the negative's disposal. It carries the potential to backfire, resulting in an affirmative win. Thus, a careful consideration of the strategic ramifications of plan disadvantage extension is essential. The response option criteria delineated above can assist the negative advocate in optimizing use of the plan disadvantage argument.

A fourth strategic concern involves the ideal speech to initiate and extend the plan disadvantage. Traditionally, the first negative constructive speech features arguments designed to minimize affirmative benefits (i.e., straight refutation, a defense of the present system, etc.) while the second negative constructive speech employed the plan disadvantage. Traditionally, the first negative constructive speech featured arguments designed to minimize affirmative benefits (i.e., straight refutation, a defense of the present system, etc.) while the second negative constructive speech employs plan disadvantage arguments to focus on affirmative costs. By contrast a more integrated

The following guidelines will assist the negative advocate in making this decision. A plan disadvantage—which (1) is a vital element in the negative's attack and (2) can be strongly extended through two additional speeches—can be maximized if presented early in the debate. The policy systems perspective, in focusing attention on the costs and benefits of alternative courses of action, enhances the importance of the plan disadvantage argument. If the affirmative position constitutes a swift and single-minded change in the present system, the plan disadvantage is likely to be the negative's strongest argument. In such circumstances it should be presented in the first negative constructive and initially extended in the second negative constructive speech. The opportunity for argument extension is precious. If a negative advocate is confident of being able to outextend an affirmative opponent on a particular issue, it makes good sense to introduce that material in the initial speech so as to provide one additional opportunity for extension.

Topicality

Topicality is one of the most potent negative argumentative options. It is one of the few issues that carries absolute impact. If the negative advocate wins the topicality argument, the debate is over. Unfortunately, topicality may be the most difficult argument for the negative to extend well. Two factors are responsible for this difficulty. First, topicality is an intricate argument. Chapter 10 discussed the theoretical dimensions of the topicality argument at some length. Second, topicality poses special problems for extension. At this time we will examine strategic considerations involved in extending the topicality argument.

First, the negative advocate should strive to optimize the use of topicality standards. Standards hold the key to topicality—they function as perceptual lenses for the evaluation of this argument genre. Thus, the advocate must initially master standards in order to master topicality. However, it is not enough to understand topicality standards. The negative advocate must apply them properly in the course of answering individual affirmative responses to topicality. This presupposes that the negative support all claims with regard to standards with cogent reasoning and illustrative examples. The use of "tag lines" (argument labels lacking in analytical development) does not constitute effective topicality extension.

FIGURE 12–2   NEGATIVE PLAN DISADVANTAGE RESPONSE OPTION
CRITERIA

IF THE AFFIRMATIVE ATTEMPTS TO DENY THE DISADVANTAGE'S LINK
  Refute affirmative's denial of the link if:
      1) you can outevidence the affirmative;
      2) the impact of the disadvantage is substantial; and
      3) you can prevail should the affirmative attempt to reverse the impact of the
          disadvantage.
  Abandon this phase of the disadvantage if:
      1) you cannot outevidence the affirmative;
      2) the impact of the disadvantage is moderate; or
      3) the affirmative didn't attempt to reverse the impact of the disadvantage.
  Grant and use affirmative responses to the disadvantage if:
      1) affirmative answers facilitate a stronger negative argument than the
          disadvantage; or
      2) the affirmative also reversed the impact of the disadvantage—and can
          outextend the negative on this issue.
IF THE AFFIRMATIVE ATTEMPTS TO REVERSE THE DISADVANTAGE'S LINK
  Refute the affirmative's reversal of the link if:
      1) you can significantly outextend the affirmative; and
      2) the impact of the disadvantage is substantial.
  Abandon this phase of the disadvantage if:
      1) you cannot outextend the affirmative on this issue; or
      2) the impact of the disadvantage is small or moderate.
  Grant and use affirmative responses to the disadvantage if:
      1) affirmative answers facilitate a stronger negative argument than the
          disadvantage; or
      2) the affirmative has also attempted to defeat the disadvantage by reversing its
          impact.

Second, the negative advocate must deal with each and every affirmative answer to topicality in a systematic, on-point and substantive manner. A common affirmative approach to topicality is to combine a limited number of quality answers with a variety of mediocre responses. Such an approach works, but *only if the negative cooperates*. In this instance, the affirmative hopes to capitalize on missed or mishandled responses later in the debate. Hence, it is imperative for the negative advocate to respond to each affirmative answer so as to "take out" the underpinning analysis and/or evidence; nothing less than systematic, on-point and substantive extension will do.

Negative advocates should be especially wary of certain types of affirmative responses to topicality. First, affirmative advocates will attempt to exploit analogies in an effort to broaden the topic, shift presumption, or escape one of the negative's standards. However, analogies usually suffer various shortcomings which negative advocates can utilize in refuting them. Second, it is common for affirmatives to claim

IF THE AFFIRMATIVE ATTEMPTS TO DENY THE DISADVANTAGE'S IMPACT
Refute the affirmative's denial of the impact if:
  1) you can significantly outextend the affirmative; and
  2) the affirmative has not also attempted to reverse the link or the impact of the disadvantage.
Abandon this phase of the disadvantage if:
  1) you cannot outextend the affirmative on this issue; or
  2) you have mounted a strong attack and can prevail in an effort to deny or reverse the link of the disadvantage.
Grant and use affirmative responses to the disadvantage if:
  1) Affirmative answers facilitate a stronger negative argument than the disadvantage; or
  2) the affirmative advocate also reversed the link of the disadvantage.
IF THE AFFIRMATIVE ATTEMPTS TO REVERSE THE DISADVANTAGE'S IMPACT
Refute the affirmative's reversal of the impact if:
  1) you can outextend the affirmative on this issue;
  2) you will have to attempt to refute the affirmative's reversal of the link, whether or not you are sure of being able to outextend the affirmative, unless prior affirmative answers can be used to deny the link or the impact of the disadvantage.
Abandon this dimension of the disadvantage if:
  1) the affirmative provides strong denial of the link or thesis of the disadvantage; and
  2) you cannot outextend the affirmative on the reversal of the impact of the disadvantage.
Grant and use affirmative responses to the disadvantage if:
  1) affirmative answers facilitate a stronger negative argument than the disadvantage; or
  2) the affirmative has used strong evidence to reverse the link or thesis of the disadvantage.

that the resolution is worded badly; hence, the blame for broad interpretation rests with the framers of the resolution, not with the affirmative. The negative advocate must nonetheless insist that the responsibility for a reasonable interpretation of a "flawed" resolution remains the affirmative's.

Third, negatives must be especially wary of affirmative claims of presumption. This claim carries *some* validity. For example, the affirmative does enjoy one original presumption; an affirmative position is presumed to be topical until such time that the negative argues to the contrary. However, any affirmative claims of presumption which extend beyond this initial assignment are dubious. If allowed, such claims would render the topicality argument moot. For example, if an affirmative advocate could simply claim that, "In the event that the outcome of topicality is close at the conclusion of this debate, the affirmative should be presumed to be topical," then the negative is destined to lose this issue. Clearly this is an unreasonable affirmative claim. There is a strong case to be made, grounded in the judicial analogy, that if jurisdiction is in doubt, then presumption should lie with the more restrictive interpretation. As Justice Jerome Frank observed in *Courts on Trial:* "Some judges say that when doubt exists whether a statute was meant to be broadly construed, the safer and appropriate course is for the courts to construe it narrowly . . ."[6] Even if negatives do not claim presumption for themselves, they must strive to limit affirmative claims of presumption to reasonable bounds.

Fourth, the negative should be alert for affirmative claims that liberal definitions are superior because they enhance the educational value of debate. The educational value of debate is most likely to flourish when an essential fairness is observed; this is not possible with overly broad affirmative interpretations which reduce negative ground and render research burdens onerous. Furthermore, a distinction must be drawn between breadth and depth. Broad interpretations may enhance the educational value of debate by expanding the breadth of discussion that is permitted within the resolution; however, broad interpretations also impair the educational value of debate by reducing the depth of discussion that is possible on any single case variant within the confines of the resolution. In short, breadth and depth stand in a tradeoff relationship.

Fifth, the negative must be prepared to deal with the affirmative claim that, "We're reasonable; that's sufficient." As indicated in chapter 10, this is not sufficient! When the meaning of "reasonable" is grounded in the lowest common denominator, it ceases to be a compelling justification. Prominent debate coaches and theorists, James J. Unger, Donn W. Parson, John Bart, and others, have criticized the all-too-common affirmative misuse of the term "reasonable" in contemporary debate.[7] We urge negatives to scrutinize any affirmative reasonability claim. When confronted with such a claim, the negative advocate should either (1) argue that the better definition perspective is superior to the reasonability standard, or (2) maintain that reasonability cannot be assessed in a vacuum—it can only be evaluated in terms of specific negative topicality standards.

The third strategic consideration concerns the optimal speech for the original presentation and extension of the topicality argument. If the argument is lengthy, extendable, and an important element in the negative's attack, it should be presented early in a debate so as to optimize extension. This scenario requires that topicality be presented in the first negative constructive speech and initially extended in the second negative constructive. An exception must be noted: if the second affirmative constructive extension reveals a new aspect of the case with topicality ramifications, then it would be appropriate to initiate the topicality argument in the second negative constructive speech.

The success of a topicality argument rests on the negative's ability to extend it well. Thus, the negative advocate must allow sufficient time to answer each of the affirmative's responses. Originating a topicality argument in the first negative constructive speech and extending it in the second negative constructive will exert tremendous pressure on the first affirmative rebuttalist. Furthermore, the approach pulls the affirmative speaker off of first-line blocks, requires substantial thought, and devours preparation time. Thus, topicality extension is optimized in the following scenario: the first negative constructive speaker initiates the argument; the affirmative opponent responds; and the second negative constructive speaker follows with systematic, on-point and substantive extension.

UNDERVIEW

We noted in chapter 11 that preemption plays an important role in refutation. Preemption is a tactic which (1) can establish the conditions for affirmative/negative clash on a particular argument and/or (2) provide anticipatory refutation of opposing argument(s). As such, preemption can prove especially helpful to negative advocates in extending intricate disadvantage and topicality positions.

NEGATIVE REBUTTAL TACTICS

Much of the theory and technique discussed in this chapter applies to the negative rebuttal speeches. Nonetheless, negative rebuttal extension tactics warrant special emphasis at this time. We will examine rebuttal tactics in greater detail in chapter 13.

The process of argument extension continues in the rebuttal speeches. Most of the techniques which foster quality argument extension in the constructive speeches continue to play an important role in the rebuttals. On-point and substantive extension, for instance, are indispensable features of constructive and rebuttal argument extension. It allows the negative advocate to maintain the initiative throughout a debate. Argument selection, however, looms as an equally significant feature of negative rebuttal prowess.

Negative advocates must continue the process of on-point and substantive extension during the rebuttals, but that in itself is not enough. Many advocates make the mistake of trying to extend too much, especially during the last negative rebuttal, thus winning many specific issues but possibly losing the debate. On-point and substantive extension *in selected areas* is essential to rebuttal success.

The bottom line is that the negative advocate must forcefully extend those argument sectors that it needs to win and those sectors that it can't afford to lose. How is this determined? The answer lies in the application of the holistic perspective to argument choices in the rebuttal periods. A holistic view makes it possible to determine which argument sectors require additional extension and which sectors do not. There are times when it is strategically counterproductive to attempt to cover every argument on the flow. The key to rebuttal success lies in knowing what must be done, doing it well, and leaving the rest. A holistic view is indispensable in this task. It enables the advocate to make wise choices from among various options. In this manner a holistic perspective directs a negative advocate's efforts to focus a debate during the rebuttal periods.

The effective use of a holistic view will lead the negative advocate to the most appropriate argument choices, extension options and evaluative perspective. It should be obvious that this view requires a genuine team approach to debate. Colleagues cannot function as individual specialists. Instead, a holistic view demands that colleagues coordinate all phases of their efforts.

SUMMARY

Chapter 10 provided an approach to negative advocacy and discussed negative case construction—the selection and implementation of strategic choices which constitute a negative position in a debate. This chapter examined the strategies and tactics of effective negative advocacy.

Initially we explored the intrinsic advantages of negative advocacy. Presumption and flexibility constitute important intrinsic advantages of arguing against most propositions. The negative advocate should attempt to capitalize on both benefits. We also discussed the strategy of wresting the argumentative terrain from the affirmative. The key to seizing and maintaining control of the argumentative terrain involves the negative position. Initially the advocate must develop the strongest possible negative position, thus assuming the initiative in critical argument areas. Then the negative must use that position to select specific arguments in order to maintain effective control.

The thrust of this chapter focused on the strategies and tactics of negative extension. We urged the utilization of a holistic view in all phases of debate: in weighing strategic options, determining which positions to advance, deciding on specific answers to affirmative responses to individual negative arguments, and evaluating the interrelationships among arguments in the rebuttal periods. We discussed the strategies and tactics of negative extension of all standard argumentative positions, including straight refutation, inherency, alternative proposals, efficacy, plan disadvantages, and topicality. We also examined negative extension and rebuttal tactics. You should now be able to construct and defend a negative case.

Notes

[1]David Braybrooke and Charles E. Lindblom, *A Strategy of Decision: Policy Evaluation as A Social Process* (New York: Macmillan Publishing Co., Inc., 1970), p. 123.

[2]Braybrooke and Lindblom, p. 239.

[3]Allan J. Lichtman and Daniel M. Rohrer, "The Logic of Policy Dispute," *Journal of the American Forensic Association,* 16 (1980), 244.

[4]Bernard L. Brock, James W. Chesebro. John F. Cragan and James F. Klumpp, *Public Policy Decision-Making: Systems Analysis and Comparative Advantages Debate* (New York: Harper & Row, Publishers, 1973), p. 160.

[5]Brock *et al.,* pp. 136–37.

[6]Jerome Frank, *Courts on Trial: Myth and Reality in American Justice* (New York: Atheneum, 1970), p. 307.

⁷For example, see: James J. Unger, "The Words of a Debate Proposition and the Debate Subject Matter: Friends or Foes," a paper presented at the Speech Communication Association annual convention, Anaheim, Cal., 14 November 1981; Donn W. Parson, "On Being Reasonable: The Last Refuge of Scoundrels," in George Ziegelmeuller and Jack Rhodes (eds.), *Dimensions of Argument: Proceedings of the Second Summer Conference on Argumentation* (Annandale: Speech Communication Association, 1981), pp. 532–42; and Donn W. Parson and John Bart, "On Being Reasonable: The Last Refuge of Scoundrels; Part II: The Scoundrels Strike Back," in David A. Thomas and Jack Hart (eds.), *Advanced Debate: Readings in Theory, Practice and Teaching,* 3rd ed., (Lincolnwood, IL: National Textbook Company, 1987), pp. 130–138.

CHAPTER THIRTEEN

REFUTATION
AND
REBUTTALS

This chapter explains the nature and purpose of refutation and rebuttal, and offers a formula for effectively refuting an argument. We will discuss the strategy and tactics of rebuttals in academic debate, with a detailed analysis of each speaker's role. We conclude the chapter with some practical suggestions for debaters in making rebuttals more effective.

DEFINITION AND PURPOSES
OF REFUTATION AND REBUTTAL

The process of attacking the opponent's case is called *refutation,* and the process of rebuilding your own case following the opponent's attack is called *rebuttal.* Both definitions assume that an advocate has already presented a case or an argument for a claim and is the target for the refutation and rebuttal processes. Refutation is the process of clashing with your opponent's case with a view toward undermining or destroying it. Rebuttal is the process of causing your opponent's attacks on your case to fail by providing new replies to them which restore your arguments to a state of acceptability.

Presenting only your side of a controversy is not enough to make up a complete debate, because your opponent may also make a persuasive case to the audience or decision maker. In addition to stating and proving your own case, you must pay attention to the opponent's case and respond to it effectively. Your case can prevail only if your opponent's arguments are defeated.

When the two competing advocates have presented their initial cases and arguments, the debate has just begun. The affirmative advocate establishes a case to convince the decision maker. The negative advocate attempts to refute the affirmative case by arguing any of a variety of approaches, such as directly denying the affirmative's key arguments, providing contradictory arguments, or suggesting some undesirable ramifications of the affirmative's position. The listener at this point cannot make a *rational* decision between the two competing sides until each one has a real opportunity to reply to the opposing arguments. It is only fair to wait until the advocates have that opportunity before weighing their cases and making a final decision.

You can see, clearly, that refutation and rebuttal play specific but very important roles in the argumentative process. Probably the greatest error most inexperienced advocates make is to fail to use refutation and rebuttal effectively. Short-sighted advocates see their own sides of the issues very clearly, but fail to realize that audiences hear *both* sides. If the advocate ignores the other side, and merely repeats the original position, the audience will be left with much doubt. The skilled advocate knows that success hinges on the ability not only to press his or her own case vigorously, but also to refute the opponent's case and to respond to the opponent's refutation.

The process of answering the opponent's arguments in the rebuttal phase should focus on two related purposes. It is important to *extend* your own arguments beyond their original status, and to synthesize the key arguments of both sides into a coherent *perspective* to facilitate the decision maker's ability to make a choice for your position, taking into account everything that has been argued in the debate.

Extensions.   Extension of your arguments in the rebuttal phase should be thought of, initially, as going beyond a simple repetition of your original position. In a quarrel between youthful playmates, the argument may consist of: "Bang! Gotcha." "You missed!" "No, I didn't." "Yes, you did!" *"NO, I DIDN'T!" "YES YOU DID!"*, and on and on in that repetitive vein. The advocates are answering each other, but they are not *extending* their positions and they do not have a rational basis for resolving their dispute. The idea of extending your argument implies that you answer your opponent's refutation with a rebuttal that not only repeats your initial claim, but also acknowledges the impact of the refutation against it. The idea is to provide a response to the refutation that removes it from seriously damaging your argument. In order to do that, you must be able to refute your opponent's refutation of your point, and to advance your initial position to some new status of understanding that goes beyond the original position, achieving a new status that would not have been possible to establish without having heard the opposing refutation first. An extension thus makes it impossible for your opponent to salvage any argumentative force from any subsequent reference to his or her point of refutation, since you have extended your position beyond that point.

The Basic Four-Point Formula.   There is a basic formula for organizing your attempts to refute your opponent, or to rebuild your own argument after attack. This formula is simply an outline of the order you should follow in making your points. Using this formula helps you keep the arguments as clear as possible in your own mind; more importantly, it makes your refutation much more understandable to the audience.

1. State the point you wish to refute (or to rebuild).
2. State the position you claim with regard to that point.
3. Provide the argument necessary to establish your claim.
4. Explain how your refutation (or rebuttal argument) affects the issue under consideration.

As an example, suppose the argument you made initially was that the electoral college is an undemocratic procedure for electing the president, and your opponent replied that the electoral college has always managed to elect the majority candidate except for three instances in all of the history of the United States. You have numerous potential answers to choose from at this point, but let's choose one as an example of how to use the formula for making your rebuttal point:

"The electoral college is undemocratic. My opponent stated that only three instances exist in American history where a minority candidate was ever elected." *(This corresponds to the first step in the formula, which is to state the point you wish to address.)* "That does not deny that the electoral college is undemocratic." *(State your claim about that position.)* "I have a couple of arguments. (1) Even if the electoral college goes along with the popular vote most of the time, the opponent's own evidence shows that in some cases, it did not. That is undemocratic. (2) It could happen again in any future election. The system has absolutely no safeguards to prevent it. Electors are not bound by the popular vote. One authority calls the electoral college a 'ticking time bomb' that could explode without warning." *(These answers show your reasoning why your claim should stand.)* "So you can see, the electoral college is not a democratic method because the electors have violated the popular vote in the past by my opponent's own evidence, and they could do so again in the future. If anything, I claim my case is even stronger now than before." *(This final remark clinches the rebuttal point and explains its importance to the debate as a whole.)*

This formula for organizing the arguments presented for the purposes of refuting opponents, or rebuilding your own case, may seem awkward and time-consuming. However, we urge any advocate to use it for the sake of clarity of the analysis. A content analysis of the transcripts of the first affirmative rebuttals given in thirteen National Debate Tournament final debates shows that all of them used this organizing technique.[1] If the formula can be applied in that intense and specialized situation, where the first affirmative rebuttal is severely compressed for time to cover numerous negative arguments, it can surely be employed in more ordinary argumentative contexts.

Extending Arguments. There are several possible ways to extend your argument. First, you may directly deny the refutation. Suppose your initial argument stated that the increased development of the country's space program would benefit the health of citizens by enabling drug companies to produce new drugs for diabetics in an ideal chemical production environment of weightlessness. Your opponent may deny the value of such an outcome as a reason for increasing the space program. There are several ways to extend your initial claim beyond your opponent's refutation.

You could point out the ways in which your opponent has failed to prove his or her own position. Probe the evidence cited against your argument to test its relevance, adequacy, or validity. Also, look at the source of the evidence used to evaluate its competence, recency, or possible bias. Look at the reasoning employed by the opponent to make inferences, and see whether the reasoning process is fallacious in any way. Determine whether the opponent's argument is consistent with other arguments and evidence he or she may have presented at other points in the case.

After you deny the validity of your opponent's refutation, your rebuttal should repeat your original position and pull it through the holes you created in your opponent's argument. This process has the effect of showing the decision maker that your initial argument still holds true, even after taking your opponent's refutation into account.

This type of extension is effective in that your original stance appears to withstand the test of opposing argument. There are other tactics of extending your argument that actually add new ground to your initial position.

Our chapters on affirmative cases provide comprehensive discussions of *turn-around refutation,* a primary method of converting negative arguments into affirmative arguments. If you can turn an opposing argument around, you not only extend your own position in light of the refutation; you also make additional points in your favor by transforming an opposing argument into a reason to support your own position. The "turn-around" tactic is a very persuasive tool—if you can succeed in turning your opponent's argument with the greatest scope around to your side, you can almost guarantee a favorable outcome from the decision maker.

Take the example of the debate over space exploration. Your initial case presented the idea that special drug manufacturing could be conducted in a space laboratory and thus provide medical relief for diabetics. Suppose your opponent argues that your proposed increase in space development would be a bad idea because it would create a false sense of confidence that other illnesses would be eradicated besides the limited advances against diabetes. You could reply that to the extent that people would have increased confidence in space-related drug manufacturing methods, more drug manufacturers would engage in high-level research efforts to bring about just such a proliferation of new cures for old troublesome medical problems. Greater research efforts in the ideal space environment could be expected to produce more actual advances, not now possible in the absence of such public (and stockholder) confidence in this setting. Thus, the negative argument of increased consumer expectations could be interpreted as an additional advantage to the proposed space program.

Since the affirmative and negative advocates are refuting cases at the same time, both sides will probably look weaker at the end of the debate than they did initially. The winning side is almost invariably the one that does the best job of buttressing and extending its original position after it has been attacked. Assuming both sides are competent in presenting initial arguments, debates (in the "real world" as well as in tournaments) are almost always won or lost in the rebuttal phase.

Attacks on Evidence and Reasoning

Recall that evidence is defined as a statement made in an argument which is intended to provide the substance or supporting material to prove the claim being advocated. As such, it is one of the basic elements necessary to establish any claim. Without evidence, a claim stands unsupported and unproven, vulnerable to overthrow by any sort of attack, denial, counterclaim, expression of doubt, or even a probing question. As a starting point for refutation, a good place to begin the analysis of an opposing argument is to examine whether any evidence is offered in its support; if not, indict the argument as being invalid on its face. The opposing advocate then must bring forth the missing support or risk the certain loss of the claim that was asserted.

Skilled advocates rarely make the mistake of asserting claims without supporting evidence to prove their point. To refute the claims, it becomes necessary to examine an argument's supporting evidence and test it against standards of evidence quality. This section of the chapter covers the principles and methods of testing evidence, with a view toward refuting it.

Chapter 7 examined a set of general tests of evidence, applicable to any type of argument. They included relevance, adequacy, consistency, recency, and acceptability to the audience.

Refuting the Relevance of Evidence.   Relevance is undoubtedly the most important quality a given statement must have in order to stand as proof for a claim, yet it is often the most violated standard. In analyzing an argument, look first to see whether the evidence has a direct bearing on the claim being made. If it doesn't, the claim is unsupported by the evidence and is unworthy of acceptance.

Refuting the Adequacy of Evidence.   The second general test of evidence is *adequacy*. The evidence offered in support of a claim must be adequate to support the claim being argued. The concept of adequacy of evidence, however, is a flexible standard which depends on the type of argument at stake. The amount or quantity of evidence needed to prove a point depends on whether the issue deals with a scientific or a rhetorical claim. Adequacy means something different when you analyze an opinion or value judgment than it does in a more empirical, factual area.

Refuting the Recency of Evidence.   The third general test of evidence is *recency*. That is, in certain kinds of arguments, the quality of the evidence may hinge on how recently it was produced. Outdated evidence is a flaw in an argument dealing with claims about rapidly changing situations. Not all kinds of claims are affected by recency of evidence. In terms of most policy claims, many factual claims, and some value claims, a good rule of thumb is that the more recent the evidence, the better.

Refuting the Acceptability of Evidence.   Finally, *acceptability* of the evidence to the audience is a very important standard to apply to your analysis of any argument. No matter what field an argument is related to, there are standards for testing the acceptability or admissibility of evidence. The obvious example is the court of law, with its detailed and rigorous rules of what evidence may even be heard. In all other fields, similar standards and rules also apply, though not necessarily the same rules as used in a courtroom and not necessarily as detailed or formalized. By knowing the nature of the claim being made and the audience to whom the claim is directed, you can refute the argument based on the acceptability of the evidence. Unacceptable evidence must be ruled inadmissible in an argument, and so the claim is left unsupported without it.

Refuting Testimonial Evidence.   In our chapter on evidence, we defined *testimony* as a statement of fact or opinion offered as proof, where the convincing quality of the evidence hinges less on the substance of the statement and more on the credibility of the source. Testimony is important as a type of evidence in both fact and value arguments, and the credibility of the source of the testimony is the key determinant of the force of the argument.

In a factual controversy, it may be that the evidence is so complex that the audience cannot understand the facts well enough to judge the issue. Arguments over value judgments, however, *must* rely on the believability of testimony. As we have previously stated, value judgments are often more deeply rooted in our central belief systems than our arguments about mere facts. In realms of artistic, moral, and political values, when controversies arise, the only proof available to shore up our personal commitments may be the testimony of others.

It is important to learn and to use the tests of testimonial evidence. These tests are directly tied in with the notion of the acceptability of evidence to a given type of audience.

Refuting the Source of Evidence. Our concern is not with trying to find an all-purpose source that anyone can accept. The key point here is that rarely does the source quoted for relevant evidence fit into a black/white, either/or category of being either "credible" or "non-credible." Instead, a given audience will find evidence to be either *more* credible or *less* credible.

The standard criteria for testing the credibility of testimonial evidence are these: Is the source qualified to testify on the subject? Is the source unbiased?

Is the statement in question the most recent available (assuming it is on an issue where recency of evidence is important)?

Is the statement in question consistent with other testimony from the same source?

You can show that the evidence is unacceptable if the answer to any of these questions is "no"; and by doing so, you can defeat the argument that is based upon that unacceptable evidence.

Refuting Generalizations Based on Examples. Whenever examples are cited as evidence, the best way to refute them is to argue that there are not enough examples, or that the examples are not typical of the general population under discussion.

Another refutational stance which can be effective against a generalization based on examples is to offer counter examples. When you introduce contrary examples, you go beyond simply asking for more proof. This attack requires the original advocate to come to grips with your contrary examples and show that they are atypical, unrepresentative, or can otherwise be explained away.

Finally, reasoning from example can be turned against an advocate by skillful refutation. Reasoning from example bears a resemblance to reasoning by analogy. The argument, "The Communication Department is brilliant because this example of a brilliant professor proves it," depends on the closeness of fit between the example and the claim. All the refutation has to do is illustrate that the designated professor is not brilliant. If the star exhibit is really a bore, a fool, or a charlatan, then the whole department must be like that. Thus, the argument is not merely disproved, but turned around against the original advocate using his or her own example.

REBUTTAL STRATEGY AND TACTICS
IN ACADEMIC DEBATE

Academic debate is a formal argumentation contest. As we noted in chapter 1, there are several forms of debate currently in use in high school and college debate tournaments. For instance, Lincoln-Douglas debate is a one-on-one contest. Standard debate and championship cross-examination debate in high school both use two-person teams. In college, both National Debate Tournament (NDT) policy debate and the Cross Examination Debate Association (CEDA) value debate leagues follow the two-person team format.

A common feature among all the different debate formats is the use of rebuttal speeches. Each debater has an opening constructive speech; at the conclusion of all the constructive speeches, each debater has a rebuttal speech. We shall now devote our attention to the rebuttal strategies and tactics employed in academic debate.

In championship-calibre debate rounds, both sides are able to present a compelling initial position. In rebuttals, superior debaters extend their initial arguments beyond their opponents' replies, and set a final perspective on the issues which compels the listener to see things from their viewpoint.

As stated earlier, the rebuttal speech has two very specific purposes: to refute the opponent's arguments, and to rebuild the case which was originally advocated. A rebuttal is not simply an additional opportunity to repeat the initial arguments and evidence, nor to present new arguments the speaker wishes to add.

A common beginner's error in debate is to drop the original case and shift to new arguments during the rebuttal. Preparation of the initial case takes most of the debater's effort, and inexperience prevents the debater from anticipating the strong arguments likely to be raised against it. When the moment comes and the opponent makes a strong clash with the case, the temptation is strong to move on to something new in the face of resistance. However, the constructive speeches in an academic debate are the only places where debaters may present their constructive cases. After that, they must stick with those initial cases, and not shift to something else.

For example, in one Lincoln-Douglas debate on the topic of the Equal Rights Amendment (ERA), the negative debater built her constructive case on the premise that the ERA is unnecessary because the states have passed laws to remove discrimination against women. Then, in her rebuttal, she added a new argument that the ERA is so vague that the Supreme Court might rule on it in any of a variety of ways, some of which even the ERA's supporters would find objectionable. While the judge of that debate agreed that the rebuttal argument was an excellent one, he could not give her any points for it because it should have been presented during constructive speaking time, rather than in the rebuttal period.

The "No New Argument" Rule

No new arguments in rebuttals are permitted. To understand this fundamental rule in the way it is meant to operate in a debate, it is helpful to explain first what it does *not* mean.

First, it does not mean that no new information can be brought forward to buttress arguments that were previously made. Another common error made by beginners in rebuttals is simply to repeat their initial arguments, or re-read certain favorite pieces of evidence. When asked why, they explain that they are not permitted to make new arguments in rebuttal. Therefore, for all practical purposes, the debate ends after the constructive speeches, since nothing new is provided by the rebuttals.

Often, a debater may be pressed by an opponent for more evidence during cross-examination, or the opponent may indict the source of the evidence that was used in an argument. It may be very important for these or other reasons to bring up new evidence in the rebuttal period. While the Lincoln-Douglas debater could not present the new argument about the vagueness of the ERA in her rebuttal, she could have brought out new examples of how states have moved to bar discriminatory practices against women. The key is that the new evidence must be related to an argument already on the floor.

Second, the rule against new arguments does not mean that a debater is helpless to refute arguments made by an opponent by giving counter arguments. If, in a standard debate, the second negative constructive speaker made some arguments against the affirmative plan, then the first affirmative rebuttal must be allowed to answer those arguments with counterarguments which have not previously been introduced. These negative rebuttal arguments, though new to the debate in the sense that they have not yet been introduced, still are considered to be admissible, since they come in direct response to arguments previously made during constructive speeches.

What is intended by the rule against new arguments is that, in effect, a debater cannot shift from the initial constructive case to a new case later in the rebuttals. Suppose the affirmative presents three comparative advantages in the constructive speech. If the negative constructive speech effectively refutes them all, the affirmative is not permitted to drop them and launch a new case built on a different set of advantages in the affirmative rebuttal. Similarly, suppose the negative strategy is to argue that the affirmative has failed to prove an inherent problem in the present system. If, after that attack, the affirmative proceeds to provide the necessary proof against the present system, it would be against the rules for the negative to shift to a counterplan strategy in the first negative rebuttal.

Sometimes the dividing line between new arguments and extensions of old arguments is indistinct. What about using previously given arguments or evidence in a new way in the final rebuttal periods? This is called "cross-applying" material in rebuttals. The current tendency among discerning judges is to permit the cross-application of material in only two ways. First, if the evidence or argument previously appeared in connection with the same *issue,* it is permissible to cross-apply it in rebuttals to another point in that issue. It is not permissible, however, to pull down an argument or a piece of evidence which initially appeared in, say, a significance argument, and cross-apply it to another issue like a disadvantage argument in the last rebuttal. It is intended that the opponent should have fair notice of what your response to an argument is going to be; if the information you cross-apply was previously given in the course of arguing about the same issue, the opponent could have seen its applicability.

Second, it is permissible to cross-apply material given in reasonable preemption arguments presented at the outset of the case. The operative term here, of course, is *reasonable* preemptions. This includes plan planks (sometimes called plan "spikes") designed to head off potential negative plan objections. The rule is not usually expanded to include the tactic of concluding with a miscellaneous group of "super cards" under the general heading of "Rebuttal Preempts," and then cross-applying them at will in the rebuttal, like cashing in so many traveler's checks. Preemptive arguments should stand in a clear and logical relation to the case or to the proposal when initially presented. If they are not, judges may not accept them as admissible arguments because they are not explained until rebuttals, in answer to an opposing argument.[2]

The Length of Rebuttals

Rebuttal speeches are usually about half the length of the constructive speeches. In standard, championship cross-examination, or NDT debate, the rebuttals are exactly half as long as constructive speeches (eight-minute constructive and four-minute rebuttal; or ten-minute constructive and five-minute rebuttal). In CEDA, some tournaments allow the rebuttals to be slightly longer than half the length of the constructives (eight-minute constructive and five-minute rebuttal). In Lincoln-Douglas debate, the time division between the constructive speech and the rebuttal is more nearly even (affirmative has a six-minute constructive speech and two rebuttals totalling seven minutes between them; negative has a seven-minute constructive speech and a six-minute rebuttal).

As CEDA debate and Lincoln-Douglas debate have increased the emphasis on persuasive speaking styles, the time allocated for rebuttal speeches has expanded relative to the time for constructive speeches. The reason debaters develop a rapid speech pattern is because there are usually too many issues to cover in very limited time. Perhaps one solution would be to provide more rebuttal time.

Rebuttal speeches should be considered as relatively brief additional rejoinders to the main body of the debate. The primary tasks are to refute the opponent's case, and to extend upon your own case, not to present a new or additional case. If an opponent has refuted an argument so that your case is jeopardized, you should have an opportunity to salvage the argument (to "rebut" it). Also, in the light of all the arguments, the opposing debaters should have an opportunity to summarize their perspectives of the debate overall.

Rebuttal Speaker Duties: The Two-Person Team

The two- versus two-person team debate has been the traditional format for academic debate for many years. Instruction for planning and conducting the rebuttal speeches incorporates the preceding points, but allocates the duties between the two members of the team in the same general division of labor that applies to the constructive speeches.

In Figure 13–1, the order in which all speeches and rebuttals are made is shown across the top of the diagram. The abbreviations used include "A" for "Affirmative" and "N" for "Negative"; "C" for "Constructive Speech" and "R" for "Rebuttal." As shown, the constructive speeches alternate sides, beginning with the first affirmative

FIGURE 13-1   TWO-PERSON TEAM DEBATE SPEAKING ORDER

1AC	1NC	2AC	2NC	1NR	1AR	2NR	2AR
	Topicality	yes	no	yes	yes	yes	yes
Plan	no	no	yes (below)	no	yes	yes	yes
Adv 1	yes	yes	no	yes	yes	yes	yes
Adv 2	yes	yes	no	yes	yes	yes	yes
Adv 3	yes	yes	no	yes	yes	yes	yes

(2NC Plan Attacks are flowed on a separate sheet to avoid confusing the flow of arguments stemming from the 1NC's attacks on the other parts of the affirmative case.)

constructive speech (1AC). The rebuttals also alternate sides; however, the first rebuttal is given by the negative (1NR). Hence, the affirmative team has the privilege of presenting both the first constructive speech, and the last rebuttal in the debate.

In the illustration diagrammed in Figure 13–1, the debate begins with an affirmative case (in 1AC) consisting of a plan and three advantages. The initial negative attack (in 1NC) launches a topicality argument, then pursues a direct refutation strategy against each of the three advantages of the affirmative case. The affirmative (2AC) answers the topicality argument and extends the three advantages. Then the negative (2NC) raises a set of objections against the affirmative plan, such as workability and disadvantages. As shown, the 2NC plan attacks should actually be recorded on a separate page for the purpose of flowing the succeeding arguments on them in rebuttals. That concludes the four constructive speeches in a two-person team debate.

Next, the debate proceeds to the rebuttals. Figure 13–1 indicates which arguments are covered in each succeeding rebuttal speech. Of course, the diagram is meant only as an illustration of a typical debate. It does not purport to be an exhaustive catalog of the types of arguments possible in a debate, nor does it necessarily match the arguments each speaker might choose to make in the constructive speeches. For instance, there may be one or more negative counterplans. The negative team might choose to reverse the order of presentation, so that 1NC begins with plan attacks and 2NC makes the other arguments. These and other variations are not shown in Figure 13–1, though they could occur in real debates.

The negative side has an artificial advantage created by the speaking order. The second negative constructive speech (2NC) is the final speech in the series of constructive speeches, but the first negative rebuttal (1NR) is the first speech in the series of rebuttals. In other words, the negative team has two speeches back-to-back in the middle of the debate, the 2NC and the 1NR. This sequence of two consecutive negative speeches is called the *negative block,* and it comprises one of the greatest single advantages for the negative side. Immediately following this powerful concentration of negative speaking time, the first affirmative rebuttal (1AR) is the first chance the affirmative has to answer the entire negative block—which works out to be about a three-to-one advantage in speaking time ratios between the affirmative and negative sides at that point.

First Negative Rebuttal.   The negative block is an advantage only if the negative uses the time strategically. The 1NR must not cover the same material as the 2NC speech. It would be the same as if the negative constructive speaker made some arguments for half of the speaking time, then repeated them for the rest of the speech. Mere repetition of an argument adds no force to it, whether you repeat your own argument or your partner repeats it.

The 1NR has more important arguments to make. Notice in Figure 13–1 that after the 1NC speech, presumably the 2AC speech responded to the initial negative arguments. What is to become of the initial negative constructive arguments? They will fall to the 2AC's responses, unless the 1NR extends the initial arguments beyond the 2AC's responses.

The 1NR should organize the sequence of arguments to extend in exactly the same order as initially presented. At this point in the debate, there are many issues on the judge's flow sheet, and the course of the debate has evolved into a complex set of arguments on both sides. It is very important for the 1NR to stick to the original outline of points as presented initially in 1NC. Invariably, the 1NR will have to be selective and decide which positions to extend and which to drop. The listener cannot read the 1NR's mind and determine those choices merely by looking at his or her own flow sheet. Worse, if the 1NR skips around between points, the judge will almost certainly become lost and will be unable to flow all of the 1NR extensions where they are intended to be applied.

In extending selected arguments against the affirmative case, it is important for the 1NR to indicate clearly what each extension accomplishes in terms of refuting some particular aspect of the affirmative case. These "clinchers" are persuasive to the critic or judge. They also signal to your partner which arguments you are highlighting for him or her to carry through in the final negative rebuttal.

In extending certain selected arguments, the 1NR should not fail to call the judge's attention to points the affirmative failed to answer, or "dropped." Once you call attention to issues the affirmative has dropped, you must be prepared to continue to flow the 1AR's replies to those points. Then, before the final negative rebuttal, confer with your partner and highlight those specific items to be sure they are nailed down in the last negative rebuttal.

If these suggestions are followed, then the negative block will consist of a solid set of new arguments by the 2NC, plus a 1NR that extends the initial negative arguments. When this strategic allocation of negative arguments between the two parts of the negative block is accomplished, then the 1AR is placed in a very precarious position. Also, the 1NR emphasizes the crucial issues which must still be addressed by the affirmative rebuttals. This helps crystallize the key points for the judge, and it sets up the final negative rebuttal.

First Affirmative Rebuttal. From the preceding discussion, as illustrated by the diagram in Figure 13–1, you can see that the main task of the 1AR is to alleviate the damages done to the affirmative case by the negative block. The 1AR is like a paramedic whose task is to diagnose the worst injuries suffered in the negative's all-out attack and apply first aid to stop the bleeding. Notice that in Figure 13–1, the 1AR is the first speech in the debate in which the speaker is expected to touch on every one of the major issues of both sides. This is truly a challenging rebuttal task for any debater to accomplish. The limited time available to answer the negative block requires the 1AR to be selective in choosing what to answer, since it is almost impossible to answer every negative point in an effective negative block.

How should the 1AR make these choices? The first part of the rebuttal should answer the arguments given by the 2NC. The last part of the rebuttal should return to the arguments extended by the 1NR. In both instances, the 1AR should follow the exact order of arguments as outlined by the negative in their original presentations. Otherwise, the judge who must evaluate the 1AR responses will almost certainly lose track of where the 1AR responses are supposed to fit into the debate, and their forcefulness will be lost.

This seemingly backward approach makes sense because the 2NC has not yet been addressed by any affirmative reply. If any of the 2NC goes unanswered in the 1AR, then the negative will have no chance to defend it if the 2AR gets to it. If any negative argument goes unanswered until the 2AR, judges will probably not listen to anything the affirmative says about it at that point. It will be too late. Moreover, some judges believe it is unethical for the 2AR to answer constructive negative arguments for the first time, since it is impossible for the negative to reply to those answers and extend their own position after the last affirmative rebuttal.

Even though the 1AR's main task is to answer the 2NC, the rebuttal should also get back to the arguments extended by the 1NR. Those are the arguments the negative chose as the ones they hoped to win. If any of the 1NR's extensions are unrefuted, then that much of the negative case will carry through to the end of the debate. Many judges will not permit the 2AR to "resurrect" any arguments dropped by the 1AR, on the same general principle as a dropped 2NC argument. Therefore, the goal of the 1AR is to cover every important argument which was extended in the 1NR. If this proves to be impossible, then the success or failure of the 1AR hinges on the quality of the choices made as to which of the arguments must be answered, and which must be dropped.

In sum, the 1AR is the most challenging speech in the debate. It has to answer the entire negative block. The best strategy is to cover all of the new arguments made by the 2NR first, then return to the arguments extended by the 1NR. In the first instance, the 1AR is *refuting* the 2NC with initial replies. In the second instance, the 1AR is *extending* on initial case arguments, which were refuted by 1NC, then extended by 2AC, and extended again by 1NR. The process of extending selected arguments through the rebuttals in this manner has the effect of crystallizing the major issues of the debate for the judge.

The Final Rebuttals. This is the final opportunity to speak in a two-person team debate. At this point, as shown in Figure 13–1, the affirmative case has been presented in 1AC, attacked in 1NC, extended in 2AC, rebutted in 1NR, and extended once again in 1AR. Also, the 2NC has levied a constructive speech against the affirmative case, (often confined to plan attacks in a policy debate), and 1AR has given responses to the main arguments. In terms of the actual time expended in the debate at this point, if the debate follows the standard format consisting of ten-minute constructive speeches and five-minute rebuttals, the 2NR and the 2AR come after 25 minutes of affirmative arguments and 25 minutes of negative arguments. In the final five minutes of each side's 30 minutes on the floor, the rebuttalist has the task of perspective drawing for the judge.

Clearly, it is almost impossible to cover every single point made in the 50 preceding minutes. For example, the affirmative case might consist of a plan with three comparative advantages. In the debate, the negative might have presented a topicality argument, a counterplan (or even multiple counterplans), and several plan objections to the affirmative plan. The number of issues generated by each side might have escalated into the dozens, so this final five minutes for the 2NR is the time for selectivity and persuasion.

If the 2NR and the 2AR continue the process of extending certain arguments, a few issues in contention will be four affirmative layers deep at the end of the debate. Certain arguments raised by the negative, such as topicality arguments or plan disadvantages, will also very likely be strongly and repeatedly emphasized. For instance, if the 2NC makes the argument that a certain disadvantage will accrue to the affirmative plan, and the 1AR argues that the disadvantage turns around, then 2NR will surely wish to address that particular argument to avoid having an initial negative position converted into an affirmative position. All these issues can only stand out for the listening audience, and particularly for the judge, to the extent that the rebuttals maintain clarity of organization.

Our discussion of the duties of the rebuttal speakers so far has avoided the content of the rebuttal speeches. Perhaps there was a time not long ago when a textbook could advise the 1AR, "Answer the plan attacks first, then return to your case-side arguments." Today, however, negative strategy may dictate that the plan attacks come out in the 1NC instead of the 2NC. Also, in CEDA debate, there is not often an affirmative plan proposed as such at all, hence, no plan attacks to answer.

Our advice is to consider the way the debate evolves through the succeeding order of all the speeches, and organize the rebuttal structure in terms of which opposing speaker to answer first, and which one last. This is our best advice, even though our discussion necessarily takes on an abstract tone as a result. Since the rebuttals must be keyed to the content of the prior speeches which are the focus of their attention, rebuttal speakers must listen carefully, keep a good flow sheet, and be flexible.

SOME PRACTICAL SUGGESTIONS FOR REBUTTALS IN ACADEMIC DEBATE

Rebuttals are usually the most crucial speeches in terms of winning or losing decisions, yet, because rebuttals are so dependent upon the situation, it is not possible to provide a complete set of guidelines for what to do in every instance. The following discussion is useful only to the extent that the suggestions fit a particular debate in which you may be participating. We have selected some of the more generally applicable suggestions for your consideration.

Think

Debate is a contest in argument skills in which a high premium is placed on your ability to refute your opponent's case, and to rebuild your own case after it has been attacked. This feature of debating can only be performed well by clear and critical thinking in the situation. "Canned" rebuttals that are prepared in advance are not useful in academic debates, since they seldom apply to the flow of issues begun in the constructive speeches.

This suggestion is easy to make, but difficult to apply under pressure of an actual debate. It is easier when:

You have a good case to begin with;
You are thoroughly familiar with your own arguments and evidence;
You have carefully anticipated the arguments your opponent is likely to make; and,
You have prepared a set of potential replies to those anticipated arguments.

This is not the same thing as working out a set speech for your rebuttal. It is also not the same as brainstorming for rebuttal points after the debate is underway. Following this approach to rebuttal preparation, you will always be prepared to say something relevant about any particular item that comes up, realizing that any two debates will ordinarily be as individual as two fingerprints, snowflakes, or chess games. With the security of having adequate preparation on all the expected arguments, along with thorough knowledge of your own material, you will be better able to notice the unexpected windfalls that your opponent presents to you, such as contradictory arguments, irrelevant arguments, unsupported assertions, or inferior arguments.

Economize

The following suggestions should enable you to cover more material within your limited rebuttal time.

Group Your Arguments.   Rather than trying to cover each of your opponent's points separately, look for ways to combine them. Two common methods of grouping arguments are according to common assumptions underlying more than one of the opponent's arguments, and according to the type of issue at stake. Grouping by common assumption simply means looking at your opponent's arguments to see whether any of them rest on a single assumption, and then refuting that assumption. For instance, "Two of the asserted disadvantages to our plan assume that the government will finance by raising taxes. Recall that in our plan, the agency will charge all users a graduated fee according to their ability to pay. The plan will not need added tax dollars to operate. Therefore, the two disadvantages must fall because we do not raise taxes."

The other method of grouping opposing arguments involves combining them according to type. For example, "The 1NC argued that the administration has three different agencies which could achieve our goals, not just the one we indicted in our plan. But recall that the reason we said the present system cannot solve the problem is because the Supreme Court has ruled that the federal government has no jurisdiction. Without the enabling legislation of our plan, none of the negative repairs will work. There could be 50 federal agencies in the field, and it would be the same problem. The present system can't solve it because the courts say the federal government lacks jurisdiction."

Select Your Arguments.   It is not always necessary to cover every argument in order to win an issue. Selectivity implies leaving out some initial arguments in order to emphasize others. For instance, if the negative team uses a counterplan strategy, a major part of the affirmative case will be granted either explicitly or implicitly. The affirmative rebuttal in this example, then, should cover the counterplan issues; but it is not necessary to spend much time or attention on those initial case arguments no longer in doubt. The affirmative rebuttal should pull through the initial case, primarily to remind the judge of its rationale, and possibly to pull through those elements of the case that are legitimate answers to some other issues brought up by the negative — for instance, evidence of the solvency of the plan, or of the significance of the advantages.

Dropping some arguments on the negative side is advisable in those instances where a lot of initial challenges were posited but answered adequately by the affirmative. Doing a few things well, as a rule of thumb, is the key to negative success.

Eliminate Wordiness.   The rebuttals in an academic debate are typically highly edited speeches, with few if any wasted words. There are several techniques to save precious time by eliminating excess words.

First, pare down the tag lines or argument labels. The ideal tag line should be as brief as five words or so. The argument tag line should consist of the subject of the argument and a characterization. For instance, on the resolution for the federal government to guarantee a minimum cash income for all citizens, one highly successful second negative debater used only two main arguments, labeled thus: "1. Cash won't work. 2. In-kind assistance is best." All of his solvency arguments and disadvantage arguments were then presented under these two tag lines. The key question is, what do you want the judge to write down? If you use lengthy tag lines, chances are the judge will not be able to get everything down. You have no control over what the judge actually writes. With a short tag line, you make it easier for the listeners (opponents and judges) to write your arguments down completely and accurately.

What about the use of evidence in rebuttals? There are several suggestions for efficiency. First, it is recommended that some evidence should be used. A content analysis of the first affirmative rebuttals given at the National Debate Tournament discovered that each of these champions used a range of four to 23 pieces of evidence.[3] It is not recommended that your rebuttal should be unsupported by evidence at all merely to conserve time. Next, make sure your references to evidence are brief. While your evidence cards themselves must be complete with full documentation, and with the context of the original evidence included, your rebuttal speech may use only a highlighted portion of it. (You should underline or highlight selected portions of your evidence for use during rebuttals under time pressure.)

Arrange Your Arguments Strategically.   It is a good idea to prepare rebuttal briefs in advance, just as you would have your case extensions on separate briefs. These briefs may be on sheets or cards, mounted in clear plastic protective carriers. A grease pencil or overhead transparency marker can be used to check the particular items from the brief you wish to actually present during the rebuttal. You can also number the selected items on the plastic cover in the order you intend to use them in the rebuttal.

Your arrangement of arguments should alternate your one-line "blips" and "presses" with your more substantive arguments and explanations. In most rounds, you will speak rapidly during the rebuttal, and it is difficult for the listener to write all your responses on a flow sheet. By interspersing your arguments with longer explanations, or with evidence cards, among the whole body of arguments, you make it easier for the listeners (both the opponents and the judge) to keep up and record your responses accurately.

Use Rebuttal Flow Sheets Wisely

Use separate notepads for different categories of arguments. Keep in mind that paper is cheap. At the beginning of a debate, you cannot predict which particular points will generate the greatest mushrooming. If you have the whole affirmative case and plan on the left margin of one page, you cannot keep a legible set of flowsheet notes on those arguments the opponent may decide to spread with 15 or 20 responses. At a minimum, use separate pages for (1) affirmative case rationale such as advantages or contentions, (2) plan arguments, (3) counterplan arguments, and (4) topicality arguments. Some debaters use a separate page for every single major contention, such as a separate sheet for each case advantage, separate pages for counterplan competitiveness arguments and for counterplan nontopicality arguments, etc. This suggestion should be taken as far as your individual notetaking aptitudes and abilities need to go.

During the actual rebuttal, partners should help each other out. If possible, use each other's flowpads (of course, this suggestion assumes you can read your partner's handwriting and vice versa). By doing this, you can concentrate on your own division of labor with regard to the issues, and let your colleague brief you on the salient parts of his or her share of the division of labor. That is, if you are the 1AR, for instance, you can concentrate on preparing your responses to the plan attacks, while your partner writes out the essential responses to the case side arguments on his or her flowsheet. (In addition to dividing flowsheet writing duties in rebuttal, partners can also serve one another as "file clerks" and retrieve specific information needed from the looseleaf brief books or evidence card file.)

Practice Comprehensibility

It is very important to be comprehensible in rebuttals. One of the reasons for the growth of Lincoln-Douglas debate in high schools and for CEDA debate in colleges is because they are seen as alternatives to some of the practices developed in standard debate. Style and delivery are important evaluation criteria in many debates. The Judging Philosophy Book of the National Debate Tournament reveals that even in that highly specialized tournament, a wide majority of the judges say they will not vote for any argument (or evidence) that is incomprehensible when first presented. To do so would allow the debater to expand the time for debate beyond the time limits, to a period after the debate during which the judge is expected to read the text of whatever was not clearly understood during regulation time. It would also place an unfair requirement on the opponent, to give a comprehensible reply to an incomprehensible argument.

Therefore, debaters should rehearse their rebuttal delivery skills in order to polish their articulation, enunciation, and diction. There is, for any speaker, an ideal delivery rate at which peak efficiency is reached. This is almost always at a point somewhat less than the actual upper limit of speaking speed for the individual. Research shows that the debaters whose speeches reach the highest word-per-minute count (or word-per-second count) are not the ones whose speeches contain the highest content load. "Speed freaks" attain their velocity by frequent repetition of pet phrases and familiar jargon, not by covering more arguments. Exceeding the speed limit risks the loss of judges' attention and patience.

When you determine your ideal rate for rebuttal coverage efficiency, you should then plan your constructive speech to cover material at about two-thirds of your ideal rebuttal rate. It will be a rare debate in which you can accomplish all your duties in the rebuttal period at the same pace you used in your constructive speech. Therefore, do not load your constructive speech with so much material that you will spread yourself out of the rebuttal just trying to manage it.

SUMMARY

Academic debate places a number of constraints on the process of refuting your opponent and rebuilding your own case. There are special rules and conventions to know, such as the "no new arguments" rule and the limited time constraints. Each rebuttalist in a debate has specific obligations and duties. These have been explained in detail earlier in this chapter.

The general principles of refutation and rebuttal apply to academic debate. The basic purposes of extending original arguments, and of providing a coherent and persuasive perspective on the debate from your own viewpoint certainly apply to academic debate. The technique of the four-point formula for dealing with any argument (state the argument, state your position, prove your point, relate the argument to the point at issue) applies as well. In particular, refutation and rebuttal will be more effective to the extent that the listener comprehends your line of thinking. This factor is very dependent on clear organization (such as "headlines" and "road-maps" to preview your rebuttal, and "clinchers" to nail down your points in an unmistakable and persuasive manner). The process of refutation incorporates the various attacks on evidence and reasoning discussed at length in the body of this chapter.

Rebuttal techniques can be enhanced by following a few practical suggestions: think on your feet; economize by argument grouping, argument selection, judicious wording, and strategic arrangement; use effective flowsheet techniques; and practice diligently. Taken together, these suggestions can increase your rebuttal effectiveness and reduce the frustrated sensation often felt after a debate, "I should have said . . ." With experience, these suggestions will become more habitual, and your success in debate will increase as a result.

Notes

[1]Ruby Daniels Rouse and David A. Thomas. "The First Affirmative Rebuttal: A Content Analysis of Thirteen NDT Transcripts" in *Advanced Debate: Readings in Theory, Practice and Teaching,* 3rd ed. David A. Thomas and Jack Hart, (eds.) (Lincolnwood, IL: National Textbook Co. 1987) 101–111.

[2]Scott L. Harris, "A Jurisprudential Approach to Final Rebuttal," in *Argument in Transition: Proceedings of the Third Summer Conference on Argumentation,* Ed. by David Zarefsky, Malcolm O. Sillars, and Jack Rhodes (Annandale, VA: SCA, 1983) 904–917.

[3]Rouse and Thomas, 104.

CHAPTER FOURTEEN

CROSS EXAMINATION

In many disputes, arguments do not progress simply by having one side present a position followed by a response from the opponents; instead one or both sides have the opportunity to interact with the other in order to ask questions about the other side's case. In legal courts, for example, the majority of the trial consists of the examination and cross examination of witnesses. In ordinary argument we often have the opportunity to ask our opponents questions, and in formal debate, there is a time period set aside for each team to ask questions of their opponents. This allows the two teams to interact directly, and allows the advocates to examine positions in greater depth than would otherwise be permitted.

There are two extreme views of the role of cross examination in argument. At one extreme is the view that cross examination is unimportant. Some advocates feel that little is accomplished in the cross examination period—it is simply viewed as a break in the debate. As a result, these individuals pay little attention to cross examination. The questions that they ask are frequently unimportant, and the cross-examination period is often devoted to asking for evidence or other methods of wasting time.

At the other extreme is the position that suggests that cross examination is the most important part of advocacy. These advocates picture themselves as famous lawyers, asking the "killer" questions and illustrating their brilliance as speakers. In the middle of cross examination they picture their opponents as breaking down and admitting that they are wrong. As in the courtroom drama, it is assumed that a good advocate can use cross examination to leave his or her opponent defenseless.

The truth probably lies between these two extremes. Cross examination can help an advocate win an argument, but it rarely wins a dispute by itself. The rare opponent who surrenders in cross examination would probably lose the argument anyway. An effective cross examination, however, could help establish ground for later arguments that could help win the dispute. To suggest that cross examination is inherently unproductive is to ignore several minutes of debate time that could prove to be helpful in winning a dispute. The question becomes, what specific goals can be achieved using cross examination? This chapter will examine the nature of cross examination by discussing three major issues. First, the goals of cross examination will be looked at from the point of view of both the questioner and the respondent. Second, guidelines for cross examination from the perspective of both the questioner and respondent will be discussed. Finally, the psychological dimension of cross examination will be studied.

THE PURPOSE OF CROSS EXAMINATION

Cross examination consists of the interaction between two individuals. One individual asks questions that the second individual will answer. These two individuals will often trade roles as the questioner responds to a question by the respondent (for example, if the respondent asks for clarification of a question), or when the questioner becomes a respondent in a later part of the dispute. A goal that both speakers will share is the desire to create a favorable psychological impression in the minds of both the judge and the other team. This goal will be discussed in greater detail in the last section of this chapter. Although both the questioner and respondent will share certain goals, they will also have different goals in mind when they prepare for the cross-examination period.

Goals for the Questioner

The questioner usually has at least one of three goals in mind when preparing for cross examination. First, the questioner should attempt to clarify positions. The advocate should make sure that he or she understands the position of the other team before advancing an argument. This is especially critical in preparing attacks on the plan of a team. Often the best attack against a case will depend upon the specific policies that are being defended by the affirmative team. Suppose that a debater were arguing against a program of gun control. Before deciding what specific arguments to make against the affirmative team, the debater may want to ask questions concerning the type of gun control that the affirmative team is defending. Are they advocating a total ban on ownership of all guns, or merely the registration of guns? Does the plan cover all guns, or merely handguns? Will the plan have exemptions? Is there a phase-in period? Will present owners of guns be compensated? The best negative arguments against the affirmative case will depend upon the answers to these questions. For example, if the affirmative team merely requires the registration of handguns, then the negative team may want to argue that this policy will not be effective. If the plan compensates owners of handguns, the negative team may wish to argue that the plan would be very costly and that the funding of the policy would lead to undesirable effects. The questions are designed to pin down the affirmative team so the negative knows what to attack. For these reasons, questions about the precise nature of a policy are often extremely important in a debate.

Clarifying positions can have other advantages in a debate round. Clarifying a position can help establish common ground for later speeches. An advocate may wish to ask about the cost of the policy, or the effect of their policy on employment or other programs. This information can be the basis for later arguments. Sometimes it is unclear what a team means by an argument, or what support (if any) they have for a position. It would be foolish to attack an opponent's position if it is unclear. A wise advocate should discover as much as possible about the exact position of an opponent before making a commitment to a strategy. The cross examination period is an ideal time to discover this type of information. In addition, cross examination can be used to help clarify your own positions; your questions can be used to set up later responses, as in the example below, where the questioner is attempting to demonstrate that laws against marijuana do not decrease the harm of the drug.

Question: You argue that marijuana should not be decriminalized since it is harmful, correct?

Answer: Yes.

Question: This would be a disadvantage to our case only if decriminalizing marijuana increased the use of marijuana, correct?

Answer: No, the fact that it is harmful means that it should not be decriminalized.

Question: But if the same number of people use marijuana under our plan as use it now, no additional people would be hurt if marijuana were decriminalized, right?

Answer: Yes.

In this example, the questioner used the cross examination period to help explain the argument that if the plan would not increase use of marijuana, this particular disadvantage would not apply.

Cross examination can also help the advocate explain arguments. Once an argument has been made clear in cross examination, less time is required in a later speech to explain the position.

A second use of cross examination is to establish the limits of an advocate's proof. Sometimes an advocate will read evidence that does not say what the advocate claims. Other advocates may introduce evidence reaching a conclusion that includes a number of qualifications. The source of the evidence might, for example, speculate that the adoption of a policy *might* produce a side effect *if* other conditions are also present. The advocate might utilize cross examination to emphasize the tentativeness of the conclusion supported by the evidence. Cross examination can be used to draw attention to the weakness of a piece of evidence or it may expose assumptions that are made by the source of the evidence. Consider the following exchange:

Question: What was your first disadvantage?

Answer: Your plan will prevent nuclear proliferation, which is desirable.

Question: To support this disadvantage, you read evidence from Cy Smith, correct?

Answer: Yes.

Question: And this evidence is the only evidence read in this round that suggests that the spread of nuclear weapons is desirable, correct?

Answer: Yes.

Question: Isn't Mr. Smith talking about a slow spread of nuclear weapons being desirable, not a rapid, unbalanced spread of nuclear weapons?

Answer: Yes.

This exchange permits the questioner to point out assumptions that are made in the evidence. If the questioner can, in a later speech, demonstrate that the affirmative plan will prevent a rapid spread of nuclear weapons, then the evidence in question would not apply in the round.

A third function of cross examination is to refute positions of the other team. Sometimes a debater might be able to defeat an entire line of argument through effective use of cross examination. Consider the following exchange:

Question: Your first disadvantage argues that our plan will cripple industry by increasing their costs, correct?

Answer: Yes.

Question: This disadvantage assumes that industry must pay for the costs of the plan, right?

Answer: Yes.

Question: Doesn't our plan mandate that the government, not the industries affected pay for the costs of our policies?

Answer: I don't think so.

Question: What does plank IIB in our plan mandate?

Answer: (Looking at the plan) It subsidizes the industries for costs incurred as a result of the plan.

Question: So our plan will not require any additional expenditures from industries, correct?

Answer: Well, no.

Question: And since the plan does not require any additional expenditures from industries, it will not cripple the industries, correct?

In this example, the entire disadvantage presented by the negative team was based upon a single assumption: that the affirmative policy required industry to spend money. The questioner used the cross examination period to demonstrate the importance of this assumption. Once the assumption was established, it was easy to demonstrate that it was incorrect.

In other cases cross examination can be used to expose contradictions in the positions of a team, as shown here:

Question: Your first disadvantage argues that our plan will cause a decrease in medical research, correct?

Answer: Yes.

Question: Your second disadvantage, however, argues that medical research is bad since experimenting with dangerous DNA could result in catastrophic effects, correct?

Answer: Yes.

Question: Then doesn't that mean our plan is good, since it would eliminate potentially harmful DNA research?

In this exchange, the questioner attempts to clarify two positions that he or she thinks are contradictory. Once the questioner is sure that the positions are contradictory, the questioner points out the contradiction. If this contradiction had been pointed out in a speech, it is possible the other team would attempt to alter their initial position; by pinning them down on both positions before observing that the contradiction exists, it is harder for the other team to explain its way out of the contradiction.

Goals for the Respondent

From the perspective of the respondent, there are at least three different purposes of cross examination. First, the respondent should attempt to explain positions. When the questioner asks a question, it gives the respondent an opportunity to introduce into the round additional information. For example, consider the following exchange on the topic, "Resolved, that plea bargaining should be eliminated":

Question: How do we know that eliminating plea bargaining is possible?

Answer: Well, according to a study conducted by the Department of Justice, plea bargaining was effectively eliminated in Alaska when a policy similar to ours was implemented.

Question: But won't eliminating plea bargaining cause the court system to be overcrowded?

Answer: Studies in both Alaska and Louisiana found that there was no adverse effect on the caseloads of the courts in those jurisdictions that eliminated plea bargaining.

In this example, the respondent was able not only to answer these questions, but also to explain the basis for the answer and even provide additional information supporting the case. This type of response has two effects. First, it helps strengthen the advocate's case by presenting new evidence to support it. Second, it enhances the advocate's credibility, since it demonstrates to the audience that the advocate is extremely familiar with the evidence on the case.

A second goal of the respondent in cross examination is to keep options open. While the questioner wants to pin the respondent down, the respondent wants to remain flexible in order to see what the other team argues before committing his or her side to a specific position. In a political debate, for example, a candidate may wish to remain flexible about what specific actions he or she will take to solve a specific problem. This may be especially true early in a campaign when the candidate may still be developing a detailed position on an issue. Rather than make a commitment to a specific policy (a commitment that may have to be altered as additional information is discovered), the candidate may wish to remain flexible in responding to a question. This does not mean that the respondent should be evasive, but it does suggest that the respondent not commit his or her side to a position until the questioner forces such a commitment to be made.

A final goal of the respondent is to avoid mistakes. It is important to make sure that incorrect answers are not given in cross examination. In both the 1976 and 1980 Presidential elections, one of the factors leading to the "loss" of the debates by Ford and Carter were errors made in response to questions. Ford's comment about Eastern Europe and Carter's handling of the nuclear proliferation issue were seized by their opponents (and the mass media) and helped undermine the effectiveness of their campaigns. To that end, it is important that the respondent become familiar with all the specifics of his or her case. It may be advisable for the members of a team to discuss potential answers to possible questions before the debate round to ensure that the answerer does not fall into traps set by the questioner.

Guidelines for the Questioner

In preparing for cross examination, there are several guidelines that the questioner should follow. First, the questioner should establish a goal for the cross-examination period. It would be foolish to assume that a debater can wait until the last minute to prepare for cross examination and then expect, as he or she walks up to ask questions, that a flash of inspiration will lead to a brilliant series of questions that will destroy the opposition. Instead, the advocate should decide prior to the round potential lines of questions. While developments in the round may modify the utility of these questions, they can help improve the quality of the questions asked. For example, an advocate might develop a series of questions that assist in explaining an argument. Other lines of questions designed to expose weaknesses in an opponent's case should be developed.

Advocates should think about cross examination *before* the debate and they *should have a definite goal in mind* before the cross-examination period. What admissions would be desirable? What positions need to be clarified? What lines of questions are likely to prove useful? Instead of asking one single question, the debaters may wish to think about potential ways of leading up to a conclusion.

This is an important stage in preparing for cross examination. The questioner should prepare a series of questions designed to promote the goal of cross examination. Rarely will a single question lead to the accomplishment of any major goal; instead the questioner should prepare a series of questions that might allow the accomplishment of his or her objectives. This series of questions will lead the respondent step by step through a series of admissions until those admissions place the respondent in a position where he or she must either contradict a previous position (and risk looking foolish) or admit a damaging conclusion. The Socratic dialogues are full of examples of this type of questioning.

In debates, a debater might develop this line of questioning by discovering the tension points in a position; those points where an advocate is faced with a choice, either one of which will lead to undesirable conclusions. For example, suppose an opponent was advocating anarchy. One problem facing such an advocate is the tension between law and order and freedom. This problem can be exposed in cross examination. The advocate might begin with the question, "How will anarchy prevent crime?" Consider two possible exchanges that might follow:

Answer: In an anarchistic state, peer pressure will prevent individuals from committing crimes.

Question: In other words, individuals will not commit crime because they will be afraid of pressure from other members of society?

Answer: Yes.

Question: Then if an individual violates a law, he or she might be ostracized, excluded from society, and punished by "peers"?

Answer: Yes.

Question: Would there be any due process afforded an individual accused of a crime?

Answer: No.

Question: How does this differ from existing punishments an individual receives in the state?

In this exchange, the questioner points out that the system used in an anarchy to prevent crime may eventually be similar to that of an organized society, though perhaps without procedural safeguards. Other answers might create other opportunities for the questioner:

Answer: There will be no crime in an anarchistic society.

Question: Why not?

Answer: Because individuals are naturally good; only society causes crime.

Question: Then why is there crime in primitive societies?

This sequence can continue with questions suggesting that humans may not be inherently law-abiding. The speaker begins with one question, and prepares for all possible responses. Follow-up questions are then designed in such a manner that any response to the initial question will open up a series of other questions that will lead an opponent into a corner.

A second guideline for the questioner in cross examination is to be organized. Consider the following exchange:

Question: Who is Dr. Jones?

Answer: I'm not sure, where did I quote her?

Question: On the third contention.

Answer: Oh, let me see. (pause) Oh, she is a lobbyist for the American Medical Association.

This sequence is extremely inefficient. Time is wasted finding the evidence and, even after the evidence is found, it is unclear what is so important about the evidence. It would be better if the exchange were organized into three steps: (1) the questioner should locate the argument on the flow; (2) the position of the other team should be established; (3) the specific focus of the exchange should be given. For example, the earlier exchange could be more clearly structured in the following manner:

Question: On your third contention [step 1] you argue that national health insurance would be expensive [step 2], correct?

Answer: Yes.

Question: Your only support for this is a quotation from a Dr. Jones, correct?

Answer: Yes.

Question: Who is Dr. Jones [step 3]?

Answer: Dr. Jones is a lobbyist for the American Medical Association.

While in the first exchange it was unclear why the admission of Dr. Jones' link to the AMA was relevant, in this exchange the questioner provides the context for the evidence, which makes the admission of Jones' biases more damaging. In addition, the respondent (and the judge) knew what the questions were about, which made it easier to understand the exchange. This can prevent misunderstandings. For example, the question, "Can the police prosecute individuals for loitering?" could mean, can they prosecute *now,* or could they prosecute *under the affirmative plan.* Unless the respondent is sure about what part of the debate the question relates to, it would be possible to interpret the question in an incorrect manner. By structuring the cross-examination period, this type of misunderstanding is avoided.

Third, the questioner should phrase questions precisely. The wording of the questions can influence the types of responses that can be made by the respondent. For example, a questioner could ask an open-ended question, such as "What is the harm of your case?" This provides the respondent with much latitude in answering the question. Most of the examples in this chapter have been leading questions that could only be answered with a yes or a no. These questions are similar in nature to true/false questions on a test; the respondent has a limited number of responses. Finally, the questioner could ask objective, factual questions. These questions (like short-answer questions on a test) give the respondent a little latitude to respond. For example, to ask a person about the cost of a plan would be an objective question.

Generally, leading, yes/no questions are the best to use in debate. These allow the questioner to remain in control. If these questions are used, however, it is important to phrase them fairly. A question like, "Are you still beating your wife?" is unfair since it makes an assumption (that the person has beat his wife in the past) that has not been established. As a result, true/false questions are best if they are part of a sequence of questions that slowly lead to a conclusion.

Open-ended questions are dangerous because they permit the respondent instead of the questioner to control the questioning period. This is undesirable, since it can prevent the questioner from channeling the period into areas of productive inquiry. If the questioner asks a broad question like "What does your case argue?" or "Explain this disadvantage?" it gives the respondent ample opportunity to ramble or to provide material that supports his or her side. It would be better to limit the respondent to a simple, brief answer.

This does not mean that open-ended questions should never be used. Sometimes a debater does not understand a position, and the open-ended question might be useful. For example, in responding to an unfamiliar set of arguments, it might be desirable to permit the opposing advocates to explain their position in depth in order to determine the best strategy to use against the case. Often, however, the questioner will know enough about the issues to make the open-ended question of little value. It would generally be wise therefore to rely mainly on narrow, objective questions in order to control the cross-examination period.

The questioner often encounters difficulties when asking objective questions. Some respondents are extremely evasive and attempt to avoid responding directly to a question. If the respondent is evasive, it is important for the questioner to remain calm so that the cross examination period does not degenerate into a shouting match. It is possible that the respondent honestly does not understand the question. To ensure that this is not the case, it is usually wise to repeat or paraphrase the question. If this is not successful, attempt to change the subject, since further attempts to pin down an evasive respondent may waste valuable time.

Sometimes the witness will waste the questioner's time by rambling about a topic. The questioner should attempt to prevent this from happening in order to retain control of the cross-examination period. There are several strategies that can be used to accomplish this. The easiest strategy is simply to ask an additional question. The questioner may also wish to break up the response by saying such things as, "I think I see the implications of what you are saying," or, "I think I understand," followed by another question. The best way to avoid being in this situation is to ask direct questions that require only short answers.

A fourth guideline for the questioner is to know the answer to the question. This may seem to be an unusual guideline, since normally when one asks a question it is to gain new information. In debate, however, the questioner is asking questions designed to promote a case. It would be a good idea to have some idea of the type of answer that will be given to a question. The usefulness of a question will often depend on the anticipated response. Consider the following two exchanges:

Question: On the third contention, [all of] your evidence is from Ms. Vavra, correct?

Answer: Yes.

Question: Who is Ms. Vavra?

Answer: I don't know.

In this example, the question served the purpose of pointing out that a critical source has no qualifications. Suppose the answer to the last question was different:

Question: Who is Ms. Vavra?

Answer: She is a leading expert in international relations. She has taught on the faculties of Harvard, Oxford, and Yale. She has been a member of numerous national and international commissions on human rights. She has published articles in. . . .

While in the first example, the question helped the questioner by pointing out the lack of qualifications of an important source of information, in this exchange the question ends up helping the respondent by permitting the respondent to bring out the qualifications of the source under question. What makes the question a good one in the first exchange but a bad one in the second exchange is that in the first exchange, the questioner knew that the source was not qualified, while in the second exchange the questioner did not have any idea what the response would be.

As with all guidelines, there are some exceptions to this rule. Sometimes the questioner cannot know the exact answer to a question, or even have an idea of what the answer will be. For example, when confronted with an unfamiliar position, questions may be asked in order to discover new information about the position. In general, however, cross examination is most productive when the questioner has some idea of the type of answer that will be given to a specific question.

A final guideline for the questioner is to use the admissions gained in cross examination in later speeches. Admissions in cross examination are useless if the team that gains these admissions does not do anything with them. Cross examination should be tied to later arguments and it should be used in subsequent speeches. Unless an advocate does this, even the best cross-examination skills will be wasted.

Guidelines for the Respondent

The respondent should follow several guidelines in preparing for cross examination. First, he or she should be familiar with the issues involved in the argument, and should anticipate potential questions and prepare responses. He or she should be familiar with all evidence read in support of his or her position and should be prepared to provide additional evidence to support these positions. Members of a team should discuss the specifics of their arguments to ensure that they are in agreement about how questions should be answered.

Second, the respondent should not be evasive in answering questions. Evasive answers cause the respondent to appear to be obstinate. Instead, he or she should appear to be open, answering the questions as they are asked. In this way, the respondent enhances his or her credibility. If you are unsure about the meaning of a question, ask for clarification. If a question seems to be irrelevant to your arguments, go ahead and answer it; after all, there is no rule requiring that all cross-examination questions be addressed to what you think are the key issues in the round. In addition, a question that may seem to be irrelevant to you may be very relevant in the mind of the judge or opponent.

Third, the respondent should be honest. The questions should be answered truthfully and in a manner that does not mislead the questioner and the judge. If you do not know the answer to a question, do not be afraid to say that you don't know; to make up an answer is dishonest and ultimately counterproductive. A good respondent gives the impression of being non-partisan. This enhances the credibility of the respondent.

Fourth, if a respondent must clarify a response, this should be done at the start of an answer. Some yes/no questions cannot be adequately answered with a simple yes or no; there may be qualifications or exceptions to the answer. If that is the case, these qualifications should be given before the yes or no. For example:

Question: Can individuals sue the government for violations of their rights?

Answer: Yes, if . . .

Question: OK, now, on your second contention, you argue your plan will solve the problem, right?

In this case, since the qualification was attempted after the yes or no response, the questioner was able to cut off the qualification. Consider what would have happened if the qualification had been given before the yes or no:

Question: Can individuals sue the government if their rights have been violated?

Answer: If they can raise the money, get witnesses, and prevent the government from claiming immunity, yes.

This time, the questioner has a difficult time cutting off the respondent, and as a result the respondent can provide a more detailed answer.

Finally, it is important for the respondent to think before answering. This does not mean that the respondent should take two minutes to think about a question before responding to it, but it is generally wise to think about the implications of various responses to a question. The respondent should ask, why is the questioner asking this question? How does it relate to their other questions? What problems will be encountered by answering the question in the expected ways? What other options are open to the respondent?

The respondent's partner should also pay close attention to the cross examination period. While debate is a team activity, many judges feel that it is inappropriate for partners to consult with each other during cross examination; when a person is being asked questions, his or her partner should remain silent. Even if a teammate makes an error, the partner should not react to the answer. If the partner to the respondent does react to a response in a negative manner it may not only create friction between the two team members, but it also alerts the opposition to the fact that an error has been made. It thus is generally advisable to remain silent during your partner's cross examination.

PSYCHOLOGICAL ASPECTS OF CROSS EXAMINATION

Much of the utility of the cross-examination period is not the logical aspects of the questioning process, but the psychological effects. The cross-examination period is the only time during the debate when the opposing advocates are in direct conflict, standing side by side and interacting directly with each other. It thus provides the judge with an excellent opportunity to compare the skills of the two teams. This direct comparison allows the team members to develop a favorable (or unfavorable) impression on the judge. In addition, the cross-examination period can have a psychological effect on the opposition, especially if the opposition is not prepared for cross examination. In the next chapter we will discuss the importance of *ethos,* or source credibility. Much of the persuasiveness of any speaker depends upon the image of the speaker created in the minds of the audience.

The credibility of a speaker is based on three factors: the speaker's knowledge about the subject, the speaker's character, and the speaker's good will toward the audience. What is important in determining a speaker's credibility is the audience's *perception* of these features, not the speaker's *actual* characteristics. Cross examination is the ideal time to establish these characteristics. The intelligence of an advocate can be established, both by the types of questions that an advocate asks, as well as the quality of the answers given. The nature of the questions asked can reveal much about the individual. Consider the following exchange:

Question: On the third contention, you read evidence from Brenner, right?

Answer: Yes.

Question: Is this from Brenner's first study, or from his 1984 revision of the study?

Answer: I don't know.

Question: Do you know what assumption Brenner made about the time lag between unemployment and the impact of unemployment on health?

Answer: I don't know.

In this case, the questioner demonstrates some knowledge, not only with the evidence, but with the potential problems with the evidence. The respondent demonstrates an unfamiliarity with the evidence. The result is that this exchange improves the ethos of the questioner, and decreases the ethos of the respondent.

Similarly, cross examination can illuminate the personality of those involved. The exchange can bring out the best and worst features of individuals. Individuals who come across as obnoxious or arrogant tend to have their ethos damaged. Those who come across as open individuals interested in the quest for the truth will tend to have high ethos as a result of the cross examination. Consider this exchange:

Question: Will your plan create unemployment?

Answer: That is irrelevant.

Question: Answer the question, you idiot.

Answer: I don't have to take that from a creep like you.

Neither participant in this exchange is likely to have high ethos after this exchange. The answerer should have answered the initial question; if the questioner wants to waste time, the respondent should permit him or her to do so. The exchange after this was inexcusable for both sides. Even if one is provoked into an insult contest, an effective advocate should remain calm. Once your opponent has demonstrated immaturity, it would be advantageous to emphasize the distinction between your credibility and that of your opponent. The advocate should attempt to retain his or her poise. A good advocate does not lose his or her temper, regardless of what the opponent does. If the opponent is rude, the more polite an advocate is, the better received the advocate will be. Any attempt to be more rude than the opposition will result in a loss of much credibility.

It is important to be courteous in the cross-examination period. Rude advocates alienate the audience and decrease their own credibility. To browbeat an opponent may make some individuals feel important, but it serves no purpose in advocacy and it undermines the activity.

Humor may be used (in moderation) to enhance a debater's credibility, although sarcasm should be avoided. The physical setting of the cross-examination period can also be used to establish credibility. The advocate should not simply stare at the opponent (although it is desirable to look at the opposition occasionally, both to see how they are reacting to the questions and as a matter of courtesy). It is important to maintain some eye contact with the audience, both to gauge the audience's reaction to the questions and answers and to create an impression that the speaker is interested in the audience. The advocate should attempt to appear confident and poised. Much of the speaker's total image is based on nonverbal elements of the speaker's presentation. Does the speaker's voice suggest sincerity? Is the speaker's posture one that suggests confidence and poise? All of these factors can help establish the advocate's credibility.

SUMMARY

Cross examination can play an important role in advocacy. In order for cross examination to be useful, however, it is important that the debater be prepared. This requires developing a set of goals for both questions and answers, and then anticipating the strategy of the opposition. The advocate needs to anticipate the argumentative situation and prepare potential questions and answers. In addition, it is important to practice cross examination with your partner. By refining the skills of cross examination, advocates can gain both a logical and a psychological advantage over their opponents.

CHAPTER FIFTEEN

STYLE
AND
DELIVERY

A decade ago, the Sedalia Conference on Forensics produced a landmark report on the goals, theories, research, and status of forensics in America. In its well-known definitional statement, the Conference said, "Forensics activities, including debate and individual events, are laboratories for helping students to understand and communicate various forms of argument more effectively in a variety of contexts with a variety of audiences."[1] Debate exists in order to train students to communicate. Implicit within the Sedalia Conference statement is the idea that communication consists of different sets of behaviors within different contexts, or with different audiences. Thus, an important aspect of learning to debate in different contexts is to learn how to adapt your communication to different audiences of listeners or decision makers.

Debate is a contest in oral argumentation, and in the end the winning debater is usually the one most successful in communicating his or her position to the decision maker. Style and delivery are the subjects of this chapter. These topics are the familiar and staple subject matters of almost all courses in rhetoric and public speaking. Our treatment here echoes many of the same principles and rules which the reader might find in a traditional textbook on the fundamentals of public speaking.

Every school debater quickly discovers that, in practice, effective style and delivery in the competitive arena are different from what is expected in many other persuasive settings. Time limits make it hard to cover all the required points by using a conversational speaking rate. Therefore, debaters often tend to develop rapid speaking rates. Also, debate places a higher premium on critical thinking and direct refutation. Many debate judges reward debaters who demonstrate those intellectual skills, even though their opponents may in fact be more communicative and persuasive by traditional rhetorical standards.

These practices tend to prevail in both high school and college tournament debates. They are also found in both policy and non-policy divisions, though they may be manifested to variable degrees in different levels and different divisions of debate. Academic debate fosters its own special behaviors.

When uninitiated observers see a school debate, the most visible behaviors of the debaters are often not their analysis, or the products of their hours and hours of research, but their patterns of speaking style and delivery. The variance between what is observed and what is expected is great, particularly when the observer's mental image of a debate is a vague memory of a televised political debate, or some other audience-oriented speech program.

To the students who participate, these stylistic and delivery patterns pose few problems once they adjust to them. To the participants involved, striving to master a different style and delivery becomes as routine as learning the techniques of library research. Debaters may, in fact, subordinate standards of rhetoric in order to concentrate more on the substantive issues. As long as participants on both sides use similar practices, and their coaches and judges are also on that same wavelength, the activity can be an effective laboratory for learning the techniques of argumentation.

Our purpose in this chapter is to present our suggestions for style and delivery techniques. It is important to place a proper emphasis on style and delivery as tools for effective advocacy within a distinctive setting. If effective style and delivery consist of the fit choice of words, aptly spoken, then conversely, ineffective style and delivery consist of the unsuitable choice of words, spoken ineptly. As traditional rhetoric teaches, what is "fit," "suitable," and "apt" is always a matter of adapting to the requirements of the situation.

THE COMMUNICATIVE REQUIREMENTS OF DEBATE: ADAPTATION

We have defined *debate* as a contest in argumentation. There are numerous contexts for debate, including political campaign debate, legal debate, and academic debate. Within each of these groups, there are sub-categories of debate, each with its own set of rules and expectations. The "contest of argumentation" in the legal environment, for example, would be judged by one set of standards if you are thinking of an attorney's final summation to a jury in a local murder trial; but it would be judged by another set of standards if you are thinking of the attorney's oral arguments during an appeal to the Supreme Court.

Similarly, the several different debate leagues that govern academic debate tournaments in high schools and colleges use a wide variety of approaches to the activity. You will find some groups that define the "contest in argumentation" as being primarily a dialectical activity in which oral persuasion is relatively unimportant, and other groups that define it as a communication exercise that happens to focus on a debate resolution.

Outside the academic debate setting, advocates in other debates such as televised political debates must also be prepared to adapt to their audiences. Some critics raise the question of whether such media events are authentic discussions of issues. The charge is made that televised debates are merely frames for candidates' images. Some images are important to the voters. What voters want to know about the candidates is how genuine, competent, and trustworthy they are.

Voters are concerned about the apparent qualities of leadership and character the opposing candidates possess. In the 1980 presidential campaign, two candidates —Democrat Edward Kennedy and Republican John Connally — lost out because the voters perceived Jimmy Carter and Ronald Reagan as being candidates with higher character and integrity.[2] The voters want to be reassured that, whatever unforeseen issues arise during the next term of office, the person elected to that office has the qualifications and judgment to deal with them in an approved manner. Viewed in this light, image-building is a positive, not a negative, function of political campaign debates.

In the academic context, student debaters are not judged on the basis of their genuineness, leadership, character, and trustworthiness. They are judged according to the opinion of the critic judge as to which side did the better debating in a given round of debate. But in an important sense, school debaters are indeed being judged on the basis of how well they fulfill the judge's expectations of what is meant by "doing the better debating." If that is true, then the process of learning how to adapt arguments to different audiences and judges can be thought of as creating an image in the judge's eyes.

If debaters can learn to anticipate the expectations that different judges have of what makes for "the better job of debating," then they can practice the art of adapting to them. The perceived purpose of the debate is the key, whether this is thought of as proving the resolution, resolving the issues that emerged, winning the election, or getting the jury's unanimous verdict. Adaptation is necessary in order to meet the expectations of the decision maker. First, the criteria of judgment being employed by the decision maker must be known. Then, the debater must behave in such a way that the criteria for judgment are met. The first step is known as audience (or judge) *analysis;* the action taken in order to meet the criteria derived from the analysis is known as audience (or judge) *adaptation.*

Judge analysis and adaptation in academic debates may be difficult, but it can be done. In some championship tournaments, a judging philosophy booklet is published. This document contains each judge's answers to some specific questions about judging preferences. Studying this booklet helps debaters determine the criteria for debate judging in use.

Another way to find out what a judge is interested in is simply to ask before the debate begins. Some judges will volunteer a brief judging philosophy orientation for you. Do not expect the judge to answer questions about whether particular arguments are valid (such as the topicality of your case). However, it may be wise to ask the judge whether he or she prefers a particular judging paradigm, or whether evidence cards will be called for at the end of the debate. Such information is useful, since it could help the debaters attempt to analyze and adapt to the judge's criteria for evaluating the debate.

STYLE AND LANGUAGE IN DEBATE

Language is the primary instrument available to debaters to communicate and persuade the audiences and judges of the superiority of their arguments. Because of the crucial importance of the skillful use of language in debate, we intend to provide a basic perspective towards the role of language in argument. No matter what debate paradigm is used, whether policy systems analysis, hypothesis testing, or stock issues, all debate consists of the words of the affirmative versus the words of the negative. Advocates who have an effective command of language in creating effective arguments, and in refuting their opponents, will have a tremendous advantage.

Ambiguity and Vagueness of Language   A useful perspective to take towards language is that it is intrinsically vague and ambiguous. The debater's essential task is to reduce vagueness and ambiguities in the most reasonable way. Let us examine this perspective more closely.

Monroe C. Beardsley defined *ambiguous* this way: "A word or phrase is semantically ambiguous in a certain context if there is more than one sense that it can have in that context."[3] All academic debate resolutions are deliberately made ambiguous in this sense: the key terms may all be interpreted in more than one way. Debaters have a lot of leeway in interpreting the resolution. This provides the opportunity for a variety of affirmative cases to be advocated legitimately.

If resolutions for a season's debate were not ambiguous, the possibilities for research and analysis might become exhausted too quickly. Better a broadly ambiguous resolution like "Police powers to investigate and prosecute crime in the United States should be significantly restricted," than a narrow one like "Capital punishment should be abolished." The more ambiguous resolution allows the affirmative to specify a reasonable interpretation of its own choosing. The topicality issue, and many other issues that arise during a debate, may hinge on what is the most legitimate interpretation of the meaning of ambiguous words or phrases. Issues of significance, efficacy, and inherency are a few of the types of arguments that stand or fall on the way debaters interpret a particular word or phrase.

Vagueness is a quality of language which is similar to ambiguity, but an important distinction must be made. Beardsley explained, "The difference between vagueness and ambiguity is that between two kinds of indecisiveness. An ambiguous statement offers you a choice between interpretations, but doesn't guide you to a correct choice. A vague statement doesn't leave you in doubt as to which quality is in question (cleanliness of air, noisiness, tallness), but only of how much of it is there. The more vague the statement, the less informative it is."[4]

Value resolutions are typically vague. For instance, in the resolution, "that unauthorized immigration into the United States is seriously detrimental to the United States," there is an ambiguous term and a vague term. The *ambiguous* term is "unauthorized immigration," which could be interpreted to mean undocumented workers from Mexico, boat people from Haiti, or even espionage agents from enemy nations anywhere. The *vague* term is "seriously detrimental," which implies a comparative degree of detriment but offers no standard for determining how much detriment is "seriously detrimental."

On factual or empirical issues, then, the advocate's task is to reduce ambiguity and clearly define the meaning of the terms. On value issues, the advocate's task is to interpret the vague terms in such a way that the audience or judge can agree with that interpretation.

Style is defined as *the communicator's choice of available options in the manner and use of language.* There are many possible choices open to an advocate, both in the language (words, sentences, arguments) and in the manner in which it is stated (delivery, tone, attitude). In theory, there could be as many "styles" as there are individuals, although we must remember that there are real limits to the number of possible stylistic choices available to anyone in a given situation. Not all stylistic options are regarded as equally good. A great deal depends on the individual's personality, and on the communication situation involved. It is possible to make better or worse choices for expressing your ideas. Debate is a specific arena for developing an awareness and mastery of an effective and appropriate style.

Written vs. Oral Style

Debate, as a communication activity, uses both oral and written language. Academic debate, as a system, is designed to emphasize written forms of language. Debaters are required to find documentary sources of evidence (books and magazines, newspapers, journals, government publications) and to extract verbatim quotations to use in contests. Yet the debate contests themselves are designed to be presented orally to a listening audience or decision maker.

It is important to recognize that there are some distinct differences between oral and written language forms. The debater who understands these differences can gain some major advantages over an opponent who fails to see them. The dual emphasis on spoken and written forms of language in debate can result in serious problems in communicating.

Consider the skills of oral communication and written communication from the standpoint of learning theory. Oral communication is learned by an infant through imitation. Babies begin to imitate the words they hear their parents saying—"Mama," "wa-wa" for "water," etc. The physical processes of speaking (making sounds with the voice) and listening (taking in sounds via the ears) are accomplished in specific locales in the brain.

In comparison, consider the process of learning the skills of reading and writing. Children are taught the skills of reading and writing in the formal schoolroom environment. The process begins several years after the child has already developed oral communication skills. Reading is taught as an internal, mental process of looking at combinations of letters on a printed page and interpreting them to mean certain words. Likewise, physical writing skill involves taking a pencil in hand and drawing letters on a blank sheet for others to read and interpret.

As learning progresses, acquisition of oral and written communication skills takes place in separate and distinct locations within the brain. There are separate "data banks" for the two sets of vocabularies, grammars, styles, etc., learned through different sense organs at different stages in life. A person's reading, listening, speaking, and writing vocabulary are all different. It is not known to what extent, if any, there is overlap between the oral and written modes of language use.

Debaters who do not realize these simple principles may believe that when they read a manuscript aloud to an audience, they are communicating with that audience. When the manuscript consists of a technical argumentative discourse written in a sophisticated, scholarly prose style, the debater is crossing over between written style (the prose manuscript) and oral style (reading it aloud to listeners). Unless the listeners have the manuscript to read, they will probably not comprehend nearly as much of it as the debater hopes. It is for this reason, as much as for any other, that debate judges keep flow sheets of the debate. They must translate the manuscript into their own printed version which they can process in the correct data banks of their minds.

Written communication presents its message in a step-by-step, sequential arrangement of letters into words, words into phrases and sentences, sentences into paragraphs, etc., which must all be read in the exact order they are printed. For this reason, written language features linear, logical thinking. It is ideally suited for argumentation, which uses linear methods of analyzing the subject matter.

Oral language, on the other hand, uses both the eyes and ears of the listener. While the logic of oral style is much looser, the power of personal presence is more likely to lead the audience to identify with the speaker and his or her message. The communicator does not rely solely on words, but also on nonverbal cues such as voice, eye contact, delivery, etc., to generate shades of meaning not possible in written form. Simultaneously, the speaker uses both verbal and nonverbal communication, all aimed at arousing a certain intended mood or feeling among the audience. Debaters who rely exclusively on written briefs are guilty of disregarding what may be the most appealing aspect of their argumentation to some listeners—the sense of trust and credibility the listener attaches to the speaker.

Oral communication is basically grounded in the immediate personal contact between the speaker and the listener. Speaking and listening are intimately social acts. Two people, the speaker and the listener, must participate and cooperate together for there to be any communication between them. Oral communication is a communal experience. In contrast, written communication is almost exclusively a solitary experience.

Let us mention some of the differences between oral and written style, paying attention to the aspects most relevant to debate.

1. A person's written vocabulary is larger than the spoken vocabulary.
2. A person's reading vocabulary is larger than the listening vocabulary.
3. Oral style is marked by the use of more personal pronouns (such as *I, you, me, we, us, our, they, he, she*) than written style. Probably this characteristic of style is directly related to the learning theory mentioned above. In oral communication, the use of personal pronouns fosters a sense of personal involvement and trust between the speaker and the listener.

4. Oral communication uses more vague and ambiguous terminology than written communication. Probably this is a function of the different oral and written vocabulary levels. When speaking, advocates use imprecise and ambiguous terms to refer to quantity ("some," "many," "a lot"). When writing, the advocate is more likely to use precise quantification terms ("42 percent," "657,444," "an F value of 3.23, which is significant at the 0.01 level.")

Other aspects of the message are also made more ambiguous in oral communication. A speaker is much more likely to insert words which make the message more conditional and less definite. A speaker is likely to say "I think" or "I feel" before making a claim. A speaker is likely to insert qualifying words like "perhaps," "often," etc., before drawing a conclusion or asserting a claim.

5. Advocates use shorter, simpler sentences when speaking than when writing. When writing a message, a person is much more likely to use complex sentences which include dependent clauses (such as "when writing a message," and "which include dependent clauses" in this sentence). When speaking, you are more likely to stick to the simple "subject-verb-object" sentence structure.

6. Written communication uses more complete idea development, including documentation of sources of evidence used in arguments. A common problem shared by most students enrolled in a course in the fundamentals of public speaking, for instance, is their inability to use evidence sources orally. Most of these students would have no problem with knowing how to handle source material in written form, in their essays and term papers, etc.

7. The formality, impersonality, and precision of written style combine to give an academic tone to a written message. On the other hand, the informality and ambiguity of oral style go to make a spoken message seem more human and conversational. To cross styles over between these two modes can lead to communication problems. To present a written manuscript orally to an audience seems academic, stuffy and dull. Obviously, some merger of the strengths of oral style and written style must be sought for effective debating. It is essential that the debater *appear* to be extemporaneous and personal in tone, even though many hours may have been devoted to research and preparation of arguments in writing.

Here are some suggestions for more effective advocacy. Assuming that debates are presented orally to audiences and/or decision makers who are physically present and listening to the debaters, the advocate should integrate as much oral style as possible into the message. Only quoted excerpts from written documents used as evidence *must* be given verbatim in their written style. All the rest can be adapted to the needs of the listener.

The main points or contentions of the case can be written in oral form by using short and simple sentence structures which feature active verb forms. If there are several lines of analysis involved in the argumentation, rhetorical devices such as parallel structure and alliterative phrasing will help the listener remember what is said.

Throughout the presentation, the advocate should use personal, conversational language such as personal pronouns. In some situations, it may be appropriate to refer to the listeners or the decision makers by name. When the advocate presents a complex argument, it helps listeners to pay closer attention when they feel personally included in the speaker's message.

During the initial stages of composing the cases and arguments, one effective technique for making the advocate's style less "essayish" is to avoid using the tools of writing. Instead, try dictating your ideas into a tape recorder. Then, transcribe what you said. A manuscript written as you actually talk to people, rather than how you write your ideas down, will sound conversational when it is read aloud.

Economy of Words and Phrases

Debate challenges the advocate to present a large number of arguments in a finite time limit. For this reason, debate places a higher premium on word economy than many other persuasive or rhetorical situations.

As we saw in chapter 13, time is most severely limited in rebuttals. Every second counts. For instance, if a case initially has three main arguments, each with three lines of analysis, then there are nine lines of argument to extend in the rebuttal. If the opponent makes three arguments against each of them, the rebuttal load escalates to 27 points.

If each outlined point is stated in sentences of 15 words, the debater must use 405 words just to state the 27 statements of lines of analysis. Time can be saved by economical phrasing. Use shorter tag lines or argument labels in the rebuttals. If an argument can be condensed to an average of five-word tag lines in the rebuttal instead of fifteen-word statements, the debater can save a lot of time. In this hypothetical example, ten words multiplied by 27 arguments saved a total of 270 words. If you speak about 150 words per minute, in a five-minute rebuttal you would save almost two minutes of speaking time.

Another suggestion for achieving word economy is to edit lengthy evidence cards. Extract only a sentence or two from a given source for actual presentation during a debate. To avoid the risk of distorting the evidence used in this manner, record the complete text of the evidence in full on the index card or brief. However, for the purpose of reading it orally, only the salient statements are used. To indicate the parts to be read, highlight them so that the context of the evidence remains clearly available.

As to what to edit, current practice in academic debate permits omission of extraneous sentences, and deletion of extraneous verbiage within statements, as long as the intended sense of the source's evidence is retained. A rule of thumb: If the author were asked to verify that the evidence had been quoted correctly, is there anything in the manner of editing the evidence that would cause the author to say that it was misquoted, quoted out of context, or the meaning was distorted?

DELIVERY SKILLS IN DEBATE

Since debate is a contest in oral argumentation, debaters must develop their delivery skills. Mastery of speaking skills is a complex and difficult goal. Effective speech delivery, even limited to the most rudimentary speaker's behaviors and motor skills, cannot be achieved in a lesson or two. Space limits do not allow us more than a few suggestions aimed at some of the unique features of debate. Delivery skills are divided into vocal and nonverbal elements.

Vocal Skills

Vocalization is the production of audible sounds by intoning the flow of air through the mouth and nasal passages. There are several variables of the human voice which the speaker can control: rate, pitch, quality, and volume. Debaters tend to develop these vocal variables in ways that are suited to the competitive arena, but are not transferable to more ordinary speaking situations.

These vocal variables all work together, of course. It is next to impossible to change one without influencing the others. Unfortunately, if a debater is guilty of abusing any of these variables, he or she will probably violate more than one. For instance, if a debater speaks unintelligibly due to excessive rate, chances are the debater will probably be too loud, too high pitched, and too shrill, all at the same time.

Yet it is possible to work on each variable separately. Improvement in only one vocal area due to conscious effort results in corresponding improvement in other variables out of sympathetic responses. For instance, a conscientious effort to lower one's pitch also results in reducing one's volume.

Rate. Vocal rate simply means the number of words the speaker articulates during the available time. Debaters cultivate a much faster rate than other speakers do. Speaking rate is the most obvious speaking variable that seems to be unique to debating, though it is not the most important one. The impulse to speak more rapidly is due to a number of factors. Debaters have more issues to cover than the limited time allows. Debaters can gain strategic advantages if they make more arguments than their opponents can cover, i.e., by talking faster than their opponents.

A fast speaking rate is neither desirable nor undesirable in and of itself. The faster the sustained rate, however, the harder it is for listeners to comprehend. Speaking rate should be matched to the audience's listening rate. There is a boundary line between comprehensible and incomprehensible speech. Intelligibility is a frequent casualty of the speaker who tries to go too fast. As mentioned in chapter 13, a good rule of thumb is to present your constructive speeches at about 70–80 percent of your optimal speech rate for a debate. Remember, you will have to present rebuttal arguments later on the basis of what you have laid out in your constructive speech. By this strategy, when you need to increase your speech rate during the rebuttal, you can cover all the points without sacrificing your intelligibility.

Moreover, a study by Vasilius has shown that debaters who speak faster than their opponents do not necessarily cover more arguments. She content-analyzed the transcripts of several debates and found that, although some debaters managed to achieve a speaking rate of more words per minute, they did so by the simple expediency of repeating meaningless jargon phrases.[5]

Pitch. Speakers have, on the average, a range of almost two full octaves in pitch. (Trained singers may have a three octave range or more.) The optimum speaking pitch is within the midrange between your highest and lowest comfortable pitch.

The problem some debaters have with pitch is that of using a basic monotone, or constant pitch level, throughout their speeches. That pitch level is often near the top of their range, i.e., a high pitch level, stimulated by the excitement of the debate. An extremely high pitch is not pleasant. Debaters who habitually speak in high pitched voices may slip into a nasal quality along with it, and create an impression of being shrill and even hysterical.

The remedy is to aim for more overall variety in oral pitch. Variations in pitch should designate points of emphasis in the speech. No speech should be presented at a constant pitch level, either high or low. Speakers whose pitch is habitually too high may need to consult a speech therapist for individual help in overcoming this problem.

Volume and Projection.   Debaters seldom have a problem of too little volume to be heard. The opposite may be true. In the heat of a championship debate tournament, the noise may reach record decibel levels. A visitor who walks down the halls of a classroom building which is being used for debates will receive a predominant impression that everyone is shouting at once. A faculty member interrupted a debate to tell the debaters to tone down their speaking because he could not concentrate on his work in his office — because of their shouting through the solid plaster walls of the classroom.

Vocal projection is not so much a matter of sheer volume as it is the breath control of vocal production. Vocal force is produced by breathing deeply from the diaphragm, rather than from more shallow chest breathing. Over the course of a tournament, debaters may strain their voices by failing to understand how to project their voices without shouting.

Vocal Quality.   The variable of vocal quality refers to the "voice print" of resonance and tone which identifies your voice as unique. Some positive descriptions of vocal quality include warm, friendly, melodious, deep, authoritative, bright, lively, sharp, and beautiful. Some negative descriptions include nasal, thick, dull, dead, breathy, harsh, raspy, wimpy, thin, shrill, whiny, tentative, and obnoxious.

The debater's goal is to develop an aura of credibility by sounding authoritative and trustworthy. Female debaters have to be aware of some potential vocal faults that male debaters typically need not worry about. On one hand, the vocal pattern of using upward (questioning) inflections at the ends of words that are not questions sounds tentative. A weak, high-pitched voice signals insecurity. Tentativeness and insecurity create a negative image that invites judges to vote for the other side.

On the other hand, the vocal pattern of aggression, firmness, and loudness, combined with combative nonverbal delivery cues, create an obnoxious impression which is unattractive to the listener. Male and female debaters are seldom judged on the same standards when it comes to exhibiting these traits. In particular, male debaters may be regarded as simply being forceful for using the types of forceful vocal cues for which female debaters are often criticized.

Probably the single most irritating negative vocal quality in both male and female debaters is nasality. In most instances, nasal vocal tones are easily corrected by becoming aware of the proper techniques for generating vocal quality, and by practicing those techniques with simple vocal drills.

Articulation and Pronunciation.   Debaters should strive for crisp, clear articulation and correct pronunciation. Articulation refers to the distinct enunciation of all the sounds and syllables that make up words and phrases. Articulation problems arise as a direct function of an excessively fast speaking rate. When sounds and syllables are omitted during articulation of words, the result is a run-together, garbled, unintelligible statement.

Pronunciation refers to the proper way a word should sound. Debaters should know the correct pronunciation of all the words in their case, particularly of the words most crucial to their arguments, or which appear most frequently in their cases. Debaters should also know the correct pronunciation of the proper names of the sources they cite. In a political science lecture, the lecturer continually referred to Rousseau as "Row-Sue." Incorrect pronunciation such as that can have a devastating effect on a debater's image of credibility. It only takes a little effort to look up the correct pronunciation and master it.

Emphasis and Variety.   Mastery of the vocal variables of rate, pitch, volume, and vocal quality can be used to manipulate the relative emphasis you give to key words, ideas, and arguments. A monotonous debater is a dull debater. In many debate rounds, however, a uniform level of pacing, intensity, pitch, and tone is apparently contagious among all the speakers. It only requires small, subtle distinctions in speech to set you apart from the others. For example, you can vary your rate by simply inserting dramatic pauses at the conclusion of each major point in your argument. Consider the difference in the impression made by these two affirmative debaters, Dave and Joan:

> **Dave:**   ". . . and so, you can see that this disadvantage turns around. It is a reason to vote for affirmative. Go now to the top of the case and consider the arguments my partner made. Begin with the case overview . . ."

> **Joan:**   ". . . and so, you can see that this disadvantage **turns around**. */pause a beat/* It is **a reason to vote for affirmative**. */pause a couple of beats/* Go now to the **top of the case** and consider the arguments my partner made. Begin with the case overview. */pause to make sure that everyone is following your transition before continuing/* . . ."

In Dave's rebuttal, he made the same points Joan made, but he gave equal emphasis to all of them. Joan's dramatic pauses made the points about the importance of the turnaround stand out, and they also invited the listeners to keep up with her as she made the transition between major sections of the argumentation. Which debater, Dave or Joan, appears to make the most favorable impact on the listeners?

Likewise, the judicious use of pitch and volume variations can serve to emphasize key words, phrases, sources, and arguments. These are the ways you can provide "vocal punctuation" to your arguments. Subtle variations in rate, volume, and pitch are the ways you create the commas, question marks, underlining, etc., for the listener. They make the difference between dynamism and dullness.

All of these suggestions are tailored to the debate situation, and not to general rhetorical communication. They are consistent with traditional rhetorical principles, and it is within your ability to control and modify them if necessary. If it is within your power to control the effectiveness of your speaking, why choose to be an ineffective speaker? Any debater can develop better vocal patterns.

Our aim in presenting these suggestions is to enable you to improve the intelligibility of your speaking during a debate, and to enhance the authoritativeness with which you present your material. If you can develop these traits, you will have two great advantages in debate.

Delivery: Nonverbal Elements

In addition to the vocal aspects of debate delivery, it is important to consider the effects of nonverbal delivery elements. Nonverbal communication can facilitate or hamper the debater's image of credibility. We will now discuss the contest trappings, eye contact, posture, movement, and gestures. In addition, we shall discuss the techniques of handling materials such as evidence cards and flow pads.

Trappings.   Debates take place within a certain milieu or environment, which always provides some guidance as to what is expected of the debaters. In the Oxford Union in England, debates sometimes require the speakers to wear tuxedos and formal evening dress. Televised political debates call for conservatively tailored business wear for both men and women. Intercollegiate and interscholastic tournaments are relatively casual, considering that rarely is there a public audience present. A rule of thumb is that, if there is an audience for a debate, say a noon debate held at the Rotarians' meeting, the debaters should wear business suits, or a slightly more dressy choice of clothing. Do not underdress for a debate, but do not overdress either.

The ideal room arrangement for a debate is to provide tables and chairs for all participants, a lectern with ample desk surface to hold reference materials during the speeches, and sufficient chairs for all observers. If it is a public debate, nameplates should be provided for each debater's table. If a sound amplification system is required, there should be enough microphones placed strategically so that all who need to speak at once may have instant access.

The debaters should begin the debate at the scheduled time. Place all reference materials where they can be reached during the debate. Arrange the scene as you need it. The tactic of making a late, dramatic entrance for some imagined one-upmanship advantage is sure to boomerang. At the end of the debate, retrieve and pack all your materials, and congratulate the opposing team. Do not continue arguing with opponents over points brought up during the debate.

If yours is a public debate, remain in your place and be prepared to field audience questions. Be gracious throughout the event, particularly when interacting with members of the audience. Do not leave until the moderator has adjourned the meeting.

In addition to the trappings, there are several important facets to understand about your delivery during the debate.

Eye Contact.   The single most important element in isolation for establishing a sense of personal connection between the judge and the advocate is eye contact. This is a very difficult skill to master in debates. There is a built-in bias toward using a great deal of printed matter, from the evidence cards and the briefs written in advance to the hand-written flow sheets of the ongoing issues during the round.

The debater must develop the ability to work within the constraints of extensive written materials without losing the ability to keep a relatively high degree of personal eye contact. Some situations are better suited to the informal, direct style than others. During cross-examination, debaters should face the decision maker, not each other.

A simple device for maintaining the illusion of eye contact, if not the reality, is to hold your materials at a level—chest high or higher—so that your face and eyes are always visible to the audience. This practice is in contrast with the common habit of placing all materials on the lectern, or worse, on a side table, and then bending over them to read from them at length. The only view the audience ever gets of the debater is the top of the head. Holding up the materials facilitates more actual eye contact with the audience. It permits a more constant surveillance of what the audience or judge may be doing. Sometimes it may be that listeners want to provide some sort of feedback, but they are frustrated if you are not watching them at all times.

Posture.   The ideal posture is to stand erect. Distribute your weight evenly on both feet. Assume an alert, forward orientation of the body toward the audience. This ideal posture is honored in the breach more often than in actual practice. It is not difficult to describe the violations of good posture rules. Jack and Ruth Kay have described some of the awkward postures debaters have used during their debates. Some debaters are like the flamingo, with all their weight perched on one foot. Some debaters speak from the stance of the vulture, head hunched over the flow pad and outstretched arms flapping.[6] To the list could be added other negative images, such as the clinging vine who leans against the lectern with his or her weight perched on one foot.

Debaters often have little concept of the appearance they present to the judge when they speak from such inappropriate postures. None of these stances is particularly comfortable or natural. Other things being equal, the debater who appears to be poised and authoritative will generate a higher ethos or source credibility. Good posture is a key component of a speaker's image.

Movement and Gestures.   The traditional advice given to speakers by teachers of public address concerning the use of movement and gestures also applies generally to debaters. Gestures should be used, along with vocal inflections and eye contact, as a means to emphasize key words and ideas. Gestures indicate transitions between points. Whatever gestures are used should be definite, followed through, executed at chest or eye level (not at the belt line or below), and spontaneous in appearance.

Negative or undesirable movements and gestures are any which unnecessarily distract from the message. Whenever any mannerisms interfere with your communication, work to eliminate them. Do not hold a pen or pencil in your hand and gesture with it while speaking. Keep your hands out of your pockets; do not rattle your keys or coins while speaking. Do not pace like a caged lion while speaking. Do not fidget nervously with your hair or clothing. All of these and similar distracting mannerisms may be unconscious devices to combat inner tensions and nervousness. It is better to replace them with deliberately planned, consciously executed gestures and movements that serve the same purpose of discharging pent-up energy, but that also serve your need to communicate effectively.

Handling Materials. Debaters must use a great deal of material during a speech, including flow pads. Prepared argument briefs and evidence cards can become jumbled and disorganized in the course of several debates. It is very important to learn the most effective methods of handling materials in view of the time pressure during the speech itself. The materials need to be in compact form for easy handling. They need to be arranged in a logical sequence.

First, the flow sheet itself should be the "road map" to the use of all other materials. It contains your outline of everything you have contended, along with your opponents' replies. Presumably, you will follow that outline as you extend your arguments and refute your opponents. But these prospective extensions and refutations will only help you if you have them in an organized and useable form.

It helps, initially, to consolidate your prepared blocks, briefs, or packets of evidence cards into unitary entities corresponding to major points on your flow sheet. If you have your prepared arguments on sheets, mount them in clear plastic carriers on which you can write with nonpermanent markers. If you use note cards, clip them together under a "table of contents" cover sheet. Whatever you can do to reduce the number of separate pieces of paper you have to handle during your speech will help. Searching and fumbling through cluttered materials as you speak will hurt your fluency and your credibility.

When you arrange your materials to use during your rebuttal, code each point on the flow pad with a number or abbreviation to indicate which piece of material you need to use in connection with that point. Before you speak, place your materials on the lectern or side table in the exact sequence you intend to use them. Then, as you speak, pick up only the piece of material you need to support the argument you are making. Do not attempt to hold all of your material in your hands at once. As you complete an argument, return it to the side of your work surface, and place it face down so you will not be tempted to pick it up again. At the end of your speech, all your material will be stacked face down in the exact order in which you referred to it in your speech.

On the affirmative, it is very useful to type a "strip flow" of your own case. A strip flow consists of an outline of each of the points in your case along a narrow strip of paper which can be clipped to a fresh flow sheet before each debate. Using a strip flow lets you avoid having to take down a new outline of your own case during each round of the tournament. This suggestion will pay off during the rebuttals, when you need to be particularly well organized.

EFFECTS OF STYLE AND DELIVERY DURING DEBATE

Other things being equal, the debater who displays skill in style and delivery presents the audience with an image of being prepared and knowledgeable. Conversely, the debater whose style is incorrect or dull, and whose delivery techniques are awkward and ineffective, appears to the audience to be unprepared and incompetent. These impressions make a difference in their willingness to believe the debater, and they do influence the final outcome of the debate, favorably or unfavorably.

The debater who is more fluent will be more comprehensible than the debater who is not. The factor of fluency will actually enable the debater to cover somewhat more ground than a less fluent debater. Style and delivery techniques have a great bearing on the degree of fluency and comprehensibility the debater can achieve, which in turn influences the outcome of the debate.

The personal credibility of the debater is influenced by his or her command of language. The debater who mispronounces key words, and who uses incorrect grammar, slang and substandard language, is shooting himself in the foot. Listeners who are distracted by how a person talks do not pay much attention to what the person is saying.

In general, the debater's mastery of style and delivery techniques enhances his or her authoritativeness. Debate is a laboratory for teaching students how to communicate arguments effectively to a variety of audiences. The forms of style and delivery most effective in debate are marks of leadership.

COMMON PROBLEMS TO AVOID IN DEBATE STYLE

Incomprehensibility

In every year's Judging Philosophy Booklets distributed at the National Debate Tournament (NDT), all judges who address the topic of style and delivery state that they will refuse to vote for an argument which is not intelligible when presented. They will not ask to see copies of the evidence to decipher anything that was garbled, cluttered, or confused.

Of course, the NDT admittedly has somewhat more specialized standards for considering what is "comprehensible" than other leagues. The Cross Examination Debate Association demands a more persuasive speaking style as a matter of preference. At the high school level, Lincoln-Douglas debate is designed to emphasize public speaking skills equally with analytical skills.

Comprehensibility is not merely a matter of slowing the rate. It is also a matter of style, organization, and the quality of thought. Some arguments cannot be comprehended, even though they are articulated very slowly and distinctly. Comprehensibility is a function of clear organization and analysis as well as fluency.

Deliberate Misinterpretation of Information

In the effort to win at any cost, some debaters may violate the code of ethics. Distortion or fabrication of evidence subverts the entire basis of debate.

Sarcasm and Disrespect

One of the important objectives of debate is to learn how to be assertive without being obnoxious, and how to be aggressive without being hostile. It is often said that in debate, one learns to disagree without being disagreeable.

Many judges penalize violations of debating etiquette. Some of the more common instances of unacceptable behavior include sarcastic or overbearing treatment of the opponent. Debaters must display courteous and respectful attitudes toward one another. Debate is not a contest of personal intimidation, but of the clash of ideas. The debaters may criticize the arguments and evidence of the opponent, but the tone and content of the criticism must never be directed toward the opponents personally.

During the 1984 televised political debate between Vice President George Bush and Congresswoman Geraldine Ferraro, the first woman in history to participate in the presidential debates, the public was more sensitive than usual to the interpersonal dynamics between the two candidates. Vice President Bush was criticized for his unbecoming behavior to her. He appeared to belittle her credentials for even appearing with him in the debate, when he waived his final rebuttal period to respond to her argument. To another question during the debate, he said he thought he might like to talk about the World Series (which was then in progress). After the debate, he said in a reporter's hearing that he had "kicked a little ass" during the debate. The overall impression he created was of being supercilious and ingratiating toward his opponent.

In contrast to his behavior, Congresswoman Ferraro maintained her dignity and poise. At one point she chided him for seeming to suggest that she could not take a responsible view of defense matters because she was a woman. These differences between the demeanor of the two contenders for the Vice Presidency were enough to lead many to feel that she had clearly won their debate, without even considering the substance of their comments on the issues raised by the panelists. This example is instructive, because it demonstrates the impact your debate etiquette (or lack of it) can have on the decision maker.

Be aware that judges do not take kindly to instances of disrespect which you indicate toward them. Act professionally during a debate toward the event, the opponents, your partner, and the audience, and you will be treated reciprocally.

Insincerity

Your ethos, the credibility you develop can be seriously jeopardized when your comments or your manner seem to indicate a basic insincerity on your part. During cross-examination, debaters sometimes "play dumb" when answering straightforward questions about their position. Although there may be strategic reasons for declining to take a specific position on certain issues, it does look suspicious when they belatedly seem to be crystal clear about them in the rebuttals, after the opponents have no more constructive speeches. The strategy of "granting out" certain arguments in order to take out others (such as admitting that the plan won't work in order to shed a disadvantage, then pulling through a case turnaround as the main justification for voting to adopt the plan) can be taken to such extremes that the judge cannot be sure of what you are advocating from one speech to the next.

Unsportsmanlike Conduct

Don't ruin the event for yourself, your colleagues, your coach, and everyone else concerned by a negative attitude or uncooperative behavior during a debate tournament.

SUMMARY

In this chapter we have discussed debate as a communicative activity. The importance of communication skills in debate cannot be overemphasized. Without communication skills, you cannot persuade your listeners of the soundness of your reasoning, or the relevance of the evidence your research has disclosed. Even though debate is a decision-making tool allied with logic and policy making, it might as well be a mystical process based on palm reading if the debater cannot be understood or believed.

In this chapter, we have explained the crucial importance of adapting the debate to the audience's (or judge's) expectations. Next, we explored the nature of language as it relates to debate. In particular, we explained the differences between ambiguity and vagueness. Much of the debatable controversy arising from policy issues stems from ambiguity of the key terms; in value issues, from vagueness of the key terms. The debater whose interpretation of the meanings of ambiguous and vague terms are accepted as most reasonable is well on the way to winning the debate. Following this preliminary insight, the chapter moved next to a discussion of the elements of style in debate. Of necessity, debate being what it is, our discussion concentrated on the distinctions between oral and written style, and offered practical suggestions for developing a winning communicative style of your own.

Not only must the debater have an effective command of the language, but there must also be a workable delivery system. Much could be said about delivery — indeed, whole courses are devoted to the subject — but our space limits forced us to narrow our focus to a few specific points about vocal and nonverbal elements of communication in debate. Our treatment is consistent with traditional rhetorical principles, considered primarily from the perspective of how to adapt these time-tested principles to debaters' needs. Our approach has been prescriptive, with an effort to balance the negative "thou shalt nots" with positive "thou shalts."

The chapter concluded with a brief encapsulation of the major communication taboos in debate. Five common problems to avoid are incomprehensible speech, ethical violations, disrespect/discourtesy, insincerity, and unsportsmanlike conduct.

Their opposites include making sense; speaking truthfully; engaging your opponents and your listeners with respect rather than as crooks or fools; maintaining your own authenticity and integrity; and exhibiting wholesome zest and enthusiasm for the intellectual game. Those are not bad ideals with which to conclude a chapter on style and delivery, or a book on debate and argumentation.

Notes

[1]James McBath (ed.) *Forensics as Communication: The Argumentative Perspective* (Skokie, IL: National Textbook, 1975) 11.

[2]"Not by Issues Alone," *Time* 12 Nov. 1984: 37.

[3]Monroe C. Beardsley, *Thinking Straight,* 4th ed. (Englewood Cliffs, NJ: Prentice Hall, 1975) 133.

[4]Beardsley, 146.

[5]Janet M. Vasilius and Dan DeStephen, "An Investigation of the Relationship Between Debate Tournament Success and Rate, Evidence and Jargon," *Journal of the American Forensic Association* 15 (1979) 197–204.

[6]Jack Kay and Ruth Kay, "Chapter 1: Style in Debate," Richard Fawcett (ed.) *Welfare Reform: A Preliminary Analysis* (Kansas City: National Federation of State High School Associations, 1984).

BIBLIOGRAPHY

1. APPROACHES TO DEBATE.

A. General Works.

Cox, J. Robert. "A Study of Judging Philosophies of the Participants of the National Debate Tournament." *Journal of the American Forensic Association,* 11 (Fall 1974) 61–71.

> The first systematic study of the nature of judging philosophies. It includes a brief discussion of the major judging paradigms.

Rowland, Robert C. "Debate Paradigms: A Critical Examination," in *Dimensions of Argument: Proceedings of the Second Annual Summer Conference on Argumentation,* George W. Ziegelmueller and Jack Rhodes, eds. Annandale, VA: Speech Communication Association, October 15, 1981, pp. 448–475.

> Critically evaluates the stock issues, policy making, and hypothesis testing paradigms.

"Special Forum: Debate Paradigms." *Journal of the American Forensic Association,* 18 (Winter 1982), 133–160. (contains five articles of debate paradigms: Robert C. Rowland, "Standards for Paradigm Evaluation"; David Zarefsky, "The Perils of Assessing Paradigms"; Allan J. Lichtman and Daniel M. Rohrer, "Policy Dispute and Paradigm Evaluation: A Response to Rowland"; Walter Ulrich, "Flexibility in Paradigm Evaluation"; and Robert C. Rowland, "The Primacy of Standards for Paradigm Evaluation: A Rejoinder.")

> Rowland attempts to develop standards for evaluating judging paradigms. These standards are critically evaluated by a representative of three of the policy making, hypothesis testing, and *tabula rasa* judging paradigms.

B. Policy Making.

"Forum on Policy Systems Analysis." David A Thomas, editor. *Journal of the American Forensic Association,* 22 (Winter 1986), 123–166. (Includes Robert C. Rowland, "The Relationship between Realism and Debatability in Policy Advocacy"; William L. Benoit, Steve R. Wilson, and Vince Follert, "Decision Rules for the Policy Metaphor"; Allan J. Lichtman, "Competing Models of the Debate Process"; William Reynolds, "Harms and Benefits: A Reappraisal"; and Jerome R. Corsi, "The Continuing Evolution of Policy Systems Debate: An Assessment and a Look Ahead.")

> Issue devoted to an evaluation and expansion of policy making as an approach to judging debate.

Hynes, Thomas J. "Can We Save Policy Making?" *Argument in Transition: Proceedings of the Third Summer Conference on Argumentation,* David Zarefsky, Malcolm Sillars, and Jack Rhodes, eds. Annandale, VA: Speech Communication Association, 1983, pp. 756–771.

Attempts to defend policy making against attacks from its critics.

Klumpp, James F.; Brock, Bernard L.; Chesebro, James W.; and Cragan, John F. "Implications of a Systems Model of Analysis on Argumentation Theory." *Journal of the American Forensic Association,* 11 (Summer 1974), 1–7.

A concise summary of some of the major parts of their book.

Lichtman, Allan J., and Rohrer, Daniel M. "The Logic of Policy Dispute." *Journal of the American Forensic Association,* 16 (Spring 1980), 236–247.

An excellent introduction to policy making, developed in more detail in the next two articles.

Lichtman, Allan J.; Rohrer, Daniel M.; and Corsi, Jerome. "Policy Systems Analysis in Debate." In *Advanced Debate: Readings in Practice and Teaching,* David A. Thomas and Jack Hart, eds. Lincolnwood, IL: National Textbook Company, 1987, pp. 216–230.

Lichtman, Allan J.; Rohrer, Daniel M.; and Hart, Jack. "Policy Systems Revisited." In *Advanced Debate: Readings in Practice and Teaching,* David A. Thomas and Jack Hart, eds. Lincolnwood, IL: National Textbook Company, 1987, pp. 231–240.

C. Hypothesis Testing.

"Special Forum: The Hypothesis Testing Paradigm." *Journal of the American Forensic Association,* 19 (Winter 1983), 158–190. (contains four articles on hypothesis testing: Jerome R. Corsi, "Zarefsky's Theory of Debate as Hypothesis Testing: A Critical Re-Examination"; Thomas A. Hollihan, "Conditional Arguments and the Hypothesis Testing Paradigm: A Negative View"; David Zarefsky and Bill Henderson, "Hypothesis Testing in Theory and Practice" [Response to Hollihan]; and Thomas A. Hollihan, "Conditional Arguments and the Hypothesis Testing Paradigm: A Negative Rebuttal.")

These articles (Zarefsky and Henderson) attempt to defend hypothesis testing against the attacks raised in the other articles.

Ulrich, Walter. "An Ad Hominem Examination of Hypothesis Testing as a Paradigm for Evaluation of Argument." *Journal of the American Forensic Association,* 21 (Summer 1984), 1–8.

Argues that hypothesis testing is internally inconsistent.

Ulrich, Walter. "Further Reflections on Hypothesis Testing: A Rejoinder." *Journal of the American Forensic Association,* 21 (Summer 1984), 14–15.

An extension of the previous article.

Zarefsky, David, "Argument as Hypothesis Testing," In *Advanced Debate: Readings in Practice and Teaching,* David A. Thomas and Jack Hart, eds. Lincolnwood, IL: National Textbook Company, 1987 *Advanced Debate,* 1979, pp. 427–437.

The best available introduction to hypothesis testing.

Zarefsky, David. "Reflections on Hypothesis Testing in Response to Ulrich." *Journal of the American Forensic Association,* 21 (Summer 1984), 9–13.

Answers the attacks on hypothesis testing raised by Ulrich in this section.

D. *Tabula Rasa.*

Dempsey, Richard H., and Hartmann, David J. "Emergent Voting Criteria and Judicial Impotence of Critics." *Journal of the American Forensic Association,* 22 (Winter 1986), 167–175.

Critical of the *tabula rasa* approach to judging debates.

Rowland, Robert C. "*Tabula Rasa:* The Relevance of Debate to Argumentation Theory." *Journal of the American Forensic Association,* 21 (Fall 1984), 76–88.

Suggests that the *tabula rasa* approach to judging debates leads to poor debate.

Ulrich, Walter. "Debate as Dialectic: A Defense of the *Tabula Rasa* Approach to Judging." *Journal of the American Forensic Association,* 21 (Fall 1984), 89–93.

A response to the previous article.

Ulrich, Walter. "In Search of *Tabula Rasa,*" in *Advanced Debate: Readings in Practice and Teaching,* David A. Thomas and Jack Hart, eds. Lincolnwood, IL: National Textbook Company, 1987, pp. 183–190.

Outlines the justification for the *tabula rasa* approach to judging: a view of debate that the judge should apply to debate the standards developed in an individual round.

E. Other Approaches to Judging.

Balthrop, Bill. "The Debate Judge as 'Critic of Argument': Toward a Transcendent Perspective," *Journal of the American Forensic Association,* 20 (Summer 1983), pp. 1–15.

Very influential article, which suggests that a judge should take an active role in evaluating arguments.

Rowland, Robert C. "The Debate Judge as Debate Judge: A Functional Paradigm." *Journal of the American Forensic Association,* 20 (Summer 1984), 183–193.

> Suggests that guidelines for debate should be developed to fit the unique nature of the debate activity

Snider, Alfred C. "Games Without Frontiers: A Design for Communication Scholars and Forensic Educators." *Journal of the American Forensic Association,* 20 (Winter 1984), 162–170.

> Develops a view of debate drawn from the theoretical work in gaming.

2. TOPICALITY

Herbeck, Dale, and Katsulas, John. "The Affirmative Topicality Burden: Any Reasonable Example of the Resolution." *JAFA,* (Winter 1985), pp. 133–145.

> Defends the reasonability standard of topicality and also attacks counter warrants.

Parson, Donn W. "On 'Being Reasonable': The Last Refuge of Scoundrels." In *Dimensions of Argument: Proceedings of the Second Summer Conference on Argumentation,* George W. Ziegelmueller and Jack Rhodes, eds. Annandale, VA: Speech Communication Association, October 15, 1981, pp. 532–543.

> Attacks the reasonability standard of topicality.

Parson, Donn W., and Bart, John. "On 'Being Reasonable': The Last Refuge of Scoundrels: Part II: The Scoundrels Strike Back." *Advanced Debate: Readings in Practice and Teaching,* David A. Thomas and Jack Hart, eds. Lincolnwood, IL: National Textbook Company, 1987, pp. 130–138.

> An extension and clarification of the previous article.

Unger, James J. "Topicality: Why Not the Best?" *Rostrum,* 56 (October, 1981), 5–9. In *AD,* pp. 139–143.

> The "best" defense of the better definition standard of topicality.

3. AFFIRMATIVE APPROACHES.

Cox, J. Robert. "Attitudinal Inherency: Implications for Policy Debate." *Southern Speech Communication Association,* 40 (Winter 1975), 158–168.

> Explores some of the problems facing affirmative teams claiming attitudinal inherency.

Goodnight, Tom; Balthrop, Bill; and Parson, Donn W. "The Problem of Inherency: Strategy and Substance." *Journal of the American Forensic Association,* 10 (Spring 1974), 229–240.

> Excellent discussion of the nature of inherency.

Kruger, Arthur. "The Inherent Need: Further Clarification." *Journal of the American Forensic Association,* 2 (September 1965), 109–119.

> A discussion of the justifications for inherency.

Lichtman, Allan; Garvin, Charles; and Corsi, Jerry. "The Alternative Justification Affirmative: A New Case Form." *Journal of the American Forensic Association,* 10 (Fall 1973), 59–69.

> Discusses the theoretical justifications for the alternative justification case.

Ling, David, and Seltzer, Robert V. "The Role of Attitudinal Inherency in Contemporary Debate." *Journal of the American Forensic Association,* 7 (Spring 1971), 278–283.

> Examines some of the limitations on attitudinal inherency.

Schunk, John. "A Farewell to 'Structural Change': The Cure for Pseudo-Inherency." *Journal of the American Forensic Association,* 14 (Winter 1978), 144–149.

> Argues that the affirmative team does not need to demonstrate that its plan will not be adopted.

Zarefsky, David. "The 'Traditional Case'—'Comparative Advantages Case' Dichotomy: Another Look." *Journal of the American Forensic Association,* 6 (Winter 1969), 12–20.

> Argues that both the traditional case and the comparative advantage cases have similar burdens.

Zarefsky, David. "The Role of Causal Argument in Policy Controversies." *Journal of the American Forensic Association,* 14 (Spring 1977), 179–191.

> Examines the nature of causal arguments in policy debates.

4. NEGATIVE APPROACHES.

Pfau, Michael. "The Present System Revisited: Part One: Incremental Change." *Journal of the American Forensic Association,* 17 (Fall 1980), 80–84.

> Develops the strategic and logical advantages of defending incremental changes in the present system.

Pfau, Michael. "The Present System Revisited: Part Two: Policy Interrelationships." *Journal of the American Forensic Association,* 17 (Winter 1981), 146–154.

> Discusses the many effects policies have on the political and social system.

5. COUNTERPLANS.

Gass, Robert H., Jr. "On Fiat Power," *Advanced Debate: Readings in Practice and Teaching,* David A. Thomas and Jack Hart, eds. Lincolnwood, IL: National Textbook Company, 1987, pp. 280–288.

Attacks Ulrich's position that the negative team is limited to the agent specified in the resolution.

Herbeck, Dale A. "A Permutation Standard of Competitiveness." *Journal of the American Forensic Association,* 22 (Summer 1985), 12–19. In *AD,* pp. 254–263.

Excellent discussion of permutations.

Hynes, Thomas J. "Study: Hope or False Promise." *Journal of the American Forensic Association,* 17 (Winter 1980), 192–198.

Critical evaluation of the study counterplan.

Hynes, Thomas J., Jr. "The Studies Counterplan—Still Hoping—A reply to Shelton." *Journal of the American Forensic Association,* (Winter 1985), 156–160. In *AD,* pp. 273–279.

An extension of his attacks on study counterplans.

Kaplow, Louis. "Rethinking Counterplans: A Reconciliation with Debate The-ory." *Journal of the American Forensic Association,* XVII (Spring 1981), 215–226.

Excellent discussion of the nature of counterplans.

Mayer, Michael. "Epistemological Considerations of the Studies Counterplan." *Journal of the American Forensic Association,* 19 (Spring 1983), 261–266.

An attack of the studies counterplan.

Shelton, Michael W. "In Defense of the Studies Counterplan." *Journal of the American Forensic Association,* (Winter 1985), 150–155.

An attempt to defend the desirability of the study counterplan.

Ulrich, Walter. "The Agent in Argument: Toward a Theory of Fiat." *Debate Issues,* XV (November, 1981), 5–7.

Argues that the negative team cannot counterplan using an agent other than the one specified in the resolution.

Ulrich, Walter. "Limitations on the Options Available to the Evaluator of Policy." *Advanced Debate: Readings in Practice and Teaching,* David A. Thomas and Jack Hart, eds. Lincolnwood, IL: National Textbook Company, 1987.

Response to Gass's article.

Unger, James J. "Investigating the Investigators: A Study of the Study Counter-plan," *Debate Issues,* 12 (February, 1979), 1–8.

The first article explaining and defending the study counterplan.

6. COUNTER WARRANTS.

Hynes, Thomas J., and Ulrich, Walter. "The Role of Propositions in Forensic Argument." *Argument and Social Practice: Proceedings of the Fourth SCA/AFA*

Conference on Argumentation, Robert J. Cox, Malcolm Sillars, and Gregg Walker, eds. Annandale, VA: Speech Communication Association, 1985, pp. 827–840.

> Suggests that whether or not counter warrants are justified depends on the wording of the resolution.

Keeshan, Marjorie, and Ulrich, Walter. "A Critique of the Counter-Warrant as a Negative Strategy." *Journal of the American Forensic Association,* 16 (Winter, 1980), 199–203.

> First major response to the theory of counter warrants.

Paulsen, James W., and Rhodes, Jack. "The Counterwarrant as a Negative Strategy: A Modest Proposal." *Journal of the American Forensic Association,* 15 (Spring 1979), 220–227. In *AD,* pp. 156–164.

> The first defense of the theory of counter warrants.

7. VALUE DEBATE.

Matlon, Ronald J. "Debating Propositions of Value." *Journal of the American Forensic Association* 14 (Spring, 1978), 194–204. In *AD,* pp. 394–407.

> The first major article to discuss the nature of value debate resolutions.

Rowland, Robert C. "The Philosophical Presuppositions of Value Debate." In *Argument in Transition: Proceedings of the Third Summer Conference on Argumentation,* David Zarefsky, Malcolm Sillars, and Jack Rhodes, eds. Annandale, VA: Speech Communication Association, 1983, pp. 822–836.

> Defends the use of examples to test value statements and compares policy resolutions to value resolutions.

Warnick, Barbara. "Arguing Value Propositions." *Journal of the American Forensic Association,* 18 (Fall 1981), 109–119.

> Develops standards for debating value resolutions.

Zarefsky, David. "Criteria for Evaluating Non-Policy Argument," *Perspectives on Non-Policy Argument,* Don Brownlee, ed. Wingate, NC: Cross-Examination Debate Association, 1980, pp. 9–16.

> Develops a system of classifying value topics, as well as a system for developing stock issues for these types of topics.

8. TRANSCRIPTS OF DEBATES.

Boaz, John K., and Brey, James R. *1986 Championship Debates and Speeches.* Annandale, VA: Speech Communication Association, 1986.

> From 1967 to 1985, the transcript of the final round of the National Debate Tournament (NDT) was published in the *Journal of the American Forensic Association.* From 1976 on, critiques of the debates were also included.

Beginning in 1986, this material will be published in a separate book, along with the final rounds of CEDA nationals (the college value debate organization) and the first place speeches in selective events at the two college individual events tournaments. This publication includes critiques of these speeches.

Dale Publishing Co., Box 151, Grandview, MO 64030

Dale sells a videotape of the final rounds of the high school National Forensic League tournament.

National Federation of State High School Associations, 11724 Plaza Circle, P.O. Box 20626, Kansas City, MO 64195.

The Federation has sample tapes of debates on the current high school topic.

Bill Henderson, Dept. of Speech, University of Northern Iowa, Cedar Rapids, IA 50613

The University of Northern Iowa has a number of video and audio tapes of sample debates on a variety of topics.

9. BIBLIOGRAPHIES.

Chandler, Robert. "Selected Bibliography on Argumentation and Debate," in *Advanced Debate: Readings in Practice and Teaching,* David A. Thomas and Jack Hart, eds. Lincolnwood, IL: National Textbook Company, 1987. pp. 539–545.

Church, Russell T., and Buckley, David C. "Argumentation and Debating Propositions of Value: A Bibliography" *Journal of the American Forensic Association,* 19 (Spring 1983), pp. 239–250.

Matlon, Ronald J., and Matlon, Irene R., *Index to Journals in Communication Studies Through 1985.* Annandale, VA: Speech Communication Association, 1987.

Ulrich, Walter. "Bibliography of Material on Argumentation and Debate," In *Debating United States Latin American Policy: A Preliminary Analysis,* Kansas City, MO: National Federation of State High School Associations, 1987, (in press).

10. COLLEGE DEBATE TEXTS.

Brock, Bernard L., James W. Chesebro, John F. Cragan, and James F. Klumpp, *Public Policy Decision-Making: Systems Analysis and Comparative Advantages Debate.* New York: Harper & Row, Publishers, 1973.

One of the first works to attempt to apply systems analysis to academic debate.

Church, Russell T., and Wilbanks, Charles. *Values and Policies in Controversy: An Introduction to Argumentation and Debate.* Scottsdale, AZ: Gorsuch Scarisbrick, 1986.

One of the first textbooks to include extensive discussion of value debate.

Ehninger, Douglas, and Wayne Brockriede. *Decision by Debate,* 2nd Edition. New York: Harper & Row, 1978.

More philosophical in nature than most textbooks.

Freeley, Austin J. *Argumentation and Debate: Reasoned Decision Making.* 6th Edition. Belmont, CA: Wadsworth Publishing Company, Inc., 1986.

Takes a traditional approach to academic debate.

Patterson, J. W., and David Zarefsky, *Contemporary Debate.* Boston, MA: Houghton Mifflin Company, 1983.

Approaches debate as a method of testing the truth of the resolution.

Perella, Jack. *The Debate Method of Critical Thinking: An Introduction to Argumentation.* Dubuque, IA: Kendall/Hunt, 1986.

Introductory textbook that emphasizes value debate.

Rybacki, Karyn C., and Rybacki, Donald J. *Advocacy and Opposition.* Englewood Cliffs, NJ: Prentice-Hall, Inc., 1986.

Introductory textbook covering both policy and value debate.

Thomas, David A., and Hart, Jack. *Advanced Debate: Readings in Theory, Practice and Teaching.* 3rd Edition. Lincolnwood, IL: National Textbook Company, 1987.

Contains many of the more influential recent articles on academic debate, including sections on debate paradigms and value debate.

Ulrich, Walter. *Debating About Values: An Introduction to CEDA Debate.* San Francisco, CA: Griffin Research, 1987.

Concentrates exclusively on value debate.

Wood, Stephen, and Midgley, John. *Prima Facie: A Guide to Value Debate.* Dubuque, IA: Kendall/Hunt, 1987.

Emphasizes value debate. Chapters contributed by a number of CEDA debate coaches.

11. BOOKS ON COACHING, JUDGING, AND ADMINISTRATING TOURNAMENTS.

Faules, Don F.; Rieke, Richard D.; and Rhodes, Jack. *Directing Forensics.* Denver, CO: Morton Publishing Co., 1976.

One of the best books on coaching forensics.

Goodnight, G. Thomas, and Zarefsky, David. *Forensic Tournaments: Planning and Administration.* Lincolnwood, IL: National Textbook Company, 1980.

Useful discussion of the mechanics of forensic tournament administration, with an emphasis on debate tournaments.

McBath, James H., ed. *Forensics as Communication: The Argumentative Perspective*. Skokie, IL: National Textbook Company, 1975.

This contains the recommendations (and several papers) from the 1974 Sedalia conference on the future of debate.

Parson, Donn W., ed. *American Forensics in Perspective: Papers from the Second National Conference on Forensics*. Annandale, VA: Speech Communication Association, 1984.

This contains papers and recommendations from the second conference on forensics, including sections on the justification of forensics, ethics, individual events, summer institutes, and similar issues.

Ulrich, Walter. *Debate Paradigms*. San Francisco, CA: Griffin Research, 1987.

Examines the nature of debate paradigms, and discusses the hypothesis testing, stock issues, policy making, and other paradigms.

Ulrich, Walter. *Judging Academic Debate*. Lincolnwood, IL: National Textbook Company, 1986.

Includes chapters, judging paradigms, value debate, evaluating debates, and other judging problems.

12. BOOKS ON INFORMAL LOGIC AND CRITICAL THINKING.

Blair, J. Anthony, and Johnson, Ralph H. *Informal Logic: The First International Symposium*. Inverness, CA: Edgepress, 1980.

Good introduction to the informal logic movement. Includes an extensive bibliography.

Copi, Irving M. *Introduction to Logic,* 6th ed. New York: Macmillan Publishers, 1982.

One of the most popular logic texts. Includes a discussion of fallacies.

Fearnside, W. Ward, and Holther, William B. *Fallacy: The Counterfeit of Argument*. Englewood Cliffs, NJ: Prentice-Hall, 1959.

Includes one of the most comprehensive collections of types of fallacies.

Govier, Trudy. *A Practical Study of Argument*. Belmont, CA: Wadsworth, 1984.

Good discussion of fallacies and the informal logic movement.

Hamblin, C.L. *Fallacies*. London: Methuen and Co., Ltd., 1970. Reprinted by Vale Press, Newport News, VA, 1986.

Considered by many to be one of the most important works in informal logic. Attempts to develop a comprehensive treatment of fallacies.

Kahane, Howard. *Logic and Contemporary Rhetoric: The Use of Reason in Everyday Life,* 4th ed. Belmont, CA: Wadsworth Publishing Co., 1984.

> Contains many good examples of common fallacies that are used in ordinary arguments.

Woods, John, and Walton, Douglas. *Argument: The Logic of the Fallacies.* New York: McGraw-Hill, 1982.

> Good text by two of the most important figures in the informal logic movement.

13. BOOKS ON ARGUMENTATION.

Cox, J. Robert, and Willard, Charles Arthur. *Advances in Argumentation Theory and Research.* Carbondale, IL: Southern Illinois University Press, 1982.

> Contains several invited essays covering a wide range of perspectives on argument.

Perelman, Chaim. *The Realm of Rhetoric.* Notre Dame: University of Notre Dame Press, 1982.

> Perelman is one of the most influential scholars in argumentation in the twentieth century. This is an abbreviated version of his more influential *The New Rhetoric* (with Olbrechets-Tyteca) (Notre Dame Press, 1970) and is a good introduction to his work.

Rieke, Richard D., and Sillars, Malcolm O. *Argumentation and the Decision Process.* Glenview, IL: Scott, Foresman Co., 1984.

> Provides a good introduction to argument, as well as an analysis of how argument "works" in a variety of fields.

Toulmin, Stephen. *Uses of Argument.* Cambridge: Cambridge University Press, 1958.

> Widely influential book in speech; basis for the Toulmin model.

van Eemeren, F.H.; Grootendorst, R.; and Kruiger, T. *The Study of Argumentation.* New York: Irvington Publishers, Inc., 1984.

> Good survey of argumentation theory by three European argumentation theorists.

Willard, Charles Arthur. *Argumentation and the Social Grounds of Knowledge.* Tuscaloosa: University of Alabama Press, 1983.

> Develops a perspective of argument as a type of social interaction.

INDEX

ACKNOWLEDGMENTS

From "Unemployment and Health" by Therman Evans in *Journal of the American Medical Association,* Vol. 237, No. 18, May 2, 1977. Copyright © 1977 by American Medical Association. Reprinted by permission.

M. Harvey Brenner, "Health Costs and Benefits of Economic Policy," *International Journal of Health Sciences,* Vol. 7, No. 4, 1977.

From "Lies, Damn Lies and Statistics" in *Time,* July 9, 1984. Copyright © 1984 by Time Inc. Reprinted by permission.

John Conyers, Jr., "Journal's Guide for Women Crimefighters," *Congressional Record,* March 24, 1977.

Leonard Greene, *Free Enterprise Without Poverty.* New York: W.W. Norton and Company, 1981.

Peter Draper, et al, "Microprocessors, Macroeconomic Policy and Public Health," *Lancet,* February 17, 1979.

Achieving the Goals of the Employment Act of 1946—Thirtieth Anniversary Review, prepared for the use of the Joint Economic Committee Congress of the United States, October 26, 1976.

From "Do Economic Slumps Increase Illness?" by William Check in *Journal of the American Medical Association,* Vol. 242, No. 12, September 21, 1979. Copyright © 1979 by American Medical Association. Reprinted by permission.

Ian Miles, "Joblessness and Health," *World Press Review,* July, 1983.

Charles L. Schultze, *The Politics and Economics of Public Spending.* Washington, DC: The Brookings Institution, 1968, p. 38.

Allan J. Lichtman and Daniel M. Rohrer, "The Logic of Policy Dispute," *Journal of the American Forensic Association,* Spring, 1980.

Allan J. Lichtman and Daniel M. Rohrer, "A General Theory of the Counterplan," *Journal of the American Forensic Association,* Fall, 1975.

Jerome Frank, *Courts on Trial: Myth and Reality in American Justice.* Princeton: Princeton University Press, 1949.